GOOD NEWS STUDIES

Consulting Editor: Robert J. Karris, O.F.M.

Volume 30

The Mission of Christ and His Church

Studies in Christology and Ecclesiology

by

John P. Meier

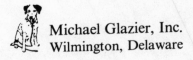

Michael Glazier, Inc.
Wilmington, Delaware

About the Author

John P. Meier received his License in Theology from the Gregorian University, Rome, in 1968, and his Doctorate in Sacred Scripture from the Biblical Institute, Rome, in 1976. Both degrees were awarded with the papal gold medal. He is the author of Matthew (New Testament Message, vol. 3, Michael Glazier), and numerous articles in scholarly journals. He is presently on the faculty of The Catholic University of America.

First published in 1990 by Michael Glazier, Inc., 1935 West Fourth Street, Wilmington, Delaware 19805.

Library of Congress Cataloging-in-Publication Data

Meier, John P.
    The mission of Christ and His Church: Studies in Christology and ecclesiology/by John P. Meier.
        p. cm. — (Good news studies: v. 30)
    Includes bibliographical references.
    ISBN 0-89453-795-4
    1. Jesus Christ—Person and offices. 2. Jesus Christ—History of doctrines. 3. Church. 4. Mission of the church. 5. Mission of the church—Biblical teaching. 6. Bible. N.T.—Criticism, interpretation, etc. 7. Catholic Church—Doctrines. 8. Church—Biblical teaching. I. Title. II. Series.
BT202.M3984   1990
262'.7—dc20
                                                                    90-30923
                                                                    CIP

Typography by Brenda Belizzone, Phyllis Boyd LeVane, Angela Meade
Printed in the U.S. by Princeton University Press.

To His Eminence
John J. O'Connor, Ph.D.
for his generous support and encouragement

*dei oun ton episkopon ... einai
... philoxenon, didaktikon*

1 Tim 3:2

Table of Contents

Acknowledgments

Grateful acknowledgment is given to the following publications for permission to reprint material:

The Catholic Biblical Quarterly for:
"Presbyteros in the Pastoral Epistles," *CBQ* 35 (1973) 323-45
"Salvation History in Matthew: In Search of a Starting Point," *CBQ* 37 (1975) 203-15
"Nations or Gentiles in Matthew 28:19?" *CBQ* 39 (1977) 94-102
"On the Veiling of Hermeneutics (1 Cor 11:2-16)," *CBQ* 40 (1978) 212-26

The Journal of Biblical Literature for:
"Two Disputed Questions in Matt 28:16-20," *JBL* 96 (1977) 407-24
"John the Baptist in Matthew's Gospel," *JBL* 99 (1980) 383-405

Biblica for:
"Structure and Theology in Heb 1:1-14," *Bib* 66 (1985) 168-89
"Symmetry and Theology in the Old Testament Citations of Heb 1:5-14," *Bib* 66 (1985) 504-33

Interpretation for:
"Matthew 15:21-28," *Int* 40 (1986) 397-402

Worship for:
"Catholic Funerals in the Light of Scripture," *Worship* 48 (1974) 206-16
"Celebration of the Word in Communal Services of Penance," *Worship* 50 (1976) 413-20

The Bible Today for:
"Liberty and Justice for All," *The Bible Today*, Part I: 87 (1976) 1032-39; Part II: 88 (1977) 1098-1103

The New York Times for:
"Jesus among the Historians," *The New York Times*, Dec. 21, 1986, pp. 1, 16-19 (expanded version printed in this book)

Harper & Row for:
"Antioch," article in the *Harper's Bible Dictionary* (ed. P.J. Achtemeier et al.; San Francisco: Harper & Row, 1985) 33-34

The Catholic Theological Society of America for:
"Jesus among the Theologians. II. Sobrino and Segundo," opening address at the annual meeting of the CTSA, Toronto, Canada, June 15, 1988 (revised version printed in this book)

Abbreviations

AAS	*Acta apostolicae sedis*
AB	*Anchor Bible*
AJBA	*Australian Journal of Biblical Archaeology*
AnBib	Analecta Biblica
ASTI	*Annual of the Swedish Theological Institute*
BAG	W. Bauer, W. F. Arndt, and F. W. Gingrich, *Greek-English Lexicon of the* NT
BASOR	Bulletin of the American Schools of Oriental Research
BDF	F. Blass, A. Debrunner, and R. W. Funk, *A Greek Grammar of the* NT
BZ	*Biblische Zeitschrift*
CBQ	*Catholic Biblical Quarterly*
CTM	*Concordia Theological Monthly*
EB or Ebib	Etudes bibliques
Est Bib	*Estudios biblicos*
ET	English Translation
EvT	*Evangelische Theologie*
ExpT or *ExpTim*	*Expository Times*
FRLANT	*Forschungen zur Religion und Literatur des Alten und Neuen Testaments*
HeyJ	*Heythrop Journal*
HTR	*Harvard Theological Review*
ICC	International Critical Commentary
Int	*Interpretation*
JB	*Jerusalem Bible*
JBC	*Jerome Biblical Commentary* (1968 ed.)
JBL	Journal of Biblical Literature
NAB	New American Bible
NEB	*New English Bible*
NICNT	New International Commentary of the New Testament

NIGTC	New International Greek Testament Commentary
NovTSup	Novum Testamentum, Supplements
NRT	*La nouvelle revue théologique*
NT or	
NovT	*Novum Testamentum*
NT	New Testament
NTD	*Das Neue Testament Deutsch*
NTS	*New Testament Studies*
OT	Old Testament
PE	The Pastoral Epistles
QD	Quaestiones disputatae
RB	*Revue biblique*
RHPR	*Revue d'histoire et de philosophie religieuses*
RNT	*Regensburger Neues Testament*
RSR	*Recherches de science religieuse*
RSV	*Revised Standard Version*
SBLDS	Society of Biblical Literature Dissertation Series
SBLSBS	Society of Biblical Literature Sources for Biblical Study
SBT	Studies in Biblical Theology
SJ	Studia judaica
SNTSMS	Society for New Testament Studies Monograph Series
SPB	Studia postbiblica
Str-B	[H. Strack and] P. Billerbeck, *Kommentar zum Neuen Testament*
TDNT	*Theological Dictionary of the New Testament* (ed. G. Kittel and G. Friedrich)
TEV	*Today's English Version*
TGl	*Theologie und Glaube*
THKNT	*Theologischer Handkommentar zum Neuen Testament*
TR or *TRu*	*Theologische Rundschau*
UBSGNT	United Bible Societies *Greek New Testament*
WMANT	Wissenschaftliche Monographien zum Alten und Neuen Testament
WUNT	Wissenschaftliche Untersuchungen zum Neuen Testament
ZNW	*Zeitschrift für die neutestamentliche Wissenschaft*

Preface

When I began to collect and edit the various studies that make up this volume, I wondered whether there would be a common thread running through the individual essays—something that would supply the semblance of a coherent whole. After all, these studies stretch over some fifteen years (1973-1988) and were originally intended for a wide variety of audiences. Most of these essays are scholarly pieces presupposing a fair knowledge of present-day Scripture research. A few attempt to present key scriptural themes on a more popular level, while a few others broach the delicate topic of pastoral application. Most have been previously published, although a few appear here in print—at least in their present form—for the first time. Hence, the question: Would I be collecting flotsam and jetsam with no common viewpoint?

As I assembled what might have proven to be just a theological jigsaw puzzle, I was surprised and delighted to notice a familiar pattern emerging. From the beginning of my studies on Matthew's Gospel, I had insisted, to the point of driving my colleagues to distraction, that the special characteristic of Matthew's work is the close connection he creates among the three themes of Christ, church, and morality.[1] To my amazement and amusement, I discovered that I had replicated the same pattern in my own writing, even though a fair number of these pieces do not have Matthew as their main focus. First

---

[1] Hence the subtitle of my *The Vision of Matthew. Christ, Church, and Morality in the First Gospel* (Theological Inquiries; New York: Paulist, 1979).

impressions, exegetical as well as personal, indeed seem to be lasting.

Unlike the First Evangelist, however, this latter-day scribe has focused mostly on Christ and his church, with relatively little space given to moral issues. This gap is not the result of an instinct for self-preservation in an ecclesiastical climate not overly propitious to the development of moral theology. Rather, it is simply a question of strategic distribution. My views on morality in Scripture demand a full treatment of Christ and church as their necessary context, and hence my exposition of morality in the New Testament appears in books rather than in individual essays, viz., *Law and History in Matthew's Gospel*[2] and *The Vision of Matthew*. When moral considerations do appear in the following studies, they naturally occur in the more popular pieces aimed at pastoral application.

The bulk of the material, instead, dwells on selected questions of Christology and ecclesiology debated today among Scripture scholars and theologians. This emphasis is due not only to subliminal influence from Matthew but also, I would suggest, to the simple fact that Christ and church have been the two great foci of study and controversy since Vatican II.

One benefit of the present volume is that it has allowed me to rethink and refine some of my own positions as I drew together essays originally written separately. A clear case in point is the triad of essays that opens the book. The first study, "Jesus among the Historians," is the original long form of a review of present-day research on the historical Jesus which, because of limits of space, had to appear in *The New York Times* Sunday Book Review section with close to two-thirds of the material cut. Subsequent to the appearance of the abbreviated form of the article, the Hartford Seminary Foundation kindly invited me to expand my reflections to include "Jesus among the Theologians," i.e., the use of Jesus-of-history-research among contemporary systematic theologians. I originally attempted to encompass treatments of Küng, Schil-

---

[2]*Law and History in Matthew's Gospel. A Redactional Study of Mt. 5:17-48* (AnBib 71; Rome: Biblical Institute, 1976).

lebeeckx, Sobrino, and Segundo all in one essay; but I was not satisfied with the result, since too much had to be compressed into too small a space. The invitation of the Catholic Theological Society of America to deliver the opening address at their convention in 1988 allowed me to rework and expand the material on Sobrino and Segundo more to my satisfaction; the result, with further rewriting, is the third essay. Happily, this present volume allowed for the correlation and interweaving of all three essays, which appear here together for the first time as a sort of trilogy on the present-day study of the historical Jesus by both exegetes and theologians. I hope it will provide a stimulus to further discussion in this vital area.

Most of the other essays have had a less complicated genesis. Since all of them had appeared elsewhere in journals, I felt it would be a falsification of the historical record to rewrite them to any great degree. Yet time, tide, and research wait for no man or woman, and so I sought some way of bringing these studies up to date, lest they seem mere museum pieces. The best solution to this problem, in my opinion, is the one offered by Rudolf Schnackenburg in his collected essays, *Schriften zum Neuen Testament*:[3] after each essay, an "Afterword" (*Nachwort*) considers recent developments and offers an updated bibliography. This is the format I have chosen to "freshen up" my own studies. Depending on the subject matter of the essay, the Afterword will supply at times further personal ruminations, at times pointers to further reading, and at times both. The fact that I supply Afterwords even to the three initial essays that are of fairly recent vintage only reminds us that, in Scripture and theology, there is no keeping up, only catching up.

Originally, I had intended to supply footnotes for all the articles, even those first printed in a popular format. As the editing proceeded, however, this approach seemed to impose a false uniformity on pieces obviously different from one another in style and tone. Hence I have decided to let the Afterwords of the popular pieces simply substitute for footnotes.

---

[3]Rudolf Schnackenburg, *Schriften zum Neuen Testament* (Munich: Kösel, 1971).

This volume would not have appeared without the help of many people; I regret that only a few can be mentioned here. Thanks are due in particular to Michael Glazier, a good friend as well as an innovative publisher. This book is wholly his brainchild. When he first broached the project to me, I was skeptical—until his irrepressible Irish enthusiasm swept all objections before it. Thanks are likewise owed to my friends, both colleagues and students, at The Catholic University of America, who supported me with their encouragement as well as their work in the tedious business of proofreading and compiling indexes.

Finally, I wish to thank Cardinal John J. O'Connor, to whom this volume is dedicated. When I asked him whether he would accept the dedication, he replied by letter: "It is hard not to sound fraudulent or Uriah Heepish in saying I'm flabbergasted. . . . Nevertheless, if you're not afraid it will ruin your reputation, I will be deeply honored . . . but [I] will understand if you come to your senses and change your mind." No such *metanoia* has set in, mainly because Cardinal O'Connor's lively support has been a key factor in my coming to Catholic University and my continued writing. It has been a privilege for me to be able to pierce through the caricatures of the media and to come to know a concerned bishop whose voracious reading habits and inquiring mind guarantee the most stimulating *Tischreden* in the whole of New York.

PART ONE

1

Jesus among the Historians

In his novel, *Roger's Version*, John Updike pits a Barthian theologian toying with skepticism against a conservative and naive student (tautology there?), in a fierce debate over whether the existence of God can be proved. As I sit at my desk, looking at a slender volume entitled *Jesus and the Word* (1926) by the skeptical and sometimes Barthian Rudolf Bultmann, and the much larger and more confident *Jesus and Judaism* (1985) by E.P. Sanders, I wonder whether the twentieth century has not witnessed a similar debate on the historical Jesus. The comparison, though, is not quite apt. Sanders, neither conservative nor naive, does not represent the antithesis to Bultmann; that role belongs to the exegetical acrobats of an earlier generation, the conservative Protestants and Catholics who wrote "lives of Jesus" that desperately sought to harmonize the discordant testimony of the four gospels at any price. The breath-taking intellectual gymnastics of the Catholic "lives" seem especially poignant today, since often they were the result of official pressure rather than personal narrowness. Scholars like Ferdinand Prat and Marie-Joseph Lagrange knew better, but they were subject to censorship and silencing by the Vatican. How times change.

Sanders' book, by contrast, represents more of a centrist approach, an honest attempt to avoid both the minimalism of an existentialist like Bultmann and the uncritical acceptance of the gospel narratives by fundamentalists who think they are watching videotape replays. Whether one prefers the Baptist Norman Perrin or the German Catholic Anton Vögtle, the post-liberal-Protestant Sanders or the Jewish expert on the Dead Sea scrolls Geza Vermes, one senses that the last forty years have produced a rough consensus on valid sources, method, and criteria in that most enduring of modern treasure hunts, the quest for the historical Jesus. Although decisions still vary greatly on the authenticity of individual sayings of Jesus, and one expert will feel more confident than the next on whether Jesus used this or that title, a surprising amount of convergence has emerged since World War II. It is symptomatic that, in a 1974 work, *Jesus in Contemporary Historical Research*, Gustaf Aulén, a Swedish bishop, was able to draw up a sketch of Jesus' message and ministry based not on his own original research but simply on basic agreements he found among a wide range of exegetes.

It is in this sense that Sanders represents the culmination of the post-World War II period in the quest for the Jesus of history. It is not that Sanders does not present new and debatable views; he does, from claiming that Jesus did not demand repentance to playing down the sayings of Jesus and totally ignoring the titles attributed to him. These challenges to the received wisdom will make his book must reading, even in Updike's mythical divinity school on the Charles. Yet the greatest value of *Jesus and Judaism* is that it acts as a summation and a watershed. It is a classic because it brilliantly embodies a whole generation's desire to avoid exaggerations from right or left, to stop portraying Jesus as a predecessor of Heidegger or Ortega or Luther or Aquinas, and to try to understand what this Jew meant to say and accomplish in first-century Palestine.

That all this should have happened since 1945 is not totally accidental. Granted, popularizers have exaggerated the importance for Jesus-of-history research of the Jewish scrolls discovered at Qumran and the gnostic codices recovered at Nag Hammadi. One easily forgets that nothing in either discovery tells us anything directly about Jesus. Still, these finds have joined forces with Greco-Roman studies, rabbinic research, and the sociology of the New Testament to nail down our picture of Jesus of Nazareth to a concrete time and place. While Qumran is actually more useful in showing us how variegated pre-A.D. 70 Judaism was, and while Nag Hammadi is more relevant to church history from the second to the fourth centuries, these discoveries have helped keep professorial flights of fancy within certain limits. As the quest in the eighteenth and nineteenth centuries shows, the historical Jesus readily becomes the clear crystal pool into which scholars gaze to see themselves. The archaeological finds since World War II have fended off this academic narcissism just at a time when New Testament researchers might have been tempted to cave in to the lotus-eating of structuralism and semiotics.

Nevertheless, no amount of archaeology guarantees objectivity in interpretation of the data. The personal pilgrimages of Sanders or Vermes have left their own lineaments on the portraits of Jesus they paint. And so it must be. Not that this inevitable influence of personal stance justifies junking objectivity in favor of a new-journalism approach to historicity—far from it. Objectivity in the quest for the historical Jesus is, to borrow a phrase from Karl Rahner, an "asymptotic goal": we have to keep pressing toward it, even though we never fully arrive. Pressing toward the goal of objectivity is what keeps us on target—along with an honest admission of one's own point of view. Without that admission, archaeology and sociology can still become mere tools of more sophisticated apologetics.

For instance, as a Roman Catholic, I must constantly be on guard against anachronistically reading back the expanded universe of church dogma into the "big-bang" moment of Jesus' earthly life. Yet I would maintain (more apologetics?) that a Catholic is paradoxically freer than, say, a conservative evangelical Protestant in pursuing the quest. For one thing, Catholics distinguish carefully between what they know by reason and what they know by faith. The question of the Jesus of history automatically brackets—*not* betrays—what is known by faith and restricts all affirmations to what is verifiable or at least arguable by historical reasoning. One can best picture the process by imagining a gathering of Catholic, Protestant, Jewish, and agnostic scholars trying to hammer out a consensus document on what they could say about Jesus from purely historical sources and arguments. A Catholic could accept the consensus without imagining that it captured the full reality of Jesus. Moreover, Catholics have traditionally rejected a Bible-only approach to faith in favor of a Scripture-plus-tradition view. For a Catholic, the full reality of Jesus Christ is mediated through multiple channels: Scripture, sacraments, Church Fathers, medieval and modern theologians, the teaching of popes and bishops, and contemporary experience. My faith in Christ does not rise or fall with my attempt to state what I can or cannot know about Jesus of Nazareth by means of modern historical research. The Jesus of history I sketch is at best a fragmentary, hypothetical, changeable reconstruction; it is not—and could hardly be—the object of the church's faith and preaching. Thus, the very restrictive nature of the enterprise is at the same time liberating. Since I am not trying to argue myself or anyone else into faith (a hopeless task anyway), I can let the historical chips fall where they may. This does not mean that there is a total dichotomy between reason and history on the one hand and faith and theology on the other. After all the historical research has been done, there remains the work of correlating the images of Jesus formed in historical reconstructions and in statements of faith. But such a project would take us far beyond the scope of this essay, which is a modest one. On this Christmas forty years after Qumran, I am simply trying to frame my own answer to the question first posed during the Enlightenment and debated ever since: What can "all reasonable people"—that Platonic will o' the wisp—say with fair probability about the historical Jesus?

Birth and Early Years

To begin with, the very notion that Jesus was born exactly 1,987 years ago on December 25th is hopelessly wrong. A sixth-century monk named Dionysius Exiguus (Denny the Dwarf) is responsible for our present B.C.-A.D. system of dating, and unfortunately his math was not as good as his piety. Jesus (Hebrew *Yeshu* or *Yeshua'* a commonly used name that was a contraction of the Hebrew form of Joshua) was born toward the end of the reign of King Herod the Great, hence somewhere around 6-4 B.C. His mother was Miriam (Mary), his putative father Joseph. That is all we can say for certain about his birth. The world-wide census under

Caesar Augustus while Quirinius was governor of Syria is the result of Luke's garbling and compressing of later events. Only one chapter apiece from Matthew and Luke speaks of a birth at Bethlehem. The rest of the New Testament knows only of Nazareth as Jesus' place of origin. Thus, Bethlehem may simply be symbolic of Jesus' status as the new David. I would not, however, be so quick to jettison some kind of Davidic descent for Jesus, as does John L. McKenzie; many different and early streams of New Testament tradition affirm it. In any event, Davidic sonship is traced through Joseph, not Miriam.

Jesus spent about the first thirty years of his life in Nazareth, an obscure hilltown in southern Galilee. We know almost nothing about this period, perhaps because nothing significant happened. Apparently there was little if anything in Jesus' background or education (if any existed) to prepare his neighbors for the shock of his later ministry. Out of the whole New Testament, only one verse tells us that Jesus was a *tekton*, most likely a carpenter, though the word can mean stonemason or smith. In this, Jesus probably followed the trade of Joseph, though the matter is by no means as clear as most people think. Presumably, Joseph died before Jesus began his ministry. At least, Joseph is not mentioned during it, in contrast to Miriam, Jesus' mother, and his brothers Jacob (James), Joseph, Judah (Judas), and Simon. Sisters are also alluded to, but not named. Since the Enlightenment, controversy has raged between Protestant and Catholics over these brothers and sisters, Protestants generally taking them to be true siblings, while Catholics usually see them as cousins. Recently, the German Catholic scholar Rudolf Pesch has favored the sibling interpretation, and the dean of German Catholic exegetes, Rudolf Schnackenburg, has written diplomatically that the question needs to be discussed further. Actually, the most disconcerting aspect of Jesus' family life is that his relatives did not believe in him during his public ministry.

The New Testament never speaks of Jesus' marital status. The idea that he remained celibate rests mostly on an argument from silence; but in the face of all the references to his father, mother, brothers, and sisters, the silence may be significant. Some scholars suggest that Jesus' reference to eunuchs who make themselves such for the sake of the kingdom (Matthew

19:12) is a reply to critics who sneered at his single status. Others propose that Jesus was consciously imitating the celibate life of Jeremiah, another prophet who called Israel to repentance at a critical juncture in its history. The influence of the "monks" at Qumran is likewise invoked, but whether celibacy was ever practiced there is still debated.

What *is* certain about Jesus' status is that he was a layman. Christian rhetoric about "Christ the high priest" has obscured the fact that Jesus the layman consorted almost entirely with other Jewish laypeople, his few encounters with priests being invariably hostile—including the final one that precipitated his death. We miss the sharp barb in the parable of the Good Samaritan if we forget it is an anticlerical joke, told by Jesus the layman to other Galilean laypeople who disliked the priestly aristocracy in Jerusalem as much as he did. Since Jesus plied his ministry for the most part among the common people of Galilee and Judea, he presumably taught in Aramaic, the ordinary language of the lower classes. His reading of Scripture in the synagogue points to a knowledge of Hebrew, and commercial transactions in Galilee may have introduced him to Greek (used perhaps with Pilate during his trial?). But there is no indication of higher education or rabbinic training (see John 7:15). Jesus, like John the Baptist, was addressed as "Rabbi," but in the early first century the title was used widely and loosely.

Baptism and Ministry to Israel

Sometime around A.D. 28-29 (see Luke 3:1), during the reign of the Emperor Tiberius (A.D. 14-37), Jesus journeyed to the Jordan River to receive a "baptism of repentance for the forgiveness of sins" from John the Baptist, a Jewish prophet known as well from the Jewish historian Josephus. (Josephus also seems to mention Jesus in two passages, but their authenticity is debated among scholars.) The embarrassing nature of Jesus' submission to a baptism of repentance conferred by John, a point increasingly played down by the four Gospels, argues for the event's historicity and its pivotal place in the life of Jesus. By accepting John's baptism, Jesus indicated he accepted John's message of the imminent disaster that was threatening Israel in the last days of its history, a disaster to be avoided only by national repentance. When Jesus struck out on his own, he continued the Baptist's warning about divine judgment soon to come. It is no accident then, that some of Jesus' closest disciples had been followers of the Baptist. Sanders rightly takes to task recent literary critics who have sought to make Jesus relevant by ignoring his emphasis on an imminent and definitive intervention of God, bringing salvation or doom. To remove this future thrust from Jesus' preaching about the coming kingdom of God is to isolate him from his first-century Jewish Palestinian matrix.

Although Jesus followed in the Baptist's footsteps, perhaps even baptizing for a while, there was a major shift in his message. While John emphasized judgment and punishment, Jesus proclaimed the good news that God, like a loving father, was seeking out and gathering in the lost, the poor, the marginalized, yes, even the irreligious. Gathering is indeed the word; for Jesus was not concerned—as nineteenth-century liberal piety often portrayed him—simply with touching individual souls. The audience Jesus sought to address was none other than all Israel. Seeing himself as the final prophet sent to a sinful nation in its last hour, Jesus sought to gather the scattered people of God back into one, holy community. In this sense, Jesus could not have intended to *found* a church because he *found* a church already existing: the *qahal*, the *'eda*, the *knesset* that Yahweh had once called together in the wilderness and was now calling together again. How the Gentiles fit into this vision is not clear. Perhaps Jesus thought that in "the last days" the *gôyīm* would come on pilgrimage to a restored Mt. Zion to be taught by Israel, as Isaiah had prophesied. In any case, Jesus saw himself as a prophet sent only to his own people. Positive encounters with individual Gentiles occurred, but they were the exceptions that proved the rule.

Jesus concretely embodied his vision of an Israel restored in the last days by selecting from his followers an inner circle of twelve men, representing the twelve patriarchs of the regathered twelve tribes. Scholars like Günter Klein and Walter Schmithals have claimed that the Twelve are a retrojection of the early church's organization into the life of Jesus. As a matter of fact, though, the group of the Twelve soon lost their prominence in the early church, which indeed had trouble even remembering all twelve names! Moreover, the Gospels' embarrassed acknowledgment that Judas the betrayer was one of the Twelve hardly sounds like an invention of church propaganda. That Jesus should choose *twelve* men to symbolize the restored Israel and not *eleven*, with himself as the twelfth, indicates that Jesus saw himself standing over against and above the nucleus he was creating. The choice of the Twelve makes clear that Jesus was not intending to found a new sect separated from Israel. His twelve "patriarchs" were rather to be the exemplars and center of a renewed people of God in the endtime. Some modern scholars, ignoring the lesson of Qumran, continue to suppose that Jesus' announcement of the end necessarily involved a lack of concern about organization and order among his disciples. That was not the case in the highly structured community at Qumran, and the appointment of the Twelve shows it was not the case among Jesus' followers.

The followers of the Nazarene extended far beyond the Twelve. Perhaps we can best imagine the situation in terms of concentric circles: the Twelve, other committed disciples who left family and employment to follow Jesus literally, and people who accepted Jesus' teaching but maintained their homes and jobs. No doubt some people passed back and forth between the outer two circles; the borders were hardly fixed. Jesus' relation to his disciples differed from that of the later rabbis in a number of ways. Jesus often took the initiative in calling people—including some not very promising candidates—to discipleship, even ordering them to forsake sacred duties to follow him: "Let the dead bury their dead." At least in his inner group, he expected commitment to himself to be a permanent affair; his disciples were not studying to be rabbis who would then leave him and set up schools of their own. Especially striking was Jesus' inclusion of women in his traveling entourage and his willingness to teach them. With both personal and financial support they stood by him—quite literally at the cross, when all the male disciples fled.

If we had only the Gospels of Mark, Matthew, and Luke (the "Synoptic Gospels"), we would get the impression that almost all of Jesus' followers came from the countryside and towns of Galilee; indeed, some scholars have referred to his supporters as "an agrarian reform movement." It is John's Gospel that reminds us that Jesus was also frequently active in and around Jerusalem—which helps explain how this supposedly agrarian movement suddenly became an urban phenomenon. John's Gospel is also correct, I think, in spreading Jesus' ministry over a number of Passovers and therefore over a number of years. Left with the Synoptic Gospels, we might easily compress Jesus' ministry into a couple of months. Fortunately, exegetes like C.H. Dodd and Raymond Brown have crusaded effectively against the Schweitzer-Bultmann dogma that John's Gospel may be safely ignored in reconstructing the historical Jesus. Only the keepers of the Bultmannian flame still reject John's statements en masse.

Teaching in Parables and in Actions

Prophet and wisdom teacher that he was, Jesus used the rich rhetorical traditions of Israel to hammer home his message. Oracles, woes, aphorisms, proverbs, but above all parables (*meshalim*) served to tease the minds of his audience, throw them off balance, and challenge them to decide for or against his claim on their lives. The parables are not pretty Sunday-school stories. They are troubling riddles, meant to destroy any false sense of security and create a fierce feeling of urgency. Any moment may be too late: you must stake all on my message now, no matter what the cost. For God is about to work his own kind of revolution: the poor will be exalted and the powerful dispossessed. This is the startling and disturbing program at the heart of the parables as well as the beatitudes. It is a promise of radical reversal, usually reduced by sermonizers to a spiritual bonbon. For Jesus, though, the revolution would be God's doing, not man's. This may be unpalatable to some liberation theologians, who are especially fond of the historical Jesus, as opposed to the Christ of dogma. Sad to say, their uncritical use of such gospel texts as Jesus' inaugural sermon at Nazareth would make the Holy Office look like Rudolf Bultmann by comparison. Indeed, in this,

Bultmann's *Jesus and the Word* may have been correct: the historical Jesus seems to have had no interest in the great political and social questions of his day. He was not interested in the reform of the world because he was prophesying its end. Whether this makes Jesus irrelevant to the academicians of the 1980s is itself irrelevant to the historical quest we are on; and it is more likely the academicians than Jesus who will change by the 1990s.

Jesus' impact did not come simply from powerful rhetoric. As with Old Testament prophets, the word (*dabar*) was also deed. Jesus consciously willed his public activity to be a dramatic acting out of his message of God's welcome and forgiveness extended to the prodigal son. He insisted on associating and eating with the religious low-life of his day, "the toll collectors and sinners," Jews who in the eyes of the pious had apostatized and were no better than Gentiles. This practice of sharing meals (for Orientals, a most serious and intimate form of social intercourse) with the religiously "lost" put Jesus in a continual state of ritual impurity, as far as the stringently law-observant were concerned. As Sanders emphasizes, Jesus no doubt shocked the pious by offering salvation to these outcasts without demanding the usual Jewish mechanism of repentance. What Sanders does not sufficiently note is that, in effect, Jesus was making acceptance of himself and his message the touchstone of true repentance. No doubt this upset the pious even more. Instead of grim works of penitence, Jesus proclaimed the joy of the heavenly banquet soon to come and already anticipated in his table fellowship with those outside the pale. In keeping with this festive mood, Jesus and his disciples did not undertake the voluntary fasts practiced by the Pharisees and the followers of the Baptist. Indeed, so blatant was Jesus' merrymaking that the devout contemptuously dismissed him as a bon vivant, "a glutton and a drunkard" (Matthew 11:19).

There was, then, on Jesus' part a conscious coherence between his words and deeds, his message and praxis. To the great discomfort of us moderns, part of his praxis was his claim to perform healings and exorcisms. At this point, many treatments of Jesus get hopelessly bogged down in a discussion of the possibility or the impossibility of miracles—which, properly speaking, is a philosophical rather than historical or even theological problem. But from the perspective of religious history, it is simply a fact that faith healers and miracle workers are common phenomena in both ancient and modern religions, from Honi the Circle Drawer and Apollonius of Tyana to the grotto of Lourdes and the televised epiphanies of Oral Roberts. How one explains such phenomena varies with both the subject studied and the observer commenting. Autosuggestion, psychosomatic diseases, mass hysteria are all possibilities, although the medical records at Lourdes do not always allow for such convenient escape hatches. In the case of Jesus, all that need be noted is that ancient Christian, Jewish, and pagan sources all agreed that Jesus did extraordinary things not easily explained by human means. While Jesus' disciples pointed to the Spirit of God as the source of his power, Jewish and pagan adversaries spoke of demonic or magical powers. It never occurred to any of the ancient polemicists to claim that nothing had happened.

For the modern interpreter, the key point is to situate Jesus' healings within the overall context of his message and praxis (something Morton Smith does not do in his *Jesus the Magician*). Jesus saw his healings not simply as kind deeds done to help unfortunate individuals; rather, like his table fellowship, they were concrete ways of dramatizing and effecting God's victory over the powers of evil in the final hour of human history. The miracles were signs and partial realizations of what was about to come fully in the kingdom. An already/not-yet tension lay at the heart of Jesus' vision. Yet, despite his stress on the imminent future of salvation, Jesus was not strictly speaking an apocalypticist; he had no interest in detailed time tables or cosmic journeys. Indeed, to the great chagrin of Christian theologians, he even affirmed his ignorance of the day and hour of the final judgment (Mark 13:32).

Jesus and the Mosaic Law

We must keep this proclamation of the present-yet-coming kingdom of God in mind when we try to understand Jesus' moral teaching. To put it in a laconic paradox: Jesus exhorts his followers to live even now by the power of a future event that has already touched and transformed their lives. Now, this is not quite the same thing as Albert Schweitzer's "interim ethics"; for Jesus gives neither a precise calendar nor any indication that his basic ethic is meant for only a short interval. The unrestricted love of God and neighbor that stands at the heart of Jesus' moral imperative is hardly a stop-gap measure for the time being. Actually, for the sake of accuracy, it should be noted that the word "love" does not appear all that frequently in the authentic sayings of Jesus. But if we gather together all of his pronouncements and parables that deal with compassion and forgiveness, the picture that results is a Jesus who stressed mercy without measure, love without limits—even love of one's enemies. To many of us, such ideals, however beautiful, seem simply un-doable. To Jesus, they were doable, but only for those who had experienced through him God's incredible love in their own lives. Radical demand flowed from radical grace. If religion becomes grace, then ethics becomes gratitude—and not just for the interim.

Trying to formulate Jesus' moral teaching into some codified, rational system is futile, especially since it is in his attitude to morality and law that Jesus proves himself the true charismatic in the classical sense. Faced with a crisis of traditional authority, the charismatic claims direct authority and intuitive knowledge that are not mediated through the traditional channels of law, custom, or established institutions. That is a perfect description of Jesus' approach; and it led to a basic tension in his treatment of the Mosaic Law. Jesus the Jew fundamentally affirmed the Law as God's will, though with a radicalizing thrust seen also at Qumran. At times, Jesus would engage in rabbinic-style debate to solve concrete problems. Yet on certain specific issues (divorce, oaths, unclean foods), he claimed to know intuitively and directly that Jewish Law or custom was contrary to God's will. In such cases, the Law had to give way to or be reinterpreted by the command of Jesus, simply because Jesus said so ("but *I* say to you"). He made no attempt to ground or authenticate such teaching in the manner of the Old Testament prophets ("the word of the Lord came to me, saying . . .") or the later rabbis ("Rabbi X said in the name of Rabbi

Y"). His peculiar and solemn introduction to various pronouncements, "*Amen*, I say to you," emphasized that he knew
and taught God's will with absolute certitude. Hence, as people
accepted or rejected his instruction, so they would be saved or
condemned on the last day. It was perhaps this unheard-of
claim to authority over the Mosaic Law and people's lives,
more than any title Jesus may or may not have used of himself,
that disturbed pious Jews and the Jewish authorities. Along
with and even more than the temple, the Torah was *the* central
symbol of Jewish religion, around which warring parties could
rally. By assuming unlimited power over the Torah and by
rescinding a key boundary marker between Jews and Gentiles,
Jesus inevitably put himself on a collision course not only with
the temple priests but also with sincere Jews in general.

Jesus and the Jewish Parties

Jesus' exact relation to the various Jewish parties of the day
is extremely difficult to fix, all the more so because most of the
rabbinic material comes from a later date. If it is naive to cite
indiscriminately Gospel texts written down one or two gener-
ations after Jesus' death, it is more than naive to quote rabbinic
texts written down hundreds of years after Jesus died, as
though Judaism had not undergone tremendous changes
during the interval. To make vague claims about the Mishna
and Talmud enshrining older oral traditions does not answer
the pivotal question: how much older? The relation of Jesus to
the various Jewish groups of the first century A.D. is thus
vastly more complicated than most popular presentations of
"Jesus the Jew" acknowledge. The problem is: what kind of
Jew? Different scholars have identified Jesus with almost every
Jewish party known to exist. The favorite designation is "Jesus
the Pharisee," but that simply shifts the question to: what kind
of Pharisee? Jesus has been painted as a nonconforming
Pharisee because of his freedom vis-à-vis the Law and tradition,
a Pharisee of the Shammai school because of his strict views
on divorce, and a Pharisee of the Hillel school because of his
humane emphasis on love of neighbor as central to the Law.

Others have seen his critique of the Pharisees' oral tradition as indicating a preference for the Sadducees. Still others suggest that, since Jesus radicalized the obligations of the Law and proclaimed the imminent end of the present age, he had ties with the sectarians at Qumran. Despite the popularity of the last suggestion since the discovery of the Dead Sea scrolls, Jesus' free-wheeling approach to written Law, his critique of purity rules, his distance from minute priestly concerns, and his openness to Jewish sinners make the identification improbable.

Then, too, there is the ever-popular attempt to present Jesus as sympathetic to armed revolt against the Romans, Camillo Torres before his time. S.G.F. Brandon was an indefatigable proponent of such a view, but much of his argument rests on seeing Jesus' nonviolent ethic as a coverup contrived by the later church. To supply the real Jesus, Brandon reads between the lines of the Gospels with more than a dollop of novelistic imagination. Naturally, if one is free to reject large portions of the gospel tradition and rewrite the rest to suit a given thesis, any interpretation of Jesus is possible. Recent essays by Ernst Bammel, C.F.D. Moule, and a host of colleagues investigating Brandon's method and individual arguments have rendered the whole Jesus-as-Sandinista approach highly dubious.

If truth be told, Jesus did not fit any of these pigeonholes, which may be one reason he wound up deserted and crucified. The Gospels may not be entirely wrong, though, in presenting the Pharisees as the group with which Jesus was most often in dialogue and debate. It is a commonplace in New Testament research today to affirm that the negative, polemical picture of the Pharisees in the Gospels largely reflects later debates between church and synagogue and do not go back to Jesus himself. Though this is largely true, the claim presupposes that we know the exact social status and religious views of the Pharisees in the pre-A.D. 70 period. Actually, both Jewish and Christian scholars still debate such questions; the groundbreaking work of Jacob Neusner on the Pharisees remains a focal point of contention, with the writings of Ellis Rivkin providing an alternative view.

On any reading, however, there were certainly points of

contact between the Pharisees and the Nazarene. Like Jesus, the Pharisees were religiously committed lay people who, disgusted with the corrupt rulers and high priests of Israel, sought personal and national reform through a fierce commitment to doing God's will in ordinary daily life. Unlike the Sadducees, their outlook was not restricted to this world; they hoped to share in a future resurrection and eternal life. The tragedy is that, while Jesus and the Pharisees could agree on the basic goal of personal reform and national restoration along spiritual lines, they were diametrically opposed on the way to achieve such renewal. As far as we can tell—and the evidence is by no means clear—the Pharisees of the pre-A.D. period emphasized the voluntary acceptance by lay people of the rules of ritual purity that bound the temple priests. Detailed regulations concerning tithing, washing, eating, and observance of the Sabbath were meant to sanctify everyday life, turning the nation into a spiritual temple by obedience to both the written Law and oral tradition. The charismatic freedom Jesus displayed toward the Law, his announcement of the imminent coming of the kingdom, and the personal claim all this implied naturally put him at odds with the Pharisees. Yet in many ways they remained the Jewish group closest to his own views, and as a party they were not directly involved in his death.

The Identity of Jesus

Looking at all Jesus said and did, we are confronted by one central question: who did Jesus think he was? Or to put the question in terms more open to verification: who did he claim to be? Jesus himself—at least in sayings that seem to be authentic—gave no clear and detailed answer. Totally absorbed in proclaiming and realizing the kingdom of God, he showed no indication of suffering an identity crisis, no need to engage in the tiresome modern hobby of finding oneself. He apparently was quite sure of who he was, though no one since has been. The crux of the problem lies in the paradox that, although Jesus rarely spoke directly about his own status, he implicitly made himself *the* pivotal figure in the final drama he was announcing and inaugurating. The kingdom was somehow already present in his person and ministry, and on the last day he would be the criterion by which people would be judged.

Jesus seems to have based such monumental claims, at least in part, on his special relationship with God. Following Joachim Jeremias, Edward Schillebeeckx has focused on Jesus' use of the Aramaic word *Abba* ("my own dear Father") in his prayer to God and the whole relationship that lies behind such prayer. The intimate address of *Abba*, foreign to the liturgy of temple and synagogue, expresses an extremely close, confident relation to God, says Schillebeeckx; it betokens the wellspring of Jesus' ministry. There is a danger here, however, of basing a great deal on very little. *Abba* occurs only once in the four Gospels and could be a retrojection of early Jewish-Christian prayer, reflecting a popular Aramaic practice not recorded in formal liturgical documents. On balance, though, Schillebeeckx is probably correct: Jesus' experience of intimate relationship with God as *Abba* was one—if not the only— basis of his mission.

Did Jesus go beyond this and actually apply any titles or categories to himself? Many a volume has been written over the past few decades cataloguing the titles given Jesus in the New Testament and weighing the possibility that some of them derive from Jesus himself. The results range from the optimistic (Oscar Cullmann) to the skeptical (Günther Born-kamm and E.P. Sanders, who both waive any detailed investi-gation). Among Jewish authors, Geza Vermes is surprisingly accepting of titles, provided they are purged of Christian ideas. At the very least, I think it safe to say that Jesus saw himself as a prophet, indeed the final prophet sent to Israel in its last days; a similar figure appears in the Dead Sea scrolls. Jesus' reputation for performing miracles may have conjured up hopes that the wonder-working Elijah had returned to prepare Israel for the end. Vermes even suggests that we see Jesus as standing in the tradition of the *hasid*, the charismatic holy man of Galilee, a product of popular folk religion rather than academic theology. Be that as it may, the title prophet was not without its dangers. In Jewish thought of the time, the image of prophet was often connected with rejection and martyrdom; and so the title was much more ominous than might at first appear.

The title Messiah ("the Christ") is often presumed to be central to Jesus' identity, but that is to read later Christian concepts and definitions back into a much more confused situation. In the early first century A.D., there was no one clear doctrine on the Messiah, and some Jewish groups that looked for the imminent coming of God dispensed completely with any such intermediary figure. Qumran expected two Messiahs, one Davidic and royal, the other—who took precedence!—Levitical and priestly. Since the word "Messiah" simply meant "anointed one," it could be applied to all sorts of sacred agents of God in the endtime, including a prophet "anointed" by the Holy Spirit. The expectation of the common people and of the Pharisees did apparently center on a king like David. If Jesus was in fact of Davidic descent, it would not be surprising if some of his followers identified him with the Davidic Messiah. There is really no other reason why the disciples' belief in his resurrection at Easter should have in turn triggered their proclamation that he had been enthroned in heaven as the royal son of David. In themselves, the two ideas of resurrection and a new King David had no intrinsic connection. That speculation about Jesus as the Davidic Messiah was well-known, even to Jesus' enemies, is supported by the charge under which he was tried by Pilate and crucified: King of the Jews. There is no proof, though, that Jesus himself ever directly claimed to be the Messiah in the royal sense; he was perhaps all too aware of the dangers of a political interpretation.

As for the title "Son" or "Son of God," it is not inconceivable that a person who addressed God as *Abba* might understand himself in some sense or other as God's Son. As a matter of fact, the titles Son of God and Son of the Most High are applied to a mysterious royal figure of the endtime in a fragmentary text from Qumran. Still, very few Gospel sayings in which Jesus calls himself the Son have much chance of being authentic. The best candidate is Mark 13:32, which affirms that the Son (=Jesus) does not know the time of the final judgment. It seems improbable that the early church went out of its way to make up sayings emphasizing the ignorance of its risen Lord. In any event, one must beware of reading into the title the meaning it acquired in later Trinitarian controversies.

Of all the titles, the most confusing is "Son of Man." As it now stands in the Gospels, it refers to the earthly ministry of Jesus, his death and resurrection, and his coming as judge (alluding to Daniel 7:13-14). The question whether Jesus ever used the title, and if so in what sense, has received every answer imaginable. Bultmann held that Jesus used Son of Man not of himself but of some other figure still to come. Norman Perrin came to believe that the title as applied to Jesus was totally a creation of the early church. Barnabas Lindars suggests that Jesus originally used Son of Man not as a title but simply as a modest circumlocution, "a man like myself"; it was the church that turned it into a title. Personally, I think it arguable that Jesus the parable-maker did use Son of Man as an enigmatic designation of himself during his ministry as the lowly yet powerful servant of God's kingdom. Faced with increasing rejection, he may also have used the title to affirm his assurance of final triumph and vindication by God. On the other hand, the use of Son of Man in the explicit predictions of Jesus' death and resurrection may well stem from the church.

As for the title Lord, there is really no problem in its being applied to Jesus during his earthly life. As we now know from Qumran, the Aramaic *mare'* could mean anything from a polite "sir" to a divine "Lord." No doubt different people addressed the title to Jesus with varying degrees of reverence, and the early church simply continued the address, in a new transcendent sense, when praying to its exalted Lord.

Going to Jerusalem to Die

The upshot of all this is that Jesus was much less interested in titles than we are. He was not primarily a theologian but a man of action. In the spring of A.D. 30 (or possibly 33), he took the decisive action of going on pilgrimage to Jerusalem for Passover, apparently determined to engage the leadership of Israel in a once-and-for-all confrontation. Two symbolic acts performed by Jesus were meant to press home the issue with the authorities: the "triumphal entry" into Jerusalem and the "cleansing" of the temple. The historicity of both events has been called into question; but if we think of limited symbolic gestures rather than Hollywood-style riots, both acts fit in with the tradition of prophecy-by-action practiced by the Old Testament prophets. The entry into Jerusalem implied but did not define some sort of messianic claim over the ancient Davidic capital. More crucial was the "cleansing" of the temple, which was probably not a call for reform but a prophecy that the present temple would be destroyed. Various sayings of Jesus point in that direction and cohere with Jewish apocalyptic thought of the time. The "cleansing" had much more ominous implications than the "entry." An attack on the temple, however figurative, would have alienated not only the priests but also many pious Jews otherwise opposed to the Jerusalem hierarchy.

As Schillebeeckx notes, given the challenge he put to the hostile authorities on their home ground, Jesus would have had to have been a simpleton not to have realized the mortal danger in which he was placing himself. He did not have to be a very far-sighted prophet to appreciate that a violent death in Jerusalem had become a real possibility. Bultmann claims that we cannot know anything about how Jesus understood and confronted his death, indeed, whether he broke down when faced with it. In recent years, Heinz Schürmann has vigorously challenged that position. Admittedly, most critics would agree that the explicit predictions of death and resurrection reflect the theology of the early church. Still, I think that some sayings which speak of his death in general terms, often with no mention of resurrection or ultimate triumph, may come from the historical Jesus.

In a number of sayings (e.g., Matthew 23:37-39; Luke 13:31-33), Jesus speaks of his possible death as that of a prophet martyred in Jerusalem, in the long line of Old Testament prophets. The lack of titles beyond the generic "prophet," the placing of Jesus on the same level as the Old Testament prophets, and the absence of any mention of resurrection or vindication make it unlikely that these sayings were created by the church. In the core parable of the evil tenants of the vineyard (Mark 12:1-8), the parable ends in unmitigated tragedy: the son (=Jesus) is killed, with no hint of reprieve or reversal. In Mark 10:35-40, James and John ask Jesus to grant them seats of honor next to him in his kingdom. In reply, Jesus uses Old Testament images to tell them that all he can promise is a share in his death. The anecdote reflects badly on the glory-hungry sons of Zebedee; when one considers that, a few years after Jesus' death, James became the first martyr among the Twelve, it seems improbable that the early church would have created such a slur on his memory. Moreover, Jesus' prophecy that John would suffer the same fate remained, as far as we know, unfulfilled. Finally, in the anecdote Jesus affirms his inability to assure seats at his right and left in the kingdom; all in all, the story does not sound like later Christian propaganda. What is especially noteworthy in all these passages is that there is no saving significance attributed to Jesus' death, no idea of vicarious sacrifice. The death of Jesus is simply predicted; it has no positive value.

If Jesus ever did give a clearer explanation of how he viewed his approaching death, the most likely occasion would have been the last opportunity he had: the Last Supper. The historicity of this last meal with his disciples is supported independently by Mark, John, special traditions in Luke, and an early formula preserved by Paul in 1 Corinthians 11. The meal took place on a Thursday evening, but the exact date differs in the Synoptic Gospels and John. John is probably correct in dating the supper on the Day of Preparation (for Passover), the 14th of Nisan. The Synoptics' presentation of the Last Supper as a Passover meal is later Christian theology. At the beginning and end of the meal respectively, Jesus used bread and wine to represent graphically his coming death, which he accepted as part of God's will for bringing in the kingdom. Jesus' interpretive words over the bread and wine are recorded in four different versions, all influenced by Christian liturgy; hence many scholars consider the original form irrecoverable. I would hazard the guess that the most likely reconstruction is: "This is my body [or flesh]. . . . This is the covenant [sealed] by my blood." If these words adequately reflect what Jesus said, then he interpreted his death as the (sacrificial?) means by which God would restore his covenant made with Israel at Sinai (cf. Exodus 24:8) and bring it to fulfillment. This *last* supper—the last in a whole series of meals of salvation celebrated with sinners—was a pledge that, despite the apparent failure of Jesus' mission to Israel, God would vindicate him even beyond death and bring him and his followers to the final banquet in the kingdom. Jesus insists that his disciples all drink from the *one* cup, *his* cup, to emphasize that they must hold fast to their fellowship with him even as he dies, if they are to share that fellowship again in the kingdom.

Trial and Death

After the supper, Jesus led his disciples outside the city to a country estate on or at the foot of the Mount of Olives (Gethsemane means "oil press"). There he was arrested by an armed band guided by Judas. The arresting police were in all likelihood controlled by the high priest, though John's Gospel gives indication of some Roman presence as well. The disciples abandoned Jesus and fled. From this point until the trial before Pilate, the succession of events is highly controverted, for three reasons: contradictions among the four Gospels, our uncertainty about Jewish and Roman law in pre-A.D. 70 Palestine, and religious apologetics that plague us still.

Sifting through the vast literature, I find three major scenarios proposed, each of which is possible. (1) A night trial was held before the Sanhedrin, presided over by Caiaphas the high priest (A.D. 18-36); this session either lasted until dawn or was followed by a brief session at dawn. This is the picture given by Mark and Matthew and is supported by Josef Blinzler and Otto Betz. (2) The Sanhedrin held only an early morning session. This is the presentation of Luke and is supported by David Catchpole. (3) An informal hearing was held by some Jewish official, perhaps Annas, the father-in-law of Caiaphas, who had been high priest A.D. 6-15; but no formal trial took place before the Sanhedrin. This scenario can be reconstructed from John's Gospel and is defended by Paul Winter.

Winter in particular appeals to the many prescriptions of the Mishna tractate *Sanhedrin* that are flouted in the Synoptic versions. The problem, though, is that we cannot be sure that the rabbinic rules in *Sanhedrin* (written down around A.D.

200) accurately reflect how the Sanhedrin conducted trials under a Roman prefect in the pre-A.D. 70 period. Although all sides want certitude on this neuralgic issue, the truth is that the historian must remain uncertain. Whether a trial or an informal hearing took place before Jewish authorities, some accusation against Jesus would have been considered. His threats against the temple, his teaching that rescinded commandments in the Law, his claim to be a prophet and perhaps something more might all have been considered; but once again we are in the dark. The ringing affirmations by Jesus that he was indeed the Messiah, Son of God, and Son of Man look like a Christological catechism drawn up by Christians.

What was no doubt not invented by Christians was Peter's cowardly denial of being Jesus' disciple, a denial which occurred sometime during the Jewish process. This event, however embarrassing, is important, since it does place an eyewitness near the first stage of Jesus' passion. At the end of the process, the officials decided to charge Jesus before Pilate. Historians debate whether the Jewish authorities had to have recourse to Pilate for a death sentence to be executed. Though the evidence is ambiguous, it seems more plausible that John 18:31 is correct: at this period, the Sanhedrin no longer had the power to execute a death sentence.

From A.D. 26-36, Pontius Pilate was *prefect* of Judea (*not* procurator, as Tacitus thinks; an inscription discovered at Caesarea Maritima in 1961 confirms that Pilate held the lower title of prefect). Scarcely interested in theological disputes, Pilate would have been concerned only with accusations involving threats to Roman rule. Hence Jesus was brought before him charged with claiming to be King of the Jews—which may indicate that the Jewish process had touched on Jesus' messiahship. It was on this charge of kingship, understood no doubt in terms of being a revolutionary, that Jesus was tried and condemned by Pilate; a placard bearing the charge may have been affixed to the cross. The whole Barabbas incident, however, may be a later theological dramatization of what was at stake in the trial.

Roman crucifixion was usually preceded by scourging, which apparently so weakened Jesus that he could not carry the crossbeam (the upright stake remained in place at the site of execution). To aid Jesus, the soldiers pressed into service one Simon from Cyrene in Africa; his sons, Alexander and Rufus, must have been well-known members of Mark's church (cf. Mark 15:21). Once again, an eyewitness is present, this time for the whole process of carrying the cross and the crucifixion. Besides Simon, sympathetic witnesses included only a handful of female followers from Galilee. The placing of the mother of Jesus and the "beloved disciple" at the cross—present only in the Fourth Gospel—may reflect the symbolic mentality of John the Evangelist.

The crucifixion naturally took place outside the walls of the holy city, at a spot called Golgotha ("Skull Place"), possibly an abandoned quarry by the side of the road. Despite our traditional references to "Mt. Calvary," the Gospels say nothing about a hill. The best archaeological candidate for the site is the Church of the Holy Sepulchre in Jerusalem; despite continuing debates over the path of Jerusalem's walls in the first century, it seems that the site of the present church lay outside the walls in A.D. 30.

None of the Passion Narratives specifies whether Jesus was tied or nailed to the cross, though nails are mentioned in accounts of resurrection appearances. The use of nails does fit in with recent archaeological discoveries of crucified bodies around Jerusalem. With regard to what Jesus may or may not have said from the cross, the historian can reach no certain conclusion. All of the "seven last words" (a later conflation, in any case) may come from subsequent Christian tradition. This includes the famous cry of abandonment, "My God, my God, why have you forsaken me?" (Psalm 22:2), a favorite among psychiatrists and spiritual writers who show no knowledge of its place in Jewish prayer.

Jesus died relatively quickly, and Jewish law (Deuteronomy 21:22-23) required that the body not be left hanging overnight—all the more so when Passover Day (the 15th of Nisan) coincided that year with the Sabbath. Joseph of Arimathea, an influential Jew, interceded with Pilate in order to provide (temporary?) burial in a tomb he owned nearby. The actual tomb, long since destroyed, probably lay in a spot now enclosed by the Church of the Holy Sepulchre. The so-called Garden Tomb of General Gordon, beloved of tourists, is a product of nineteenth-century romanticism. The Galilean women at the cross also witnessed the preparations for burial, though the only name constant in all the traditions is Mary Magdalene. The story of setting a guard at the sealed tomb to prevent a grave-robbery stems from later Jewish-Christian debates; it is intriguing, though, that neither side in later polemics thought to deny that the tomb was soon empty.

As for the Shroud of Turin, up until very recently scholars were divided in their judgments, especially since the "relic" was first documented in the fourteenth century, when many dubious relics were flooding the West. Even if the shroud had been shown to go back to the time of Jesus, that would hardly have settled the case. Thousands of Jews were crucified in Palestine in the first centuries B.C. and A.D. with barbaric tortures similar to those suffered by Jesus. Even if the shroud had been that of a first-century Palestinian Jew, a multitude of unfortunate candidates could have qualified. As it is, recent carbon-14 tests on pieces of the shroud performed in England, Australia, and the United States show, according to the report delivered to the Archbishop of Turin, that the shroud was woven in the fourteenth century and so cannot be the shroud of Jesus. Only those fundamentalists who are constantly tempted to prove faith by pseudo-science will be upset.

Since the "Jesus of history" is by definition the Jesus open to empirical investigation by any and all observers, the resurrection of Jesus, of its very nature, lies outside the scope of this essay. This does not mean that the resurrection is not real, but simply that it is not an ordinary event of our time and space, verifiable in principle by believer and nonbeliever alike. All that history can say is that, starting in the early 30s of the first century, people who had known Jesus during his earthly life and who had deserted him out of fear did a remarkable about-face after his disgraceful death and affirmed that Jesus had risen and appeared to them. That these people were not raving lunatics is shown by their skillful organization and propagation of the new Christian movement. That they were sincere is demonstrated by their willingness to die for what they claimed. How any of us reacts to all this is a question not only of historical investigation but also of existential decision. In the end, there is the hermeneutics of belief and the hermeneutics of unbelief. What is beyond dispute is that Jesus of Nazareth is one of those perennial question marks in history with which mankind is never quite done. With a ministry of two or three years he attracted and infuriated his contemporaries, mesmerized and alienated the ancient world, unleashed a movement that has done the same ever since, and thus changed the course of history forever.

꙳

Afterword

Work continues apace in "history of Jesus" research. I have written a more technical article on the Jesus of history that can be found in *The New Jerome Biblical Commentary* (ed. R. Murphy, J. Fitzmyer, and R. Brown; Englewood Cliffs, NJ: Prentice Hall, 1990). I hope in a few years to publish a book-length treatment of the question in the Doubleday Anchor Bible Reference Library series.

Attention in the popular press has focused especially on the meetings of the "Jesus Seminar" organized by Prof. Robert Funk. At the end of a discussion of papers on given sayings of Jesus, a vote is taken as to the authenticity of the material. Recently, for example, a majority of the scholars voted that Jesus never taught the Lord's Prayer; at best it contained individual phrases he had used. Personally, I find this voting system curious. What is important is the argumentation pro and con; that is what the interested reader should know and be able to evaluate. A vote in itself is little more than an attention-getting gimmick, especially when, as in the case of the Lord's Prayer, the vote was split three ways. When consulting previous authorities on an issue, theology used to quote the maxim: "Authorities are to be weighed, not counted." The same might be said about Jesus research: it is the weight of arguments, not the number of votes, that counts. Some examples of the type of work done by members of the Jesus Seminar can be found in Charles W. Hedrick (ed.), *The Historical Jesus and the Rejected Gospels* (Semeia 44; Atlanta: Scholars, 1988). I would not share the optimism of some of the authors that the extracanonical literature can yield fruitful data for the quest for the historical Jesus. Perhaps the best essay in the volume is that of M. Eugene Boring, "The Historical-Critical Method's 'Criteria of Authenticity': The Beatitudes in Q and Thomas As a Test Case," pp. 9-44. Another member of the Jesus Seminar, Paul Hollenbach, surveys some recent works on the historical Jesus in "The Historical Jesus Question in North America Today," *BTB* 19 (1989) 11-22. Needless to say, I do not share Hollenbach's view that Christianity is a "mistake" which Jesus research must "overthrow."

2

Jesus among the Theologians:
I. Küng and Schillebeeckx

In my first essay, "Jesus among the Historians," I tried to summarize what most impartial historians might be able to say in summary about the "historical Jesus." Needless to say, however, no matter how objective the "quest for the historical Jesus" is pursued, there is almost always some philosophical or theological agenda lurking in the background—indeed, supplying the motivation that spurs on the search. Inevitably, after conclusions are reached about the historical data concerning Jesus, some theologian will try to press it into service for his or her theological program.

Now, there is nothing wrong with this. In fact, since theology, according to St. Anselm, is nothing else than "faith seeking understanding," it is only natural that theologians should reflect on results of the "quest" in order to gain further understanding of the mystery of the Incarnation. If Christians claim that, in Jesus of Nazareth, "the Word became flesh and dwelt among us," then they must grapple with the question of how this affirmation of faith relates to what we can know about the historical Jesus. Catholic theologians in both the First and Third Worlds have recently accepted this challenge with gusto. The question that a student of the Bible must ask is how these systematic theologians have understood and used the Jesus of history in their larger project of reflecting on faith in the context of the modern world. Both the present and the following essays will attempt to grasp and evaluate the assimilation of the historical Jesus into the theologies of four contemporary Catholic systematicians. Admittedly, the project I propose may raise objections. Some may feel that an exegete like myself is not competent to judge how systematicians integrate the historical Jesus into their work. I stress therefore that I do not presume to pass judgment on the entire work of the systematicians I shall discuss in this and the following essay. My focus will be solely the way in which they use the historical Jesus. A limited goal, to be sure. But still, it may be of some use to have Dr. Frankenstein comment on what the townspeople have done with his creation.

Still, even with this narrowing of perspective, a topic like "An exegete looks at the historical Jesus of theologians" remains terribly broad, in view of the unabated flood of books on the subject. I was pondering how further to specify the scope of these essays when I happened to come upon a sentence of Albert Schweitzer that I had first read some 15 years ago. In the new 1950 preface to the sixth German edition of his classic work, *The Quest of the Historical Jesus (Geschichte der Leben-Jesu-Forschung* [2 vols.; Munich/Hamburg: Siebenstern Taschenbuch, 1966]), which was first published in 1906, Schweitzer concludes his preface with the ringing affirmation that "research on the life of Jesus is an act of honesty [*Wahrhaftigkeitstat*] on the part of Protestant Christianity." That is certainly true. Roman Catholic scholars neither initiated the critical quest nor fostered it in the nineteenth and most of the twentieth century.

The reason for this absence is not difficult to discover. The anti-Modernist suppression of Catholic Scripture scholarship, which began around 1905 under Pope Pius X (first serious negative response from the Biblical Commission; see Denziger-Schönmetzer # 3372-73), put an end to practically all critical research on the Bible by Catholics—and therefore, *a fortiori*, put an end to any serious quest for the historical Jesus by Catholic exegetes. Great minds like Ferdinand Prat and Marie-Joseph Lagrange were reduced to writing harmonizing "lives of Christ." During this period, the Catholic response to

Protestant life-of-Jesus research was almost entirely negative and apologetic. Endless ink was spilt to prove how the genealogies of Matthew and Luke did not contradict each other, how all four accounts of the public ministry really coincided, how all of the discourses in John's Gospel were just as much the historical words of Jesus as were the sayings in the Synoptics. (One feels a twinge of sadness when one reads J.A.T. Robinsons's last book, *The Priority of John*; one begins to suspect that Robinson finally arrived where Catholics had been stuck in the 20s and 30s.)

Granted this long dark night of the anti-Modernist suppression, which reached into the 1940s and enjoyed a short revival around 1960, it is no surprise that when Catholic exegetes reemerged into the light, like the prisoners in Beethoven's *Fidelio*, they did not immediately rush to tackle the sensitive question of the historical Jesus as the first item on their agenda. Many initial skirmishes had to be fought and many other territories pacified before that front could be opened up. All this may sound exaggerated and melodramatic until one remembers that the "grandfather" of all German Catholic exegetes, Anton Vögtle, had to have his article on "Jesus Christ" censored before it could be published in the *Lexikon für Theologie und Kirche*—in 1960! The dark days are not all that distant.

Fortunately, though, they are past. In recent decades, Catholic exegetes and theologians have hurled themselves into the quest for the historical Jesus with a naive gusto that might raise a few eyebrows among their older and wiser Protestant colleagues. Since the Catholics are largely "playing catch-up," they have naturally learned and borrowed heavily from previous Protestant scholarship. Now that fact raises an interesting set of questions. To what extent have Catholic questers harvested the best in Protestant research? And to what extent have Catholics merely repeated their Protestant forebears to the point of repeating their mistakes? And to what extent have Catholic questers put their own Catholic "spin" on the questions? Here, at least, was a precise, contemporary, and ecumenical question that merited personal reflection and interfaith dialogue.

In the present and following essay, therefore, I propose to consider four contemporary Catholic scholars who have labored in or raised questions about various dimensions of "Jesus-research" (to use the phrase favored by James H. Charlesworth). For the sake of contrast, two of the authors will be European, and two Latin American. As an ecumenical offering, I hope to point out what these Catholic authors have learned from and perhaps contributed to the *Wahrhaftigkeitstat*, that act of honesty on the part of Protestant Christianity, so beloved of Albert Schweitzer.

As we begin to review Catholic works on the historical Jesus during the past decade-and-a-half, it is perhaps symptomatic that the contemporary Catholic quest did not first burst upon the public scene as a result of books by Catholic Scripture scholars. Ordinary Catholics were much more likely to have become aware of the historical-Jesus question from the controversial works of Catholic systematicians. Within out time frame, the earliest and best-known of these were Hans Küng and Edward Schillebeeckx. This predominance of systematicians may be no accident. As a result of previous run-ins with authorities, Catholic Scripture scholars have tended to write highly technical articles and books for their colleagues; not too many of them have authored wide-ranging popular syntheses on the historical Jesus. Indeed, with the exception of a few scholars like Raymond Brown, Catholic exegetes are not terribly well-known to the Catholic public at large. Küng and Schillebeeckx, to the contrary, tried to absorb Scripture studies on the historical Jesus into a larger theological whole and make the results available to the Catholic in the street. In the process, they got into trouble.

It is too simplistic, however, to yoke Küng and Schillebeeckx so closely together. Their projects are not the same, nor is their approach to the historical Jesus. Each must be treated separately.

I

Küng's treatment of the historical Jesus forms the centerpiece, though not the whole project, in his *On Being a Christian* [German ed. 1974; ET 1976]. Here I am interested not in the book's overarching project, with all the controversies it aroused, but rather in its portrait of the historical Jesus.

Küng is at pains to dispel all popular misconceptions about Jesus—but especially those held by the pious or marginal believer. After briefly addressing the skeptic by pointing to Jesus' historical reality in a concrete time and place, Küng spends a good deal of time developing his portrait of Jesus by a *via negativa*: Jesus wasn't a priest or theologian, a tool of the establishment, a violent revolutionary, a monk or professional religious, or a pious legalist. One can see a great deal of Küng's own agenda in what is thus excluded. Positively, Küng presents Jesus as proclaiming the kingdom of God, signifying its coming through his actions and his teaching, which emphasized that the true will of God is not legalism. Jesus rather aimed at the humanization of the individual and society, proclaiming not a new God but a revolution in our understanding of God. Now I suppose the academician might shrug his or her shoulders and ask what is new here. Yet the startling popularity of Küng's book both here and in Europe (one year after its publication in Germany it was in its sixth edition) indicates that it addressed a real need. In that sense, Küng achieved what every "Jesus book" should do: present Jesus to a new generation in a way that will be both intelligible and challenging.

And yet there are real problems with Küng's presentation. It may be unfair to harp on the fact that the criteria for judging historicity are referred to only briefly and that arguments about individual sayings are waived in favor of a supposed consensus about the general pattern of Jesus' life and teaching. His book is, after all, a work addressed to the public at large. But the omission of a detailed discussion of criteria and their application—a discussion one does find in some popular works—creates real problems. If we are never sure about the historicity of any individual saying, how do we ever arrive at certainty about the big picture, the overall pattern of Jesus' words and deeds? A chain is as weak as its weakest link.

To take an example: Küng states that Jesus put himself

above the Mosaic Law by rescinding prescriptions on clean and unclean food, as well as the regulations concerning divorce, oaths, and retaliation. Now this may ultimately be true; I think a good argument can be made for the authenticity of at least some of these sayings. But the relevant texts, mostly from Matthew, are simply cited by Küng in his footnotes, with no argumentation about their authenticity. Indeed, verses that are widely viewed as Matthean creations (for example, Mt 5:20, "Unless your justice exceeds that of the scribes and Pharisees, you shall not enter the kingdom of heaven") are cited alongside of sayings that may well come from Jesus himself, e.g., the prohibition of divorce. Moreover, precepts of Jesus which do not really oppose the Mosaic Law, such as love of enemies, are listed along with the prohibition of divorce and retaliation as examples of revocation of the Law.

One has to stop and ask: Why is this popular presentation becoming simply an inaccurate presentation? What are the unspoken criteria of historicity operative here? It seems to me that, for Küng, the real arbiters of historicity, the real representatives of the scholarly consensus he adopts, are largely Günther Bornkamm and Küng's colleague at Tübingen, Ernst Käsemann. This becomes especially clear when the Pharisees' theology is presented mainly in terms of the question of merit, with Jesus naturally being portrayed as strongly against merit, despite his well-attested use of the terminology of "reward" (*misthos*). As E.P. Sanders has suggested, this whole scenario, this whole way of approaching the question, may owe more to disputes during the 16th-century Reformation than to the teaching of a first-century Jesus. Küng learned much from his German Lutheran confreres; he also took over their particular prism for viewing Judaism and Jesus in terms of Catholic-Protestant debates.

Another sign of Küng's dependence on German post-Bultmannians may be his *a priori* exclusion of John's Gospel from serious consideration as a source for Jesus' words and deeds, except for the period of the Passion. Now, I certainly do not want to defend the uncritical harmonizaion of John with the Synoptics that we see in J.A.T. Robinson's last book, *The Priority of John*. But I do think that the work of moderate scholars like C.H. Dodd and Raymond Brown has made the wholesale exclusion of the Fourth Gospel from serious consideration an outmoded and biased position, though one still found among German post-Bultmannians and Americans under their influence.

Along with this dependence on the post-Bultmannians, Küng adopts a position much at variance, in my opinion, with a basic dictum of Martin Kähler and Rudolf Bultmann, the dictum that the object of Christian faith must be the Christ proclaimed in the Gospels and the church's preaching, and not a hypothetical Jesus of history reconstructed by modern scholars. Küng, as a matter of fact, does not in general operate with a strict Bultmannian dichotomy between the historical and the historic (*historisch* and *geschichtlich*). He prefers to speak of the historic (*geschichtlich*) Jesus, who is the real (*wirklich*) Christ. Küng's ringing affirmation that the Jesus of history and the Christ of the Gospels are not two different entities is certainly good Catholic theology, but in practice that principle lies uneasy alongside of Küng's trust in historical-critical research's ability to recover for us the "real Christ." Küng states that "the stories of Jesus lead us to ask for his real history ... for what really happened." Thanks to historical-critical research, he says, we can ask about the "true, real, historical Christ" in a way not possible in former centuries.

Now Küng is careful to deny that critical research can establish or prove faith, or is even necessary for faith. Yet the easy way in which the "real, historical" Jesus whom Christians believe in and who is the norm of what is truly Christian is equated with Küng's historical reconstruction of Jesus makes me uneasy. Paradoxically, this follower of the post-Bultmannians almost seems at times to be marching into the camp of Joachim Jeremias. I wonder whether, for all the influence of the post-Bultmannians, Küng is not finally propelled by a fierce Catholic drive to show that faith does not contradict reason and indeed that the two can be correlated into a higher synthesis. That is a noble project, but in *On Being a Christian* it may result in a questionable identification of Küng's hypothetical reconstruction of Jesus with the Christ of faith, with the former being the dominant factor. One's ultimate impression is that of a mixed bag, a valiant attempt to assimilate empirical, historical exegesis into Catholic systematic theology. But the marriage of Bornkamm's Jesus to post-Vatican II theology remains a shotgun wedding.

II

When we turn to the Belgian Dominican systematician, Edward Schillebeeckx, we immediately notice similarities to and yet differences from Küng. Both wrote their major works in the same year, 1974 (though the English edition of Schillebeeckx did not appear until 1979). Both produced mammoth books on Jesus Christ that proved to be religious best sellers. Both sought to mesh contemporary exegesis, especially the quest for the historical Jesus, with Catholic systematic theology, in order to create a modern, intellectually respectable Christology within the parameters of the Catholic faith.

Still, the differences, I would hold, are greater than the similarities. Schillebeeckx, in my view, is the more subtle and learned scholar; and he has produced a more profound and complex book, one focused more completely on the person and work of Jesus. Schillebeeckx's basic question, like Küng's, is one of relevance: What does salvation in Jesus, coming to us from God, mean to us now? Yet, despite this ultimate concern for relevance, Schillebeeckx wisely realizes that relevance is a goal to be pursued, not an all-determining starting point. Schillebeeckx's starting point is instead a slow, almost ponderous 100-page mapping-out of method, in which his program of confronting and correlating historical research and the Catholic faith is clearly articulated.

Almost from the beginning we sense that Schillebeeckx has a much better grasp of the complexities of early Christological traditions than does Küng. There is much more discussion of the redactional tendencies of Mark and Q, Matthew and Luke, much more appreciation of the many varied Christological models and titles afloat in the early church—and hence the problem of discerning any one "historical Jesus" amid all the primitive Christological pluralism. Schillebeeckx readily admits that, from the beginning, even prior to Easter, there were different "images" of Jesus (an echo of his dictum that there is no experience apart from initial interpretation). While a plurality of images is legitimate, every image must be tested for legitimacy by being referred back to the historical phenomenon of the real Jesus of Nazareth. Our own projections, he says, must be corrected by that reality, or otherwise Jesus becomes a mere receptacle for our own predilections, an arbitrary cipher that we manipulate. Hence the necessity of the quest.

With his philosophical mind, Schillebeeckx defines the concept of the historical Jesus very carefully. The historical Jesus is that which the methods of historical criticism enable us to retrieve of Jesus of Nazareth. Unlike the positivistic historicism of the 19th-century, we must appreciate that what can be reconstructed historically (i.e., the historical Jesus) does not coincide with the full reality of the Jesus who lived in the first century. So notice: unlike Küng, Schillebeeckx resolutely refuses to identify any or all historical reconstructions with the real Jesus—and in this he is methodologically superior. Schillebeeckx realizes that the historical Jesus is no less a Jesus-image than is the Christ of the believer. They cannot be sharply opposed because, as images, they both derive from the full reality of Jesus. What really occurs in history is broader than the history recoverable by a historian. And so a faith-interpretation of Jesus can express a part of the reality of Jesus inaccessible in principle to purely historical-critical methods.

Yet Schillebeeckx holds that it is absolutely essential that Christianity concern itself with the quest today, for a radical breach between Christian faith and what we know by historical research is untenable. Here Schillebeeckx articulates a typically Catholic emphasis. Thus, he firmly rejects a total opposition between the historical Jesus and the Christian kerygma, be it from the viewpoint of Rudolf Bultmann, David Strauss, or Herbert Braun. At the same time—ever in search of balance— Schillebeeckx rejects any attempt to validate Christian faith by historical study. Historical study gives a concrete content to faith. "One cannot go on forever believing in ideas," he says (p. 75); "a kerygma minus the historical Jesus is vacuous...." Still, the historical Jesus can never be a verification of faith. A historian cannot demonstrate that in Jesus some truly saving activity on God's part has occurred. What a historian can do is trace a line of continuity between a Christology after Jesus' death and Jesus' message and life before Calvary. But this does not prove Christian faith.

Schillebeeckx's independent position, the product of his own thought, is clear in his remark that "scholars who are also believing Christians usually claim too much regarding the historical Jesus ... even a punctilious historian like ... Bornkamm fails to avoid this in his already somewhat aging study of 'Jesus of Nazareth.'" One cannot imagine Küng making such a remark against a leading post-Bultmannian.

Also unlike Küng, Schillebeeckx explores the criteria of historicity at length. A true internationalist from Belgium, Schillebeeckx pointedly observes that one has to look at German, English, Scandinavian, and French exegetes on this point, for different groups tend to emphasize different critieria. His own list of criteria are as follows: (1) traditions that go against the redactional tendencies of the evangelist; (2) discontinuity with Judaism and the church; also sayings and actions of Jesus which would embarrass the church; (3) multiple attestation in different sources and literary genres; (4) consistency or coherence with other authentic Jesus material; (5) and most characteristically of Schillebeeckx, the criterion of the rejection of Jesus' message and praxis, leading to his execution. Here Schillebeeckx touches on a point many miss: A historical understanding of Jesus' life and message is possible only when it is shown why they result in his crucifixion. A bland, platitudinous Jesus, an academic spinner of riddles and symbols, a tweedy professor of Semitic rhetorical forms, would not end up impaled on a cross by Roman soldiers. A good deal of what goes on today in American Jesus-research might well take Schillebeeckx's final criterion to heart. In itself, this criterion of Jesus' rejection does not discover anything authentic, but it does sharpen and concentrate our inquiry on certain types of material.

Schillebeeckx's independent stance, divorced from traditional apologetics, is shown in his rejection of certain popular criteria of historicity. Against J. Jeremias and Matthew Black, Schillebeeckx questions the usefulness of detecting Aramaic language and Palestinian color behind sayings of Jesus.

Aramaic-speaking or bilingual Christians abounded in Palestine for a generation after Jesus' crucifixion; they could easily have created material seen to have an Aramaic substratum. The same can be said for parables. Jesus was not the only Jew ever to teach in parables; some of his talented disciples could cetainly have imitated his style. One must show, not presume, that the particular parable under study comes from the historical Jesus.

Schillebeeckx then proceeds to apply his criteria to a fairly full sketch of Jesus' message, manner of life, rejection, and death. He again stresses the importance of the final events of Jesus' life for an interpretation of the whole. Instead of arguing over what exact words Jesus may or may not have pronounced over the bread and wine at the Last Supper, Schillebeeckx stresses the overall attitude of Jesus as he celebrated this farewell meal. Despite the looming, brutal separation, Jesus used the supper to affirm that God would renew table fellowship between Jesus and his disciples in the kingdom. Jesus used the supper to dramatize his unconditional obedience to the Father and his loving service to his followers even to the point of death. Schillebeeckx claims that it is this self-understanding of Jesus in the face of death that creates the possibility and lays the foundation for later Christian interpretation of Jesus' life and death. There is no gap, says Schillebeeckx, between Jesus' self-understanding and the Christ proclaimed by the church. The critical question is: Is this self-understanding correct? The answer, of course, cannot be given by historical investigation, but only by the response of belief or unbelief.

Nevertheless, Schillebeeckx does not end his historical quest here. He continues by exploring the earliest Christological creeds preserved in the NT. These various independent interpretations of Jesus have evident points of contact with particular facets of Jesus' life on earth, however one-sided they may be. Indeed, *the* central point Schillebeeckx makes about these earliest Christological statements is the historical continuity between each distinctive kerygma and a particular aspect of the earthly Jesus. Schillebeeckx isolates four primitive creeds and correlates each with some historical foundation in Jesus' life: (1) the maranatha or parousia Christology, which he correlates with Jesus as the proclaimer of the imminent rule of God, bringing definitive salvation; (2) the *theios aner* Christology, linked with Jesus as Davidic Messiah, which he correlates with Jesus' activity as healer and exorcist; (3) various wisdom Christologies (Jesus the humble servant of wisdom or Jesus as wisdom incarnate), which he correlates with Jesus the teacher of wisdom and of a true relation with God as Father; (4) "Easter Christologies," which he naturally correlates with the historical fact of Jesus' crucifixion and the later claim of the disciples that they had seen Jesus after his death.

Schillebeeckx stresses that all these different creeds could coalesce into one Christian gospel because they all referred to the same historical person. They all acknowledged salvation in the person of Jesus, which, for Schillebeeckx means that they all identified Jesus with the eschatological prophet, which he calls "the basic creed of all Christianity." Indeed—and this is a linchpin of his whole project—Schillebeeckx makes the category of eschatological prophet "the matrix" of all the other honorific titles and creedal strands. "That the link between the earthly Jesus and the kerygmatic Christ is the recognition, common to all creedal strands, of the earthly Jesus as the eschatological prophet . . . and that this identification . . . was most likely made prior to Easter, has enormous consequences. It points to a considerable continuity between the impression that Jesus made during his earthly days and the apparently "advanced Christology' of the church's *kerygmata* or affirmations of belief after his death" (p. 479). Amid all the various Christologies, "the unity turns out to be more universal and profound than the pluralism."

The broad scope and sweep of Schillebeeckx's project, as well as his adept handling of the vast literature on the topic, is breathtaking and has many strong points. (1) It presents a more careful mapping-out of problem and method, compared with Küng's work. (2) Schillebeeckx has a more international outlook, using a broad spectrum of both Catholic and Protestant exegetes. He thus appreciates the labyrinthine nature of the scholarly disputes. He is not a captive of German exegesis, especially the post-Bultmannian variety—although, as we shall see, the exegetes he leans on at pivotal points are Protestants. (3) Knowing the wide spectrum of opinions, he has to argue his case more on individual texts; hence there is more genuine exegesis in his discussion. (4) For all the ecumenical scholarship, the book remains truly Catholic in its drive to see a link, a continuity, amid all the discontinuity between the historical Jesus and the Christ of faith. Indeed, the latter seems to emerge "organically," despite all the transformations, out of the former. Perhaps for the first time in Catholic theology, we have in Schillebeeckx's *Jesus* a genuine integration of the quest for the historical Jesus into a systematic Christology. Whatever its failures, this is the book's claim to lasting fame. In the future, no Catholic Christology can turn the clock back to the pre-Schillebeeckx era and still hope to be taken seriously.

Still, there are problems. (1) Precisely because Schillebeeckx treats exegetes and their exegesis in such detail, one must ask why he chooses to side with this or that exegete on a given question. His choice is not always justified; and, though he would deny it, he seems to pick whichever exegete suits his program at that point. Here we touch the ongoing problem of the sophisticated theologian taking over the work of a given exegete. Such borrowing is unavoidable in an age of functional specialization in theology. No one can be the Renaissance man, competent in all fields. But the questions remain: which exegetes? and why this exegete in this case?

(2) More specifically—and here I become quite subjective in my criticism—I think that at major points in his argument, Schillebeeckx relies on the wrong exegetes, notably Klaus Berger for Christological titles, Siegfried Schulz for the Q document, and Theodore Weeden for Mark. By the way, let me emphasize that I do not think that these three are the wrong choices because all three happen to be Protestants. As I have said, that coincidence is rather a sign of one of the book's strengths: its knowledge of the wide spectrum of opinions.

But the problem involved in his choice of these three particular exegetes cannot be denied. In my view, Klaus Berger is much too impressionistic and uncritical in his assembling of various strands of Christological traditions. He moves too quickly back and forth among widely separated centuries to create rather artificial blocks of tradition. This defect is reflected in some of Schillebeeckx's Christological models. For example, the eschatological prophet is a pivotal figure for the whole of Schillebeeckx's argument about continuity between the historical Jesus and the Christ of faith. Yet Richard Horsely has recently pointed out ("'Like One of the Prophets of Old': Two types of Popular Prophets at the Time of Jesus," *CBQ* 47 [1985] 435-63, esp. 437-43) that such a figure was by no means widespread or well-known in first-century Palestine.

As for Siegfried Schulz's reconstruction of all the stages of tradition and redaction of the Q document and his attempt to assign each saying of Jesus to a particular stage, I must admit that I can just about manage a basic belief in Q's existence. But to do what Schulz wants to do would require the omniscience of God himself. Schulz wants to know more about Q than I think I can ever know about the historical Jesus; this is trying to explain the obscure by the more obscure. Still more problematic is Schulz's reconstruction of a Q community, whose whole theology is summed up in a Q document without any passion-death-resurrection kerygma. This is to create an academic phantom, for there is no solid empirical evidence that such a community with such a limited kerygma ever existed. We have enough professorial poltergeists as it is.

As for Theodore Weeden's views on Mark, exegetes have already seen something of a reaction against his radical approach to Mark. Carl Holladay (*Theios Aner in Hellenistic Judaism* [SBLDS 40; Missoula, MT: Scholars, 1977]) has pointed out how questionable it is to use *theios aner* to describe a miracle worker in first-century Palestinian Judaism. Similarly, Ernest Best (*Mark. The Gospel as Story* [Edinburgh: Clark, 1983.]) and others have shown that the totally negative depiction of the disciples in Mark is a one-sided reading.

(3) Most problematic from a Catholic view—though this takes us outside of a consideration of the historical Jesus—is Schillebeeckx's treatment of the resurrection. He interprets it as a conversion experience of Peter and the other disciples, who sense once again God's forgiveness coming to them in Jesus, who must therefore be alive. The whole thing sounds too much like an academic consensus reached after discussion in a German university seminar.

Still, in spite of all these reservations, I think Schillebeeckx's book is a more significant work than Küng's, especially because it shows a wider knowledge and use of both Catholic and Protestant questers, all absorbed into an original synthesis. As I have indicated, for better or for worse, the ecumenical scholarship appears notably in Schillebeeckx's dependence on three prominent Protestant exegetes at three pivotal points in his argument. Indeed, it may be a crowning achievement of ecumenical scholarship that, while the two most important Christologies of the 1970s were written by Catholics, neither could have been completed without the Protestant exegesis on which both heavily rely.

❧

Afterword

No work since Schillebeeckx's *Jesus* has attempted such a massive survey of New Testament exegesis with a view to incorporating it into a contemporary Christological synthesis. Perhaps the limitations of Schillebeeckx's own fine work showed that no one theologian today can hope to be the Renaissance man competent in all fields. What we may need for the next *Jesus* book of the Schillebeeckx type is the collaborative work of a New Testament exegete, a historical theologian, and a systematician. Such a joint work might prevent the theologians involved from adopting idiosyncratic or out-dated views—something that regrettably happens at times in Schillebeeckx's *Jesus*.

This is not to say that theologians have not continued to absorb and employ good exegesis in their systematic reflections. Two examples that broaden out the Christological question to Trinitarian and ecclesiological horizons respectively are Walter Kasper, *The God of Jesus Christ* (New York: Crossroad, 1984); and Francis Schüssler Fiorenza, *Foundational Theology. Jesus and the Church* (New York: Crossroad, 1984). A more popular, but solid, work that focuses on the relation of the historical Jesus to the origins of the church is Gerhard Lohfink, *Jesus and Community* (Philadelphia: Fortress; New York/Ramsey, NJ: Paulist, 1984). An introductory survey of the many different contemporary approaches to the study of Jesus can be found in William M. Thompson, *The Jesus Debate. A Survey and Synthesis* (New York/Mahwah, NJ: Paulist, 1985). The use of recent studies of narrative in Christology is explored by Robert A. Krieg, *Story-Shaped Christology. The Role of Narratives in Identifying Jesus Christ* (New York/Mahwah, NJ: Paulist, 1988).

3

Jesus among the Theologians:
II. Sobrino and Segundo

In the preceding essay, I examined the use to which two noted First-World theologians put the results of the quest for the historical Jesus. Now, just as American theologians have been eager to declare their intellectual independence from Europe, so too theologians of the Third World have been struggling during the past two decades to enunciate their particular approach to theology, in a context of oppression and a need for liberation. The fact is, though, that "liberation theology" has become a vague umbrella-term, beneath which many different approaches find shelter. Part of the problem is the elasticity of the phrase "Third World": in reality, the cultural, social, and economic situation in Brazil or Uruguay is vastly different from that of South Africa or various parts of Asia. Then, too, some of the concerns of feminist and black theologies intersect with liberation theology. The resulting mix is all the richer, but all the more difficult to survey.[1]

---

[1]Even in the restricted area of the exegetical underpinnings of feminist theology, research is constantly on the move, making generalizations dangerous. For example, most people would automatically turn to Elisabeth Schüssler Fiorenza's *In Memory of Her* (New York: Crossroad, 1983) for a classic articulation of New Testament feminist theology. Yet, like any scholar, Schüssler Fiorenza is always testing and developing new positions. For example, her more recent article, "Rhetorical Situation and Historical Reconstruction in 1 Corinthians" (*NTS* 33 [1987] 386-403) seems to take a darker view of Paul vis-á-vis the freedom and egalitarianism of the Corinthian community than does *In Memory of Her*, 226-33. It is precisely to avoid broad generalizations about a whole movement that, in this essay, I concentrate on specific works of two liberation theologians—realizing that they may indeed move on to more developed positions.

Granted this diversity, I am faced with the practical problem of choosing one type or branch of liberation theology to use in my probe of theological appropriations of the historical Jesus. Of all the possible candidates, the type that intrigues me the most is Latin American liberation theology,[2] notable for its fierce desire to ground its reflection and praxis in the message and praxis of the historical Jesus, as reflected in the canonical Gospels, as well as for its clear intention to root its reflection in the "popular Catholicism" actually lived out by a native population over centuries of oppression.

Hence, I think it appropriate to focus on the special use that Latin American theologians have made of the historical Jesus. These theologians have brought a breath of fresh air to theology in general, Christology in particular, and the historical Jesus most especially. I say this without any disparagement of the fine work done in the area of Christology by the First-World scholars I studied in the previous essay, Hans Küng and Edward Schillebeeckx. As I stressed there, Schillebeeckx's books, in particular, show an amazing command of a wide range of exegetical opinions, Catholic and Protestant alike. But, for all their newness, Küng and Schillebeeckx still reflect the context of Christology as taught in European universities; even the ecumenical scholarship is part of that context.

We seem to breathe a different atmosphere when we turn to the use of "Jesus-research"[3] displayed by Latin American liberation theologians. In saying this, I do not mean to fall into the naive claim that liberation theology is free of academic influence from the First World. Many of the Latin American liberation theologians studied in Europe and/or the United States. To take as examples the two scholars I intend to study

---

[2]I readily admit, therefore, that one could easily cast the net farther afield to explore the Christology of liberation theologies in other *Sitze im Leben*; see, e.g., in a South African context, Albert Nolan, *Jesus before Christianity* (Maryknoll, NY: Orbis, 1976; 9th printing, 1987). Limitations of space, as well as the constantly changing theological scene, demand some practical choices.

[3]This is the phrase that James H. Charlesworth prefers to the loaded phrases, "the quest" or "the search for the historical Jesus" (implying that we have lost something that we may or may not find); see his *Jesus within Judaism* (Anchor Bible Reference Library; New York: Doubleday, 1988) 1-2.

in detail, Jon Sobrino attended St. Louis University and then the Hochschule Sankt Georgen in Frankfurt, while Juan Luis Segundo studied at Louvain in Belgium and the Sorbonne in Paris. Interestingly, their footnotes and bibliographies reflect dependence largely on European rather than U.S. authors. Thus, one does not see the total break with continental scholarship that is sometimes assumed. Sobrino himself points this out in the English-language preface to his early book, *Christology at the Crossroads.*[4.]

Yet there *is* a difference as we cross into the Third World. The Christologies of Sobrino and Segundo have been forged in the furnace of oppression, violence, and the need for a liberating praxis and theology in San Salvador and Uruguay respectively. They represent a fierce drive to make academic theology speak to and be responsible to the lived Christianity of a suffering people yearning for liberation from political, social, and economic enslavement. Within the Catholic Church, no group prior to the liberation theologians had spotlighted so intensely the past misuse of religion to prop up oppressive structures and the need to re-speak Catholic faith and theology to support instead the liberation of the oppressed.

This is a genuine achievement that cannot be gainsaid— least of all by me. If, in this essay I do subject some liberation theologians to the same sort of critique that I have applied in the previous essay to Küng and Schillebeeckx, I do so not out of any disdain for Latin American theology. It is all too easy for armchair exegetes in the safety of the United States or Canada to criticize Latin American authors who daily risk their lives by writing with a relevance that could be deadly to themselves. I yield to no one in admiration for their personal courage and scholarly achievements under great pressure and restrictions. However, theologians like Sobrino and Segundo have chosen to write not simply inspiring popular literature and stirring homilies. They have chosen to take up the discourse and trappings of academic scholarship, complete with learned footnotes and references to noted exegetes to bolster

---

[4] *Christology at the Crossroads* (Maryknoll, NY: Orbis, 1976; ET 1978) xxix.

their positions and debate their confreres. If, to support one's argument, one chooses to play the academic game, then one has to be willing to be judged by the rules of that game. What I propose to do, therefore, is to take a brief look at how a few liberation theologians are incorporating the quest for the historical Jesus into their Christologies.

I stress *a few* liberation theologians, since there is no one homogenized liberation theology—as even recent documents from the Vatican have recognized.[5] I do not presume to make judgments valid for all writers in the field. I rather propose to examine the two theologians already mentioned—Jon Sobrino and Juan Luis Segundo—because they are prominent liberation theologians who have recently written specifically on the question of the historical Jesus as the basis of liberation theology. Even in such a limited area, though, one cannot presume that an author's opinions have remained unchanged from book to book. Hence I will restrict myself to two recent publications: (1) *Jesus in Latin America*, by Sobrino,[6] with a glance back at his earlier *Christology at the Crossroads*; and (2) *The Historical Jesus of the Synoptics* by Segundo.[7]

I

Sobrino himself, with admirable honesty, warns the reader in his preface to the English language edition of *Christology at the Crossroads* that there are problems with his use of Scripture: ". . . the scriptural texts introduced in this book stand in need of more solid exegetical grounding, for this particular

---

[5]So the "Instruction on Certain Aspects of the 'Theology of Liberation,'" issued by the Congregation for the Doctrine of the Faith and dated 6 August 1984 (*Origins* 14 [1984]) 193, 195-204, esp. Section III par. 3 on p. 196: "As with all movements of ideas, the 'theologies of liberation' present diverse theological positions. Their doctrinal frontiers are badly defined." Though the popular press presented this instruction as highly critical of liberation theology, what is perhaps surprising is how much good the Congregation is willing to see in the movement.

[6]*Jesus in Latin America* (Maryknoll, NY: Orbis, 1987; Spanish original, 1982).

[7]*The Historical Jesus of the Synoptics* (Jesus of Nazareth Yesterday and Today, vol. 2; Maryknoll, NY: Orbis, 1985; Spanish original, 1982).

Christology purports to be based on the historical Jesus." That is the key point for both of these authors: the historical Jesus does not enter in tangentially; he is basic to the whole project. Sobrino continues: ". . . I have tried to take due account of what exegesis has to say about the various passages used here. . . . But the exegetical analysis needs to be worked out in greater detail."[8]

In fact, very few important exegetes are cited at length in *Christology at the Crossroads*, and those who are cited are not the most recent authors. It is symptomatic of the book that Rudolf Bultmann is the most quoted exegete, and often he is referred to more for his general hermeneutics and theology. There are also scattered references to Schnackenburg, Thüsing, Jeremias, Käsemann, and Cullmann, with a few pointers to Bornkamm and Herbert Braun. Notice, by the way, that almost all of these authors are German. The wide range of recent exegetical literature used by Schillebeeckx in his *Jesus* book simply is not there.

But this is not the most serious flaw of *Christology at the Crossroads*. Sobrino's whole presentation of liberation theology claims to be based on the historical Jesus; and that is where it is most seriously lacking. Nowhere in the book is there any extended, critical discussion of what the phrase "the historical Jesus" means or what criteria we are to use to discern authentic material. One almost gets the impression that the historical Jesus equals the full reality of the pre-Easter Jesus, with no awareness of all the difficulties that simplistic equation involves. At times, the historical Jesus seems to be Jesus insofar as he fits into Sobrino's program of liberation theology. For all the talk of a new approach, we are not all that far from the proof-text use of Scripture in the old Catholic manuals of dogmatic theology.

Indeed, Sobrino's work is very much a product of dogmatic and systematic theology, so much so that even when he is speaking about the historical Jesus, most of the writers he cites are German systematicians, especially Rahner, Pannenberg, and Moltmann.

[8]Sobrino, *Christology at the Crossroads*, xxvi.

In his more recent book, *Jesus in Latin America*, Sobrino seeks to reply to criticisms of *Christology at the Crossroads.* Unfortunately, the concept of the historical Jesus continues to remain fuzzy, at times being equated with a Christology that emphasizes the humanity of Jesus or Jesus' earthly career. Even within this fuzzy context there are problems. Sobrino constantly emphasizes Jesus' partisanship and favoritism toward the poor, the oppressed and sinners. These various groups tend to be lumped together as the object of Jesus' favor, and solidarity with them is seen as the cause of opposition to Jesus and finally of his death. Yet E.P. Sanders, in his fine book *Jesus and Judaism,*[9] points out that it is illegitimate to treat all these groups as one. There is no proof that Jesus' concern for economically poor or uneducated people caused a major scandal or persecution, or was the major reason for his execution. Matters may have been different with his free offer of forgiveness to public sinners who were considered to have broken with Judaism. Here Jesus may have offended *many* sincere and zealous Jews, and not just the rich or powerful. Since such people as tax collectors were not necessarily the poorest members of the community, and indeed some like Zacchaeus (Luke 19:1-10)[10] may have been wealthy, Jesus' scandalous free-wheeling offer of forgiveness to these economic oppressors cannot be simply equated with his care for the economically deprived. (This is a key point, and I will come back to it when I look at Segundo.)

---

[9]*Jesus and Judaism* (Philadelphia: Fortress, 1985).

[10]I purposely use the phrase "some like Zacchaeus," since this is not the place to enter into a full discussion of the historicity of the Zacchaeus incident. Favorable to at least a historical core are J. Ernst, *Das Evangelium nach Lukas* (RNT; Regensburg: Pustet, 1976) 512-13; J. Fitzmyer, *The Gospel According to Luke (X-XXIV)* (AB 28A; Garden City, NY: Doubleday, 1983) 1218-19; W. Grundmann, *Das Evangelium nach Lukas* (THKNT 3; 7th ed.; Berlin: Evangelische Verlagsanstalt, 1974) 358-59; I. H. Marshall, *The Gospel of Luke* (NIGNTC; Grand Rapids: Eerdmans, 1978) 694-95; M.-J. Lagrange, *Evangile selon Saint Luc* (EB; 4th ed.; Paris: Gabalda, 1927) 487-90; A. Plummer, *The Gospel According to St. Luke* (ICC; Edinburgh: Clark, 1969) 432. Even M. Dibelius hesitates over the question of historicity (*Die Formgeschichte des Evangeliums* [6th ed.; Tübingen: Mohr (Siebeck), 1971] 114-15. R. Bultmann seems in a hopeless minority when he declares the story "an ideal scene, a variant developed out of Mark 2:14" (*Die Geschichte der synoptischen Tradition* (FRLANT 29; 8th ed.; Göttingen: Vandenhoeck & Ruprecht, 1970) 34.

Thus, for all the socioeconomic trappings, Sobrino's treatment of the historical Jesus is socioeconomically naive. What brought Jesus to the cross may have been no one aspect of his ministry, but rather the fact that his ministry offended *so* many groups—including pious Jews—in *so* many different ways that he had few influential supporters when the final clash came between himself and the rulers in Jerusalem over his attacks on the temple. Like Sanders, Sobrino recognizes the importance of the temple question, though he fails to appreciate that such attacks probably alienated not just the Jerusalem priests but also a good many devout Jewish lay people. Just as it is too simplistic to say that all of Jesus' audience was economically poor, so it is too simplistic to say that Jesus offended only the rich and the powerful. Again, I will return to this point when I come to Segundo.

One corollary of these observations is that the precise reason or reasons *why* Jesus was arrested and finally crucified, and the precise grounds on which he was tried, are by no means clear, as Sobrino himself admits.[11] Yet Sobrino proceeds to reconstruct the scenario of Jesus' Jewish and Roman trials, complete with a trial before the Sanhedrin. In all this, Sobrino's theological theses seem to be the guiding rule for deciding what in the Gospel narratives is historical. Once again, we are proof-texting. Having recently spent three days at a colloquium between Christian and Jewish scholars discussing the historical

---

[11]It is surprising to see how little discussion there is on the complicated historical question of the trial(s) of Jesus in Sobrino and Segundo. For basic orientation and bibliography, see E. Bammel (ed.), *The Trial of Jesus* (SBT 2d series 13; London: SCM, 1970); O. Betz, "Probleme des Prozesses Jesu," *Aufstieg und Niedergang der römischen Welt* (ed. W. Haase; Berlin/New York: de Gruyter, 1982) II/25. 1, 564-647; J. Blinzler, *Der Prozess Jesu* (4th ed.; Regensburg: Pustet, 1969); S.G.F. Brandon, *The Trial of Jesus of Nazareth* (Historical Trials Series; New York: Stein and Day, 1968); R.E. Brown, *The Gospel According to John (XIII-XXI)* (AB 29A; Garden City, NY: Doubleday, 1970) 791-802; D. Catchpole, *The Trial of Jesus* (SPB 18; Leiden: Brill, 1971); M. Hengel, *Crucifixion* (Philadelphia: Fortress, 1977); H.W. Kuhn, "Die Kreuzesstrafe," *Aufstieg und Niedergang der römischen Welt*, II/25. 1, 648-793; E. Rivkin, *What Crucified Jesus?* (Nashville: Abingdon, 1984); A. Sherwin-White, *Roman Society and Roman Law in the New Testament* (Grand Rapids: Baker, 1963) 24-47; G. Sloyan, *Jesus on Trial* (Philadelphia: Fortress, 1973); A. Strobel, *Die Stunde der Wahrheit* (WUNT 21; Tübingen: Mohr (Siebeck), 1980); P. Winter, *On the Trial of Jesus* (SJ 1; 2d ed. rev. by T. Burkill and G. Vermes; Berlin/New York: de Gruyter, 1974).

events surrounding the trial of Jesus, I can only marvel at the simplistic treatment Sobrino gives this complex problem. Let me give one example.

While Sobrino, in good Germanic fashion, sometimes omits consideration of the Fourth Gospel from his treatment of the historical Jesus, he does bring in John's Gospel on this question of the persecution of Jesus unto death. Sobrino makes an initial acknowledgment of John's redactional tendencies, but then misses the very point of those tendencies by saying that John makes the whole Jewish people responsible for the persecution of Jesus, and not just their leaders. Actually, the phrase "the Jews" in John's Gospel, when used in a pejorative sense, does not usually mean the whole Jewish people, but rather the hostile authorities in Jerusalem. Worse still, Sobrino proceeds to cite the Johannine texts that refer to the Pharisees' deadly opposition to Jesus and their excommunication of those who acknowledge Jesus as Messiah. Nowhere in all this is there a glimmer of realization that the presentation of the Pharisees as *the* ultimate power in Judaism, before whom even the rulers must tremble, is a post-A.D. 70 picture and hardly reflects the historical Pharisees of Jesus' day. Contrary to Sobrino, the Pharisees probably had nothing to do as a group with Jesus' death. Faced with the horrors of 20th—century anti-Semitism, one should be more careful when dealing with the historical question of who actually was involved in the death of Jesus.

Sobrino's new book, *Jesus in Latin America*, does mark a step forward in his thought, in that he does attempt some definition of what he means by the historical Jesus. The attempt, though, is not auspicious. Sobrino states simply: "Latin American Christology understands the historical Jesus as the totality of Jesus' history...."[12] Of course, that is precisely what the historical Jesus cannot be. As Schillebeeckx points out so well in his *Jesus* book, the historical Jesus is that which the methods of historical criticism enable us to retrieve

[12]"The Importance of the Historical Jesus in Latin American Christology," *Jesus in Latin America*, 65.

of Jesus of Nazareth.[13] Unlike the positivistic historicism of the 19th century, we must appreciate that what can be reconstructed historically (i.e., the historical Jesus) does not coincide with the full reality of the Jesus who lived in the first century. What really occurs in history is broader than the history recoverable by a historian. As a result, unlike Küng and certainly unlike Sobrino, Schillebeeckx resolutely refuses to identify any or all historical reconstructions with the *real* Jesus—and in this he is methodologically superior. The Gospels hardly give us the totality of Jesus' history, and a quest for the historical Jesus must be highly selective amid the data the Gospels do provide. Hence the *real* Jesus, i.e., the total reality of Jesus of Nazareth as he lived in the first century, is no longer accessible to us by scholarly means. It is this basic insight which touches off a quest for the historical Jesus, and it is this basic insight that is lacking in Sobrino's approach.

Sobrino himself readily acknowledges that Latin American Christology has not reflected at length on the methodological problems involved in appealing to the historical Jesus. In the last few pages of his essay on "The Importance of the Historical Jesus in Latin American Christology," he attempts such a reflection. While recognizing that the factual data concerning Jesus are not directly accessible from the Gospels, Sobrino observes that Latin American Christology is not especially interested systematically in determining data about Jesus with exactitude. It does not make a Christology based on the historical Jesus depend on the *ipsissima verba* or *ipsissima facta* of Jesus. "Its interest rather consists in discovering and historically insuring the basic structure of Jesus' practice and preaching, an end through which the basic structure of his internal historicity and his person are likewise discernible."[14]

Sobrino notes that Latin American Christology does not share the radical skepticism of some; rather, it shares "the common heritage of other current Christologies (including the

---

[13]Edward Schillebeeckx, *Jesus. An Experiment in Christology* (New York: Seabury, 1979) 67-71.

[14]"The Importance of the Historical Jesus," 73-74.

European)."[15] Sobrino then proceeds to give a thumbnail sketch of such a common heritage—and the problem of appealing to such a supposed common heritage becomes evident. The picture is basically that of the Synoptic Jesus: e.g., there is simply one journey to Jerusalem toward the end of Jesus' life. Yet this is mixed up with a strange borrowing from John, namely the idea of a crisis toward the middle or end of Jesus' public life—one element from John that is historically dubious. A good deal of this common heritage is distressingly vague: e.g., Jesus shared "some kind of meal with those close to him" before he was arrested; Jesus showed "certain attitudes toward the Jewish Law and the Temple."[16] Sobrino is no doubt aware that if he gets any more specific than this, his presumed common heritage may evaporate; but without more specificity, these vague snippets are useless.

In this recent essay, Sobrino does at least examine a few criteria of historicity. Like Harvey McArthur,[17] and unlike Norman Perrin,[18] he finds the criterion of multiple attestation to be the best. Two other criteria, discontinuity with the NT church and the consistency of Jesus' death with what is narrated of his life, are considered indirect verifications of the first criterion.

Yet Sobrino never bothers to use these criteria in any detail. In this there appears a real tension between his awareness of the historical-critical problem and his desire to get on with his project of liberation theology. He states that it is more than likely that the Gospels are in part the fruit of the imagination of the NT communities. But he thinks that it is "rather unlikely" that the Gospels are such in their totality. Then, with a rhetorical wave of the hand, he continues: "At all events, Latin American Christology holds a presupposition in favor of the basic historicity of the gospel narratives. . . . To anyone

[15] Ibid, 74.

[16] Ibid.

[17] Harvey McArthur, "A Survey of Recent Gospel Research," *Interpretation* 18 (1964) 39-55, esp. 48; idem, "The Burden of Proof in Historical Jesus Research," *Expository Times* 82 (1970-71) 116-19, esp. 118.

[18] Norman Perrin, *Rediscovering the Teaching of Jesus* (London: SCM, 1967) 39-43.

living and suffering history on the South American continent it seems altogether probable that 'Jesus was like that.'"[19] In short, if it enjoys verisimilitude in the eyes of Latin Americans, it is judged historical.

It is telling that Sobrino admits that his position is a problem from the standpoint of historical criticism, but an advantage from the standpoint of systematic reflection. And that, it appears, is all Sobrino is really interested in. In a sense, Sobrino feels justified in proceeding this way because he is convinced that Latin American communities replicate in their experience the first Christian communities that produced the Gospels. This is simply naiveté once removed. The first Christian communities were by no means all the same in their experience or Christology, and to recapture their historical situations is hardly less taxing than recapturing the historical Jesus.[20] In the end, Sobrino substitutes unsubstantiated generalizations for the hard work of Jesus-research. The basic problem is never really engaged, and one is left wondering how, if at all, the Bible has really been a source of theology for Sobrino—or for liberation theology in general.

II

The problem of the historical Jesus cetainly *is* engaged— and at great length—by Juan Luis Segundo, who has written a sizable treatise on liberation theology and the historical Jesus. In its English translation, it takes up a whole volume, entitled *The Historical Jesus of the Synoptics.*[21] To my knowledge,

[19]"The Importance of the Historical Jesus," 74-75.

[20]See. e.g., Raymond Brown and John Meier, *Antioch and Rome* (New York: Ramsey, NJ: Paulist, 1983); Raymond Brown, *The Churches the Apostles Left Behind* (New York: Ramsey, NJ: Paulist, 1984).

[21]Juan Luis Segundo, *The Historical Jesus of the Synoptics* (Jesus of Nazareth Yesterday and Today, vol. 2; Maryknoll, NY: Orbis, 1985; ET of the first part [pp. 1-284] of *El hombre de hoy ante Jesus de Nazareth. Vol II/1, Historia y actualidad: Sinopticos y Pablo* [Madrid: Cristiandad, 1982]). While I quote in this article from the English translation, I have compared the English with the Spanish original. Such a comparison reveals some flaws in the translation, but the sentences I consider in detail are present in the same form in the Spanish.

Segundo is the only Latin American liberation theologian who has dedicated an entire book to the question of the historical Jesus.

But precisely because his treatment of the historical Jesus is so much more extensive than that of Sobrino's, the problems of the whole approach become more glaring. At least Sobrino was aware of the deficiencies of his use of Scripture; Segundo seems unaware of the same problem in his own work.

This may sound like a harsh judgment, but time after time throughout *The Historical Jesus of the Synoptics*, Segundo proves to be haphazard and eclectic, as he meshes together and selects from the Synoptics, John, and Paul to construct his portrait of Jesus the political agitator. The more unusual his judgments become, the less he tries to ground them with data and arguments. For example, in justifying Paul's creativity in formulating the gospel message, Segundo says: "Like the authors of the fourth Gospel, the Letter to the Hebrews, and the Book of Revelation, Paul clearly perceives the distance between the historical Jesus and the interpretations of Matthew, Mark, and Luke. So he feels free to create his own gospel... " (p. 21). The astounding claim that Paul, writing in the 50s, both knew the three Synoptics and perceived their distance from the historical Jesus remains unsubstantiated— as indeed it must.[22] To take another example: although most exegetes point out that John's Gospel lacks any detailed interest in ecclesiology, Segundo declares John the most ecclesial of the Gospels.[23] At times Segundo seems to have an

---

[22]The claim implicit in Segundo's statement goes far beyond the revisionist views proposed by J.A.T. Robinson in his *Redating the New Testament* (Philadelphia: Westminster, 1976) and *The Priority of John* (Oak Park, IL: Meyer-Stone, 1985); and at least Robinson spent hundreds of pages trying to prove his idiosyncratic theories.— Segundo's attitude toward the historicity of the Fourth Gospel oscillates between general rejection and occasional acceptance when it suits his purposes. The same sort of hesitant attitude can be seen in his more recent *Teologia Abierta. III. Reflexiones Criticas* (Madrid: Cristiandad, 1984) 35-128, esp. pp. 46-47 and n. 8 on p. 47.

[23]See, e.g., the remarks of Raymond Brown in his *The Community of the Beloved Disciple* (New York/Ramsey/Toronto: Paulist, 1979) 155-62. In my opinion, Brown's mature reflections modify somewhat his views on ecclesiology in the Gospel of John as presented in the first volume of his commentary on the Gospel (*The Gospel According to John* [AB 29; Garden City, NY: Doubleday, 1966] CV-CXI.

tetchy   p 62

scrofulous   p 70

sozzled   p 104

cretaceous   p 115

mastodons   p 194

unerring sense for the wrong text to prove his point. To show that Jesus demonstrated partiality toward the poor, Segundo cites the parable of the Pharisee and the publican praying in the temple. The publican, not the Pharisee, goes home justified—fine! But the publican, the tool of the government in extracting tolls or excise taxes, was hardly the economically poorest person in Israel, and he belonged on the side of the oppressors rather than the oppressed. If anything, the parable overturns Segundo's, as well as the Pharisee's, theology.[24]

Amid all the confusion, one is relieved when Segundo attempts to articulate a detailed method in treating the historical Jesus—something Sobrino does not do. Segundo enunciates three criteria of historicity: (1) one must distinguish pre-Easter from post-Easter statements;[25] (2) one must distinguish pre-ecclesial from post-ecclesial statements (the criterion of discontinuity); and (3) historicity is supported by multiple attestation. Sad to say, the criteria are not often used in practice. Sayings are often accepted without much reasoning if they fit Segundo's political program; often texts that exegetes would assign to the creative redaction of the evangelists are attributed to the historical Jesus (e.g., Matt 17:12-13, the descent from the mount of transfiguration). The most blatant example of this occurs when Segundo reads Mark's redactional theme of the messianic secret back into Jesus' life. William Wrede must be turning over in his grave.

There is also uncritical meshing of disparate texts. Like some other liberation theologians, Segundo is fond of referring to a Galilean crisis, which seems to result from conflating

[24]It is true, as Segundo points out in *Teologia Abierta. III.*, 90, that publicans could be poor too. Yet it is interesting to notice how, while various people and groups in the New Testament are portrayed as poor (noticeably widows and orphans), no tax collector is every portrayed as poor (cf. Levi throwing a party for Jesus and inviting a large crowd in Mark 2:15). More to the point, nothing in the Lucan parable indicates that the publican is any poorer than the Pharisee; at any rate, the point of the parable hardly rests on such an unsubstantiated assumption.

[25]Actually, this is more of a general principle than an exact criterion that enables one to distinguish authentic from unauthentic material in particular cases. Given the general principle, one must still ask: And how do we know in particular cases what is prepaschal? The individual criteria (e.g., discontinuity, multiple attestation) seek to answer that question. On this point, see also his *Teologia Abierta. III.*, 45-46.

Peter's confession of faith at Caesarea Philippi in Mark and Matthew with a different profession of faith by Peter at Capernaum in John 6. Indeed, one is left wondering whether Segundo understands his own criteria. He misses the point of the criterion of multiple attestation when he appeals to the fact that a given narrative (e.g., Peter's confession at Caesarea Philippi) appears in much the same way in Mark, Matthew, and Luke. He conveniently overlooks the obvious reason for this agreement, namely, that Mark is *the* source which both Matthew and Luke copied. Hence there is no attestation by multiple *sources*, and no argument for historicity simply from agreement among the three Synoptics.

As one goes through this book, it is not just the portrait of the historical Jesus that becomes increasingly problematic, but also the portrait of historical Judaism in the first century A.D. Instead of a carefully differentiated picture of a highly diverse religion, we get oversimplifications and even caricatures. in practice, for Segundo, the Judaism presented by the four Gospels *is* the historical Judaism of the time of Jesus, period. The recent work of scholars who have investigated the history of first-century Judaism is simply not considered. For example, Segundo claims that among the groups Jesus addressed were the Zealots—ignoring the claims of some historians that the Zealots as a distinct group with that precise name emerged only during the First Jewish War, or at least that they were dormant during the time of Jesus.[26]

Leaning on John's redactional tendencies (esp. chaps. 11 and 18 of the Gospel), Segundo presents the Pharisees and Sadducees plotting together in Jerusalem to arrest and condemn Jesus. Actually, an investigation of the earliest Passion traditions shows that the Pharisees as a group were probably not involved in Jesus' death. The Pharisees are inserted into a few episodes of the Passion by the redactional activity of Matthew and John. Especially disturbing is Segundo's accep-

---

[26]See, e.g., Shaye Cohen, *From the Maccabees to the Mishnah* (Library of Early Christianity 7; Philadelphia: Westminster, 1987) 164-66; Richard Horsley and John Hanson, *Bandits, Prophets, and Messiahs* (Minneapolis: Winston, 1985) 216-43; cf. the earlier article of Morton Smith, "Zealots and Sicarii: Their Origins and Relations," *HTR* 64 (1971) 1-19.

tance of Matthew's polemic against the Pharisees in a post-A.D. 70 situation as historically reliable for the time of Jesus. Segundo affirms that the Pharisees are Jesus' enemies par excellence; or better, "they are the enemies par excellence of the God that Jesus reveals.... Everything we know about the Pharisees from the Gospels and the extrabiblical sources shows them to be a sincere and fanatically religious group. (Sincerity and fanaticism very often accompany the ultimate stages of bad faith.) Theirs is a terrible legalism. And if they are guilty of hypocrisy,... it ultimately stems from hardness of heart ..., which is translated into an insensitivity to the evident needs of their neighbor...."[27] All one can say is that Segundo is woefully ignorant of all the work done in the last decade or two by both Jewish and Christian scholars to recover a more accurate religious and social description of the Pharisees.

The same criticism can be made of his treatment of the Sadducees. Segundo describes them as follows: "... rather than being a sincerely religious sect in opposition to the Pharisees, the Sadducean party seemed to be much more concerned about their own power ... than about the purity or profundity of their religious opinions."[28] At this point Segundo should have remembered his own hermeneutic of suspicion. Almost everything we know about the Sadducees at the time of Jesus we know from their enemies: the Pharisees, the Essenes, and the Christians. History gets written by the survivors.

In all of this, I am not claiming that Segundo is intentionally anti-Semitic. Rather, I think he lets his reconstruction of first-century history be dictated by his desire to draw parallels between the political oppression of Jesus' day and political oppression in Latin America today. Historical parallels over the chasm of twenty centuries are seldom so simple. Indeed, although Segundo berates exegetes for their lack of concern with the social, political, and economic dimension of the Gospel, he seems unaware of all the work done by North American scholars on the sociology of the NT. This is part of

---

[27] *The Historical Jesus of the Synoptics*, 99.
[28] Ibid, 101.

a larger problem; as his notes and bibliographies show, Segundo leans heavily on European exegetes of the 50s and 60s; strictly exegetical works from the 1970s are few and far between—and very few come from North America. Again, the contrast with Schillebeeckx's wide knowledge of various exegetes is striking.

There is one area in which Segundo's failure to appreciate the Jewish context at the time of Jesus calls his whole political approach into question. This is his treatment of "the poor."[29] One would never guess from Segundo's presentation that "the poor" had long since become more than a mere socioeconomic designation in Palestinian Judaism. Through the spirituality of the Psalms and the prophets, *'anawîm*, "the poor ones," along with similar Hebrew adjectives, had become a description of those who had seen through the illusory security of this world and had learned to trust in God alone for their salvation. At times no particular socioeconomic connotation is attached to *'anawîm*; a prime example of this can be found in the Book of Ben Sira. In 3:17-18 (for which we have Hebrew fragments), Ben Sira exhorts his audience—presumably the sons of the well-to-do in Jerusalem—to walk in *'anawa,* for God reveals his mystery to the *'anawîm*.[30] Here the poverty-vocabulary is coming to mean humility, meekness, almost Matthew's "poor in spirit." Indeed, according to some scholars, Matthew's very phrase has now been found in the documents of Qumran (ironically, in the War Scroll!).[31] As the quintes-

---

[29]For his treatment of the poor, Segundo relies, among others, on A. Myre, "'Heureux les pauvres,' histoire passeé et future d'une parole," in P.-A. Giguère, J. Martucci, and A. Myre, *Cri de Dieu. Espoir des pauvres* (Montreal: Editions Paulines & Apostolat des Editions, 1977) 67-134; it should be noted that the title of this article is incorrectly given in the bibliography of the English translation, p. 223. Although I admire Myre's work, I would construct the tradition history of the beatitudes in a different way.

[30]For the Hebrew text, with Greek, Latin, and Syriac versions, see *Ecclesiastico* (Pubblicazioni del Seminario di Semitistica, Testi I; Naples: Istituto Orientale di Napoli, 1968) 17; indeed, Manuscript A from the Cairo Geniza reads: "My son, *in your wealth* walk in *'anawa*"! The use of *'anawa* for humility can also be found in many Qumran texts, notably the Manual of Discipline (Rule of the Community); see 1QS 2:23-25; 3:8-9; 4:3; 5:3; 5:24-25; 9:22-23; 11:1.

[31]See 1QM 14:7, where E. Lohse (*Die Texte aus Qumran* [2d ed.; Munich: Kösel, 1971] 212) vocalizes the Hebrew text (unfortunately incomplete) to read *ube'anwe*

sentially pious group, the Essenes called themselves "the poor of God." They provide the prime example of the theology of poverty applied to a whole Jewish sect at the time of Jesus. It may be that the same type of group-designation was applied to the Jerusalem church.[32] I am not arguing here that the vocabulary of poverty had totally left its socioeconomic moorings; many of these people *were* economically poor. I am simply pointing out that the theological use of terms for the poor makes an analysis of the NT data more complex than Segundo claims.

More troubling is Segundo's affirmation, taken over from Joachim Jeremias, that the economically poor and ignorant in Israel (the *'amme ha-ares*) were viewed as sinners.[33] Jewish scholars rejected such an equation decades ago, and now E.P. Sanders has clearly shown its falsehood in his *Jesus and Judaism*.[34] "Sinners" were the wicked who sinned willfully and heinously and who did not repent; they renounced the covenant. Sinners included people in disreputable professions, such as tax collectors. The scandalous point of Jesus' mission was that he directed himself notably to sinners, i.e., to the wicked. Jesus also was concerned with the poor. But, in Jewish eyes,

---

ruah ("and by the humble [or poor] of spirit. . . . " This was the reading preferred by J. Dupont in his earlier article, "Les pauvres en esprit," *A la rencontre de Dieu: Mémorial Albert Gelin* (Le Puy: Mappus, 1961) 265-72. Later, however, Dupont changed his view: the Hebrew should rather be vocalized as *'anawî ruah*; see his "Le ptochoi to pneumati de Matthieu 5, 3 et les *'anawî ruah* de Qumran," *Neutestamentliche Aufsätze* (J. Schmid Festschrift; ed. J. Blinzler, O. Kuss, and F. Mussner; Regensburg: Pustet, 1963) 53-64. The use of *'anawa* for humility can also be found in many other Qumran textrs, notably the Manual of Discipline (the Rule of the Community); see 1QS 2:23-25; 3:8-9; 4:3; 5:3; 5:24-25; 9:22-23; 11:1.

[32] So possibly in Rom 15:26: *eis tous ptochous ton hagion en Ierousalem*, though exegetes still fight over whether the genitive is partitive ("the poor members of the Christian community in Jerusalem," so Bultmann, Munck, Georgi, Käsemann) or epexegetical ("the whole Christian community in Jerusalem that constitutes 'The Poor,'" so Lietzmann, Dahl, Bammell, Hahn, Cerfaux).—Granted his own emphasis on the poor, Segundo makes an intriguing point in *Teologia Abierta. III.*, p. 122, when he suggests that, speaking anachronistically, Jesus and his disciples came from the lower middle class and were not among the desperately poor of Palestine.

[33] Joachim Jeremias, *New Testament Theology. Part One. The Proclamation of Jesus* (London: SCM, 1971) 108-13.

[34] *Jesus and Judaism*, 176-79. Segundo repeats the equation of poor and sinners in *Teologia Abierta. III.*; see, e.g., p. 78.

the damaging charge against him was not that he associated with the poor, but that he associated with the wicked. It is a mistake to think that the Pharisees were upset because Jesus ministered to the ordinarily pious common people and the economically impoverished. There is no passage in the whole of rabbinic literature that states that the super-pious in Israel considered ordinary people to be *ipso facto* wicked. As Sean Freyne has pointed out in his book *Galilee from Alexander the Great to Hadrian*,[35] Galilean peasants were basically loyal Jews, loyal to the Jerusalem temple and to basic tenets and practices of Judaism, though not attracted to the special rules of the Pharisees. In short, Segundo's picture of Jesus' Galilean audience is simplistic and outdated. Not only is he weak in his exegesis, he is weak precisely in his analysis of the religious and socioeconomic situation in Galilee at the time of Jesus.

Segundo's desire to interpret Jesus in a this-worldly political key also leads him to play down or reinterpret those sayings of Jesus which look to a transcendent eschatological future, sayings that imply some divinely caused break with the history of this present world. The rejection of transcendent future eschatology in favor of a restructuring of society in this world is curiously reminiscent of the very founder of the quest for the historical Jesus, Hermann Reimarus.[36] This political interpretation of Jesus has had a long history down to our own day, including notably the books of S.G.F. Brandon, such as *Jesus and the Zealots*[37] and *The Trial of Jesus*.[38] Brandon, like Segundo, denied that Jesus was a Zealot, yet Brandon thought that Jesus sympathized with the aims of the Zealots. Ernst Bammel shrewdly notes how a number of liberation theo-

---

[35] *Galilee from Alexander the Great to Hadrian 323 B.C.E. to 135 C.E.* (Wilmington, DE: Glazier, 1980) 208-97. In *Teologia Abierta. III..*, 61-62, Segundo makes the startling statement that because Jesus was a Galilean and an artisan, he was looked upon from the start by the religious authorities as a heretic. In general, Segundo too easily retrojects the Judaism of the Mishnah and the Talmud back into early 1st-century Palestine.

[36] Hermann Reimarus, *Reimarus: Fragments* (ed. Charles Talbert; Philadelphia: Fortress, 1970).

[37] *Jesus and the Zealots* (New York: Scribner's, 1967).

[38] *The Trial of Jesus* (Historical Trials Series; New York: Stein and Day, 1968).

logians have become intrigued by Brandon's theory. The whole book in which Bammel's essay appears (*Jesus and the Politics of His Day*)[39] exposes the many difficulties under which Brandon's theory labors; academically, being intrigued by Brandon may prove a fatal attraction. In all this there is a strange irony: While out of touch with the best of recent work on the historical Jesus, especially that of Protestant exegetes, Segundo and his confreres, in a limited sense, have unwittingly reached back to the father of the quest, that great skeptic of the Enlightenment, Reimarus, a Protestant progenitor the Latin American theologians might not care to own. One is reminded of George Santayana's quip that those who are ignorant of history are condemned to relive it.[40]

I fear that my view of the use of Scripture by Sobrino and Segundo may lead some readers of this essay to think that I am simply opposed to liberation theology. That is certainly not the impression I want to leave. I have picked these two liberation theologians for consideration precisely because I admire their personal dedication and scholarly production. I see liberation theology as holding great promise for the renewal of both theology and church life, and I would like to aid it by fraternal correction, not hostile criticism. There is surely room for the former. After all, by the measuring rod of patristic and scholastic theology, liberation theology is still in its infancy and needs to grow in a sophisticated use of the sources of theological reflection—especially the Bible, and most especially that scholarly will-o'-the-wisp, the historical Jesus.

[39]Ernst Bammel, "The revolution theory from Reimarus to Brandon," *Jesus and the Politics of His Day* (ed. Ernst Bammel and C.F.D. Moule; Cambridge: Cambridge University, 1984) 11-68.

[40]Among the more sophisticated approaches to the social and political framework of Jesus' ministry, see R. Horsley and J. Hanson, *Bandits, Prophets, and Messiahs. Popular Movements at the Time of Jesus* (Minneapolis: Winston, 1985); and R. Horsley, *Jesus and the Spiral of Violence. Popular Jewish Resistance in Roman Palestine* (San Francisco: Harper & Row, 1987). The first volume is perhaps the more sober and successful of the two; the latter tends toward highly speculative theories and, at times, a convoluted exegesis that forces a text to fit a predetermined thesis (see, e.g., the exegesis of the coin-of-tribute pericope on pp. 306-17). In short, the second volume is a more erudite form of what Sobrino and Segundo are trying to do, with all the pluses and minuses that involves.

Along with criteria of historicity that must be more carefully defined and employed, I think liberation theologians must rethink a larger Christological question: Is it wise, when doing Christian theology, and more specifically Christology, to focus so intensely, almost exclusively, on a protean Jesus of history? What is wrong with using, yea, reveling in, the full Christology of each of the Gospel writers, whom we affirm in faith to be writing under divine inspiration? Just because I happen to think that Jesus' inaugural homily at Nazareth in Lk 4:16-30 is largely Luke's creative redaction of Mark, or just because I think the great scene of Jesus judging the sheep and the goats in Matt 25:31-46 owes a great deal to Matthew's creativity, do these inspired texts lack revelatory power as a source for present-day Christology and Christian praxis—whether or not the historical Jesus ever spoke them?

Perhaps the liberation theologians are all too quickly going down the primrose path Hans Küng took, the path that naively equates the historical (*geschichtlich*) Jesus with the real (*wirklich*) Christ and then elevates *that* Jesus to the canon within the canon. The nuanced, differentiated, many-tiered approach of Schillebeeckx is more faithful to the complexity of the biblical witness and the Catholic tradition. It is by embracing, celebrating, and appropriating that complexity that I hope that liberation theologians will make the whole Bible— and the whole Bible's witness to the whole Christ—a true source for their theology and their liberating praxis.

❧

Afterword

Studies in liberation theology continue with great gusto. Juan Luis Segundo has completed his theological Summa

with a volume on the "humanist Christology of St. Paul"—
actually a treatment of the Epistle to the Romans, chaps. 1-8.
Whether Paul's Christology can actually be grasped from only
eight chapters of one of his epistles is doubtful. Moreover, the
problem of jejune and out-dated bibliography that plagues
The Historical Jesus of the Synoptics dogs *The Humanist
Christology of St. Paul.* Jon Sobrino has likewise continued to
publish, but his more recent writings do not include a major
work on the historical Jesus. On the question of the events of
the Passion Narrative and their interpretation in liberation
theology, see Leonardo Boff, *Passion of Christ, Passion of the
World* (Maryknoll, NY: Orbis, 1987).

4

Structure and Theology
in Hebrews 1:1-14

In New Testament research, the relationship of the structure of a given book to that book's theology is a problematic variable. In a work like 1 John, for instance, the very existence of a clear structure is disputed;[1] and so a close nexus between the book's structure and its theological content becomes very difficult to establish. Lying close by in the traditional canon but at the opposite end of the structural spectrum is the Epistle to the Hebrews. Its intricate structure and dense theology are so tightly interwoven that an investigation of Hebrews' literary design inevitably draws one into the heart of its theology.[2] The work of L. Vaganay,[3] C. Spicq,[4] A. Descamps,[5] W. Nauck,[6] O.

[1]See the treatment by R. Brown, *The Epistles of John* (Garden City, NY 1982), 116-129.

[2]For an overview of various theories on the structure of Hebrews, see A.Vanhoye, *La structure littéraire de l'épître aux Hébreux* (Paris-Bruges 1963) 11-32.

[3]L.Vaganay, "Le plan de l'épître aux Hébreux", *Mémorial Lagrange* (Paris 1940), 269-277.

[4]C. Spicq, *L'épître aux Hébreux* (2 vols., Paris 1952 and 1953), especially I:27-38; Spicq is favorable to Vaganay's approach. A short summary of these two volumes, with revised bibliography, can be found in Spicq's one volume work, also entitled *L'épître aux Hébreux* (Paris 1977), especially 32-34. Unless expressly noted, subsequent references in this article will be to Spicq's two volume work.

[5]A. Descamps, "La structure de l'épître aux Hébreux", *Revue diocésaine de Tournai* 9 (1954) 251-258, 333-338, as reported by Vanhoye, *La structure*, 31.

[6]W. Nauck, "Zum Aufbau des Hebräerbriefs", *Judentum, Urchristentum, Kirche* (ed. W. Eltester; Berlin 1960) 199-206.

Michel,[7] and above all A. Vanhoye[8] has made this abundantly clear. What E. Grässer has written about Heb 1:1-4 could be applied to almost the whole of the Epistle: "For [the] exegesis [of Heb 1:1-4] it is, I think, of the greatest importance that one understand that the stylistic care and meticulously composed structure are a factor in the author's intention. We are therefore interested in the analysis of the literary structure not simply as something *alongside of* exegesis, but precisely *as* exegesis."[9] While Grässer had only the first four verses of the Epistle in mind, I think his remarks apply equally well to the whole of the first chapter. Commentators have tried repeatedly to grasp the exact connection between the exordium (1:1-4)[10] and the catena of seven Old Testament citations (1:5-14).[11] Much of the previous work contains valid insights, but I think some important links—both structural and theological—have been overlooked. The purpose of this article is to investigate the structure of Hebrews 1 and to suggest a new way of looking at its literary design. More precisely, this article will suggest that there is both a numerical symmetry and a symmetry in the

[7]O. Michel, *Der Brief an die Hebräer* (Göttingen [6]1966) 29-35; also his "Zur Auslegung des Hebräerbriefes", *NT* 6 (1963) 189-191, where he favors the approach of Vaganay and Vanhoye.

[8]Besides *La structure*, see his *Der Brief an die Hebräer. Griechischer Text mit Gliederung und deutscher Übersetzung* (Fano 1966), which is also available in other modern languages; *Situation du Christ* (Paris 1969); and his Latin notes on individual sections of the epistle: *Exegesis Epistulae ad Hebraeos. Cap. I-II* (Rome 1968); *De Epistola ad Hebraeos. Sectio Centralis (Cap. 8-9)* (Rome 1972). For a critique of Vanhoye's approach see Nauck, "Zum Aufbau", and also J. Bligh, "The Structure of Hebrews", *HeyJ* 5 (1964) 170-177.

[9]E. Grässer, "Hebräer 1:1-4. Ein exegetischer Versuch", *Text und Situation* (Gütersloh 1973) 183; emphasis his, translation mine.

[10]Ibid., 187, for the justification of the designation "exordium". Cf. W.Wrede, *Das literarische Rätsel des Hebräerbriefs* (Göttingen 1906) 6.

[11]So, e.g., J. Moffatt, *The Epistle to the Hebrews* (New York 1924) 9; Spicq, *L'épître*, II, 15, with a remarkable quotation from Aquinas that foreshadows some of the points in this article; L. Dey, *The Intermediary World and Patterns of Perfection in Philo and Hebrews* (Missoula 1975) 146-147; O. Hofius, *Der Christushymnus Philipper 2:6-11* (Tübingen 1976) 86, 88-89; G. Hughes, *Hebrews and Hermeneutics* (Cambridge 1979) 7-8; J. Thompson, "The Structure and Purpose of the Catena in Hebrews 1:5-13", *The Beginnings of Christian Philosophy* (Washington, DC 1982) 128-140.

movement of theological thought between 1:1-4 and 1:5-14. It is hoped that a proper appreciation of the literary structure [12] and flow of thought in Hebrews 1 may also shed light on such varied and disputed questions as the Christology of the Epistle, the precise Christological reference of various Old Testament citations in chapter one, and the supposed presence of traditional hymnic material in Heb 1:2-4.

I. Numerical Symmetry in Hebrews 1:1-4 and 1:5-14

That there are numerical patterns in Hebrews in general and in Hebrews 1 in particular is widely admitted.[13] Almost all commentators point to the catena of seven Old Testament citations in Heb 1:5-14 as an indisputable example. What is less frequently noted is that there is a "chain" of Christological designations in the exordium (1:1-4), namely in 1:2b-4. The question of a possible correlation between these two chains arises, but first one must face the problem of properly isolating and enumerating the Christological designations or predications in 1:2b-4. Then one may attempt to grasp the order of thought, if any, in the chain and to correlate it with the chain in 1:5-14.

First, let us take a quick glance at the exordium as a whole. The chain of Christological designations is found in what is probably the most beautiful periodic sentence in the New Testament, Heb 1:1-4.[14] The continuity, discontinuity, and superiority of the revelation of the new covenant vis-à-vis the old is affirmed in the main clause (*ho theos lalēsas ... elalēsen,*

---

[12]It should be made clear from the beginning that, when I speak of structure, I am speaking of the structure consciously intended by the author—hence, the "surface structure" as opposed to the "depth structures" investigated by certain structuralists.

[13]See, e.g., the numerical patterns Michel detects within chap. 11 (*Brief*, 414-415, 419 n. 7).

[14]Spicq, *L'épître aux Hébreux* (one volume 1977 work) 56: " ... une seule période, qui constitue sans doute la phrase grecque la plus parfaite du Nouveau Testament ... ". See Also BDF #464; such periods are rare in the NT outside of Hebrews. For the author of Hebrews as a master of rhythmic prose, see F. Blass, *Brief an die Hebräer. Text mit Angabe der Rhythmen* (Halle 1903) 1-3. Moffatt, *Hebrews*, LVI-LVII, compares Hebrews' rhythm and rhetoric to that of Isocrates.

1:1-2a). In all the subsequent dependent clauses (relative and participial, vv. 2b-4) the claim of 1:1-2a is Christologically grounded and explicated. As the periodic sentence proceeds, one notes a gradual shift in the agent/subject: in vv. 1-2a God is the grammatical subject and primary agent of revelation. Indeed, the Son is not even mentioned in v. 1. The Son appears for the first time at the end of v. 2a in the role of instrumental agent of revelation (*en* carrying an instrumental sense, like the Hebrew *be*).[15] In v. 2b, the Son, installed as heir, is the recipient of God's action (accusative case), while in v. 2c he is again the instrumental agent (*di'hou*), this time of creation. From v. 3a to the end of v. 4, the Son is the grammatical subject and the chief agent. God being mentioned only indirectly by pronouns or periphrasis. On the one hand, then, from a rhetorical viewpoint it is true that the whole of 1:1-4 divides neatly into two parts: vv. 1-2 (God as subject) and vv. 3-4 (the Son as subject).[16] Yet, when one attends to the increasingly Christological slant of the whole period and notes the carefully ordered list of Christological designations, another kind of caesura, Christological as well as rhetorical, might be placed at the end of v. 2a, where "Son" is first mentioned. Everything that follows is grammatically dependent (directly or indirectly) on *huiǭ* and forms a chain of varied descriptions of the Son, referring to either his character (nature) or his action (creative and redemptive work).[17] As Vanhoye notes, the author of Hebrews purposely omits the definite article before *huiǭ* in v. 2a, so as to raise questions and expectations that are answered by the relative and participial clauses that follow.[18]

[15]While admitting the possibility of a semitism here, Vanhoye prefers to stress the sense of "in". God does not simply order the prophets to speak; He himself speaks *in* them (*Exegesis Epistulae ad Hebraeos, Cap. I-II*, 35; *Situation*, 58-59).

[16]See Vanhoye, *Situation*, 12:52; cf., Grässer, "Hebräer 1:1-4", 189. As Grässer notes, the very development of the period shows that our author develops the theology of 1:1-4 precisely as Christology.

[17]Grässer ("Hebräer 1:1-4", 189) claims that all the relative clauses of vv. 2b-3 have only one function: to qualify the Son as the eschatological Word of God to us. But that is to narrow the focus of the catena unduly.

[18]Vanhoye, *Situation*, 61. In *La structure*, 67, Vanhoye admits that, while God is till the subject of the relative clauses in v. 2bc, the two affirmations concern the Son and thus prepare the way for the second half of 1:1-4.

At this point, a critical problem arises: How many distinct designations or predications of the Son should we count in vv. 2b-4? Commentators disagree on what constitutes a single Christological designation and consequently on how many designations occur. F.F. Bruce, for example, counts seven "facts . . . about the Son of God".[19] Bruce, however, restricts the enumeration to vv. 2b-3. Hence, for him, the seven designations are: (1) God appointed the Son heir of all things (v. 2b); (2) through the Son, God made the worlds (v. 2c); (3) the Son is the effulgence of God's glory (v. 3a); (4) and the very image of his substance (also v. 3a); (5) the Son upholds all things by the word of his power (v. 3b); (6) the Son made purification of sins (v. 3c); and (7) the Son sat down at the right hand of the majesty on high (v. 3d).[20] As is clear, Bruce omits v. 4 from his list of "seven facts", even though in his commentary he places it with the first three verses, over against 1:5-14. J.H. Davies, on the other hand, counts only six clauses expounding the uniqueness of the Son.[21] Davies arrives at the number six by counting the whole of v. 3a ("being the effulgence of his glory and the image of his substance") as one clause and designation. At the same time, Davies, like Bruce, excludes v. 4 from the enumeration of those clauses that expound the uniqueness of the Son. Thus he arrives at the number six.

Amid these disagreements, what we must ask is whether there are objective criteria for identifying and enumerating these clauses of Christological predication. One obvious objective criterion is the grammatical structure of 1:1-4, a structure that is clearly the product of painstaking composition by our author. The author has carefully made *huiǭ* at the end of v. 2a a grammatical pivot. All the clauses following *huiǭ* depend directly or indirectly upon it, and all these clauses are linked to *huiǭ* by either a relative pronoun or a participle. The natural thing to do, therefore, is to count as a unit of Christological designation each clause linked to *huiǭ* by a relative pronoun

[19]F.F. Bruce, *The Epistle to the Hebrews* (Grand Rapids 1964) 3.
[20]Ibid., 3-8.
[21]J.H. Davies, *A Letter to Hebrews* (Cambridge 1967) 19-20.

or a participle.[22] Hence I think it not subjective or arbitrary to lay out vv. 2b-4 in the following pattern of units, with the relative pronouns and participles emphasized.[23]

v. 2a *en huiǭ*

(1) 2b HON *ethēken klēronomon pantōn,*
(2) 2c DI'HOU *kai epoiēsen tous aiōnas,*
(3) 3a [HOS] ŌN *apaugasma tēs doxēs kai charaktēr tēs hypostaseōs autou,*
(4) 3b [HOS] PHERŌN *te ta panta tǭ rhēmati tēs dynameōs autou,*
(5) 3c [HOS] *katharismon tōn hamartiōn* POIĒSAMENOS
(6) 3d [HOS] *ekathisen en dexią̌ tēs megalōsynēs en hypsēlois,*
(7) 4a *tosoutǭ kreittōn* GENOMENOS *tōn aggelōn*
    4b *hosǭ diaphorōteron par'autous keklēronomēken onoma.*

This schema does no violence to the grammatical structure by omitting v. 4 from the rounded period—a questionable procedure which reaches a climax of grammatical violence when some commentators detach v. 4 from vv. 1-3 and place it with vv. 5-14.[24] If, instead, we follow the lead of the writer, we are presented with seven clauses, each one depending directly or indirectly on *huiǭ*, each one tied to *huiǭ* by a relative pronoun or participle, and each one expatiating on one aspect of the Son's nature or work. Thus according to the criterion enunciated above, the complex clause introduced by *genomenos* in v. 4 deserves to be included in this list of predications as much as the clauses introduced by *ōn, pherōn,* or *poiēsamenos.*[25] There are thus seven designations.

Against this count of seven predications, some might object

---

[22]Strictly speaking, the participles modify *huiǭ* through the relative clause introduced by *hos.* But the rhetorical arrangement and thought content clearly show that each clause forms a distinct unit expressing a distinct aspect of the Son's nature or work.

[23]While the relative *hos* is positioned at the beginning of v. 3a, it is of course the subject of *ekathisen* in v. 3d; hence the brackets.

[24]So, e.g., P. Teodorico, *L'epistola agli Ebrei* (Turin 1952) 47; P. Hughes, *A Commentary on the Epistle to the Hebrews* (Grand Rapids 1977) 50.

[25]This point could be supported by more detailed considerations of thought-content, but for methodological reasons a full consideration of the theological content of these clauses is reserved to a following article.

that the presence of both the participle *genomenos* and the correlative *hosǭ* in one verse demands that we recognize two separate Christological designations in v. 4. But v. 4 is an example of *synkrisis*, a figure of speech beloved of our author, who is fond of "proportional" or "analogical" thinking.[26] As is clear from a simple reading of the period, v. 4 encapsulates one comparative thought, which both rounds off 1:1-4 and introduces 1:5-14. Hence it should be counted as one Christological designation or predication, despite the presence of both a participle and a correlative pronoun in the same verse. Grammatically, it is *genomenos* which—through *hos* in v. 3a—refers back to *huiǭ* in v. 2a and ties v. 4 to the larger structure.

One other objection could be raised against the count of seven Christological statements in 1:2b-4. While Davies counts the whole of v. 3a (*ōn apaugasma tēs doxēs kai charaktēr tēs hypostaseōs autou*) as one clause, Bruce divides v. 3a into two separate "facts" or Christological designations. Davies seems to have made the better choice. First, if we use the rule of thumb that an introductory participle or relative pronoun signals a new unit, both *apaugasma* and *charaktēr* are predicative nominatives of the one participle *ōn*. Second, while *doxēs* seems naturally to call for an *autou*, the author thinks it sufficient to place one *autou* at the end of the whole clause, after *hypostaseōs*. The one *autou* really qualifies both *doxēs* and *hypostaseōs*, and so nicely rounds off the entire clause.[27] Third, the two nouns are simply two alternate expressions of the Wisdom/Law/image speculation seen in Prov 8:22-36, Sir

---

[26]On *synkrisis*, see Bruce, *Hebrews*, 2 n. 6 and XLVIII n. 111, where it is also called an *a fortiori* argument and compared to the rabbis' *qal wahomer*. Grässer ("Hebräer 1:1-4", 225) points out the use of similar constructions in 7:20-22; 8:6; 10:25; one might add 3:3. See also R. Williamson, *Philo and the Epistle to the Hebrews* (Leiden 1970) 93-95. Commentators debate over whether "proportional", "analogical", "correlative", or "comparative" is the best designation of our author's mode of thought when he uses *synkrisis*. This semantic quarrel does not obscure two basic points: (1) the figure of *synkrisis* demands that the two parts of the comparison in v. 4 (*tosoutǭ ... hosǭ*) be taken together as expressing one thought and one Christological designation; (2) the whole of v. 4 is attached to the rest of the period and to *huiǭ* in particular only through *genomenos*.

[27]Admittedly, this second argument would not be valid for those who see *doxēs* as a semitism, reflecting the absolute *kābôd* as a periphrasis for God. Even in this case, though, the other two arguments are still probative.

24:1-23, Wis 7:25-26, Bar 3:9-4:4 as well as in Philo—a Wisdom speculation various New Testament authors use to describe the preexistent and creative Christ (e.g., Jn 1:1-18; 2 Cor 4:4; Phil 2:6-11; Col 1:15-20).[28] Finally, one may appeal to an independent and coincidentally concurring authority. In his structural analysis of the Greek text of Hebrews, Vanhoye, who is not concerned with the question of the exact number of Christological designations, naturally places the whole of v. 3a together on one line.[29] In sum, a division of v. 2b-4 into seven Christological designations seems to do the most justice to the objective grammatical signals in the text.

We are in a position, then, to take the first step in our correlation. On the one hand, we have seen that the carefully composed exordium of the Epistle lists seven Christological predications, describing the nature and work of the Son. On the other hand, almost all commentators acknowledge that the rest of chap. 1, the first doctrinal "paragraph" of the Epistle,[30] is made up of seven Old Testament citations, along with some introductory and concluding comments on the citations. Indeed, with his use of *palin* (vv. 5-6) *men . . . de* (vv. 7-8), *kai* (v. 10), and *de* (v. 13), the author himself seems intent on counting the number of quotations. His artistic disposition of the seven citations shows that he has not strewn them at the end of chap. 1 without an eye to order.[31] The only possible objection to counting seven Old Testament quotations is the fact that the author of the Epistle inserts a *kai* between the two lines of LXX Ps 44:7 in Heb 1:8bc. The insertion, though, is probably for the sake of rhetorical balance and emphasis.[32] It hardly carries the same weight as the *kai* at

---

[28]For further references, especially in Philo, see Bruce, *Hebrews,* 4-6; Williamson, *Philo,* 36-41 and 74-80.

[29]Vanhoye, *Brief,* 8. Spicq (*L'épître,* II, 8) also seems to be in favor of taking 1:3a as one unit. According to him, *apaugasma* and *charaktēr,* joined without any definite article to the same participle, express "two complementary aspects of the same idea".

[30]For the structural delimitation, see Vanhoye, *Situation,* 119-120.

[31]See Vanhoye, *Situation,* 121; and *Brief,* 8-9. Vanhoye sees an alternating pattern of contrast: Son—angels (vv. 5-6), angels—Son (vv. 7-12), and Son—angels (vv. 13-14). It might be asked, though, whether the third contrast (vv. 13-14, angels—Son) is as clear as the others.

[32]On this addition of the *kai,* see Moffatt, *Hebrews,* 13 n. 1. Vanhoye (*Situation,* 175) remains hesitant on whether *kai* is meant to create a separation or a closer connection.

the beginning of v. 10, which separates the lengthy citation of LXX Ps 44:7-8 from the even lengthier citation of LXX Ps 101:26-28. The insertion of *kai* in Heb 1:8c is rather on a par with the author's other minor editorial changes in these citations (e.g., moving the emphatic *sy* to the beginning of LXX Ps 101:26 in Heb 1:10).

Consequently, we can reasonably claim that there is a carefully worked-out numerical symmetry in Hebrews 1. The exordium (1:1-4) extols the superiority and uniqueness of Christ, the mediator of revelation, redemption, and creation, by qualifying the Son (v. 2a) with seven designations (vv. 2b-4). This Christological claim then receives its Scriptural grounding in seven Old Testament citations (vv. 5-14).[33] The further question, which must now be raised, is whether this symmetry is merely numerical. Does the correspondence of the two groups of seven simply aim at rhetorical neatness and aesthetic satisfaction, perhaps conjuring up a sense of Christ's perfection (*teleiotēs*) by the use of seven's? Or is there also a theological symmetry in the two groups of seven, a correspondence in the movement of Christological thought-patterns? That is the question we must now investigate.

II. Theological Symmetry in Hebrews 1:1-4 and 1:5-14

By a theological symmetry in Heb 1:1-4 and 1:5-14, I mean that one finds the same general pattern and movement of Christological thought in the seven designations of Christ and in the seven quotations used to ground those designations. Obviously, to demonstrate such a symmetry one must first indicate the exact meaning of each of the seven Christological designations and of each of the Old Testament citations (as interpreted Christologically by our author). Only then can a

---

[33]So Grässer, "Hebräer 1,1-4", 202-203: "The close literary and material dovetailing of 1:1-4 and 1:5-14 is so articulated that both sections relate to each other as thesis to interpretation. The predications of dignity in vv. 2-4 are verified point-for-point in section vv. 5-14, and indeed with the help of OT citations ...". Unfortunately, Grässer's attempt at seeing a point-for-point verification does not materialize; his observations do not adhere strictly to the order of designations in Heb 1:2b-4.

correlation be shown. Hence, I shall first briefly indicate the theological significance of each member in the seven Christological designations and then ask whether there is a correspondence with the seven citations.

The Seven Christological Designations   *v. 2b*

(1) The first Christological designation speaks of "[the Son] whom he [God] appointed heir [*klēronomon*] of all [things]". Along with O. Hofius and M. Bourke, I think it best to see here a reference to the exaltation of Jesus, which is further described in vv. 3d-4 as enthronement at the right hand.[34] Indeed, the substantive *klēronomon* of v. 2b returns as the verb *keklēronomēken*, at the end of v. 4, where the context shows that "inheriting the name" is connected with the exaltation at the right hand. Admittedly, it is possible to take *ethēken* in v. 2b as an eternal declaration by God—as a few exegetes do.[35] But such an interpretation fits neither the immediate context nor the general thought of the Epistle, which identifies the decisive act of redemption with the death-exaltation of Jesus. Indeed, the whole central section of the Epistle (8:1-9:28) is dedicated to explicating this pivotal event of bloody sacrifice and triumphal entrance into the heavenly sanctuary.[36] The immediate context likewise argues for interpreting 1:2b in reference to exaltation. As the author begins in 1:5 to comment on his Christological designations with the first of the Old Testament citations, he chooses Ps 2:7 in which God addresses the *enthroned* King as Son. In the next verse of the psalm (not quoted in Heb 1:5), God goes on to promise the enthroned Son: "Ask of me, and I will give you the nations as your

---

[34]Hofius, *Christushymnus,* 76 along with n. 5; M. Bourke, "The Epistle to the Hebrews", *JBC* II. 383: "His being made heir is not an event outside time, previous to the incarnation; it took place when he entered glory after his passion (cf. Rom 8:17)". See also Michel, *Brief,* 103.

[35]So B. Westcott, *The Epistle to the Hebrews* (London 1889) 7; also, with hesitation, Moffatt, *Hebrews,* 5.

[36]J. Héring, *L'épître aux Hébreux* (Neuchâtel 1954) 21 holds that the two interpretations (from all eternity and at the exaltation) need not exclude each other; similarly, Davies, *Hebrews,* 19.

inheritance [*klēronomian*] and the ends of the earth as your possession [*kataschesin*]" (Ps 2:8). In a sense, this verse of the psalm simply explicitates the terse *klēronomon pantōn* of 1:2b. A similar idea occurs in the author's exegesis of LXX Ps 8:5-7 in Heb 2:5-9. In commenting on Ps 8:7 ("you have placed all things [*panta*] under his feet"), the author observes that this verse is not yet true of humanity in general (Heb 1:8); but in some sense it is true even now of Jesus (Heb 1:9). For a little while (during his earthly life), Jesus was made lower than the angels. But now, because of his exaltation, he is "crowned with glory and honor" (Ps 8:6), with all things—in fact or in promise—[37] under his feet. It seems likely, therefore, that Heb 1:2b refers to Christ's exaltation after his death.[38] In 1:2bc taken together, the author's thought is moving from the eschatological to the protological.[39] It is probably the failure to appreciate this "retrogressive" order in the author's Christological thought that leads some commentators to understand *ethēken* as an eternal decree. It probably seems to them the only logical interpretation of a clause coming just before a reference to creating the worlds (v. 2c). The question, though, is: "logical" by whose logic? Our author is apparently proclaiming the Son to be, not the Alpha and the Omega, but the Omega and the Alpha.

---

[37]Hofius (*Christushymnus*, 96-98) argues forcefully that the universal subjection is a full fact at the exaltation. Vanhoye, on the other hand, claims that the reference to universal domination fits the function Jesus will obtain at the last judgment (*Situation*, 291). But even this interpretation is not in conflict with the affirmation that God *constituted* Jesus *heir* of all things at the exaltation. Perhaps it would be helpful in this matter to distinguish between two types of eschatology in Hebrews, as G. Hughes does in *Hebrews and Hermeneutics*, 66-74: the Christological-doctrinal sections of the Epistle tend to stress realized eschatology, while the ecclesiological-parenetic sections tend to stress futurist eschatology. In chap. 1, a Christological passage, the emphasis is on all that is already realized.

[38]For the dispute over whether Heb 1:2b means that Jesus enters into actual ownership and possession of all things at his exaltation, see Hofius, *Christushymnus*, 77 n. 8 and 95-101; and Vanhoye, *Situation*, 62-64.

[39]So, correctly, Grässer, "Hebräer 1,1-4", 214; and Michel, *Brief*, 94. Michel notes (p. 94 n. 1) that Ephraem, Chrysostom, and the Greek exegetes in general refer the *ethēken* to the exaltation. While Spicq (*L'épître*, II, 5) observes that the Son in one sense always had full right over the universe, he adds that Christ as man does not exercise sovereignty before the ascension. A similar line of argument is pursued by H. Montefiore, *The Epistle to the Hebrews* (London 1964) 34.

(2) The time-reference of 1:2c is much clearer: "through whom also he made the worlds [*aiōnas*]". The Son, the eschatological heir of all things and mediator of redemption is such precisely on the ground of his being the mediator of creation.[40] The plural form *aiōnas* may be intended to conjure up both the present age/world (*ton kairon ton enestēkota* of Heb 9:9) and the future age/world (*tēn oikoumenēn tēn mellousan* of Heb 2:5). As the exalted Son, Christ rules over what he created in the beginning: both the old world doomed to pass away and the heavenly world which lies before a redeemed humanity as the goal of its pilgrimage. In short, the word *aiōnas* of v. 2c, for all its difference in theological nuance, is basically identical with the *pantōn* of v. 2b.[41] At his exaltation, the Son in his perfected humanity, is constituted heir of what the preexistent Son created *kat'archas* (Heb 1:10).[42] As we have already seen, what is startling in v. 2bc taken together is that the thought moves in reverse: from the definitive act of exaltation to the initial act of creation. Our author characteristically views the various moments in the Christological drama from the vantage point of exaltation.[43]

(3) Having moved back from exaltation to creation, our author will ultimately move forward again to exaltation in the relative clause beginning with *hos* and ending with *ekathisen ... en hypsēlois* (1:3d). But his movement is neither so simple

[40]*Kai* in 1:2c could simply mean "also". But, after a relative pronoun it can carry a sense of "precisely as such"; cf. Grässer, "Hebräer 1,1-4", 214. There may thus be a note of logical nexus or correspondence; see also Spicq, *L'épître*, II, 6; Moffatt, *Hebrews*, 5. Whether *aiōnas* carries a temporal or spatial meaning need not detain us; the word probably includes both (so Hofius, *Christushymnus*, 78 n. 11). The view of F. Schierse (*Verheissung und Heilsvollendung* [Munich 1955] 67-75, which seeks to restrict *aiōnas* to the invisible world, is unlikely and has not received wide support.

[41]So, rightly, Moffatt, *Hebrews*, 5.

[42]These remarks are indebted to Hofius, *Christushymnus*, 78-79. As Hofius observes, it is this interplay of eschatology and protology that explains the curious vision of our author: the preexistent Son becomes Son at the exaltation. It is almost a Christological adaptation of the NT baptismal parenesis to the Christian: become what you are. For the view that both messiahship and mediation of creation are rooted in the author's idea of Christ's sonship, see F. Büchsel, *Die Christologie des Hebräerbriefs* (Gütersloh 1922) 14.

[43]This point, so well made by Thompson ("Structure", 128-140) in reference to Heb 1:5-14, can be legitimately extended to the whole of our author's Christological thought.

nor so direct. After the mention of creation in v. 2c, there is—if one may so speak of matters beyond the grasp of reason—a further move "backward" into the eternal existence of the Son in his relationship to God (his Father):[44] "being the effulgence of [his] glory and the image of his being".[45] The first thing to be noted about this clause in 1:3a is what comes first: the present participle *ōn*. One notable manifestation of our author's mastery of Greek rhetoric throughout the Epistle is his subtle use of Greek tenses and moods. Heb 1:1-4 is already a prime example. The present tense of the participle *ōn* is striking. With one exception,[46] *ōn* is surrounded in 1:1-4 by verbs in the aorist or perfect tenses: *lalēsas, elalēsen, ethēken, epoiēsen, poiēsamenos, ekathisen, genomenos,* and *keklēronomēken.* All of these verbs speak of particular events within (or, in the case of *epoiēsen*, at the beginning of) the historical drama of salvation. In the mythic language and thought-modes of the author, all the actions of God and the Son can be placed on a time-line reaching from creation to exaltation and all refer either to unique past acts determining the flow of salvation history (the aorists) or to the permanent triumphant state of Christ flowing from the past event of being exalted (the perfect, *keklēronomēken*). Amid this string of discrete past actions, the present stative participle *ōn* stands out like a metaphysical diamond against the black crepe of narrative. As previously noted, we have here an example of the Wisdom speculation already present in the Hebrew Old Testament (Prov 8), developed in Palestine in second-century B.C. "proto-Pharisaic" theology (Sir 24), given more Greek-philosophical expression in Septuagintal/Alexandrian Judaism (Wis 7:26, *apaugasma gar estin* [*sophia*] *phōtos aidiou*), and reaching its culmination in Philo of Alexandria. Granted, R. Williamson

---

[44]Though it is obvious that the author considers God *(ho theos)* to be the Father of "the Son"—otherwise the two OT citations in Heb 1:5 make no sense—, the author strangely avoids directly giving God the title *ho patēr* in reference to Jesus; see, however, the title, "the Father of spirits", in 12:9.

[45]The much debated and still unresolved question of whether in 1:3a *apaugasma* carries an active meaning (radiance, so Bruce) or passive meaning (reflection, so Bourke) need not detain us; see the commentaries, *ad loc.;* and Williamson, *Philo,* 37.

[46]*Pherōn,* which denotes an act which, while not existing from all eternity, will continue forever, granted the perdurance of the heavenly world.

is perfectly correct in stressing the theological differences between Philo and Hebrews and the danger of facilely taking
verbal parallels for identical thought.[47] The Jewish philosophical tradition of Alexandria is recycled by the author of
Hebrews to express his own unique synthesis of Christian
theology. Nevertheless, if one pushes this valid insight too far,
it is all too easy to fall into an apologetic stance that creates an
unbridgeable gulf between the good revelation of the New
Testament and the evil philosophy of the Greeks (and, implicitly, of the patristic period). It is high time that we recognize
that in a few startling passages in the New Testament like Heb
1:2-3 and Jn 1:1-3, the thought of some first century Christians
began, ever so tentatively, to move beyond purely historical
modes of conception and narration and to probe the speculative, philosophical implications of their tremendous affirmations about God, Christ, and humanity. In the case of
Hebrews, it is not true that the author took over from
Alexandrian Judaism only individual, isolated words, with
totally changed meanings. He also took over a *Weltanschauung*, a whole group of philosophical underpinnings and
presuppositions which can be vaguely labeled "middle
Platonism". It is not without a certain justification that J.
Thompson entitles his collection of essays on Hebrews *The
Beginnings of Christian Philosophy*. It is a historical fact that
the middle Platonism of Hebrews was also the major philosophical milieu in which the pre-Nicene Fathers thought and
wrote, especially when they struggled over Christological
questions raised precisely by such texts as Heb 1:1-4 and Jn
1:1-18. There is no magical dividing line at A.D. 100, cordoning
off the pristine New Testament from the scruffy Fathers. For
better or for worse, Hebrews 1 and John 1 share the same
philosophical bed as Justin Martyr and Origen.

All this is said by way of rejecting the nervous tendency of
some commentators to explain away or pass over quickly the
metaphysical weight and thrust of Heb 1:3a in favor of the

---

[47]On *apaugasma,* see Williamson, *Philo,* 36-41; on *charaktēr,* 74-80. Williamson's
general conclusions can be found on pp. 576-580.

Son's *heilsgeschichtliche* function.[48] The fact of the matter is that a certain first-century Christian author, steeped in Alexandrian-Jewish theology, was able to integrate speculation about eternal existence and relationship with God into more traditional and historical New Testament affirmations about Jesus Christ. In this he went beyond most of New Testament thought, but by that very fact he pointed the way into the patristic period. We need not be surprised, then, that in 1:2b-3a, the author has moved consistently "backward" from exaltation (*ekathisen*) to creation (*epoiēsen*) and to timeless preexistence (*ōn*).[49]

(4) In Heb 1:3b, the train of Christological thought, having moved backward from exaltation through creation to timeless preexistence, now begins to "round the turn". It moves forward from timeless preexistence to the Son's role in preserving the world he helped create: "sustaining, [*pherōn*] all things by his[50]

---

[48]See, for instance, the intriguing oscillation in the remarks of H. MacNeill (*The Christology of the Epistle to the Hebrews* [Chicago 1914] 56-63). On the one hand, MacNeill affirms that 1:3 does set forth "the inner or essential relation of the preincarnate Son to God" (p. 60). On p. 62 he states: "And yet, though sharing in and expressing the glory of God and picturing in himself at once metaphysically, mentally, morally, and spiritually the very nature and being of God, he is continually dependent on God, alike in his historical manifestation as Jesus and in his pre-existent life as Son". It comes as a surprise to read on the same pages that the author of Hebrews may not have thought "any more definitely of the person of the preincarnate Son than Philo thought of the person of the Logos or than the writer of Wisdom of Solomon thought of the person of Wisdom..." (p. 61). It is true, as MacNeill says, that we are dealing here with a metaphor (p. 61); but that is equally true of Hebrews' description of Christ's earthly work and heavenly exaltation. How else is one to speak of such things? Presence of metaphor does not prove absence of serious thought. It is true that Hebrews has not developed the full-blown patristic doctrine of the Son's "eternal generation" (p. 63); but the thrust of Hebrews' philosophical affirmations will in due time raise the question.

[49]Obviously, to speak of moving "backward" into "timeless preexistence" is to speak metaphorically or mythically. But this is precisely what our author is doing. This article seeks to grasp *his* thought, not a modern hermeneutical reformulation of his thought.

[50]On the textual difficulty involved in *autou* and its possible connection with the following clause, see Grässer, "Hebräer 1,1-4", 185; B. Metzger, *A Textual Commentary on the Greek New Testament* (New York 1971) 662. The dispute over whether *autou* in 1:3b refers to the Son (so Grässer, 185; Westcott, *Hebrews*, 14; Moffatt, *Hebrews*, 8), or to God as in v. 3a (so B. Weiss, *Der Brief an die Hebräer* [Göttingen 1897] 45), or possibly to either (Vanhoye, *Situation*, 79) need not detain us.

mighty word".[51] We have in *pherōn* the only other present tense in the exordium. However, the sense of the present tense in *pherōn* is slightly different from that in *ōn*. The participle *ōn* spoke of a timeless preexistence of the Son with God, prior to and capable of existing apart from any relation to the created worlds. As soon as *ta panta* (= *tas aiōnas*) is reintroduced into the picture, we are back to a consideration of the Son's relation to created time and space. The Son's conserving function did begin at some point (creation, v. 2c), and so in that sense it is not timeless or eternal. Yet, once creation occurs, the Son continues to uphold creation now and forever—at least as regards the world which is to come (Heb 2:5), the lasting city which is still to come (from our viewpoint) but which is already present in heaven (13:14 and 12:22). Thus, the present tense of *pherōn* indicates this ongoing action of upholding creation, an action which will always continue but which did not always exist. Looking backward, we can see that *pherōn* had a beginning. This is not true of *ōn*, which refers to what is eternal in the strict sense, without beginning or end. Consequently, *pherōn*, despite its present tense, does imply a return from the outer limits of theological speculation—timeless, eternal existence with God—back toward the Son's function in the world and history.[52]

(5) The fifth Christological designation places us squarely within salvation history, indeed at the heart of the decisive saving event: "having brought about [*poiēsamenos*] the purification of sins" (1:3c)—i.e., having purified believers from their

---

[51]Besides the plain idea of carrying, upholding, conserving, *pherōn* may also connote a directing of creation to its appointed goal (so Bruce, *Hebrews*, 6; cf. Moffatt, *Hebrews*, 7; Hughes, *Hebrews*, 45 n. 22). Hofius (*Christushymnus*, 83) stresses that governance as well as conservation is included. This position is rejected by Grässer ("Hebräer 1,1-4", 221), who insists that the true meaning is found in the "parallel" of Col 1:17 (*synestēken*). One might ask whether the *pherōn* of Heb 1:3 includes not only the *synestēken* of Col 1:17 but also something like the *eis auton ektistai* of Col 1:16. At the very least, *pherōn* is more than simply a repetition of Heb 1:2c, as Williamson correctly observes (*Philo*, 97).

[52]So, rightly, Grässer, "Hebräer 1,1-4", 220: "While the first pair of predications of dignity were more oriented toward the relation of the revealer to God, the next lines of the hymn are more [oriented] toward [his relation] to the world" (translation mine). It is strange, then, that Grässer claims that the "temporal aspect" of *pherōn* is not emphasized (p. 221).

sins. In the terse and dense message of the exordium, the author skips over the idea of incarnation and moves immediately to what concerns him most about the earthly Jesus: his sacrifice. Strangely, this is the only clause in the exordium which touches upon this main doctrinal theme of Hebrews: the redeeming work of Christ the high priest in offering himself once and for all as a sacrifice for sins (see esp. 4:14-5:10; 7:1-10:18). The once-and-for-all, *ephapax* nature of Christ's sacrifice, which is hammered home by the author in his latter exposition (cf. *ephapax* at 7:27; 9:12; 10:10; and *hapax* at 9:7, 26, 27, 28) is perhaps hinted at here by use of the aorist participle *poiēsamenos*. In fact, the first use of *ephapax* in the Epistle occurs with the aorist form *epoiēsen* 7:27): "Unlike the high priests, [Jesus] does not need daily to offer [present infinitive] sacrifices, first for his own sins, then for the [sins] of the people; for he did this once and for all [*epoiēsen ephapax*], by offering [aorist participle] himself". The fact that, for the author, Christ's sacrifice is constituted not only by the bloody death on the cross but also by the entrance into the heavenly sanctuary[53] may explain why, for this time alone in the exordium, he has shifted the participle to the end of the clause: rhetorically and theologically *poiēsamenos* is juxtaposed to the finite verb *ekathisen*.[54]

[53]So, correctly, Vanhoye, *De Epistola ad Hebraeos. Sectio Centralis (Cap. 8-9)*, 198. See also Hofius, *Christushymnus*, 85-86, especially nn. 42 and 43, against Grässer, "Hebräer 1,1-4", 224, who plays down the death on the cross ("an episode") in favor of the exaltation, the real goal. Yet, in a somewhat contradictory way, Grässer later states that 1:3c is the most important sentence in the exordium, because it indicates *the* theme of Hebrews: the atonement of sins (p. 224).—Bruce errs in the opposite direction, by practically reducing the sacrifice to the cross (see, e.g., *Hebrews*, 200-201). In Bruce's favor, it must be admitted that the sacrifice does not continue in heaven after Jesus' entrance with his blood, a point Vanhoye also stresses. On this whole subject, see also J. Jeremias, "Zwischen Karfreitag und Ostern. Descensus und Ascensus in der Karfreitagstheologie des Neuen Testamentes", *Abba* (Göttingen 1966) 323-331; Jeremias' concern with reckoning days is, of course, foreign to our author's thought.

[54]Cf. D. Hay, *Glory at the Right Hand* (Nashville 1973) 143. Note the joining of the two events of sacrifice (or death) and exaltation in 10:12: *mian hyper hamartiōn prosenegkas thusian eis to diēnekes ekathisen en dexiq tou theou;* and in 12:2: *Iēsoun, hos. . . hypemeinen stauron aischynēs kataphronēsas en dexiq te tou thronou tou theou kekathiken.* As can be seen the author is capable of using either the aorist or the perfect when referring to the session at the right hand, depending on whether the definitive, once-and-for-all climax of the drama or its perduring effect is uppermost in his mind.

(6) With 1:3d we arrive at the finite verb of the relative clause introduced by *hos*, which reaches all the way back to *huiǭ*: "[the Son] who . . . sat down at the right [hand] of the Majesty on high". It is exegeting the obvious to say that v. 3d refers to the exaltation of Christ after his death. The chief Scripture text behind v. 3d is LXX Ps 109:1, which is explicitly quoted for the first time in 1:13. The idea of the "heavenly sitting" or exaltation dominates the thought of the Epistle much more than citations of or allusions to Ps 109:1 or 4 (Heb 5:6,10; 6:20, 7:17,21; 8:1; 10:12; 12:2) would lead one to believe.[55] The whole argument of the Epistle revolves around the idea of the Son who has become the perfect high priest by his death and exaltation.[56] It is fitting, therefore, that the main verb within the relative clause should be the one which affirms Christ's seat at the right hand.

(7) The seventh and final Christological designation is expressed by the complicated *synkrisis* of 1:4: "Having become (*genomenos*) as superior (*kreittōn*)[57] to the angels as the name (*onoma*) he has inherited is [superior] to theirs". This final designation speaks of one consequence of the Son's exaltation at the right hand. Because of his exaltation, his position in the heavenly world has become clearly superior to that of the angels and this corresponds nicely to the fact that he has inherited (*keklēronomēken*) a name or title that is superior to the name "angel".

We should notice first of all that v. 4 speaks of an event

[55]In a sense, the whole theological achievement of the author rests on the fact that he alone among NT writers read "theologically" beyond the first verse of Psalm 109 (the most frequently quoted verse in the NT), noticed the claim of v. 4, connected it with v.1, and drew out the implications for Christology and soteriology.

[56]See Michel, "Der theologische Wille des Hebräerbriefes", *Brief*, 58-83, especially 74: ". . . Jesus dies as a victim, to create by that act the presupposition for his service as high priest in heaven. . . . The act of dying is necessarily incorporated into his priestly office, while his priestly service in the proper sense begins only after the exaltation" (translation mine).

[57]*Kreittōn* occurs thirteen times in Hebrews (out of nineteen NT uses). It expresses vhe superior quality of the name and status of the Son; the better hope Christians have; the superiority of the new covenant, founded on better promises; the superior sacrifice of Christ; the better, heavenly possession Christians hope for, the superior life of the resurrection; the more powerful intercession of Jesus' blood—in short, the superiority of the new economy of salvation Jesus has inaugurated. See Grässer, "Hebräer 1,1-4", 225-226.

involving what the Son "became" (*genomenos*). Apparently this "becoming" takes place at or immediately subsequent to the exaltation, if one may judge both from the position of v. 4 immediately after v. 3d and from the very idea of becoming superior to someone else in the heavenly sphere. To translate *genomenos* as "showing oneself" or "proving himself to be", as some modern versions do, does not do justice to the thought here and avoids the contrast with *ōn* in 1:3a. It is simply a translator's attempt to smooth over the clash of ideas in 1:2-4. Heb 1:2-3a spoke of the preexistent Son, creator of the world and perfect image of God's being. Now, v. 4 speaks of him as having inherited, at the time of his exaltation, a name superior to that of the angels. The clash is the result of two different streams of Christological traditions flowing into one channel. What the author is doing is bringing together in one periodic sentence a Christology of preexistent Wisdom (e.g., Phil 2:6; Jn 1:1) and a Christology of Jesus who is enthroned as Son or Lord at the time of his resurrection/ascension (e.g., Rom 1:4; Acts 2:34-36; 13:33; Phil 2:9-11). As the example from Philippians 2 shows,[58] the author of Hebrews is not alone in this theological tendency.[59] But, with the quasi-metaphysical

[58] As is clear from the comparison, I maintain that Phil 2:6 does contain a reference to preexistence. In this I disagree with the stimulating works of J. Murphy-O'Connor ("Christological Anthropology in Phil. II, 6-11", *RB* 83 [1976] 25-50, C. Talbert ("The Problem of Pre-existence in Philippians 2,6-11", *JBL* 86 [1967] 141-153), and especially J. Dunn in his fascinating book, *Christology in the Making* (Philadelphia 1980). While Dunn's work demands a thorough reply, let me simply note here that I think Dunn overplays the Adam references in Paul's thought. but, even granting the Adam-reference in the Philippians hymn, there are problems with Dunn's thesis. The hymn clearly presupposes a before (2:6f) and an after (2:7-8) in Christ's transition to the status of dying servant. Indeed, a transition from before to after is essential to the Adam story. What is this "before" in the situation of Christ if not preexistence? Where do we have the idea in the NT that for some period Jesus dwelt in a perfect Adamic existence on earth before he freely chose to take on our suffering? If the Adam story is the referent in the hymn, Dunn will have to do better in explaining the "before" situation of Christ. The natural candidate remains preexistence.

[59] A number of recent works situate Heb 1:2-4 in the context of NT hymns: e.g., Bornkamm, "Bekenntnis", 197-198; R. Deichgräber, *Gotteshymnus und Christus-hymnus in der frühen Christenheit* (Göttingen 1967) 138; R. Martin, *Carmen Christi* (Cambridge 1967) 305 n. 8; J. T. Sanders, *The New Testament Christological Hymns* (Cambridge 1971) 19; Hofius, *Christushymnus*, 92-102. These authors are certainly correct in seeing parallels, though at times the parallels are overdrawn and the differences ignored. As shall be seen, I am skeptical about identifying a traditional hymn in Heb 1:2-4; see Part III below.

claim about the Son in 1:3a, the clash between ontological and functional Son-Christology in 1:2-4 strikes the modern reader as harsh.[60] O. Michel is probably correct in suggesting that our author thinks of a gradual perfection or realization of Christ's sonship in steps or stages.[61] Indeed, the juxtaposition of these two different types of Christology almost demands some kind of "process-Sonship" as a way towards synthesis. Unfortunately, the author of Hebrews never explains in detail how this sonship can be realized progressively through the stages of the saving drama without any attenuation of the truth of 1:2-3a. He never seems to sense our problem. Yet, whether he does or not, the author poses a problem with his Son-Christology that will loom large throughout the patristic period.

The main point for us, though, is that v. 4 speaks of the event of becoming superior at or immediately following upon the exaltation, an event connected with a name (*onoma*). The name that is inherited is in all probability the title Son.[62] The previous and subsequent contexts both speak for this identification. It was just after the first mention of "Son" in 1:2a that the author first used *klēronomon*, the inclusion *keklēron-*

---

[60]On this, see F. Büchsel, *Christologie*, 7. It is artificial to try to avoid the clash by claiming, as Käsemann does (*Gottesvolk*, 59, and following him, Grässer, "Hebräer 1,1-4", 215 n. 209; Thompson, "Structure", 131 n. 4), that the references to the Son in passages like 1:2 and 5:8 are merely "proleptic". Especially in the case of 5:8, the whole argument depends on Jesus being the Son before his exaltation: "Son though (*kaiper*) he was, he learned obedience from what he suffered. . . ." The point lies in the shock of the Son undergoing suffering. On this, see U. Luck, "Himmlisches und irdisches Geschehen im Hebräerbrief", *NT* 6 (1963) 192-215, especially 205.

[61]Michel, *Brief*, 106 n. 1. Westcott (*Hebrews*, 16-17) interprets the thought with the later Chalcedonian model of two natures; similarly, Spicq, *L'épître* II, 12. On the tension between the eternal Son and the salvation-historical Son, see Hofius, *Christushymnus*, 92-93, who sees a parallel with the proclamation of Yahweh's kingship in the OT psalms and prophets. Hofius observes that Yahweh is and always has been king, yet in an eschatological context the promise is made that Yahweh will become king on the last day.—But does this parallel do justice to the personal, existential "perfecting" that the Son undergoes through suffering (e.g., Heb 5:5-10)? On the whole question, see MacNeill, *Christology*, 56, 96, 102, 407. MacNeill feels that the author of Hebrews never adequately fused adoptionistic and metaphysical sonships. More sympathetic to Hofius' approach is D. Peterson, *Hebrews and Perfection* (SNTSMS 47; Cambridge: Cambridge U., 1982) 119.

[62]So, rightly, Bruce, *Hebrews*, 8. As Bruce observes in n. 36, this differentiates Heb 1:4 from Phil 2:9, where the *onoma* is probably *kyrios*. Also in favor of taking *onoma* as Son are Bornkamm, "Bekenntnis", 196; Hofius, *Christushymnus*, 90; P. Hughes, *Hebrews*, 51; and Käsemann, *Gottesvolk*, 58.

omēken, implies that *onoma* is to be understood as the title Son. The flow of thought into the first Old Testament citation also suggests that *onoma* be understood as "Son." Immediately after saying: "he has inherited a name" (v. 4), the author asks rhetorically in v. 5: "*for* to which of the angels did he ever say, 'My son [*huios*] are you: I this day have begotten you': and again: 'I shall be a father to him and he shall be unto me a son (*huion*)'".[63] Given this Scriptural explanation and grounding (*gar*) in v. 5 of the statement in v. 4, to try to avoid taking *onoma* as the title Son is an exercise in avoiding the obvious. True, many different titles and designations are given to Jesus in 1:5-14, in chap. 2, and throughout the rest of the Epistle.[64] But the flow of thought in Heb 1:1-5 seems to indicate that, for the author of Hebrews, Son is *the* title of Jesus which embraces all the rest. As F. Büchsel says so well: "All the statements about Jesus in the Epistle to the Hebrews are rooted in the idea that Jesus is the Son of God. . . . God calls him Son: that is the name by which he ranks above even the angels (1:4,5)".[65]

We have come to the end of our brief survey of the seven Christological designations in Heb 1:2b-4. If our analysis of the meaning of the individual designations is correct, then a certain pattern and movement of thought emerge. The author begins to describe the Son (*huiō,* v. 2a) in terms of his exaltation to the status of heir (v. 2b), then moves back to the Son's mediation of creation (v. 2c), then "moves back" still farther to the Son's eternal, timeless relationship to God (v. 3a). Then the author turns around and moves forward to the Son's conservation of what he helped create (v. 3b), then forward again to the Son's sacrifice for sins (death and entrance

---

[63]Notice the skill of our author in choosing and arranging two Psalm quotations which yield an inclusion with the word "Son" *(huios mou——eis huion).* With such an emphasis on *huios,* it is extremely difficult to take *onoma* as meaning anything else.

[64]A valid point made by Vanhoye, *Situation,* 93-94. See also Westcott, *Hebrews,* 17: "By the 'name' we are to understand probably not the name of 'Son' simply. . . but the Name which gathered up all that Christ was found to be by believers. . .". Similarly, but more cautiously, Moffatt, *Hebrews,* 8: ". . . it [*onoma*] carries the general Oriental sense of 'rank' or 'dignity'. . . it is needless to identify *onoma* outright with *huios,* though *huios* brings out its primary meaning"; so too MacNeill, *Christology,* 36; similarly, Dey, *The Intermediary World,* 147.

[65]Büchsel, *Christologie,* 5 (translation mine); cf. Grässer, "Hebräer 1,1-4", 206.

into the heavenly sanctuary, v. 3c), then forward again to his being seated at the right hand in heaven (v. 3d), and finally to the consequence of his exaltation: his perduring[66] superiority vis-à-vis the angels (v. 4). Putting all of this into a diagram, we arrive at something like a "ring structure", a ring that describes the Son from the viewpoint of exaltation as starting point and exaltation as goal.

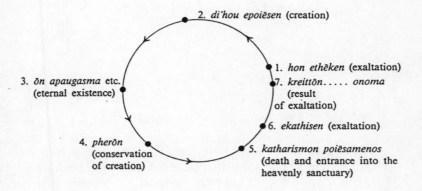

It is this ring structure that is the key to the movement of the author's Christological thought in 1:2b-4. Without it one misses the retrogressive and then progressive flow of designations. It may be that many commentators on Hebrews have been puzzled by the exact import of the string of designations in 1:2b-4, especially in relation to the whole of chap. 1, precisely because they have not grasped the ring structure which the author is using.

---

[66]The perfect tense of *keklēronomēken* makes a subtle point. The eternal Son did, for a little while *(brachu)* become lower than the angels (2:9) by entering into this world as man (10:5). But his exaltation is that event (now past) which guarantees him permanent superiority (in functional, salvation-historical terms) over the angels.

5

Symmetry and Theology in the Old Testament Citations of Hebrews 1:5-14

I. The Seven Old Testament Citations in Hebrews 1:5-14

In my previous essay ("Structure and Theology in Heb 1, 1-14"), I attempted to show that there is a numerical symmetry between the seven Christological designations in Heb 1:2b-4 and the seven Old Testament citations in 1:5-14. Moreover, we saw that the seven designations in 1:2b-4 form a definite ring pattern, moving from exaltation back through creation to preexistence and forward again through creation to exaltation. In the present essay I pose the further question: Is the symmetry between 1:2b-4 and 1:5-14 merely numerical, or do the seven Old Testament citations correspond to 1:2b-4 not only in number but also in general movement of thought? Is the parallel not only numerical but also theological? To answer this question, I shall investigate in this essay the theological import and thrust of each of the seven citations.

One point, however, should be made clear before we start. In Heb 1:2b-4 the author was free to write what he wanted, down to the individual words, and to arrange what he wrote in whatever order and pattern pleased him. Obviously, in the case of a catena of OT quotations, he does not enjoy the same absolute freedom. He is not free to undertake a massive rewriting of the OT texts; this would undermine the very purpose of quoting the OT as an authority. Rather, the author can insinuate his theological program by means of the order he gives the catena and by the interpretative remarks he makes in an introduction or a conclusion. Granted the "given" nature of the OT citations, we may not always be sure exactly how much of the quotation is being pressed into service for the author's theological message. What we must ask, therefore, is whether the general movement of thought in the seven quotations corresponds to the general movement of thought in the seven designations. To be more precise: in light of the natural constraints on our author as he quotes OT texts, I am not claiming a one-for-one correspondence between each designation and the numerically equivalent citation, but rather a general correspondence in the over-all movement of thought. With this in mind, let us look at the individual quotations.[1]

(1) and (2). I have already examined the first two citations in reference to v. 4 in my previous essay. We have seen that they are directly connected with v. 4 by *gar,* indicating that the OT texts somehow support or ground what is said in v. 4. But v. 4, as we now know, refers to the superior status Christ enjoys vis-à-vis the angels as a result of his exaltation at the right hand (v. 3d). Consequently the flow of thought seems to indicate that God is speaking to the Son at or immediately after the exaltation.[2] The "today" when God "has begotten the Son" is the day of enthronement at the right hand. Efforts, therefore, to connect Hebrews' use of Ps 2:7 with such events

---

[1] For a general orientation on the use of the OT in Hebrews, see S. Kistemaker, *The Psalm Citations in the Epistle to the Hebrews* (Amsterdam 1961); and R. Reid, *The Use of the Old Testament in the Epistle to the Hebrews* (typewritten thesis; NY: Union Theological Seminary, 1964). For general considerations of form, function, sources, and theology of Heb 1:5-14, see O. Hofius, *Der Christushymnus Philipper 2:6-11* (Tübingen 1976) 86, 88-89; D. Hay, *Glory at the Right Hand* (Nashville 1973) 39, 144-145; E. Grässer, "Der Hebräerbrief 1938-1963", *TR* 30 (1964) 138-236, especially 208-209; C. Spicq, *L'épître aux Hébreux* (2 vols.; Paris 1952 and 1953) 2, 15; H. Montefiore, *The Epistle to the Hebrews* (London 1964) 43-44; G. Hughes, *Hebrews and Hermeneutics* (Cambridge 1979) 7-8; J. Thompson, "The Structure and Purpose of the Catena in Hebrews 1:5-13", *The Beginnings of Christian Philosophy* (Washington, D.C. 1982) 128-140; L. Dey, *The Intermediary World and Patterns of Perfection in Philo and Hebrews* (Missoula 1975) 146-147; O. Michel, *Der Brief an die Hebräer* (Göttingen 1966) 109, 125.

[2] So Thompson, "Structure", 131.

as Christ's eternal generation, the annunciation, the nativity, the baptism by John, or the transfiguration, miss the particular cast of our author's thought.[3] He is closer to the homily of Paul addressed to Hellenistic Jews in a diaspora synagogue in Acts 13:33[4], where Ps 2:7 is applied to the resurrection. The idea that Jesus is constituted Son at the resurrection/exaltation is also clear in the pre-Pauline creedal formula of Rom 1:3-4.[5] That Ps 2:7 is to be understood in terms of exaltation is confirmed by our author when he brings together Ps 2:7 and Ps 109:4 in Heb 5:5-6 as two proclamations of God to Christ, apparently spoken at the same time.[6] From the whole theology of the Epistle it is clear that Christ becomes priest by his death and entrance into the heavenly sanctuary: "If he were on earth, he would not be a priest" (8:4). Hence, in the mind of our author, Ps 109:4 is spoken by God to Christ at or around the time of his death-exaltation. Since the author ties Ps 2:7 so closely to Ps 109:4 in 5:5-6, he seems to envision the same setting for the proclamation of sonship. And, if Ps 2:7 refers to the exaltation in Heb 5:5, there is no reason to think it refers to something else in 1:5.[7] Once we have established this time-

---

[3]So correctly A. Vanhoye, *Situation du Christ* (Paris 1969) 140-142.

[4]One cannot help remarking on the similarity of *Sitz in Leben* between Paul's homily and the homily that is the Epistle to the Hebrews.

[5]Similar in thought is the climax of Peter's Pentecost speech in Acts 2:36, but here Lord and Christ are used as titles of exaltation, not Son.

[6]Michel (*Brief,* 219) rightly observes on 5:5-6: "By two statements in the Psalm, God himself has conferred on him [Christ] the dignity of Son and Priest" (translation mine). Yet Michel hesitates over whether the oracles refer to Christ as exalted or as preexistent; on p. 110 he seems to decide in favor of a primordial event. Bruce is better on this point (*Hebrews,* 94): "... 'this day' in our author's mind is the day of Christ's enthronement ... And, says our author, the same God who acclaimed Jesus as His Son also acclaimed Him as perpetual high priest"; see also his remarks on p. 13. Peterson (*Hebrews and Perfection,* 85) is also strong on enthronement. B. Westcott (*The Epistle to the Hebrews* [London 1889] 21) speaks in terms of resurrection and ascension; so too, P. Hughes, *Hebrews,* 54. Contrary to most, J. Moffatt (*The Epistle to the Hebrews* [New York 1924] 9-10) claims that no specific time or event is envisaged in the "today I have begotten you."

[7]So D. Peterson, *Hebrews and Perfection* (SNTSMS 47; Cambridge: Cambridge U., 1982), 118-119; *contra* Montefiore (*Hebrews,* 44), who applies the text to the eternal generation of the Son; so too, J. Bonsirven, *Saint Paul. Épître aux Hébreux* (Paris 1943) 190. It is interesting to see how Montefiore appeals to what must be the "logical" progression of thought: "he [the author] starts at the beginning". One sees the importance of grasping that the "logic" of our author can take the shape of a ring.

frame for Ps 2:7 in Heb 1:5, the same would hold true for the citation of 2 Sam 7:14 in the second half of the same verse. The second quotation simply repeats the content of the first in different phrases. Indeed, it is difficult to see what 2 Sam 7:14 really contributes to the argument except a deft inclusion (*huios . . . huion*); everything important has already been said by Ps 2:7.[8] One wonders whether this "back-up" citation is included merely to bring the number of quotations in the catena up to the desired seven.

(3) The third citation brings with it a number of problems involving both the introductory formula and the text itself. What seems clear from the start is that the OT text is a command from God that all the angels of God adore *him*, presumably the Son. But when is the command issued? The introductory formula is opaque: "But when again he brings the first-born into the [inhabited] world, he says (*hotan de palin eisagagē ton prōtotokon eis tēn oikoumenēn, legei*)". Commentators' suggestions with regard to the time of speaking and "bringing in" range from preexistence through Christ's nativity to his exaltation or parousia.[9] One fairly firm starting point comes from our author's use of *oikoumenē*. In Hebrews, *oikoumenē* does not mean this empirical, visible, inhabited world of ours, as general and NT Greek usage would lead us to expect. Rather, the "humane", "civilized" sense inherent in *oikoumenē* and its use in the LXX lead our middle-platonic author to apply it to the true world, where the holy assembly lives (12:22-24; cf. 13:14). This is the "upper", heavenly world, the *oikoumenē* which, from the perspective of those on this earth, is still to come (*tēn mellousan* of 2:5, where there is again a negation of the angels' supposed superior status: *ou gar aggelois*).[10] By contrast, when our author speaks of the

---

[8]It is interesting to observe how the commentaries generally spend a great amount of time reviewing the original meaning of the text and of various OT parallels. Having explained how Ps 2:7 functions in Hebrews 1, they find very little to say about the function of 2 Sam 7:14.

[9]For the various opinions, see Vanhoye, *Situation,* 152. What follows is indebted to his treatment on pp. 152-156.

[10]Commentators often quarrel over whether the theology of Hebrews is dominated by a gnosticizing *Weltanschauung* which thinks spatially of the world above and

preexistent Son coming into this empirical world of ours, he uses *kosmos* (10:5). Indeed, *kosmos* at times can take on the pejorative meaning of sinful humanity (11:7,38). Our author does not use *oikoumenē* in such a sense.

If *oikoumenē* in 1:6 does mean the heavenly world, what event could be described in terms of "when again he [God] brings the first-born [Christ] into the heavenly world"? It can hardly be the nativity of Christ on earth, given the meaning of *oikoumenē* in Hebrews. Besides, in Luke 2:13-14, the angels do not adore Christ but praise the Father—to say nothing of the dubious procedure of using the special infancy-narrative material of Luke to exegete Hebrews[11]! A reference to the parousia is also unlikely. The normal scenario for the parousia demands that Christ come from heaven back to earth, not that he be led into heaven. Moreover, the adoration of Christ by the angels is not a usual motif in descriptions of the parousia.[12] Could the reference be to an event in the Son's preexistent state, as in the *prōtotokos pasēs kitiseōs* in Col 1:15? Since the author has already spoken of the Son's mediation of creation and of his eternal existence with God, it is difficult to understand how or why God would "bring him into" the heavenly world, when the Son would have existed prior to the heavenly world and would have helped create it. By a process of elimination, then, the most likely reference is to the exaltation. This is not surprising, since the theme of Christ's *entrance* into the heavenly sanctuary and his enthronement there are at the

---

below or by a Jewish-apocalyptic mentality which thinks in terms of present versus future. The opposition is a false one. The author has synthesized gnosticizing and eschatological currents of thought. What is now present in the world above remains the future goal of believers still living in this world. It is a commonplace of Jewish apocalyptic that the goods of the end-time are already present and reserved for the faithful in heaven.

[11]This is precisely the mistake of A. Cernuda ("La introducción del Primogénito, según Hebr 1:6", *Est Bib* 39 [1981] 107-153), who goes so far as to see in 1:6a a veiled reference to the virginal conception! It might be observed, with regard to this question, that, for Hebrews, the time of Jesus' earthly life is the time when he is lower than the angels, not the time when he is adored by them (2:9).

[12]Cf. F. Schierse, *Verheissung und Heilsvollendung* (Munich 1955) 95. I would therefore disagree with Michel (*Brief*, 113), who seems to prefer a reference to the parousia, although he also mentions the birth of Christ. J. Héring (*L'épître aux Hébreux* [Neuchâtel 1954] 25) also opts for the parousia.

heart of the Epistle's theology.[13] *Prōtotokos* therefore has nothing to do with the usage in Luke 2:7 or Col 1:15.[14] Although this occurrence in Heb 1:6 is unique in the NT since *prōtotokos* is used here absolutely, a genuine parallel in thought can be found in Col 1:18, *prōtotokos ek tōn nekrōn*.[15] The one obstacle to this interpretation is the presence of *palin*, "again", in the introductory formula. What does it mean to say that God "again" brings the Son into the heavenly world? The phrase could refer to the *descensus-ascensus* schema: the preexistent Son left the heavenly world (*oikoumenē*) for awhile, entered this visible world (*kosmos*, 10:5), became for a short while lower than the angels (2:9), then through death and exaltation re-entered the heavenly world. More probable, in my opinion, is the position that *palin* properly goes with *de* and functions as a connective word linking together the various citations of the catena—as do *palin* in v. 5, *men...de* in vv. 7-8, *kai* in v. 10, and *de* in v. 13. Granted, the presence of *palin* in the *hotan* clause strikes one as unusual, if *palin* is meant to tie the whole clause—and the whole citation—to what precedes. But two considerations help explain the position of *palin*. (1) If *palin* is taken with *de*, then the whole connecting phrase is *de palin*. But *de*, being a postpositive, necessarily goes after the first word of the sentence, in this case *hotan*. *Palin* simply follows along after *de*, which must stand within the *hotan* clause. (2) The construction is not totally without parallel; a somewhat similar case occurs in Wis 14:1. The author of Wisdom has been discussing idolatry and the sense-

---

[13]In support of this it should be noted that almost all the occurrences of *eiserchomai* in the Epistle refer to entrance into the heavenly sanctuary or rest, or into their earthly types (earthly tent, promised land). The sole exception is 10:5, which refers to the incarnation. In favor of enthronement, but with a convoluted explanation of the thought, is P. Andriessen, "La teneur judéo-chrétienne de He I,6 et II, 14B-III, 2", *NT* 18 (1976) 293-313. Also in favor of enthronement are J. H. Davies, *A Letter to Hebrews* (Cambridge 1967) 22; F. F. Bruce, *The Epistle to the Hebrews* (Grand Rapids 1964) 17; Peterson, *Hebrews and Perfection*, 214 n. 19.

[14]*Contra* Montefiore, *Hebrews*, 46.

[15]See also *ho prōtotokos tōn nekrōn* in Rev 1:5; the *prōtotokon en pollois adelphois* of Rom 8:29 also occurs in a general context of resurrection and glorification. There is, of course, a slight difference in meaning in Hebrews, since Christ's exaltation rather than his resurrection is the main theological category.

lessness of making and worshiping an idol (13:10-19). As he begins a new example of idolatry, he says in 14:1, *ploun tis palin stellomenos.* The sense is not: "One preparing again to sail...," but rather "Again [to use another example], one preparing to sail..."[16]. Although *palin* occurs within the participial clause, it really functions "in front of" the clause, acting as a connective which enumerates. The same is true of the *palin* in Heb 1:6a.[17] The use of the aorist subjunctive with *hotan,* which often carries the sense of future action or habitual action, need not rule out a reference to the exaltation. The exaltation is a future event when viewed from the time of the original utterance of the prophecy; Scripture attests that God predicted this event.[18] All things considered, therefore, 1:6a is best taken as referring to the exaltation/enthronement of the Son, before whom the angels bow down in worship. The *prōtotokos* theme is apparently continuing the Davidic-enthronement motif of the first two citations. If so, the use of *prōtotokos* in 1:6a may allude to LXX Ps 88:28: "And I will make him the first-born (*prōtotokon*), the highest among the kings of the earth,"—perhaps picking up the allusion to Ps 2:8 standing behind *hon ethēken klēronomon pantōn* in 1:2b.[19]

The sense of 1:6 is thus fairly clear.[20] When God brings the

[16]So, with variations, RSV, NAB, NEB, and JB. Bruce, *Hebrews,* 15 n. 71, rightly rejects the objections of Westcott (*Hebrews,* 21-22), who takes *palin* closely with *eisagagē* and sees a reference to the parousia.

[17]While basically agreeing with this line of argument, Vanhoye (*Situation,* 154) prefers to see in *palin* in 1:6a an added sense of opposition ("on the other hand", "on the contrary"), while *palin* in v. 5 simply expressed coordination. Spicq (*L'épître,* 2, 17) also considers this possibility. Bruce (*Hebrews,* 15 n. 72) rejects a "strongly adversative" sense in 1:6a; see also Thompson, "Structure", 132 n. 18. Strangely, Moffatt (*Hebrews,* 10) takes *palin* as a connective but then applies the citation to the incarnation or the parousia; similarly, E. Grässer, "Hebräer 1:1-4. Ein exegetischer Versuch", *Text und Situation* (Gütersloh 1973) 216, who opts for the parousia, following Käsemann, *Gottesvolk,* 59-60, 68.

[18]So Vanhoye, *Situation,* 152-153; P. Hughes, *Hebrews,* 58.

[19]So Vanhoye, *Situation,* 158. See also Bruce *Hebrews,* 15), who unnecessarily brings preexistence into consideration here. I would not agree with Käsemann and Grässer, who see in *prōtotokos* a reference to the Gnostic Anthropos-myth; see, e.g., Grässer, *Der Glaube im Hebräerbrief* (Marburg 1965) 209; also G. Theissen, *Untersuchungen zum Hebräerbrief* (Gütersloh 1969) 62, 122.

[20]The question of the exact source of the conflated quotation (LXX Deut 32:43 and LXX Ps 96:7) in Heb 1:6b does not touch upon our problematic. For the light that the

crucified and exalted Son into the heavenly throneroom and seats him at his right hand, he bids all his angels adore him.[21] The "all" (*pantes*) is no doubt important to our author; the Son is *kreittōn aggelōn*, without exception. Their *proskynēsis* ritually confirms that fact.

(4) The introduction to the fourth citation (LXX Ps 103:4) offers only one problem. The preposition *pros* is used here with a verb of saying to mean, not "to", but rather "with regard to", "concerning". Not only is this usage philologically possible; it also seems demanded by the citation, which speaks of the angels in the third person. The usage is startling only for those who take the *pros* in v. 8a to mean "to", as it surely does mean in v. 13.[22] In the citation itself, our author construes the meaning of the text differently from the most probable sense of the MT.[23] The MT conveys the idea that God makes the winds his messengers and flaming fire his servants. The verse is part of a nature-hymn praising God the Creator in lyric terms: the natural elements obey God's commands. The LXX opens up the possibility of a different interpretation by placing definite articles before *aggelous* and *leitourgous*, which can now be read as the direct objects instead of the predicate accusatives[24]. The author of Hebrews adopts such a reading: "He who makes his angels winds [or possibly, spirits] and his

Deuteronomy fragment from Cave 4 at Qumran throws on the problem, see P. Skehan, "A Fragment of the 'Song of Moses' (Deut 32) from Qumran", *BASOR* 136 (1954) 12-15; Idem, *Studies in Israelite Poetry and Wisdom* (Washington 1971) 67-77, especially 77; P. Katz, "The Quotations from Deuteronomy in Hebrews", *ZNW* 49 (1958) 213-223; P. Hughes, *Hebrews*, 59; Vanhoye, *Situation*, 161-163; Reid, *The Use*, 57-58.

[21]Needless to say, this key Christological point is what forces the author to write the OT citation with *aggeloi theou* as the subject, while the LXX of Deut 32:43 reads *huioi theou*. Since the whole point of the catena is the superiority of the one Son to all the angels, it simply will not do to cite a text in which the angels are called "all the sons of God". Kistemaker (*Psalm Citations*, 74) allows for the possibility that our author knew a variant reading of the Greek OT.

[22]See Michel, *Brief*, 117. Some connect this dispute with the debate over the meaning of *ho theos* in v. 8b; see below.

[23]This is disputed by Westcott, (*Hebrews*, 24), who hold that the LXX correctly interprets the MT; so also *Str-B* 3.678-679, who point out that certain rabbinic passages reflect the interpretation of the LXX and Hebrews.

[24]Cf. Kistemaker, *Psalm Citations*, 77; Vanhoye, *Situation*, 170; Bruce, *Hebrews*, 17.

servants [i.e., the angels] a flame of fire". The imagery of the verse could refer to the rarefied "stuff" of which angels were thought to be composed, or to the rapidity of the angels' flight as they carry out commissions, or to the ancient idea that angels presided over or even were embodied in natural phenomena such as wind and fire. In the context of such speculation, Jewish thought sometimes stressed the ongoing nature of God's creative activity upon the angels. That there was speculation about the creation and composition of the angels before, during, and after the time of our author is clear from Jewish sources. In the Thanksgiving Psalms of Qumran, in the slightly mutilated text of 1QH 1:9-11, God the Creator is said to create every spirit (or wind, *rwḥ*), as well as the heavens and the hosts, and the spirits (*rwḥwt*) of might, "before they become angels [of holiness] and spirits [*rwḥwt*] of eternity". In 4 Ezra, in the context of a prayer to God the Creator, it is said in the Syriac version that at God's command the angels "are changed to wind and fire" (RSV, 2 Esdras 8:22). Later rabbinic material includes *b. Ḥag.* 14a ("Every day ministering angels are created from the fiery stream [of God's throne] and utter song and cease to be") and *Yal. Šimʻoni* 2.11.3 ("God changes us [the angels] hour by hour...sometimes he makes us fire, and sometimes wind").[25]

Similarly, in Heb 1:7 the subordination of the angels is reaffirmed and specified: the Creator can cause his angels to change, and indeed change often. The angels are creatures, subject to fluctuation, while the Creator (by implication) is above such a change. The theme of the sixth citation is already being subtly introduced. There is, of course, another alternation in the meaning of the Psalm verse. The OT text, in its original sense, obviously referred to Yahweh. But in the catena of Heb 1:5-14, it is the Son who is mentioned in every OT text, either in second or in the third person. Indeed, in the sixth quotation (1:10-12), while God (the Father) is the speaker, he is never referred to in the text; only the Son is mentioned. Unless we are to think that the fourth citation forms a strange

---

[25]For these texts, see Bruce, *Hebrews,* 18 n. 81; Westcott, *Hebrews,* 25; Moffatt, *Hebrews,* 12.

exception, *ho poiōn* has to be taken as referring to the Son, not God (the Father). Thus, as in the third quotation, our author boldly and without further ado or justification applies an OT text which speaks of Yahweh to the Son. Like God (the Father), the Son is superior to the angels, who are subject to change; that much is clear. But the vocabulary of the citation may suggest a further point as well. Granted what the author has already said in chap. 1, *ho poiōn*, as applied to the Son, may carry the weighty meaning of "create": "he who creates his angels as winds, and his servants as a flame of fire". This is not impossible, since the Son's mediation of creation in v. 2c was proclaimed with the help of the verb *poieō*; the *aiōnas* which he helped create would certainly include the angels. Taken in this full sense the fourth quotation moves beyond the first three not only by affirming the superiority of the enthroned Son over the worshiping angels, but also by grounding this superiority in the unchanging Son's act of creating changeable angels.[26] Indeed, the present participle *poiōn* could be understood to refer to a continuing act of creation, something Jewish speculation would support. Thus, the thought of the catena shifts subtly from exaltation to creation.

(5) The *pros* in the introduction to the fifth quotation can be taken in the sense of "of," "concerning" (so NAB, NEB, RSV, TEV, Goodspeed, and Phillips) or "to" (so KJV and JB). Actually, this choice does not necessarily determine the sense of the quotation.[27] Most of the English versions which translate *pros* as "of" or "concerning" proceed to take the quotation as direct address, with the first *ho theos* understood as a substitute for the vocative. The choice of "of" or "concerning" seems dictated rather by a desire to keep the same meaning for *pros* in v. 7 and v. 8.

Both the MT and the LXX forms of Ps. 45:6-7 (vv. 7-8 in the

---

[26]Cf. Kistemaker, *Psalm Citations,* 79: "[Heb 1:7] indicates first, that the Son was present and active at the time of creation. Thus, while the Son is designated as Lord of creation, it follows that the angels are but mere creatures. Second, it stresses the unchangeableness of the Lord". According to Westcott, the Greek Fathers laid great stress on *poiōn* as distinguishing the created angels from the uncreated Son *(Hebrews,* 25). For a somewhat different interpretation, see P. Hughes, *Hebrews,* 62.

[27]A point missed by G. Buchanan, *To the Hebrews* (Garden City, NY 1972) 20.

MT; LXX Ps 44:7-8) bristle with problems of text and interpretation. Fortunately, many of the problems do not concern
our line of investigation. The most important question for us
is how one should read the first line of the citation in Heb 1:8.
If we accept the text of *UBSGNT*, the best translation is: "Your
throne, O God, [is/ stands] forever and ever".[28] The Son is thus
addressed directly as God, the nominative with article sub-
stituting for the vocative.[29] Such a use of *theos* for the Son is
not very startling after the statements about creation, eternal
preexistence, and conservation of creation in 1:2b-3b. The
usage is not far removed from John 1:1,18; 20:28—though
John is not citing an OT text. Some commentators, however,
would prefer to avoid this attribution of *theos* to the Son by
translating: "Your throne is God forever and ever", or "God is
your throne forever and ever". Whatever be the meaning of
the MT and the LXX, such a translation does not make terribly
good sense in the context of the theology of Hebrews. The
Son is always portrayed by our author as sitting at the right
hand of God (e.g., 1:3d). Indeed, in 8:1 our author expands on
the image by specifying that the Son "sat at the right hand *of*

---

[28]The text of Heb 1:8 in the third edition of *UBSGNT* is the same as that of the first
edition. The one variant noted is at the end of v. 8: *autou* (papyrus 46, Sinaiticus,
Vaticanus) for *sou* (Vast majority of witnesses); *sou* in preferred but is given only a C
rating (considerable degree of doubt). Indeed, the 20th edition of Nestle-Aland,
Novum Testamentum Graece et Latine (Stuttgart 1961) preferred *autou*. The wording
of the 26th edition of Nestle-Aland, *Greek-English New Testament* (Stuttgart 1981) is
identical to the third edition of the *UBSGNT*, as is also the wording of the ninth
edition of A. Merk, *Novum Testamentum Graece et Latine* (Rome 1964). For the
debate on *sou* versus *autou* and resulting translations, see B. Metzger, *A Textual
Commentary on the Greek New Testament* (New York 1971) 662-663. In favor of
reading *autou* and taking *ho theos* as the subject of the sentence is Kistemaker, *Psalm
Citations*, 25, including n. 1; see also Westcott, *Hebrews*, 25-26. In favor of taking *ho
theos* as vocative are F. Büchsel, *Die Christologie des Hebräerbriefs* (Gütersloh 1922)
22; Michel, *Brief*, 118; Montefiore, *Hebrews*, 47; P. Teodorico, *L'epistola agli Ebrei*
(Turin 1952) 51; Bruce, *Hebrews*, 19; P. Hughes, *Hebrews*, 64; and possibly Moffatt,
Hebrews, 13 n. 1, who points out this creates a perfect parallel with *kyrie* at the
beginning of the sixth citation in 1:10. Vanhoye *(Situation*, 176-177) gives a detailed
vindication of the vocative understanding and answers Westcott's objections. He
points out the vocative sense of *ho theos* in the citation of LXX Ps 39:9, in Heb 10:7.

[29]The vocative *thee* occurs only in Mt 27:46 in the NT and is rare in the LXX.
Contrast Mark's *ho theos mou ho theos mou* in 15:34, with Matthew's *thee mou thee
mou* in 27:46. Elsewhere in the NT *ho theos* is used for the vocative; cf. BDF #147, (3);
and Vanhoye, *Situation*, 176.

the throne of the majesty in the heavens [*ekathisen en dexią tou thronou tēs megalōsynēs en tois ouranois*], an obvious expansion on the phrase in 1:3. God (the Father) has a throne in heaven, *at the right of which* the Son sits. Granted this key image, it is difficult to understand what it would mean to our author to say that God (the Father) *is* the eternal throne *on which* the Son sits. Taking *ho theos* as equivalent to the vocative is by far the simplest interpretation. Once we understand *ho theos* as an address to the Son, the reference to the eternal throne must be taken in its widest sense: it symbolizes not just the exaltation after Christ's death, but rather the eternal rule which the preexistent divine Son has exercised from all eternity. The citation then goes on to praise the Son's eternal rule (*basileia*) as one guided by uprightness (v. 8c). This upright rule is the result of the divine king's love of justice and hatred of evil. Vanhoye wishes to see in the aorists *ēgapēsas* and *emisēsas* (v. 9a) a reference to Christ's life and struggle on earth.[30] This is possible, but the aorists could be taken simply as literal translations of the Hebrew stative perfect followed by the *wayyiqtōl* form, both with a present meaning.[31] Here we run up against the problem of how far we can press the wording of these OT citations for precise Christological references.[32] Are we to see a specific reference to the anointing of *Christ* (hence *echrisen*) as king and priest at his exaltation? Or is the reference general: the anointing belongs in timeless eternity, as does the throne and the kingdom? In this case, it is simply a symbol of supreme happiness. One reason it is difficult to evaluate the precise sense of *echrisen* is that the author of Hebrews never uses the word again. He does not speak of the exaltation/enthronement in terms of anointing; it is one element in the allegory of becoming a priest that he omits.

[30]Vanhoye *Situation,* 186-188; similarly, Michel, *Brief,* 119.

[31]P. Joüon (*Grammaire de l'hébreu biblique* [Rome 1923; reprinted 1965] #118p, p.325) uses this verse to exemplify a stative *qatal* with a present sense followed by a *wayyiqtōl* with a present sense. So the RSV's translation of Ps 45:7: "You love righteousness and hate wickedness"; similarly, with variations in the wording, Goodspeed, JB, and NAB.

[32]P. Hughes wisely remarks: "There is no necessity to seek particular significance in every part of a somewhat extended quotation for our immediate context" *(Hebrews,* 66).

Perhaps the absence of any *chriō*-terminology in the author's own statements indicates that the *echrisen* in this citation holds no precise reference for him.[33]

On the other hand, a precise reference may be found in the *metochous* of v. 9c. Granted the context, which emphasizes the superiority of the Son over the angels, the *metochous* is best taken as the angels. True, all the other uses of *metochos* in Hebrews refer to Christians (3:1,14; 6:4; 12:8); but this is a perfect example of immediate context determining sense. In chap. 1, the main point is the relation of the Son to the angels, not to Christians.[34] What is affirmed throughout is the Son's absolute superiority over the angels. Hence, *metochous*, if it has any precise meaning, refers to the angels gathered around their king, and *para* probably carries an exclusive rather than a truly comparative sense: the Son is anointed, the angels are not.[35] In sum, while the author may or may not see some references to Christ's earthly life and exaltation in the fifth

---

[33]In favor of taking the anointing to refer to the ascension or exaltation is Spicq (*L'épître*, 2.19); Westcott, *Hebrews*, 27; P. Hughes, *Hebrews*, 65. Vanhoye *(Situation*, 192) relates the anointing to the theme of the perfection of Christ. But where is that connection made by our author? The tendency of Vanhoye to press every word of the OT citation for precise Christian meaning can be seen in his suggestion—made, however, with much hesitation—that the rod or scepter in Heb 1:8 refers to the cross (pp. 194-195). Bonsirven *(Épître*, 196) prefers to see the anointing as an expression of the eternal divine generation.—As for the *ho theos ho theos sou* of Heb 1:9, the sense could be either "God, your God has anointed you" (subject and noun in apposition) or "Your God has anointed you, O God" (subject of sentence and vocative; so Vanhoye, *Situation*, 189). Though the latter may sound strange, a similar dialectical use of *theos* in one sentence for both Father and Son is found in John 1:1 and probably (following *UBSGNT*) in John 1:18. The problem of the exact meaning of 1:9b is not as important for the general thesis of this article as is the meaning of *ho theos* in v. 8. For a defense of taking *ho theos* as vocative in both v. 8 and v. 9, see Bruce, *Hebrews*, 18-20

[34]So, correctly, Moffatt, *Hebrews*, 14. Some commentators claim the reference here is only to Christians; so, e.g., Bonsirven, *Épître*, 197; Bruce, *Hebrews*, 21. Michel (*Brief*, 119) says the reference is first of all to human beings, but also allows a possible reference to angels. In favor of angels alone is Héring *(L'épître*, 26); Moffatt, *(Hebrews*, 14, if our author has anything particular in mind); and Theissen *(Untersuchungen*, 101 n. 27). P. Hughes *(Hebrews*, 66) is doubtful about imposing too precise a value on *metochous*. Vanhoye *(Situation*, 193-194) prefers an inclusive sense: all those associated with Christ in heaven, excluding neither angels nor Christians. But does that fit the problematic of Heb 1:5-14?

[35]So, citing this text, *BAG*, 616; likewise, M. Zerwick-M. Grosvenor, *A Grammatical Analysis of the Greek New Testament* (Rome 1981) 655.

citation, the most astounding and salient aspect of his use of this psalm is the application of the name *theos* to the Son. The Son is God, and therefore his throne stands forever and ever and his rule is necessarily righteous. The emphasis seems to be on the Son's divinity and preexistence, as expressed in our author's mind in v. 8b; this provides the supreme argument for the superiority of the Son over the angels. What was implicit in the *proskynēsatōsan* of v. 6 becomes explicit in the *ho theos* of v. 8: the angels must adore the Son their Creator, because he is the eternal God.[36]

(6) The sixth citation expands upon the divine status of the Son. One necessary corollary of being God is being the immutable Creator, as opposed to mutable and perishable creatures. This theme was already implied in 1:7; now it is clearly proclaimed. The constraints of a set OT text prevent any explicit reference to the angels in vv. 10-12, but they are obviously included in the *pantes* of v. 11.

We have already been told that the Son made the angels (*ho poiōn,* v. 7), and their mutability has been hinted at.[37] The author now applies the words of LXX Ps 101:26-28 to the Son, who is accordingly addressed as *kyrie,* Lord.[38] He was active in the beginning (*kat'archas,* reminiscent of John 1:1 *en archē*[39]

---

[36]Cf. the pointed summation of Montefiore *(Hebrews,* 47): ". . . here [in Heb 1, 8] the verse [of the psalm] is used to show the Son's superiority to the angels is based on his divine nature". One weakness of Thompson's exclusive emphasis on exaltation in the catena ("Structure", 133-138) is that he does not give much theological weight to the statements about the Son's eternal, divine preexistence. At times it sounds as though Thompson is saying that the Son becomes eternal and immutable only at the exaltation. That does not do full justice to the complex thought of our author in Hebrews 1. Contrast H. MacNeill *(The Christology of the Epistle to the Hebrews* [Chicago 1914] 32-35, 49-51), who remarks that we would naturally want the author of Hebrews to be clearer "on what may be called the past eternity of Christ" (p. 51).

[37]The simple *kai* at the beginning of v. 10 also indicates that we simply have here a continuation of the contrast explicitated by the introductory rubrics in v. 7a and v. 8a; cf. Moffatt, *Hebrews,* 15.

[38]There is no equivalent to the LXX's *sy kyrie* in the MT Ps 102:26. B. W. Bacon ("Heb 1:10-12 and the Septuagint rendering of Ps 102, 23", *ZNW* 3 [1902] 280-285) tries to explain our author's application of LXX Ps 101 to Christ by the changes the LXX translator made on the Hebrew text. Bruce *(Hebrews,* 22) accepts Bacon's explanation, but Vanhoye's remarks *(Situation,* 199-203) are simpler and more satisfying.

[39]Michel *(Brief,* 121) suggests an echo of Gen 1:1. However, it should be stressed that neither here nor elsewhere in the Epistle is the Son ever explicitly called *ho logos.*

when he laid the foundations of the earth; the heavens, too, are the works of his hands. All creation therefore, proceeds from and depends on the preexistent Son. Since our author is here working under the constraints of the wording of the psalm, there is no reference to God the Father's act of creation *through* the Son, as in 1:2c.[40] The Son is here the chief agent of creation, and in this the idea is somewhat closer to the Son's conservation of creation in 1:3b. The "qualitatively infinite" distance between Creator and creature is expressed by the stark, terse juxtaposition of v. 11a: "They shall perish, but you remain [or, shall remain]".[41] Creation is subject to change and dissolution like a garment;[42] "but you are the same" (*ho autos;* cf. 13, 8, "Jesus Christ, the same [*ho autos*] yesterday and today and forever"). The final line in 1:12d, "and your years shall not fail [or, end]", is a fitting inclusion with 1:10a: "You, O Lord, in the beginning". Be it the beginning or the end of the visible creation, from protology to eschatology, the Son who is creator is present, active and unchanging. The sweep of the whole of creation's history, over which the Son presides in a timeless present (*ho autos ei*), is intimated by the movement through aorist (*ethemeliōsas*), present (*eisin*), and future (e.g., *apolountai, allagēsontai*). This, rather than a detailed concern with the apocalyptic events of the end-time, seems to be the main point of vv. 10-12.[43]

---

[40]Buchanan (*Hebrews,* 22) misses this point. He claims that, if the *kyrie* does refer to Jesus, Jesus is being thought of "as a sort of demiurge through whom God created the heaven and earth as well as the ages (1:2.10)". This is correct for v. 2, but not for vv. 10-12. Vanhoye (*Situation,* 207) sees this well.

[41]Since the original text carried no accent marks, one cannot be sure whether our author took *diameneis* as present or future; Kistemaker (*Psalm Citations,* 26) prefers the present. If we read the present, we have an interesting movement of ideas from preexistence and creation *(kat' archas ... ethemeliōsas),* through timeless present *(diameneis ... ho autos ei)* to endless future *(ta etē sou ouk ekleipsousin).* For the alternation of verbs and a possible concentric pattern, see Vanhoye, *Situation,* 198-199.

[42]For the insertion of *hōs himation* in Heb 1:12b, see Metzger, *Textual Commentary,* 663. The problem does not concern our investigation.

[43]Thompson ("Structure", 137) opposes Michel (*Brief,* 121), who sees in v. 11 a reference to apocalyptic catastrophes. It should be noted, though, that Michel says that the eschatological drama is only hinted at in Heb 1:10-12, while it is described at greater length in 12:26-29. Once again, Thompson sees 1:10-12 only as an "exaltation

(7) The seventh and final citation brings us full circle. Having started with the naming of Christ as Son at his enthronement, as described in Ps 2:7 (Heb 1:5bc), we conclude with the Son's enthronement/exaltation as described in Ps 109:1.[44] The two royal Davidic psalms of enthronement frame the whole catena. This inclusion is underlined by the fact that the seventh citation, like the first, begins with the rhetorical question: "For to which of the angels did he [God the Father] ever say...?"[45] As we have seen, Ps 109:1 supplies the starting point of our author's theological reflection. By connecting Ps 109:1 with Ps 109:4 and by drawing out the implications, he grounds his basic thesis: the exalted Son (Ps 109:1) is the eternal priest like Melchizedek (Ps 109:4). Heb 1:14 then supplies a conclusion to the catena and a transition to the first parenetic section (2:1-4).[46] The verse emphasizes for the last time that the Son, who is the heavenly enthroned king, is obviously superior to the angels. Far from being seated in power, like the Son, *all* the angels,[47] as ministers (*leitourgika,* reminiscent of *leitourgous* in

text" and plays down the references to a divine, immutable existence which precedes creation and therefore any act of exaltation. By contrast, Vanhoye (*Situation,* 194-207) emphasizes in vv. 10-12 the theme of the role of the exalted Christ at the end of the world. Indeed, on p. 226 he stresses that the whole of chap. 1 is drawn up from an eschatological perspective; again, the preexistence-motif is played down. I think instead that the major point of vv. 10-12 is the a-temporal, immutable existence of the Son, as seen in his creation of all things and his continued control over them as they change and disappear. In all this, there may be an echo of *pherōn te ta panta* (1:2), especially if *pherōn* does include the idea of governing all things and guiding them to their appointed goal.

[44] Actually, the seventh citation is unique in not having a Christological title mentioned either in the introductory formula or in the OT text. By this time, it is not necessary. Both the inclusion with 1:5 (pointing to the title Son) and the well-known initial words of LXX Ps 109:1 ("the Lord said to my Lord") make it clear that the addressee is the Son and Lord addressed in the previous citations.

[45] Cf. Kistemaker, *Psalm Citations,* 80. On p. 99 Kistemaker draws attention to the parallel between 1:13 and 1:3d; so too, Bruce, *Hebrews,* 23.

[46] Vanhoye (*Situation,* 220) observes that the author does not use another citation to enunciate the position of angels in v. 14. Instead, for the first time since the beginning of the paragraph (at 1:5), he himself composes a whole sentence. One wonders whether the author refrains from citing another OT text about the angels (of which there were many still available) precisely to keep the number of quotations at seven, thus matching the seven designations in 1:2-4.

[47] Notice the *pantes* in v. 14, which recalls the *pantes aggeloi* of v. 6 and perhaps the *pantes* (which certainly has a wider reference than the angels but no doubt includes them) in v. 11; cf. P. Hughes, *Hebrews,* 71.

v. 7c), are sent to serve Christian believers, who are destined to inherit salvation (*klēronomein,* recalling *klēronomon* in v. 2b and *keklēronomēken* in v. 4). The *tous mellontas klēronomein* captures perfectly the Epistle's interplay of Christological-realized eschatology (especially in doctrinal sections) and ecclesiological-future eschatology (especially in parenetic sections). What the Son-become-man already is on the basis of the past act of exaltation (*hon ethēken klēronomon, keklēronomēken*), the believing community is called to be at the end of its pilgrimage towards the heavenly city (*tous mellontas klēronomein*).[48]

Before we proceed to a correlation of exordium and catena, we should pause to ask one question: Why is the whole catena—and in a sense, the whole of chap. 1—dedicated to showing that the Son is superior to the angels? Various suggestions have been made: the author is fighting a type of angel-worship seen also in Colossians,[49] or he is countering a veneration of angelic priests or intercessors, reflected in some of the Dead Sea documents[50] and in other intertestamental literature (e.g., *T. Levi* 3:5; *T. Dan* 6:2; *1 Enoch* 9:3; 15:2; 39:5; 40:6; 47:2; 89:76),[51] or he is polemicizing against the idea of

[48]Some commentators speculate on who the enemies mentioned in the citation of v. 13 are. Given the author's treatment of angels here and elsewhere (e.g., 12:22), they are certainly not the angels. More likely candidates are the devil and his power over men through fear of death (2:14-15), Christian apostates (10:26-31), and persecutors (10:32-39; 11:35-38; 12:1-12); see Hofius, *Christushymnus,* 99-100, as well as the earliest patristic interpretation, found in *1 Clem.* 36:6.

[49]So Bornkamm, "Bekenntnis", 198 n. 22, against Käsemann; the idea is considered simply as a possibility by Moffatt, *Hebrews,* 9.

[50]H.-M. Schenke ("Erwägungen zum Rätsel des Hebräerbriefes", *Neues Testament und Christliche Existenz* [Tübingen 1973] 421-437) suggests a link with a type of merkabah mysticism reflected in 11Q Melch. For a full treatment of this document in reference to the NT in general and Hebrews in particular, see P. Kobelski, *Melchizedek and Melchireša'* (Washington, D. C. 1981). P. Hughes (*Hebrews,* 52-53) suggests that the Hebrew Christians to whom the author is writing have been influenced by teachings similar to those held by the "Dead Sea Sect". According to these teachings, both of the Messiahs would be subordinate to the Archangel Michael; hence the necessity to "demonstrate the supremacy of Christ over all angelic beings".

[51]All these texts may be conveniently found in R. Charles, *The Apocrypha and Pseudepigrapha of the Old Testament in English. Volume 2: Pseudepigrapha* (Oxford 1913). For a more recent edition of Enoch, see M. Knibb, *The Ethiopic Book of Enoch. 2. Introduction, Translation, and Commentary* (Oxford 1978). For a more

multiple intermediaries with interchangeable functions, an idea which was widespread in middle platonism and is seen in Philo.[52] Others would rather explain the concern in terms of a scene of royal enthronement, with the angels as the court audience.[53] In connection with this, some would even see the three steps of an Egyptian enthronement ritual in the catena of 1:5-14.[54] Some of these suggestions, such as the Egyptian enthronement ceremony, seem farfetched.[55] While other suggestions cannot be categorically denied (e.g., a polemic against syncretistic or gnosticizing ideas about angels and their priestly

recent edition of the Testaments, see *Testamenta XII Patriarcharum* (ed. M. De Jonge; Leiden 1964). In this "editio minima" of de Jonge, the key texts read as follows. *T. Levi* 3,5; *en tǭ met' auton hoi aggeloi eisi tou prosōpou kyriou, hoi leitourgountes kai exilaskomenoi pros kyrion epi pasais tais agnoiais tōn dikaiōn. Prospherousi de kyriǭ osmēn euōdias logikēn kai anaimakton prosphoran. T. Dan.* 6,2: *eggizete de tǭ theǭ kai tǭ aggelǭ tǭ paraitoumenǭ hymas hoti houtos esti mesitēs theou kai anthrōpōn epi tēs eirēnēs Israēl.* In individual cases, notably in the *T. Levi,* there are disputes over possible Christian interpolations or even Christian authorship; see, e.g., M. De Jonge, "Notes on Testament of Levi II-VII", *Studies on the Testaments of the Twelve Patriarchs* (ed. M. De Jonge) (Leiden 1975) 247-260. But the similar ideas from Qumran and from Tobit (12:11-15) prove that such motifs were known in Judaism in the first centuries B.C. and A.D.

[52]Cf. Dey, *Intermediary World,* 127, 146-147.

[53]So Käsemann, *Gottesvolk,* 60; Grässer, "Hebräer 1,1-4", 226.

[54]The pattern is explained by E. Norden, *Die Geburt des Kindes* (Leipzig 1924) 116-128. The three acts comprise the elevation of the king to divine life, the presentation of the new god to the circle of the heavenly beings, and the enthronement. Relying on Norden, Schierse (*Verheissung,* 96 n. 100) claims that the ritual pattern is found in Heb 1:5-14. One of the great popularizers of this three-step pattern is J. Jeremias; see his *Jesus' Promise to the Nations* (London 1958) 38; and *Die Briefe an Timotheus und Titus* (Göttingen ⁹1968) 23-25. The idea has been accepted, at times with variations, by Spicq (*L'épître,* 2,23), Michel (*Brief,* 109 n. 1, 116-117), and R. Martin (*Carmen Christi* [Cambridge 1967] 243-244).

[55]See, e.g., the criticism by Hofius, *Christushymnus,* 30, 89 n. 60. Whether we can reconstruct all the steps of an Egyptian enthronement ritual which supposedly remained basically the same throughout the centuries, to what degree this ritual influenced the enthronement ritual of Israelite kings, whether indeed we can reconstruct the exact steps of the Israelite ritual, and finally whether this ritual pattern would have been known to a first-century Christian author are all questions that are rarely asked. See the sober remarks by O. Keel, *The Symbolism of the Biblical World* (NY 1978) 256. I think that seeing three distinct steps of an enthronement ritual in Heb 1:5-14 takes more than a little imagination. If the seven texts were re-ordered in various combinations, I do not doubt that some would see the same three steps of exaltation, presentation, and enthronement. The fact that the seventh citation in 1:13 simply returns to the theme of enthronement of the Son struck in 1:3 makes a pattern of three progressive steps most unlikely.

functions),[56] the major reason for the stress on the superiority of the Son to the angels is best seen in the internal logic of the Epistle's argument. The son's superiority grounds the first exhortation, in 2:1-4. In an *a fortiori* (or *qal waḥomer*) argument, our author reasons that, if the Mosaic revelation, mediated through angels, had such fearful sanctions, how much more fearful is the punishment that awaits those who neglect the definitive revelation and salvation offered in the Son. The Son's superiority to the angels is simply the first in a series of *a fortiori* arguments. Moses, Joshua (by implication), and the Jewish high priests all suffer the same fate. Indeed, if we grasp that the whole purpose of chap. 1 is to ground the claim that the Son is the supreme revealer-and-revelation, even the quasi-metaphysical designation in 1:3a takes on a salvation-historical function. He who is eternally the effulgence of God's glory and the image of his substance is alone the adequate revealer and content of revelation.[57]

Having investigated the meaning of each of the seven citations, we are now in a position to say something about the movement of thought in the catena as a whole. As I pointed out earlier in this essay, the blocks of quotations, drawn from fixed texts, can hardly enunciate the neat, precise, terse schema of the author's own composition in 1:2b-4. Yet a certain general pattern does emerge. The author's Christological thought does begin with and emphasize exaltation (1:5-6, the first three citations). With the fourth citation (v. 7), one hears the first

[56]One objection against the presence in chap. 1 of a polemic concerning angels performing liturgical functions is the author's willingness to use *leitourgous* (v. 7) and *leitourgika* (v. 14) of the angels in the very chapter in which he is arguing for the Son's superiority to them. Granted, these Greek words are by no means limited to a "liturgical" or cultic meaning, and our author does not intend such a sense in chap. 1. But these words are open to a cultic meaning, as our author knows full well (cf. 8:2,6; 9:21; 10:11). If his precise purpose in chap. 1 had been to attack the idea that the angels fulfilled liturgical functions, I think he would have avoided terminology that could have played directly into the hands of his supposed opponents.

[57]In favor of understanding the argument over angels as an argument over the superior revelation given through the Son are MacNeill, *Christology,* 36-37; O. Kuss, *Der Brief an die Hebräer* (Regensburg 1953) 22-23; G. Hughes, *Hebrews and Hermeneutics,* 7-8; and Thompson, "Structure", 139. As M. D'Angelo observes (*Moses in the Letter to the Hebrews* [Missoula 1979] 260), such a revelation-Christology brings us very close to the position of the fourth gospel, especially John 1:18.

hint of the idea that the Son is superior to the angels because he creates them—if *ho poiōn* may be taken in that weighty theological sense, a sense *epoiēsen* certainly has in v. 2c. In v. 8b the fifth citation begins with and emphasizes the divinity of the Son (*ho theos*) and the eternity of his rule. The subsequent lines in v. 9 may refer to Christ's earthly life and exaltation, but such a reference is not certain. The sixth citation begins in v. 10 by emphasizing the creative activity of the Son in the beginning (*kat' archas...ethemeliōsas*), a creative activity which continues into the present (*erga tōn cheirōn sou eisin hoi ouranoi,* v. 10b), an activity which will continue as the Son guides the old creation to its appointed goal of dissolution (vv. 11-12), while the Creator himself knows no change or diminution (*diameneis, ho autos ei, ouk ekleipsousin*). Finally, the seventh citation brings us back to the theme of enthronement (v. 13), illumined by a concluding comment of our author, who contrasts the Son's royal status with the inferior position of the angels as servants (v. 14).

I would therefore maintain that, while the correspondence is not one-for-one, there is a general symmetry between the movement of thought in the seven Christological designations in Heb 1:2b-4 and the movement of thought in the seven OT citations in 1:5-14. In each case, the train of thought begins with Christ's exaltation (1:2b; 1:5-6), moves back to creation (1:2c; 1:7), moves "farther back" to preexistence, divinity, and eternal rule (1:3a; 1:8bc), moves forward again to creation as well as governance and guidance of creation (1:3b; 1:10-12), moves all the way up to exaltation again (1:3d; 1:13), and draws a final conclusion comparing Christ's exalted status to the angels' inferior role (1:4; 1:14). The ring closes where it opened. Needless to say, the symmetry is not perfect in every detail. The reference to the Son's "purifying from sin" (1:3c) finds no correlative in the seven citations[58], perhaps because the OT quotations are focused solely on the Son's status vis-à-vis the angels, while purification from sin concerns human beings. But, seen as a whole, the two "cycles of seven" do seem

---

[58] Heb 1:9a might be a candidate, but as we have seen the reference is too vague and the value of the tenses too problematic. The same is true of 9bc.

to correspond in the general movement of their Christological thought. The whole of chap. 1 is thus a monument to our author's ability to weld together OT citations and NT kerygma, literary structure and Christological thought.

II. A Traditional Hymn in 1:1-4?

There is, I think, a significant corollary to the symmetry we have investigated. The corollary concerns the traditional hymn which many exegetes find somewhere within Heb 1:1-4. So widespread is this opinion today that G. Hughes can speak of a "wide consensus that material from older and different sources has been incorporated [into 1:2-4]"[59]. Besides Hughes, this opinion is favored, with varying degrees of certitude and nuance, by E. Norden[60], G. Bornkamm[61], E. Grässer[62], O. Hofius[63], U. Luck[64], R. Martin[65], K. Wengst[66], R. Deichgräber[67], J. T. Sanders[68], and J. Thompson[69]. Most speak in general terms of traditional material or a set hymn, while Bornkamm also terms the tradition a confessional formula (*Bekenntnis*)[70]. Most of these writers admit, however, that it is difficult to delimit the hymnic tradition precisely. For instance

---

[59]G. Hughes, *Hebrews and Hermeneutics*, 6.

[60]E. Norden, *Agnostos Theos* (Stuttgart 1913; reprint 1956) 380-387, especially 386.

[61]Bornkamm, "Bekenntnis", 197-199.

[62]Grässer, "Hebräer 1:1-4", 190-198, 225.

[63]Hofius, *Christushymnus*, 80-87.

[64]U. Luck, "Himmlisches und irdisches Geschehen im Hebräerbrief", *NT* 6 (1963) 200.

[65]Martin, *Carmen Christi*, 19, 305 n. 8; Martin never commits himself explicitly to a traditional hymn in Heb 1:1-4.

[66]K. Wengst, *Christologische Formeln und Lieder des Urchristentums* (Gütersloh 1972) 166-167.

[67]R. Deichgräber, *Gotteshymnus und Christushymnus in der frühen Christenheit* (Göttingen 1967) 137-140.

[68]J. T. Sanders, *The New Testament Christological Hymns* (Cambridge 1971) 19.

[69]Thompson "Structure", 129.

[70]Deichgräber (*Gotteshymnus,* 137 n. 2) rejects Bornkamm's label of *Bekenntnis* in favor of the designation "Christ-hymn".

many agree that, while v. 4 contains traditional material, it has been redacted by the author of Hebrews.

Verse 4 is indeed a good place to begin our investigation of the "wide consensus". Taking the opposite side of the argument, I claim that there is no indication of traditional material in v. 4. The vocabulary, structure, and thought are all typical of our author, as has already been shown in my previous essay. The *synkrisis,* expressed by *tosoutǭ. . .hosǭ* or some similar construction, occurs elsewhere (e.g., 7:20, 22; 8:6; 10:25). *Diaphoros* occurs four times in the NT, three of which are in Hebrews (1:4; 8:6 [*diaphorōteras*]; 9:10). *Kreittōn* occurs nineteen times in the NT, thirteen of which are in Hebrews, which regularly uses it to express the superiority of the new economy of salvation. The words of inheritance (*klēronomos, keklēronomēken, klēronomein*) act as a repetition to stitch together 1:2,4,14; they also occur, in various forms, in 6:12,17; 9:15; 11:7,8; 12:17. The preposition *para* occurs ten times in Hebrews; *ginomai* occurs thirty times. *Onoma* occurs four times in Hebrews, and here supplies the pivotal theme for the string of titles and designations in the catena. Indeed, the whole of v. 4, with its enunciation of the thesis of the superiority of Christ to the angels, supplies the "superscription" for 1:5-14. In short, there is not a shred of evidence in favor of attributing v. 4 to a traditional hymn. To say that our author has heavily redacted the hymn in v. 4 is to assert the unprovable and to avoid the simpler explanation. The supposed "hymnic character"[71] of v. 4 simply reminds us that our author is a fine stylist capable of writing elevated, rhythmic prose[72].

Having failed to find a traditional fragment in v. 4, let us go to the other end of the supposed hymn, 2b or 2c. Here too, exegetes are vague in their comments, many saying that v. 2 contains traditional material, but material taken from a source different from the hymn they discern in v. 3. Again, this assertion is without foundation. Every single word in 1:2bc

---

[71]So Deichgräber *(Gotteshymnus,* 138), though he qualifies the description with "zum Teil". He argues for tradition from the parallel mention of the conferral of a name in the Philippians hymn.

[72]So, e.g., Norden, *Agnostos Theos,* 386; Grässer, "Hebräer 1:1-4", 190 n. 58.

occurs elsewhere in Hebrews, as do certain key concepts: Christ as heir (1:4), Christ as Creator (1:10), the use of *aiōn* in the plural in the context of creation by the word of God (11:3). The presence of relative clauses does not in itself indicate traditional material or hymns, as Grässer readily admits[73]. Especially in such a refined writer as the author of Hebrews, carefully constructed relative clauses, marked by rhythm and sometimes interwoven with participles, are to be expected; as a matter of fact, they are found elsewhere in the Epistle (e.g., 1:1-4,10,14-15; 4:12-13; 5:5-10; 7:26-27; 8:1-2; 9:6-10,11-12; 10:19-22,24-25). True, a relative clause that has no grammatical antecedent or that breaks the context may indicate the insertion of traditional material (e.g., 1 Tim 3:16). But in Heb 1:2 the relative pronouns have an obvious antecedent in *huiǭ* and do not disturb the line of thought. Once again, there is not a shred of evidence for a traditional hymn or confessional formula in 1:2.

This leaves us with 1:3, which indeed is the one verse on which all of the above-named authors agree when they try to delimit the traditional hymn. Some, in fact, limit the original hymn to v. 3 alone[74]. So certain is Deichgräber on this point that he boldly affirms that v. 3 was taken over by the author of the Epistle without additions.[75] Nevertheless, as we examine the arguments in favor of a hymn in 1:3, we get a sense of *déjà vu:* many of them have been already discredited in our treatment of v. 4 and v. 2. Rhythm, elevated prose, complicated constructions involving relative pronouns and participles—all these are the stock and trade of a rhetorician like our author, especially in an exordium. The relative *hos,* like *hon* and *di'hou* before it, has a clear antecedent in *huiǭ*. Realizing this, Grässer emphasizes the argument from unique or rare words in v. 3.[76] Actually, there are two NT *hapax legomena* in 1:3a:

[73]Grässer, "Hebräer 1:1-4", 192, 194.

[74]Wengst, *Christologische Formeln*, 166; Martin, *Carmen Christi*, 19.

[75]Deichgräber, *Gotteshymnus*, 137.

[76]Grässer, "Hebräer 1:1-4", 194-195; he also appeals to the parallels with other NT Christological hymns.

apaugasma and *charaktēr*. However, since all scholars admit that the author of Hebrews reflects the Jewish-Hellenistic intellectual milieu of Alexandria (*apaugasma* in Wis 7:26; both words in Philo), the simplest explanation is that he is drawing upon the vocabulary of his general religious background rather than on some otherwise unknown and undemonstrable Christian hymn. Put simply: *apaugasma* and *charaktēr* do occur in Jewish Alexandrian literature; they do not occur in any NT hymn. The choice of the more likely background seems clear. Almost all the other words in 1:3 occur elsewhere in Hebrews. *Katharismos* does not occur again, though *katharizō, katharos,* and *katharotēs* do, in contexts of ritual or spiritual cleansing. And, by common admission, 1:3c expresses a key concern of the author throughout the Epistle. Indeed, v. 3c and v. 3d, taken together, give the clearest expression within the exordium of the theme of the whole work. Even v. 3a and v. 3b, with their themes of divinity, preexistence, and continuous creative activity, are echoed in 1:7-12 and ultimately ground the claim of the superiority of Christ's revelation in 2:1-4.

To support the presence of hymnic material, Deichgräber appeals to the clear break between 1:2 (with God as the subject) and 1:3 (with the Son as the subject).[77] But this is to miss the subtle shift of thought engineered by the author throughout vv. 1-3. In v. 1 God is the subject who reveals, without any reference to the Son. In v. 2, the Son is first mentioned as the mediator of revelation, redemption, and creation, while God still remains the subject and principal agent. In v. 3, the Son becomes the principal agent, while God is mentioned *in obliquo* by pronouns (*autou*) or pious periphrasis (*doxēs, megalōsynēs*). By a carefully constructed slant in the movement of thought and language, theo-logy gradually becomes christo-logy. What Deichgräber calls a clear break is rather a clever and smooth progression.

A final argument in favor of a traditional hymn is the close similarity between the movement of thought in Heb 1:1-4 and the kind of Christology in the hymns found in Phil 2:6-11, Col

---

[77]Deichgräber, *Gotteshymnus,* 138.

1:15-20, and 1 Tim 3:16. But all this need show is that our author comes out of a Christian background formed by Jewish and Jewish-Christian speculation on Wisdom and is acquainted with Christological traditions reflected in the hymns which use the Wisdom myth. This in no way proves that he is citing one particular Christian hymn, known or unknown. In sum, while the arguments for a traditional hymn may look more substantial in v. 3 than in v. 4 or v. 2, they are still too weak to convince.

Moreover, I would maintain that the thesis of the present article supplies an additional argument against the consensus favoring a traditional hymn in the exordium. As we have seen, our author has carefully constructed a symmetrical pattern embracing the seven Christological designations in the exordium and the seven OT citations in the catena. Moreover, the symmetry is not only formal-numerical but also material-theological. Each group of seven moves in the same general ring-like pattern: from exaltation back to creation, back farther to divinity/preexistence, forward again to creation and guidance of creation, and forward still farther to exaltation and superiority to the angels. It strains credulity to imagine that a traditional hymn (whatever its extent), inserted into the exordium, just happened to fit perfectly into this numerical and theological symmetry. To explain such a neat fit one must again appeal to heavy redactional activity by our author. Indeed for such a snug fit, the redactional activity would have to be so heavy that the supposed traditional material would, for all practical purposes, disappear into the composition of the author of the Epistle. We are left wondering why anyone would insist on expending so much time and effort on such a weak hypothesis when the simpler solution is also the obvious one: Heb 1:1-4 is the composition of our author, from start to finish.[78]

---

[78]This position, while definitely a minority one, is not without its supporters. D. Robinson ("The Literary Structure of Hebrews 1, 1-4", *AJBA* 2 [1972] 178-186) argues against the hymn on structural grounds. Unfortunately, the structures Robinson discerns in Heb 1 are highly questionable. He follows Bruce in counting seven "facts about Christ' in 1:2-3, thus amputating v. 4 from a literary structure and a thought-unit to which it clearly belongs. The seven-fold pattern is dismissed as unimportant, and no connection with the pattern of seven psalms is seen. The chiasm

III. Conclusions

We can now bring this essay to an end by marshaling our conclusions and adding some corollaries.

(1) The view that the author of Hebrews is both a consummate stylist and a profound theologian is confirmed by a structural analysis of the first chapter. More specifically, we have seen that the author creates two "cycles of seven": seven Christological predications or designations in 1:2b-4 and seven OT citations grounding the Christological predications in 1:5-14.

(2) The symmetry, however, is not purely numerical. There is also a global parallel as regards the movement of Christological thought in the seven designations and in the catena of citations. In 1:2b-4, the thought moves in a "ring-structure" backwards and then forwards again. Starting with the exaltation of the Son, the author moves back to creation, back farther to eternal preexistence, forward again to conservation and guidance of creation, purification from sins, exaltation/enthronement, and consequently superiority to the angels. A similar theological "ring-structure" is visible in the catena: exaltation as Son, back to creation (specifically, of angels), back to divinity and timeless existence, forward to creation, to exaltation/enthronement, and to a concluding remark of the author about the inferiority of angels to the Son. The parallel is not a perfect one-to-one correspondence of each designation to the numerically equivalent citation; it is rather a general correspondence in the themes and movement of thought. Granted the numerical symmetry of the two lists of seven's, the symmetry in thought hardly seems accidental. Weaving together numerical structure and theology at the very beginning of his presentation the author may be subtly indicating by a kind of "Christological rhetoric", the perfection (*teleiotēs*) that the Son has achieved—seven being the number of perfection.[79]

---

he discerns in vv. 2b-3 is artifically constructed. J. Frankowski ("Early Christian Hymns Recorded in the New Testament", *BZ* 27 [1983] 183-194) also rejects a traditional hymn in v. 3; he thinks that the verse was freely composed by our author from Christological motifs well known in the first century.

[79]The importance of the concept of perfection to the Epistle to the Hebrews need

(3) If the author of Hebrews himself has carefully composed the numerical and theological symmetry we have found in Hebrews 1, then two well-known theses that touch on this chapter are called into question. G. Theissen has tried to claim that *1 Clement* 36 represents independent Christian tradition and so is literarily independent of Heb 1. He supports part of his thesis by presuming a traditional hymn in Hebrews 1 which is also reflected in *1 Clement* 36.[80] The rejection of any traditional hymn in Heb 1:2-4 notably weakens his thesis and makes the literary dependence of *1 Clement* 36 on Heb 1 much more likely. Indeed, if one decides that the whole of Heb 1 is the composition of our author, it seems almost impossible to deny that the writer of *1 Clement* knew the Epistle to the Hebrews. *1 Clement* is simply too close in language and thought to Hebrews 1.[81]

A similar conclusion must be reached about the thesis of those authors who explain the seven citations in Heb 1:5-14 as coming from some testimony-book. The seven citations and their precise order fit too neatly into the schema of Hebrews 1 to be taken *en bloc* from a book of OT citations.[82] In particular, those who argue that a testimony-book must have been used because OT citations fit so poorly into the literary and theological context of the Epistle[83] have failed to understand

---

not be documented here; see Peterson, *Hebrews and Perfection,* with its bibliography on pp. 294-304; also Michel, *Brief,* 225-229; Spicq, *L'épître,* 2,214-230. From all that we have seen, it is difficult to agree with Spicq (2:2) that the seven Christological designations in 1:2-4 are "without order". It is simply a question of understanding that the author's order is not our order.

[80]Theissen, *Untersuchungen,* 50.

[81]So G. Cockerill, "Heb 1:1-4, 1 Clem 36:1-6 and the High Priest Title", *JBL* 97 (1978) 437-440. Cockerill points out the background of Theissen's position in the work of Käsemann, Grässer, and Schierse. See also P. Ellingworth, "Hebrews and 1 Clement: Literary Dependence or Common Tradition?", *BZ* 23 (1979) 262-269. Ellingworth basically agrees with Cockerill.

[82]So Montefiore (*Hebrews,* 43), who tries to distinguish between the original meaning of the citations in the traditional catena and the redactional meaning in Hebrews. The results are highly speculative. Even more speculative is the claim of F. Synge (*Hebrews and the Scriptures* [London 1959] 53) that the author of Hebrews "has no notion where [in the Bible] his citations come from", since he is quoting from a testimony-book.

[83]So Hay, *Glory,* 39, in support of Theissen. Against the theory of a testimony-book behind Hebrews 1 is Grässer, "Hebräer, 1:1-4", 208-209.

the catena's true function.

(4) The fact that both ring-structures begin and end with exaltation confirms the thesis of J. Thompson that exaltation is the vantage point of the catena[84] —and indeed, the vantage point of the whole of chap. 1 and of the author's theology. It seems to me, however, that Thompson's stress on exaltation prevents him from doing full justice to the statements about the Son's role in creation, his divinity, and his preexistence.[85] In saying this, I do not mean to deny that the author's dominant viewpoint throughout the Epistle is exaltation. But from that vantage point the author does look back to creation and preexistence and does speak, mythologically of course, of those "events" or "stages". They do play a role in his total theological vision, although the emphasis is elsewhere.

(5) The fact that the Son's divinity, preexistence, and role in creation do have a place in the author's theology poses a difficulty for the thesis of J. Dunn in his excellent work, *Christology in the Making*.[86] Along with some other recent scholars, Dunn claims that there is no affirmation of a real, personal preexistence of Christ before John's gospel.[87] Dunn's radical thesis is refreshing, and forces one to rethink a great deal of what NT exegesis often takes for granted. I am not convinced, though, when Dunn claims that the Epistle to the Hebrews affirms something like OT Wisdom theology. Wisdom is simply the personification of God's activity in the world, says Dunn; and Hebrews simply says that this divine Wisdom became embodied in the person of Christ. It does not seem to me that such a position adequately describes the Christology of Hebrews. I do not think it irrelevant that all seven Christological designations depend directly or indirectly on *huiǭ* in 1:2a. The Son in and by whom God spoke historically "in

---

[84]The position is enunciated clearly on p. 129 of Thompson's "Structure".

[85]See, e.g., Thompson, "Structure", 133-138.

[86]J. Dunn, *Christology in the Making* (Philadelphia 1980) especially pp. 206-209 for Heb 1:1-3. It should be noted that Dunn seems to accept the hymn-hypothesis, at least for 1:3, possibly for v. 2b; see p. 338 n. 194.

[87]Dunn, *Christology,* 249: "...the Fourth Evangelist was the first Christian writer to conceive of the personal preexistence of the Logos-Son...."

these last days" (v. 2a) is then said, *first of all,* to be enthroned as heir at his exaltation (v. 2b), *then* to be the mediator of creation (v. 2c), *then* to be of eternal divine status (v. 3a), *then* to conserve and guide all creation (v. 3b), *then* to have purged sins (by his death and entrance into heaven, v. 3c), *then* to have sat down in heaven (v. 3d) as one greater than the angels (v. 4). Surely Dunn would not dispute that the author of Hebrews thought of the exalted Son, the dying Son, and the enthroned Son as the same real person, despite the different stages of his "career" and despite his different metaphysical "locations" (heaven or earth). Indeed, Dunn, like Thompson, stresses that "the author is thinking primarily of the exalted Christ".[88] With this I agree. But is there any reason to believe that, *in the mind of this first-century Christian author,* stages 2, 3, and 4 (vv. 2c, 3a, and 3b) involve a purely "ideal" figure, a personification of God's activity or (in Philo) God's mind, rather than the real person of stages 1, 5, 6, and 7 (vv. 2b, 3c, 3d, and 4)? The flow of the ring-structure does not seem to give any basis for such a differentiation between "ideal" and "real" existence. For this middle-platonic Christian theologian, what is in heaven is supremely real, be it the exalted Son or the preexistent Son. Consequently, I cannot agree with Dunn's judgment on Heb 1:1-3: "The thought of preexistence is present, but in terms of Wisdom Christology it is the act and power of God which properly speaking is what pre-exists; Christ is not so much the pre-existent act and power of God as its eschatological embodiment".[89]

I think my interpretation of Christ's preexistence in Heb 1:1-4 is confirmed by the catena of OT citations. Our author presents God (the Father) as addressing the Son directly in the second person singular in 1:5bc (*huios mou ei sy, egō sēmeron gegennēka se;* similarly in 1:13). Without any indication of a change in the nature of the address, God is said to use the same second person singular in addressing the preexistent Son in 1:8 (*ho thronos sou, ho theos*) and in v. 10 (*sy kat' archas, kyrie, tēn gēn ethemeliōsas*). There is no indication here that

[88] Dunn, *Christology,* 208.

[89] Dunn, *Christology,* 209.

our author is merely indulging in poetic personification or that he is distinguishing between the Son's "ideal" and "real" existence. Reciprocally, the same Son who can speak to God "in the day of his flesh" (5:7), and who can plead before God for us now in his exalted state (7:25), can also speak to God as he (the Son) enters the world at his incarnation (10:5-10). It seems to me that Dunn's distinction of the ideal and real existence of Christ is a modern *hermeneutical* distinction, made to aid the modern mind as it grapples with the implications of Hebrews' theology. That is a legitimate hermeneutical undertaking. But the prior, more narrow, *exegetical* question must first be faced: Did the author of Hebrews, thinking and writing in the first century A.D., conceive of the preexistent Son as a real person in his preexistence? I think that, when the question is posed in this specific way, the data of the Epistle favor an affirmative answer. As Williamson never tires of saying, the author of Hebrews did not take over all of Philo's theology when he took over certain words and phrases and—as Thompson would add—certain metaphysical assumptions. In Hebrews, the middle platonism of Philo is fused with Christian faith-traditions concerning a concrete, historical figure, Jesus of Nazareth, who had lived perhaps not more than a half-century before our author wrote. The fusion of middle platonism with the Jesus-traditions produced a theological *novum* that broke old categories and world-views. Thompson is quite correct in seeing in Hebrews "the beginnings of Christian philosophy". In short, I do not think that Dunn has completely grasped the *novum* of Hebrews. But then, has anyone? The present essay has simply tried to make a very modest contribution to the ongoing task of grasping the most subtle and recondite mind in the NT.

Afterword

Those wishing a readily accessible guide through this difficult epistle might consult the revised commentary by Myles M. Bourke in *The New Jerome Biblical Commentary* (ed. R. Murphy, J. Fitzmyer, and R. Brown; Englewood Cliffs, NJ: Prentice-Hall, 1990). Harold Attridge has published the commentary on the Epistle to the Hebrews in the Hermeneia series (Philadelphia: Fortress, 1989). Prof. Attridge is especially equipped to tackle this epistle, since he is an expert on the relation of the New Testament material to Hellenistic Judaism and Greco-Roman literature. On the general and slippery question of the middle Platonism that many claim forms a background to the epistle, one may consult Robert M. Berchman, *From Philo to Origen. Middle Platonism in Transition* (Brown Judaic Studies 69; Chico, CA: Scholars, 1984). The old classic of Ernst Käsemann, *The Wandering People of God,* is now available in English translation (Minneapolis: Augsburg, 1984). The heavy emphasis on Gnosticism may now seem passé to some, but the work remains a milestone in twentieth-century research on Hebrews.

Part Two

6

Salvation History in Matthew: In Search of a Starting Point

The question of salvation history in Matthew has received a good deal of attention in the past decade, especially in Germany. It is the great merit of R. Walker that he has underscored the importance of salvation-history for Matthew and has attempted to draw up a complete schema of Matthew's conception.[1] Of course, Walker's contribution is not a *creatio ex nihilo*. G. Strecker had already pointed out the importance of salvation-history in the "historicizing" view of Matthew, who consciously distances himself from the "sacred past" of the "life of Jesus."[2] This position of Strecker has not gone

---

[1]R. Walker, *Die Heilsgeschichte im ersten Evangelium* (Göttingen: Vandenhoeck & Ruprecht, 1967). But we cannot agree with Walker's schema, which demands a mission to Israel up to A.D. 70, after which the mission to the Gentiles *begins* and the mission to Israel *ceases*. Walker admits that Mt 28:18-20 lies in tension with this conception, since the mission to the Gentiles is seen here as commencing immediately after Easter. Walker simply dismisses the problem by saying that Matthew did not bother to bring the traditional material in 28:18-20 into harmony with his redactional view of things. Yet, as Walker himself admits, 28:18-20 shows strong Matthean redaction. In fact, if there is any place in the gospel where Matthew clearly expresses his view on what stage of *Heilsgeschichte* begins with the resurrection, it is Mt 28:18-20. Other passages should be judged from it, and not vice versa. As O. Michel says in "Der Abschluss des Matthaus-evangeliums," *EvT* 10 (1950) 21, Mt 28:18-20 is the key to the understanding of the whole gospel.

[2]For this thesis of G. Strecker, see his *Der Weg der Gerechtigkeit*[3] (Göttingen: Vandenhoeck & Ruprecht, 1971) 86-123, and also the convenient summary of his book in his article, "Das Geschichtsverständnis des Matthäus," *EvT* 26 (1966) 57-74. See also W. Trilling, *Das Wahre Israel*[3] (Munich: Kösel, 1964) 102-105 and 137-139.

without its critics. R. Hummel, seconded to a degree by K. Stendahl, has objected to an over-historicizing interpretation of Matthew that borrows heavily from H. Conzelmann's view of Luke.[3] And so, while there has been great interest in salvation-history in Matthew, we cannot claim that there is a consensus on precisely *what* is Matthew's schema of salvation-history. Consequently, in trying to sketch Matthew's schema, it would be wise to start from data that are fairly well agreed upon and then to move out slowly towards points that might be more controversial.

I. *Relation between 10:5-6; 15:24; and 28:16-20*

As our point of departure, then, we shall choose the data exemplified by 10:5-6; 15:24; and 28:16-20—all three belonging to the special material of Matthew (=M). Mt 10:5-6 and 15:24 are expressions of a very conscious attempt on Matthew's part to limit Jesus' public ministry to the territory and the people of Israel. Jesus himself is sent only to the lost sheep of the house of Israel (15:24) and his missionary charge to his disciples during the Galilean ministry warns them not to go to the Gentiles or Samaritans, but only to the lost sheep of the house of Israel. The repetition of *pros (eis) ta probata ta apolōlota oikou Israēl* is significant. Here we have two expressions of the same tradition, which may have arisen from the milieu of strict Jewish-Christianity during the debates in the early

---

Walker, *Heilsgeschichte* 111, goes so far as to say that Mt 28:18-20 revokes the mission to Israel; but it is questionable whether such a position can be substantiated from the text.

[3]R. Hummel, *Die Auseinandersetzung zwischen Kirche und Judentum im Matthäusevangelium*[2] (Munich: Kaiser, 1966) 168. But Hummel admits on pp. 268-269 that Matthew does have a view of Jesus' earthly life as a "normative past"; K. Stendahl, in *The School of St. Matthew*[2] (Lund: Gleerup, 1968) viii n. 3, simply states that he thinks Hummel's question about whether Strecker interprets Matthew through Luke is "valid." H. Conzelmann, in "Present and Future in the Synoptic Tradition," *Journal for Theology and the Church* 5 (1968) 34 n. 34, shows he shares Strecker's basic view: "Matthew and Luke, each in his own way, are the first to envision periods of church history and *Heilsgeschichte*." For a critique of Strecker's interpretation of the *Reflexionszitate* by means of this "historicizing" tendency, cf. W. Rothfuchs, *Die Erfüllungszitate des Matthäus-Evangeliums* (Stuttgart: Kohlhammer, 1969) 15-17.

Church over a mission to the Gentiles. If this be the case, Matthew's use of this tradition is most instructive for an understanding of the general principle according to which he works Jewish-Christian material into his gospel. The sayings themselves are preserved in all their vigor, not to say harshness. But they are taken up into a higher synthesis of salvation-history where they play a part in only one stage of *Heilsgeschichte.* The same Jesus who, during his earthly ministry, forbids the Twelve a mission among the Gentiles and Samaritans is also the Jesus who, as the risen Lord, commands the Eleven to make disciples of *panta ta ethnē*. There is here no sloppy, eclectic, or schizophrenic juxtaposition of contradictory material. Rather, Matthew is quite consciously ordering an "economy" of salvation: to the Jews first, and then to the Gentiles. The public ministry of the earthly Jesus stands under geographical and national limitations: the gospel is to be preached only to Israel, and only in the promised land. After the death and resurrection, however, this "economical" limitation falls at Jesus' all-powerful command (Mt 28:16-20). The very same persons (the Eleven) who were previously forbidden to evangelize the Gentiles and Samaritans are now solemnly commissioned (by the same Person who issued that prohibition) to extend their activities to all the nations. Matthew's intention to set up a schema of salvation-history on the basis of a limited ministry to Israel that is broadened (after the death-resurrection) to all nations can thus serve us as a working hypothesis.[4]

Note, too, that, although the ministry to the Gentiles is reserved in principle to the time after death-resurrection, Matthew does allow a symbolic anticipation of this ministry in the two cases of the centurion (8:5-13, in which Matthew

---

[4]Another indication of this schema is the fact that, while Jesus is presented as teaching during his public ministry (4:23; 5:2; 7:29; 9:35; 11:1; 13:54; 21:23; 22:16; 26:55—especially in redactional summaries!), the disciples are not portrayed as teaching until the great commission (28:20—*didaskontes*). This is particularly significant when one considers that, in the missionary discourse (ch. 10), Jesus explicitly gives the disciples authority to imitate his ministry in casting out devils, healing, performing other miracles, and even preaching (*kēryssete*—vs. 7). The one element that is eloquent by omission is teaching.

inserts the Q-logion about many coming from east and west to the eschatological banquet) and the Canaanite woman (15:21-28, which serves paradoxically as the context for 15:24). The pericopes concerning the removal to Capharnaum (4:12-17) and the Gadarene demoniacs (8:28-34) also hint at this theme. Hummel points out that another symbol of the future call of the Gentiles is the welcome Jesus extends to tax-collectors and sinners (cf. the Jewish-Christian equation of Gentile and tax-collector in 5:46-47 and 18:17).[5] Thus, the loosening of restrictions that is to take place after the death-resurrection is already hinted at and proleptically realized in the limited public ministry. We should keep this in mind, since what is true of the geographical and national limitations might prove true of another kind of limitation as well.

We have then our first firm datum: Matthew consciously draws up a schema of salvation-history which widens the geographical and national restrictions of Jesus' public ministry into a universal mission after the death-resurrection. But this datum leads us immediately to a second indisputable fact. In the final missionary command of Mt 28:16-20, the author quite obviously sees the universal mission as dispensing with circumcision. Even G. Bornkamm implicitly admits this point.[6]

---

[5]Hummel, *Auseinandersetzung*, 25.

[6]G. Bornkamm, "Der Auferstandene und der Irdische," in *Überlieferung und Auslegung im Matthäusevangelium*[5] (Neukirchen: Buchhandlung der Erziehungsvereins, 1968) 309: "Here also we find the fact confirmed that for Matthew the old question of the claim of the Gentiles to salvation (a question still quite relevant for Paul) is no longer a problem. The understanding of the people of God that was fought for in the arena of Hellenistic-Jewish Christianity—an understanding that included the Gentile nations as well—is here completely presupposed and no longer subject to doubts." Bornkamm is not too precise here. The question about the heathens was not in its essence whether the heathens could be saved, but whether they could be saved without circumcision or at least observance of the food laws. But Bornkamm is right in saying that the whole Pauline problematic is a thing of the past. On pp. 309-310, Bornkamm states that Paul and Matthew shared to a great degree the missionary understanding of Hellenistic Christianity. Bornkamm is clearer in n. 2 on p. 303: "One should beware of making parallel texts of Gal 2:11ff and Mt 16:18f., for neither the question of circumcision nor fellowship at table between Jews and Gentiles plays any kind of role in Matthew's day." In a similar vein, cf. G. Barth, "Das Gesetzesverständnis des Evangelisten Matthäus," in *Überlieferung und Auslegung* 153—although he puts down Matthew's passing over the question of circumcision to his sources. How Barth can then go on to say that Matthew emphasizes in an overall way the enduring validity of Law and Prophets for the Church is not clear; cf. Michel, "Der Abschluss" 25-26.

Yet what does this mean? How can we say that Matthew conceives Jesus as one who gives the Mosaic Law a new interpretation, and that Matthew wishes the Church to be faithful to the substance, or even the letter (5:18-19) of the Mosaic Law, when he portrays the risen Lord as giving a mandate that strikes at the very heart of the Mosaic Law? If the Church is going to admit Gentiles as full-fledged disciples of Christ, disciples who are to observe all whatsoever *(panta hosa,* a typical Matthean emphasis) Jesus commanded during his public ministry; and if, nevertheless, the Church is to use baptism rather than circumcision as the essential initiation-rite for these proselytes, then we cannot honestly speak of either the Matthean Christ or the Matthean Church as commanding faithful observance of the Mosaic Law *qua* Mosaic in the post-resurrection period. For rabbinic Judaism, a faithful observance of the Mosaic Law that dispensed *in principle* with circumcision was a contradiction in terms.[7]

Putting these two pieces of data together, we get the fol-

---

[7]Note that we say *in principle.* We do not deny that at least some Jews might allow for exceptions in extraordinary cases (e.g., hemophilia, special political pressures). For the gravity of the law of circumcision, cf. G. F. Moore, *Judaism in the First Centuries of the Christian Era,* (N.Y.: Schocken, 1971) I, 198: "The violation of these ordinances [circumcision and sabbath] is rank apostasy in the Book of Jubilees. . . . The Judaism of the Book of Jubilees is unimpeachable." In II, 16, Moore writes: "The two fundamental observances of Judaism are circumcision and the sabbath . . . these are coupled by R. Eliezer as the fundamental commandments . . . the precedence belongs to circumcision . . . (p. 18): [circumcision was] so inseparably connected with the covenant promises that it is not only the sign of the covenant (Gen 17, 11), but is itself called the covenant . . . (p. 19): Among the measures which Antiochus Epiphanes adopted to annihilate the Jewish religion none struck so directly at its very (p. 20) existence as the prohibition of circumcision. . . . Circumcision, like the prohibition of idolatry, is one of the commandments for which Israelites deliver themselves to death rather than obey a conflicting edict of the government. . . . All the more bitter was the feeling toward the apostates who in effacing the physical evidence of their Judaism, renounced the religion itself and openly united themselves to the gentiles." In I, 331, while discussing the circumcision of a proselyte, Moore quotes a rabbinic adage: ". . . if a proselyte takes upon himself to obey all the words of the Law except one single commandment, he is not to be received."—H. Gollwitzer, in a comment attached to G. Harder's article, "Jesus und das Gesetz (Matthäus 5, 17-20), *Abhandlungen zum christlich.-jüdischen Dialog 2* (Munich: Kaiser, 1967) 205, raises the fundamental question: just how far could Jesus or anyone push the "sharpening" of the decalogue and the neglect of the ceremonial law without breaking with Judaism? We might answer that, wherever the breaking-point lies, dispensing in principle with circumcision in a universal mission to the Gentiles lies on the far-side of the break.

lowing Matthean schema. During his public ministry, Jesus restricted himself in principle to the land and people of Israel, though there were a few prophetic exceptions that signified what was to come after the death-resurrection. Correspondingly, during his public ministry, Jesus proclaimed his stringent fidelity to the Mosaic Law (5:17-20 fits here), although some of the antitheses and *Streitgespräche* also point forward to what was to come after the death-resurrection.[8] After his death-resurrection, the Lord abolishes those limitations of territory and people that had clung to his public ministry. Correspondingly, his command to make disciples of all nations by baptizing them implicity rescinds the command of circumcision and so rescinds that fidelity to the Mosaic Law which marked his public ministry. In all this, there is a natural, inner logic. A ministry restricted to the land and people of Israel could hardly be carried out otherwise than with fidelity to the Mosaic Law, just as an unrestricted mission to the Gentiles would hardly be conceivable—let alone successful—without the rescinding of such Mosaic prescriptions as circumcision.

II. The Death-Resurrection as die Wende der Zeit

Throughout the first part of this article we have taken for granted that it is legitimate to speak of the "death-resurrection" as basically one event and to treat it as a critical, eschatological turning point. We have claimed that Jesus' death-resurrection means for Matthew the passing of the *heilsgeschichtliche* restrictions of Jesus' public ministry, both as to territory and people (and as to correlative commands in the Law of Moses). But is this view of Christ's death-resurrection as a single eschatological event signifying the passage of the old and the breaking-in of the new anything more than our own subtle deduction from Matthew's schema—or to be more blunt, anything more than the product of our own theological imagi-

[8]Hopefully, the impact of these views on the interpretation of the antitheses and the *Streitgespräche* will be treated at a later date. The idea of anticipation of what is to come in the life of the Church after the resurrection has some connection with the distinction between historicity and transparency developed by U. Luz in "Die Jünger im Matthäusevangelium, "*ZNW* 62 (1971) 141-171.

nation?

It is our contention that this view of Christ's death-resurrection as *die Wende der Zeit* is firmly grounded in Matthew's own depiction of the death-resurrection of Christ, especially in 27:51-54; 28:2-3; and in the appearance of the Son of Man in Mt 28:16-20. First let us look at 27:51-54. Here, with the full panoply of apocalyptic imagery, Matthew portrays the death of Christ as the end of the OT cult, as the earth-shaking beginning of the new aeon (bringing about the resurrection of the dead), and as the moment when the Gentiles first come to full faith in the Son of God. Let us take these three points one by one.[9] (1) Mt 27:51a is taken over almost word-for-word from Mk 15:38. The precise meaning of the sign is disputed. Is the sense of the passage that now all have free access to God through the sacrifice of Jesus (cf. Heb 9:3; 10:20), or that the destruction of the Temple and Jerusalem in A.D. 70 is seen as a punishment for the death of Christ, or more precisely, that the Temple cult will be brought to an end as a result of Christ's death? The problem with symbols is that

[9]For what follows, cf. the various commentaries *ad. loc.*, especially W. Allen, *The Gospel according to St. Matthew*[3] (ICC: Edinburgh: Clark, 1912); J. Schmid, *Das Evangelium nach Matthäus*[5] (RNT; Regensburg: Pustet, 1965); E. Lohmeyer, *Das Evangelium des Matthäus* (Göttingen: Vandenhoeck & Ruprecht, 1967); A. Schlatter, *Der Evangelist Matthäus*[3] (Stuttgart: Calwer, 1948); J. Schniewind, *Das Evangelium nach Matthäus*[12] (NTD; Göttingen: Vandenhoeck & Ruprecht, 1968); also, D. Senior, "The Passion Narrative in the Gospel of Matthew," in *L'Évangile selon Matthieu: Rédaction et Théologie* (ed. M. Didier; Gembloux: Duculot, 1972) 343-357; and A. Descamps, " Rédaction et christologie dans le récit matthéen de la Passion" in the same volume, 359-415. To these apocalyptic signs we could also add the darkness of vs. 45, which Matthew takes over from Mark; Schniewind, *Matthäus* 270, refers to Amos 8:9 on the darkness on the day of Yahweh. Other OT passages referred to in the commentaries on these apocalyptic signs include Jer 15:9; Ez 37:12; and Dan 12:2. Lohmeyer is quite strong on this point; cf. *Matthäus* 395: "But in all this the signs say only one thing; the consummation has broken in, the door to the coming age has opened, and it is the death of Jesus, which has brought about this eschatologically decisive event." Cf. also H. Bartsch, "Die Passions- und Ostergeschichten bei Matthäus," in *Entmythologisierende Auslegung* (Hamburg-Bergstedt: Evangelischer Verlag, 1962) 80-92—although we cannot agree with his view that behind Matthew's presentation lies an original identification of cross and resurrection with parousia and that the angel at the tomb was originally the risen Christ. More to the point is the remark of W. D. Davies, *The Setting of the Sermon on the Mount* (Cambridge: C.U.P., 1966) 85: "... The resurrection of the saints ... is here concerned ... with eschatology of the time, which looked forward to a resurrection of the dead in the Messianic Age or Age to Come." Davies refers to Amos 8:1-9,10.

they are by nature polyvalent, and so perhaps it would be wrong to pick any of these as the one meaning. But notice that all of these suggestions involve in one way or another the cessation of the Jerusalem cult as a result of the death of Christ. The end of the Temple cult was a grievous blow to the pious Jew, who, according to a rabbinic dictum, considered the world to be built on three foundations: "on the Law, on worship, and on deeds of personal kindness."[10] Now one of the props of the old creation was being pulled out, at least in principle, at the death of Christ. (2) Mt 27:51b, not in Mark, is a Matthean addition. The earthquake is a well-known apocalyptic motif from the OT, the apocrypha, and the rabbinic literature.[11] It symbolizes God's wrathful judgment on the old aeon and his powerful intervention to bring in his rule and kingdom. Note, by the way, the skillfully assembled chain of cause and effect: the earthquake splits the rocks, the splitting of the rocks opens the tombs, the opening of the tombs allows the dead to come forth.[12] (3) Mt 27:52-53 is purely Matthean. In bold apocalyptic terms, Matthew depicts the resurrection of the dead as taking place proleptically at the death of Christ. The apparently awkward fact that the saints are raised at the death of Christ and yet do not appear in the holy city until after his resurrection *(egersin autou* certainly refers to Christ's own resurrection, at least in Matthew's redaction) has caused all sorts of speculation on the original position and meaning of the pericope.[13] The earthquake has at times been identified with the earthquake in 28:2 (which indeed is an apocalyptic motif there as well), with the result that the original position of 27:52-53 has been put in the context of Christ's own resurrection. According to this view, when Matthew moved the

[10]An aphorism of Simeon the Righteous, quoted in Moore, *Judaism* I 268.

[11]Cf. Trilling, "Der Tod Jesu, Ende der alten Weltzeit," in *Christusverkündingung in den Synoptischen Evångelien* (Munich: Kösel, 1969) 195; also his article, "Die Auferstehung Jesu, Anfang der neuen Weltzeit," in the same volume, 222.

[12]Note the use of the passive voice to indicate God's action, cf. Walker, *Heilsgeschichte* 72 n. 111. Trilling, "Der Tod Jesu," 195 states: "In the death of Jesus there already occurs the revolutionary changeover to the new age."

[13]Cf. A. M'Neile, *The Gospel according to St. Matthew* (London: Macmillan, 1915) 423-424; Descamps, "Rédaction," 411 n. 104.

motif of the resurrection of the saints back to the crucifixion, he added the phrase about their not appearing until after *his* resurrection to keep Christ as the "first-fruits of the dead" (1 Cor 15:20).

Even if this speculation on Matthew's redactional activity is correct, it does not explain *why* Matthew decided to move back the resurrection of the saints to the crucifixion. We would do well to prescind from such hypotheses about the pre-redactional tradition and accept the simple datum that Matthew has quite skillfully woven together the death and resurrection of Christ to make one eschatological event. The proleptic resurrection of the saints is associated with the eschatological event of the crucifixion. Yet both the *idea* of the resurrection of the saints caused by the life-giving death of Christ and the *manner* of its portrayal (accompanied by the apocalyptic motif of the earthquake) tie it together with the resurrection of Christ in Mt 28. We are justified, then, in speaking of the death-resurrection in Matthew as one eschatological event. If all these images and themes mean anything, they mean that, in a definitive sense, the *basileia* breaks into this age at the death-resurrection of Christ. (4) In 27:54 Matthew makes a significant addition to Mk 15:39. Whereas Mark has only the centurion confessing Jesus as Son of God, Matthew says that the centurion and *those standing guard over Jesus with him* confess that "truly this (omitting Mark's 'man') was God's Son." Again, while in Mark the centurion is moved to this confession by seeing the way Jesus died, in Matthew the centurion and those with him see the earthquake and the subsequent phenomena *(ta genomena)* and are seized with a fear in the face of the holy *(ephobēthēsan)*. The Gentiles' experience of the apocalyptic signs accompanying the eschatological event of Jesus' death leads them to the Easter confession of Jesus as Son of God.[14] Here we have a proleptic realization of the goal of the risen Lord's missionary mandate in 28:16-20: the Gentiles have become disciples (cf. 14:33 for the same confession in the mouth of disciples).

As we have already mentioned, the Matthean insert in 28:2-3

---

[14]Walker, *Heilsge schichte* 72.

extends the apocalyptic imagery to the resurrection. The task
of clothing the resurrection with apocalyptic events may have
caused Matthew a bit of difficulty. Tradition forbade a
description of the resurrection itself, and even most of the
appearance-stories lack any real apocalyptic color. Matthew
solves the problem by associating the apocalyptic theme with
the angel—an element in the tradition that readily lent itself to
apocalyptic interpretation. An "angel of the Lord" (not the
young man of Mark) is introduced by a great earthquake. He
is not sitting or standing by the tomb to begin with, but
descends from the heavenly sphere to deliver his revelation.
The angel is specifically mentioned as performing the mighty
feat of rolling back the sealed rock. The description of the
angel (confirming him as an apocalyptic stock-figure) is
vaguely reminiscent of the description of Jesus at the Transfiguration (Mt 17:2; cf. also Dan 7:9; Apoc 1:14-16; Apoc
10:1). The guards are shaken with fear *(phobos)* at this apocalyptic scene. They become as dead men. The women, too, are
said to be seized with fear before the holy *(phobeomai)*. (An
interesting side-point: the reaction of both groups before the
apocalyptic vision is called fear—and yet how different is the
fear in each case! For each group, the holy is a *mysterium
tremendum et fascinans*. But for the unbelieving guards the
tremendum is dominant. For the believing women, the
fascinans is stronger than the *tremendum*.)

III. A Second Look at 28:16-20—"Proleptic Parousia?"

This consideration of 27:51-54 and 28:2-3 brings us back to
the conclusion of the gospel. Here the Risen Lord's appearance
is only the introduction to the main point of the pericope,
namely the Risen One's three-point declaration of his own
enthronement (18b), of his missionary charge to the Eleven
(19-20a), and of his constant presence to the Church (20b).
The three parts, though not strictly a full-blown enthronement
hymn, have traces of such a literary form.[15] The first part

---

[15]Cf. Trilling, *Das Wahre Israel* 46, and the literature by O. Michel and J. Jeremias
cited there. But the whole pericope, in its present state, is so much the product of

presents the risen Lord in a way reminiscent of the eschatological Son of Man in Dan 7:14. C.H. Dodd even referred to Matthew's scene in 28:16-20 as a "proleptic parousia."[16] A. Vögtle has objected to such a term, and has questioned the influence of Dan 7 on our text.[17] But his arguments are not very convincing. (1) Vögtle points out that Mt 28:18 is, from a linguistic point of view, not especially similar to Dan 7:13-14. Yet his argument, strangely enough, is based on the Theodotion text of Daniel; the LXX is much closer to Matthew's form.[18] (2) The perspective is totally different in Matthew, says Vögtle. In Daniel, after the destruction of the evil kingdoms of this world, the Son of Man comes on the clouds of heaven to

---

Matthew's redactional activity, so *sui generis*, that a form-critical category (dealing with the *typical*) can hardly be assigned to it.

[16]C. H. Dodd, "Matthew and Paul," in *New Testament Studies* (Manchester: M.U.P., 1967) 56; he himself borrows the phrase from R. H. Lightfoot. Barth, *Gesetzesverständnis* 125, also states that the reference is to Dan 7:14. Some scholars have objected to the phrase "proleptic parousia" as not in keeping with Matthew's use of *parousia*. In what follows, we defend the reference to Daniel in Mt 28:18, the view of Christ's death-resurrection as the breaking-in of the *basileia*, and the presence of a goodly amount of realized eschatology in Mt. All this, and the data that support it, is much more important than a quarrel over the phrase "proleptic parousia."

[17]A. Vögtle, "Das christologische und ekklesiologische Anliegen von Mt. 28:18-20," in *Studia Evangelica* 2 (1964) 266-294, especially p. 268 for the objection against Dodd's judgment. We cannot agree with his argument on p. 267: "If, in the understanding of the evangelist, Mt 28:18ff. proclaimed the fulfillment of Dan 7:14 now, Dan 7:13 would have to be considered as already fulfilled or, on the other hand, be left out of consideration as meaningless. Neither of these two possibilities can be satisfactorily brought into line with Mt. After the successful fulfillment of 7:14, one could no longer await intelligently the coming of the Son of Man on the clouds of heaven, as a kind of belated, supplementary fulfillment of an act preceding the enthronement." A *priori*, this either-or approach leaves no room for Matthew's use of Dan 7:13-14 in a new, creative way. Of course, even for Matthew the full manifestation of the Son of Man coming on the clouds of heaven is reserved to the *synteleia*. But those who through faith live even now the eschatological existence made possible by Jesus' death and resurrection already see in faith the enthroned Son of Man invested with all power (cf. Mt 26:64, *ap'arti*; cf. also Descamps, "Rédaction," 409-410). The task of the Eleven is to persuade all men to submit in the free obedience of faith to this power already possessed by the Son of Man, lest they fall unwillingly under his coercive power on the last day.

[18]Curiously, Trilling, *Das Wahre Israel* 22 n. 5, notes the difference between Theodotion and the LXX, admits the LXX's *exousia* instead of *basileia* is in Matthew, but nevertheless follows Vögtle's general argument. An examination of Matthew's OT citations shows that he was familiar with both Greek versions of Daniel (cf. R. Gundry, *The Use of the OT in St. Matthew's Gospel*, Leiden: Brill, 1967).

usher in the end-time. Yet, precisely on the grounds of what we have seen in this article, Matthew's adaptation of such an eschatological image to the Risen Lord is perfectly consonant with the general structure of Matthean theology; the powers of sin and death have been defeated, at least proleptically, at least in principle, by the death-resurrection of Christ. The risen Lord appears as the one to whom *pasa exousia* was given *(edothē)* in heaven and on earth, who therefore can command a universal mission to the Gentiles that prescinds from circumcision, and who can promise his abiding presence (like the *Shekinah*) to the Church (cf. 1:23 and 18:20). Of course, Vögtle is correct in seeing Matthew's use of *exousia* during the public ministry as well as Mt 11:27 as influencing the conclusion of the gospel. But we should object to a complete paralleling of 11:27 and 28:18 on the grounds that their themes differ (revelation of apocalyptic secrets by the Son *vs* the royal power of the enthroned Kyrios—so J. Schmid, in his commentary, *ad loc.*). We think it is no accident that the noun *exousia* and the adjective *pas*, used separately in reference to Jesus during the public ministry, are now united in one phrase to describe the risen Lord. The earthly Jesus, to whom all revealed knowledge *(panta)* has been given, did indeed exercise *exousia*; but to the risen Lord *pasa exousia* has been given. The death resurrection has brought in an era of realized eschatology.[19]

---

[19]Cf. Trilling, *Das Wahre Israel* 50: "Our consideration of the question of the delay of the parousia came only to the conclusion that the delay of the parousia as a theological problem seems to be alien to Matthew. This result is to be connected with the character of the whole section as 'realized eschatology.' The words are penetrated with the awareness of the fulfillment of salvation." Cf. p. 46 : "With Easter begins a new age of the world.... The Lordship of God is established in Jesus the Messiah." Cf. also E. Käsemann, "The Beginnings of Christian Theology," in *Journal for Theology and the Church* 6 (1969) 30: "... The imminent apocalyptic expectation is as little characteristic of Matthew personally as is enthusiasm."—On the other hand, Conzelmann, "Present and Future in the Synoptic Tradition," in *Journal for Theology and the Church* 5 (1968) 38, sees—incorrectly, we think—a reintensification of the imminent expectation of the parousia in Matthew. J. Lambrecht, "The Parousia Discourse. Composition and Content in Mt., XXIV-XXV," in *L'Évangile selon Matthieu: Rédaction et Théologie* 309-342, also holds that Matthew thinks the parousia is near. But, despite Lambrecht's statements on p. 329, Mt 24:48 and 25:5,19 make this view untenable. After surveying the eschatology of Qumran, Davies, *The Setting* 220, states: "... we have emphasized the difference between the 'realized eschatology' of Matthew ... and the 'expectant eschatology' of the sectarians." Hummel seems to contradict himself on the question of the delay of the parousia in

Our examination of 27:51-54; 28:2-3; and 28:16-20 has confirmed our hypothesis that Matthew sees the death-resurrection as an eschatological event in which the kingdom breaks into this aeon in a new, fuller way.[20] This explains why the limitations of territory, nation, and Mosaic Law should be observed during the public ministry of Jesus, while all these restrictions fall away after the death-resurrection, after the enthronement of the Son of Man (which is not coterminous with the complete ending of the old aeon).[21] These restrictions belonged to the old economy, the old aeon, and have been transcended for the believing disciple. This basic concept of Matthew must be kept in mind when we examine Matthew's statements on the Law, particularly Matthew's redaction of 5:17-20.

A final note of caution. We have argued above that there is much more "realized eschatology" in Matthew's theology than is usually admitted. This is not to say that Matthew is another John.[22] But there is more realized eschatology in Matthew

Matthew. In *Auseinandersetzung* 160, he affirms the delay of the parousia is a problem in Matthew, while on p. 170 (second edition) n. 64, he says that the disappearance of an expectation of an imminent parousia causes Matthew no pressing problems.

[20]We do not deny that, for Matthew, the kingdom is present in some sense in the person of Jesus from the beginning. But the death-resurrection is most certainly a powerful breaking-in of the kingdom, as the démarche of 28:16-20 shows.

[21]Hence we cannot agree entirely with Barth, *Gesetzesverständnis* 138: "Thus it is unthinkable for Matthew, that the law should be annulled with Jesus' death, even if he sees in Jesus' life and death the *plērōsai pasan dikaiosynēn* (and indeed in the place of sinners! 3:15)." On this point, Trilling's position does not seem to be wholly consistent. In *Das Wahre Israel* 186, he says: "Matthew seems to connect no christological problem in the narrower sense with the law-question (Christ the end of the law), so that Jesus' death and resurrection would have created a new situation in this respect." Yet his two essays on the Synoptics, "Der Tod Jesu, Ende der alten Weltzeit," and "Die Auferstehung Jesu, Anfang der neuen Weltzeit," while not touching especially the question of law, emphasize precisely the turning of the aeon at the death-resurrection. Are we to suppose that for Trilling this turning of the aeon has no impact on the situation of the law?

[22]On the other hand, more attention should be given to the similar views that can be found in Matthew and John. Trilling *Das Wahre Israel* 190 and 213, mentions two points of similarity: the reworking of a story to stress the interpreting word, and the free reworking of material, without too much concern for historical tradition, in order to make the material more fruitful for the life of the Church. This may be why these two gospels proved to be especially important in the life of the Church.—Actually, it is not particularly strange that there should be similarities in thought between Matthew

than in, say, the early Paul or in Mark. Matthew may indeed be moving toward John's position, but he certainly has not arrived there. Mt 28:20b should be enough to warn us against an exaggerated position. Matthew still awaits the *synteleia tou aiōnos* (a phrase which, in this precise form, is peculiar to Matthew in the NT). The breaking in of the kingdom has put an end to the old aeon in principle, but not in full-blown reality. The old age continues, the world is a *corpus mixtum* in which the devil as well as the Son of Man can plant seed (Mt 13:36-43)[23] The final, visible separation that destroys the old age once and for all still lies in the future, since the harvest is expressly said to be the *synteleia aiōnos* (vs. 39, repeated in vs. 40).[24] But as most exegetes admit, the expectation of the imminent parousia has receded in Matthew, so that the emphasis in 28:20 is on the abiding presence of the enthroned Lord *pasas tas hēmeras,* rather than on the *synteleia tou aiōnos.* There is not even a Lucan ascension on the clouds with a promise that Jesus will come again the same way. Yet, despite the fact that Matthew is not concerned with an immi-

and John. It may well be that both gospels were edited by Gentile Christians not too far removed in time and place. Cf. Stendahl, "Quis et Unde?" in *Judentum, Urchristentum, Kirche* (Berlin: Töpelmann, 1960) 104 n. 44. On contacts between Matthew and John in the passion and resurrection narratives, cf. P. Benoit, "Marie-Madeleine et les disciples au tombeau selon Joh 20, 1-18," in the same Festschrift, *Judentum* etc., 145 n. 15. Rothfuchs, *Erfüllungszitate* 151-177, gives a detailed comparison between Matthean and Johannine "formulas of fulfillment."

[23]Despite affirmations that the Church is the *corpus mixtum* referred to in the explanation of the parable, vs. 38 states that the field is the world; so the world seems to be the kingdom of the Son of Man in vs. 41. On this point, cf. A. Kretzer, *Die Herrschaft der Himmel und die Söhne des Reiches* (Würzburg: Echter, 1971) 139; and J. Dupont, "Le point de vue de Matthieu dans le chapitre des paraboles," in *L'Évangile selon Matthieu: Rédaction et Théologie* 229.

[24]Another reason why the establishment of the kingdom cannot be identified with the cross and resurrection *simpliciter* is that Matthew sees the destruction of Jerusalem in A.D. 70 as also part of the eschatological drama; cf. the two articles of A. Feuillet, "Le Discours de Jésus sur la Ruine du Temple," *RB* 56 (1949) 61-92 and "La Synthèse eschatologique de Saint Matthieu," *RB* 56 (1949) 340-364. But Feuillet also recognizes that everything is already present in principle in the death and resurrection of Christ; cf. also what we said above about Mt 27:51. But, while Matthew sees the destruction of Jerusalem in eschatological colors, it is certainly not for him the *synteleia tou aiōnos*; cf. Walker, *Heilsgeschichte* 58-59. Strecker, *Der Weg* 123-127, notes that even the earthly Jesus is portrayed in an eschatological light; but Strecker also stresses the great eschatological tone Matthew gives to the passion; cf. pp. 182-184.

nent parousia, Christian experience is for him no less basically conditioned by the eschatological event than it was for the earliest Christians. In fact, the present existence of the Christian is eschatologically conditioned in two ways. (1) The death-resurrection as eschatological event has thrown down the limitations of territory, nation, and Mosaic Law that belonged to the old aeon.[25] The Christian lives even now by the power of the kingdom, while he awaits the definitive passing of this age. (2) But the passing of the old age does indeed remain in the future, and with it the eschatological judgment of the Son of Man. The Christians of Matthew's Church do not differ in this regard from the first Christians: expectation of the end does give an eschatological quality to present existence. The difference lies in the fact that, for Matthew, the stringency of judgment has taken the place of the temporal imminence of judgment as the great motive in parenesis.

[25]W. D. Davies, in his intriguing essay, "Matthew 5:17-18," in *Mélanges A. Robert* (Paris: Bloud et Gay, 1957) 428-456, has attempted an interpretation of the trouble-some passage 5:17-18 in the light of Christ's death and resurrection seen as the eschatological event. But Davies is concerned with the intention of the historical Jesus, who, according to Davies, was aware that he was the Messiah in the sense of the suffering servant of Yahweh. Obviously, we cannot enter into such a complicated question here. But it might be better, methodologically, to begin from the firm data of Matthew's redaction and to move first to a judgment of what *Matthew* meant by 5:17-20. This is a more modest goal, but perhaps the results will be more verifiable. We hope to take up this question at a later date. For an interesting treatment of the relation of Matthew's eschatology to the Law-question, especially 5:17-18, see O. Hanssen's "Zum Verständnis der Bergpredigt," in *Der Ruf Jesu und die Antwort der Gemeinde* (ed. E. Lohse; Göttingen: Vandenhoeck & Ruprecht, 1970) 94-111.—Among the many studies on the attitude of the historical Jesus to the Law, see K. Berger, *Die Gesetzesauslegung Jesu. Teil I: Markus und Parallelen* (Neukirchen-Vluyn: Neukirchener Verlag, 1972). For older studies, cf. W. Kümmel, "Jesus und die jüdische Traditionsgedanke," *ZNW* 33 (1934) 105-130, and H. Schoeps, "Jésus et la loi juive," *RHPR* 33 (1953) 1-20. It must be admitted, however, that neither of these two studies is sufficiently critical in distinguishing original event, tradition, and redaction. For an even earlier attempt to delineate Jesus' position to the law—but one that would strike us today as too heavily "psychologizing" in the liberal mode—see the essay by A. von Harnack, "Hat Jesus das alttestamentliche Gesetz abgeschafft?" in *Aus Wissenschaft und Leben* (Giessen: Töpelmann, 1911) II 227-236.

❧

Afterword

Different views continue to be held on the question of salvation history in Matthew. The debate is reviewed by Donald Senior in his splendid little survey, *What Are They Saying About Matthew?* (New York/Ramsey, NJ: Paulist, 1983) 28-36. Senior himself supports the view of Jesus' death as a pivotal turning point in his article, "The Death of Jesus and the Resurrection of the Holy Ones (Mt 27:51-53)," *CBQ* 38 (1976) 312-29. As Senior points out, the major alternative to my view of salvation history in Matthew is that of Jack Dean Kingsbury, who sees only two "epochs": the time of Israel and the time of Jesus. He defended this view on redaction-critical grounds in his first major book on the question, *Matthew: Structure, Christology, Kingdom* (Philadelphia: Fortress, 1975) 25-39. He has more recently sustained this opinion in *Matthew as Story* (2d ed.; Philadelphia: Fortress, 1988) 40-42, which uses the method of modern literary or narrative criticism. It still seems to me that, in Matthew's presentation, the death-resurrection and the new mandate of Jesus to his disciples in 28:16-20 constitute too much of a change from the situation prevailing during the earthly life of Jesus to put both periods under one heading.

7

Nations or Gentiles
in Matthew 28:19?

Introduction

In Mt 28:19, the risen Jesus commands the Eleven to make disciples of *panta ta ethnē*. Are these Greek words to be translated "all the nations (peoples)" or "all the Gentiles"? Two noted Matthean scholars, Douglas R. A. Hare and Daniel J. Harrington, have defended the view that Matthew meant "all the Gentiles," i.e., only non-Jews.[1] While Hare and Harrington presented many strong arguments for their position, I should like to register some doubts about their interpretation of certain Matthean texts containing *ethnos/ethnē*. In the present essay, I hope to show that there are solid grounds for taking *panta ta ethnē* in Mt 28:19 as "all the nations," or, perhaps better put, "all (the) peoples." Granted, certainty is hard to come by in this kind of debate. Yet I think it can be argued that the translation of "all the nations (peoples)" enjoys the weight of preponderant evidence.

Since I have no quarrel with the observations of Hare and

[1]D. Hare and D. Harrington, " 'Make Disciples of All the Gentiles' (Matthew 28:19)," *CBQ* 37 (1975) 359-369. The article is a synthesis of two papers presented during the CBA Task Force on Matthew, August 19-22, 1974: D. Hare, "'Nations' or 'Gentiles' in Matthew 28:19?" and D. Harrington, "*Ethnos* in Matthew's Gospel." I should like to thank all the members of the Task Force for their suggestions and criticism; they have contributed greatly to the formulation of my own position.

Harrington on the use of *gôyīm/ethnē* in Judaism or the Patristic period, I shall focus my attention on the occurrences of *ethnos/ethnē* in Matthew. For the sake of clarity, I shall divide these occurrences into three types: (I) cases where the word clearly refers only to Gentiles: (II) cases where I consider it unclear whether the word refers only to Gentiles; (III) cases where I consider it clear or highly probable that the word does not refer only to Gentiles.[2]

The Occurrences of *Ethnos/Ethnē* in Matthew

I. We can deal quickly with the seven cases that seem to refer clearly to Gentiles alone. (1) in Mt 4:15 (a citation of Isa 8:23), *Galilaia tōn ethnōn* obviously refers to the large number of Gentile inhabitants in Galilee. (2) The second occurrence, Mt 6:32 (*panta gar tauta ta ethnē epizētousin*) is not quite so clear, if taken by itself. But in the context of Jesus' addressing his Jewish disciples and the Jewish crowd, the pejorative comparison implied in *ethnē* makes "Gentiles" the probable meaning (cf. the pejorative comparison in the use of *ethnikoi* in Mt 5:47). (3) In Mt 10:5, *eis hodon ethnōn mē apelthēte* obviously refers to the Gentiles, since it is parallel to the Samaritans and opposed to the lost sheep who are the house of Israel (*oikou Israēl* being an epexegetical genitive). (4) In Mt 10:18 (*eis martyrion autois kai tois ethnesin*), it is the *autois* which is not entirely clear (the Jews who institute the persecution or the governors and kings?).[3] The *ethnesin,* since

---

[2]I can waive an ordering of occurrences according to sources (Mark, Q, M, or redaction), since Hare and Harrington have already rendered that service in their article, pp. 361-363.

[3]On this, cf. Hare, *The Theme of Jewish Persecution of Christians in the Gospel according to St. Matthew* (Cambridge: Cambridge University, 1967) 106-108. Hare argues in favor of *autois* referring to the governors and kings; so too, W. Grundmann, *Das Evangelium nach Matthäus* (3d ed.; Berlin: Evangelische Verlagsanstalt, 1972) 293. I am inclined, however, to agree with W. Trilling (*Das wahre Israel* [3d ed.; Munich: Kösel, 1964] 128): the interpretation "to the rulers and to [the rest of] the Gentiles [who are under these rulers and receive the Christian witness through them]" is unnecessarily complicated. With the laconic *autois kai tois ethnesin* Matthew simply sums up the two audiences with which his whole theological problematic is concerned: Jews and Gentiles.

they seem distinct from the people who scourge the Christians in *their* synagogues (v 17—the Jews, obviously), must be Gentiles. (5-6) In Mt 12:18-21 (a citation of Isa 42:1-4), there are two cases of *ethnē* (vv 18 + 21). That they both refer to non-Jewish nations is most likely, since that is the original sense of the *gôyīm* and *'iyyîm* ("coastlands," the far-distant abode of the Gentiles) in the MT—a sense which Matthew does not seem to alter by his use of *ethnē* for both Hebrew words. (7) In Mt 20:19 (the third passion prediction), the *ethnesin* into whose power Jesus is delivered are obviously the Gentiles, since the ones doing the delivering are the high priests and scribes (v 18). This interpretation is of course confirmed by Matthew's passion narrative.

We have, then, seven certain or highly probable cases where *ethnē* means "Gentiles," and Gentiles alone. We should note, however, that three out of the seven cases occur in explicit OT citations. When we observe further that 6:32 comes from Q (=Luke 12:30), 20:19 comes from Mk 10:33, 10:18 arises from a reworking of Mt 13:9-10, and Mt 10:5-6 is generally judged to be pre-Matthean tradition rather than Matthew's redactional creation,[4] we come to the conclusion that none of the clear cases of *ethnē*=Gentiles stems purely from Matthew's redactional creativity. This fact should at least make us cautious about deciding what the *panta ta ethnē* in Mt 28:19 must mean.

II. We pass now to the two cases whose meaning I would, at least initially, consider doubtful. (1) In Mt 20:25-26, Jesus uses a comparison to rebuke the twelve for their concern about rank and honor: *hoi archontes tōn ethnōn katakyrieuousin autōn kai hoi megaloi katexousiazousin autōn, ouch houtōs estin en hymin.* Who are *hoi archontes tōn ethnōn?* At first glance, we would naturally suppose that they are the rulers of the Gentiles, as opposed to the Jewish speaker and his Jewish

---

[4]So Trilling, *Israel*, 99-101, with further bibliography. J. Lange, *Das Erscheinen des Auferstandenen im Evangelium nach Matthäus* (Würzburg: Echter, 1973) 251-252, favors Q as the source, though he acknowledges that many other critics prefer a special source (p. 251 n. 12). On the other hand, H. Frankemölle, *Jahwebund und Kirche Christi* (Münster: Aschendorff, 1973) 129, argues that Matt 10:5-6 is a Matthean creation. In my opinion, neither Lange nor Frankemölle offers solid arguments for his view.

audience. But further considerations call this view into question. First, is it true that most of the Israelite kings, Hasmonean rulers, and half-breed Herodians had been noticeably different from Gentile rulers with regard to making their power felt? One could hardly differentiate the Hasmoneans and Herodians from other Oriental rulers when it came to concern for rank and power. Secondly, and more importantly, the rulers *tōn ethnōn* are not being contrasted with Jews in general, but with the Twelve (*hymin*) and, through them, with later Christian leaders. The opposition seems to be between the rulers of this world and the Christian rulers in the church. The former try to make their power felt, while the latter must become humble servants. Given this contrast, we should probably understand *hoi archontes tōn ethnōn* as the rulers of the nations, i.e., the rulers of this world, worldly rulers, as opposed to servant-rulers in the Christian community.[5] But I admit that the case is not all that clear. "Rulers of the Gentiles" remains a possible translation,[6] and so I assign Mt 20:25 to the "doubtful" category. (2) The second doubtful case is Mt 24:9: *kai esesthe misoumenoi hypo pantōn tōn ethnōn.* Matthew has added *tōn ethnōn* to the simpler statement of Mk 13:13 *kai esesthe misoumenoi hypo pantōn.* Here I agree with Trilling:[7] there is no reason to play off Mt 10:17ff. against 24:9, as though the former referred only to Jewish persecutions while the latter referred only to Gentile persecutions. Both texts of Matthew, dependent on Mk 13:9-13, point in the same direction: a general law, a common situation, found to be true among both Jews and Gentiles. Nothing in the context indicates a contrast between the two groups of persecutors. Hare and Harrington admit that 24:9 need not be restricted to Gentiles;[8] but they favor the restriction on the grounds that

---

[5]This seems to be the understanding of the *NEB:* "You know that in the world, rulers lord it over their subjects . . . ."; so too, the *Bible de Jérusalem:* "les chefs des nations . . . ."; and Luther's translation: "die weltlichen Fürsten . . . ."

[6]As seen in the *RSV, NAB,* and *JB.* Hare and Harrington do not seem to see any other possibility; they simply state that *ethnē* in Matt 20:25 means "Gentiles," without any arguments being given ("'Make Disciples,'" 362).

[7]Trilling, *Israel,* 27.

[8]Hare and Harrington, "'Make Disciples,'" 362.

otherwise Matthew's addition to Mark seems superfluous.[9]
For the moment, I shall leave 24:9 in the "doubtful" category,
though I think a consideration of the other uses of *ethnōs*
/*ethnē* in Mt 24:7-14 will help to make the sense of 24:9
clearer. Consequently, I shall return to this verse in the following section.

Again, we should note that our two doubtful cases are not
pure Matthean creations. Mt 20:25 is simply a repetition of
Mark, and Mt 24:9 arises from the compression of Mk 13:9-13.

III. We now pass to those cases where, in my judgment,
ethnos/*ethnē* does not mean simply " Gentiles."

(1) The clearest case is Mt 21:43, a Matthean insert (and
probably a redactional creation) in the Marcan parable of the
evil tenants of the vineyard: *dia touto legō hymin hoti arthē-
setai aph' hymōn hē basileia tou theou kai dothēsetai ethnei
poiounti tous karpous autēs.*[10] From the whole context of the
parable, this *ethnos*[11] (not "nation" but " people") is not some
political unit or national state, but the new people of God, the
community of Jesus, the *mou tēn ekklēsian* of Mt 16:18.[12]
And nothing is clearer from the whole of Matthew's gospel
than that the church of Jesus is made up of both Jews and
Gentiles. It is this Jewish-Gentile church that Matthew calls
ethnos. Any attempt to create a monolithic Matthean use of
ethnos, always equaling Gentile nation(s), trips over the stone
of scandal in Mt 21:43. Here, if nowhere else in Matthew,
ethnos must mean something other than Gentile nation(s).
And here also we see that Matthew is capable of using *ethnos*
in a creative way, beyond any traditional usage he inherited
from the LXX. For what Matthew is expressing in 21:43 is the

[9]Ibid., 366. Trilling, *Israel,* 27, sees the reason for the addition in the fact that
Matthew gives only a condensed version of Mk 13:9-13 in Matt 24:9, and therefore
casts the phrase in "eine allgemeinere Fassung."

[10]For a full treatment of this parable and this verse, cf. Trilling, *Israel,* 55-65. Here
we concentrate on the one word, *ethnos.*

[11]Matthew uses the singular only here and in 24:7.

[12]This reality is also referred to by Matthew as *ton laon autou* in 1:21. This should
warn us against making air-tight distinctions between *ethnos* and *laos* in Matthew. As
Trilling, Israel, 61, notes correctly: "[in the matter of *ethnos* and *laos*] Matthew has no
firm technical usage like the Septuagint or Luke." For an exposition of 1:21 which
points up well the connection with 16:18 *(ekklēsian mou),* 20:21 *(basileia sou),* and the
whole conception of the new people of God, see Frankemölle, *Jahwebund,* 211-218.

concept of the church as a *tertia gens,* another people which cannot be neatly categorized as either Jewish or Gentile. Any attempt to solve the problem of *panta ta ethnē* in 28:19 must take seriously the complicating factor of 21:43. Furthermore, the fact that the kingdom is taken away from the Jewish people and given to an *ethnos* that will bear its fruits can be taken to imply that the Jews are in some sense an *ethnos*—the *ethnos* that refused to bear the fruits of the kingdom. It is difficult to avoid this comparison implicit in 21:43.

(2) Mt 24:7, the other case of the singular form of *ethnos* in Matthew, confirms the suspicion that Matthew could think of the Jewish people as an *ethnos: egerthēsetai gar ethnos epi ethnos.* In the context of Jesus' prediction of the destruction of the temple (24:2) and the first part of the disciples' question (24:3), it is extremely difficult to avoid a reference to the Jewish revolt (A.D. 66-70) in v 7.[13] Granted that reference, we have a clear case in which Matthew uses *ethnos* to refer to the Jewish people, precisely as opposed to some other *ethnos* engaging it in war. The question therefore arises: if both the Jewish people and some other (obviously Gentile) people can both be subsumed under the label *ethnos,* why cannot Matthew be referring to both Jew and Gentile when he speaks of *panta ta ethnē*? In fact, faced with the evidence of 24:7, by what right do we exclude the Jewish people from *panta ta ethnē*?

(3) In Mt 24:14, we have the most explicitly universalistic use of *ethnos* in Matthew: *kai kerychthēsetai touto to euaggelion tēs basileias en holę tę oikoumenę eis martyrion pasin tois ethnesin.* T. Zahn rightly observed long ago: just as *holę hē oikoumenē* does not mean the world minus Palestine, so too *panta ta ethnē* does not mean mankind minus Israel (i.e., the Gentiles).[14] *Holę hē oikoumenē can mean only "the whole*

---

[13]So Grundmann, *Das Evangelium nach Matthäus,* 503. This does not mean that we must restrict the reference to the Jewish revolt; what we may have here is the Jewish revolt "blown up" and projected onto an apocalyptic screen as an archetypal cosmic event. But this does not allow us to dismiss the testimony of 24:7 as an "apocalyptic cliché" (Hare and Harrington, "'Make Disciples,'" 362). Though the verse obviously draws on OT terminology (Isa 19:2; 2 Chr 15:6 —not specifically apocalyptic!), it still witnesses to the fact that Matthew could refer to the Jewish people as *ethnos.*

[14]T. Zahn, *Das Evangelium des Matthäus* (Leipzig: Deichert, 1903) 655 n. 7. I do not agree with Hare and Harrington ("'Make Disciples,'" 366) that Zahn's argument lacks cogency; cf. n. 16 below.

inhabited earth."[15] When such an all-encompassing phrase qualifies the preaching of the gospel to *pasin tois ethnesin*, the latter phrase must include the Jewish people.[16]

Having decided that both 24:7 and 24:14 use *ethnos/ethne* in a sense that includes the Jews, we can perhaps take a second look at an intervening verse which we provisionally placed in the doubtful category: 24:9. As I indicated above, I favored the view that in 24:9 *hypo pantōn tōn ethnōn* meant "all the nations," including the Jews. When we see now that this use of *ethnōn* falls between two verses (7 + 14) which definitely use the word in its most universal sense, we have sufficient reason to move 24:9 from the second (doubtful) to the third (definitely universal) category.

(4) Mt 25:32 (and the whole scene of the last judgment [17] in 25:31-46) is so hotly disputed today that some might prefer to leave it in our second category. I readily admit that some points of interpretation are unclear: e.g., whether the "least of my brethren" refers to Christians in the pagan world, Christian missionaries, or all the poor and suffering of mankind.[18] But,

---

[15]So. W. Bauer, *A Greek-English Lexicon of the New Testament and Other Early Christian Literature* (trs. W. Arndt-F. Gingrich; Chicago: Chicago University Press, 1957) *sub voce*, Ia.

[16]I fail to see the force of Hare's and Harrington's objection to Zahn's reasoning ("'Make Disciples,'" 366): "The assumption underlying 24:14 (and Mk 13:10) is that the Jewish nation has *already* heard the gospel." Be that as it may, the whole question in 28:19 and this present debate is whether the gospel will continue to be preached to the Jews. We must use 24:14 to solve that question, not *vice versa*. Hare and Harrington seem to be assuming what is to be proved. Moreover, in the immediate context of 24:14, there is no explicit mention of an earlier separate mission to the Jews. The immediate context of 24:14 is the problem of the apparent delay of the consummation while evils multiply. Faced with such disappointments and trials, one must persevere (v 13), for the end is not yet (v 14c), since the gospel must first be preached to all the nations in the whole inhabited world (v 14ab). Given this context and the sweeping, programmatic nature of v 14, I think it is impossible to infer a new Matthean "exceptive clause": *parektos logou Ioudaiōn*.

[17]A scene to which the label "parable" is best not applied.

[18]We think the reference to all men in need is most likely; so Grundmann, *Das Evangelium nach Matthäus*, 527; P. Bonnard, *L'Evangile selon saint Matthieu* (2d ed.; Neuchatel: Editions Delachaux et Niestlé, 1970) 366; E. Schweizer, *Das Evangelium nach Matthäus* (Göttingen: Vandenhoeck & Ruprecht, 1973) 312; J. Jeremias, *The Parables of Jesus* (London: SCM, 1963) 207. For other views, see L. Cope, "Matthew XXV 31-46. 'The Sheep and the Goats' Reinterpreted," *NovT* 11 (1969) 32-44; W. D. Davies, *The Setting of the Sermon on the Mount* (Cambridge: Cambridge University, 1966) 98. For further discussion and literature, cf. Lange, *Erscheinen*, 295-301, especially n. 137 on pp. 299-301; and J. A. T. Robinson, "The

again, I can see no solid reasons for excluding Jews from the *panta ta ethnē* of 25:32. What we have in 25:31-46 is the climactic scene (*not* a parable on the same level as 24:45-51, 25:1-13, or 25:14-30) which Matthew uses to crown his baroque expansion of the Marcan eschatological discourse. Granted the place and weight of this final pericope, the most natural supposition is that *panta ta ethnē*, in the context of final judgment, means "all the nations" without restriction. The responsibility for proving otherwise lies on the side of those who favor a restriction. To prove a restriction, Hare and Harrington employ two arguments. (a) Hare and Harrington observe that the OT and the intertestamental literature know no uniform view of one universal judgment addressed to all humans as individuals. Rather, there are often two judgments, one for the Gentiles and another for Israel; this view may also be reflected in some NT passages.[19] Consequently, Matthew need not have seen the judgment described in 25:31-46 as applying to all human beings—Jews, Christians, and pagans. It is more probable, say Hare and Harrington, that *panta ta ethnē* refers to non-Christian Gentiles only, who cannot be judged on the same basis as Jews or Christians. (b) This last suggestion is supported by another argument: the pericope assumes that those being judged have had no direct contact with Jesus, either positive or negative (e.g., 25:37). The *panta ta ethnē* are therefore all the pagans. The good pagans are saved by their acts of love for the least of men (or Christian missionaries?) in whom Jesus is present and served.[20]

I find neither of these two arguments convincing. (a) Whatever may be said for the OT and the intertestamental literature, Matthew does seem to have the concept of one judgment for all, good and bad alike, Jew and Gentile alike. Such is the case in 8:11-12 (Gentiles will enter into the kingdom while Jews are excluded); 11:20-24 (it will be easier for Tyre and Sidon on the day of judgment than for the cities of Galilee); 12:41-42 (the men of Nineveh and the queen of the South will rise up at the

'Parable' of the Sheep and the Goats," in *Twelve New Testament Studies* (Naperville: Allenson, 1962) 76-93.

[19]Hare and Harrington, "'Make Disciples,'" 364-365.
[20]Ibid., 365.

judgment and condemn "this generation," i.e., unbelieving Israel); 13:36-43 (at the end of the age the final separation of good and bad will affect the whole *kosmos*).[21] It is this one, general judgment *en hēmerā kriseōs* (11:22) that is depicted in 25:31-46. Consequently, it is almost impossible to take *panta ta ethnē* in anything but its most universal sense, which includes the Jews. (b) Is it true to say that the "passage assumes that those being judged had no direct contact with Jesus, either positive or negative"[22] (with appeal to their surprised question to prove the point)? Nothing in the passage leads one to believe that *panta ta ethnē* have not previously known (or at least known about) this Son of Man who now judges them. No introductions are necessary, and their surprised questions do *not* concern the fact that it is Jesus of Nazareth, the Son of Man, who is judging them. Their surprise is rather directed at the astounding revelation that this majestic judge was present in the least of men, that what the *panta ta ethnē* did to the least they did to the judge, and that therefore their deeds of kindness to the poor (or lack thereof) are the all-decisive criterion of judgment. Such a state of affairs does not indicate that the *panta ta ethnē* have, up until this day of judgment, been ignorant of Jesus. What they have been ignorant of is the hidden identification of Jesus with the least of his brethren. That, not the person of Jesus, is what is now revealed for the first time on the day of judgment. There is no reason, therefore, to restrict *panta ta ethnē* to "non-Christian Gentiles."[23]

---

[21]Lange, *Erscheinen*, 298, gives these passages their due, and yet wishes to restrict the *panta ta ethnē* to the Gentiles. Accordingly, he is reduced to suggesting that in 25:31-46 Matthew does not advert to the difficulty that elsewhere (in the passages we list above) he *does* place Israel at the last judgment. A strange lapse of memory! That a future judgment still awaits the already condemned Israel is also indicated by such passages as 19:28 and 23:39 —which, in the light of the texts cited above, should not be understood as a totally separate judgment for Israel, kept apart from the general judgment of mankind. To sum up: the various phases of the judgment and condemnation of Israel within history (chap. 23, the death-resurrection of Jesus, the destruction of the temple) do not exclude the meta-historical judgment *en hēmera kriseōs*.

[22]Hare and Harrington, "'Make Disciples,'" 365.

[23]Ibid.

Conclusion

I began this investigation by saying that the position I espoused enjoyed not absolute certainty but the weight of preponderant evidence. Reviewing the evidence, I think that the claim has been justified. Of the seven cases where *ethnē* means "Gentiles," three were explicit OT citations, and none was a pure redactional creation of Matthew. Likewise, of the two occurrences which were initially judged to be doubtful, neither was simply a Matthean creation. It was only when we examined cases where *ethnos/ethnē* could not be restricted to "Gentiles" that we found a completely redactional creation of Matthew. Mt 21:43 was not only a creation of Matthew but also the vehicle of a new meaning for *ethnos:* the *tertia gens,* the people of God made up of both Jews and Gentiles, the church. Mt 24:7 (=Mk 13:8) showed that both the Jewish people and an opposing people could be designated *ethnos (ethnos epi ethnos).* This led to the question: what could be more natural than for Matthew to understand *panta ta ethnē* as including both Jews and Gentiles? Mt 24:14 re-edited Mk 13:10 with the all-important addition, *en holę̄ tę̄ oikoumenę̄,* which made a restrictive interpretation of *pasin tois ethnesin* extremely improbable. Granted this interpretation of both 24:7 and 24:14, we then decided to revise our judgment on 24:9 in view of its larger context and place it among those occurrences of *ethnos/ethnē* which most probably are not restricted to Gentiles. Finally, we argued that Mt 25:32 (be it special tradition or redactional creation) speaks of *panta ta ethnē* in the context of the one final judgment, that nothing indicates these *ethnē* have as a group been previously ignorant of Jesus, and that therefore there is no reason to restrict the reference to non-Christian Gentiles. Summing up, we have seven cases where *ethnē* clearly means "Gentiles," one case that is doubtful, and five cases where the sense cannot be limited to "Gentiles." But, on further examination, we find that the latter five cases not only show the most creative activity on the part of the redactor but also contain three out of the four occurrences of *ethnē* modified by *panta ta.* The fourth occurrence is precisely

Mt 28:19, which is set in a pericope which is either heavily[24] or totally[25] redactional. I would submit, then, that the weight of preponderant evidence is in favor of taking the fourth occurrence of *panta ta ethnē*, like the other three, to mean "all the nations," or "all peoples." Israel, the unique chosen people of God, is indeed an entity of the past for Matthew; it had its hour of critical choice, and failed to choose rightly. But the *Ioudaioi* remain a present reality for Matthew's church (28:15: *para Ioudaiois mechri tēs sēmeron*). In Matthew's eyes they no longer enjoy the former privileged status of the chosen people of God (21:43). But they do qualify in Matthew's vocabulary as an *enthos* (24:7). And so they do fall under the mandate of the risen Jesus to make disciples of *panta ta ethnē* (28:19).

❧

Afterword

Scholars defending both positions can still be found. The editorial board revising the *New American Bible's* New Testament decided that the translation "nations" was more probable.

---

[24]So G. Strecker, *Der Weg der Gerechtigkeit* (3d ed.; Göttingen: Vandenhoeck & Ruprecht, 1971) 208-210. I shall defend a similar view in the following essay. Cf. also B. Hubbard, *The Matthean Redaction of a Primitive Apostolic Commissioning* (Missoula: Scholars Press, 1974). As the title indicates, Hubbard thinks he can detect the narrative of a post-resurrection commissioning behind 28:16-20. On the question of the meaning of *panta ta ethnē*, Hubbard follows Trilling; see *Matthean Redaction*, 84-87.

[25]This is one of the main theses proposed throughout Lange's *Erscheinen*.

This translation has also been accepted by various recent commentaries; see, e.g., Francis W. Beare, *The Gospel According to Matthew* (Peabody, MA: Hendrickson, 1981) 543-44; and Daniel Patte, *The Gospel According to Matthew* (Philadelphia: Fortress, 1987) 400. Monographs on Matthew that, in varying ways, defend this translation include Jane Schaberg, *The Father, the Son and the Holy Spirit* (SBLDS 61; Chico, CA: Scholars, 1982); and Terence L. Donaldson, *Jesus on the Mountain* (JSNTSup 8; Sheffield; JSOT, 1985) 183-84 and n. 74 on pp. 281-82. Lest I seem to be claiming that all the nations have rallied to my opinion, I should note that Pheme Perkins prefers "Gentiles"; see her *Resurrection* (Garden City, NY: Doubleday, 1984) 134-35 and n. 83 on p. 147. She appeals to the view of S. Brown in his article, "The Matthean Community and the Gentile Mission," *NovT* 22 (1980) 193-221.

8

Two Disputed Questions
in Matthew 28:16-20

There are certain great pericopes in the bible which constantly engender discussion and research, while apparently never admitting of definite solutions. Mt 28:16-20 seems to be such a pericope. The one thing scholars are agreed upon is the pivotal nature of these verses.[1] Indicative of the pericope's riches is the fact that, after so much has been written on the subject, J. Lange could still author a monograph of 573 pages on these five verses,[2] only to be followed by B. Hubbard, who has given us a more modest (yet more satisfying) 187 pages simply on the pericope's *Gattung*.[3] And yet what Lange and, to a degree, Hubbard have done is to provide us not with definitive solutions, but with more material for debate. The purpose of the present essay is to take issue with Lange on the question of tradition and redaction, and with Hubbard on the question of *Gattung*.[4] I am convinced that larger questions such as the

---

[1]O. Michel ("Der Abschluss des Matthäusevangeliums," *EvT* 10 [1950] 21) says that Mt 28:18-20 is the key to the understanding of the whole gospel.

[2]J. Lange, *Das Erscheinen des Auferstandenen im Evangelium nach Mattäus* (Würzburg: Echter, 1973); a full bibliography on Mt 28:16-20 can be found on pp. 513-536 of this monograph.

[3]B. Hubbard, *The Matthean Redaction of a Primitive Apostolic Commissioning: an Exegesis of Matthew 28:16-20* (SBLDS 19; Missoula: Scholars Press, 1974).

[4]I use "form" and *Gattung* interchangeably here, although I realize that some scholars have suggested a distinction between the two. The problem is that different scholars make different distinctions.

dominant Christology of Mt 28:16-20 and the pericope's function within the whole gospel can be properly dealt with only after these two pedestrian but pivotal questions are solved. And, as we shall see, it is not by accident that our two questions are treated together. They are interrelated and, in particular, the question of *Gattung* demands a prior solution to the question of tradition and redaction.

I. Tradition and Redaction

Did the evangelist use previous traditions in the composition of Mt 28:16-20, or is it his own redactional creation pure and simple? Since we lack any direct synoptic parallel, we have to rely largely on word statistics and stylistic peculiarities. Although this approach supplies us only with a rough rule-of-thumb, it is the best canon we have.[5] A heavy concentration of words, style, and thought that are peculiarly Matthean is a good sign of Matthean redaction. The absence of these elements may indicate earlier tradition—especially, if we can find motifs or phrases untypical of Matthew, or ideas which stand in tension with the Matthean context.

It must be admitted from the start that the results of this method are not unambiguous. Two Matthean scholars, G. Strecker[6] and J. Lange,[7] have applied this criterion of vocabulary and style to 28:16-20, with differing results. Both would agree on the clear presence of Matthew's heavy editorial hand. But, while Strecker would hold for some pre-Matthean tradition, Lange thinks the whole pericope is a Matthean creation, modeled on the Q-saying in Mt 11:27. Indeed, he calls 28:16-20 a new edition of 11:27. Since I think Strecker has the better part of the argument, I shall first present a verse-by-verse

---

[5]I think this canon is preferable to Hubbard's approach *via* the criterion of *Gattung*. The reason for the preference will be clear at the end of this chapter.

[6]G. Strecker, *Der Weg der Gerechtigkeit* (3rd ed.; Göttingen: Vandenhoeck & Ruprecht, 1971) 208-214.

[7]Lange, *Erscheinen,* 488-506 (summary of thesis). While Hubbard also pays attention to Matthean vocabulary and style, the data in Strecker and Lange are more complete.

argumentation of a position similar to Strecker's, and then confront the opposite position of Lange.[8]

A. THE ARGUMENT FOR TRADITION

(1) *V 16: hoi de hendeka mathētai eporeuthē san eis tēn Galilaian eis to oros hou etaxato autois ho Iēsous.* (a) Matthew tends to identify *hoi mathētai* with *hoi dōdeka*;[9] and Matthew, alone among the four evangelists, gives within the passion narrative a detailed story of the end of Judas (27:3-10). The precise designation of the group of disciples as *hoi hendeka mathētai* thus fits in well with Matthean tendencies. (b) The words *eis tēn Galilaian* take up the phrase that Matthew repeats from Mark in Mt 28:7: *kai idou proagei hymas eis tēn Galilaian, ekei auton opsesthe*—a phrase that is repeated almost word-for-word in the rather otiose apparition of Jesus to the women running from the grave (a pericope only in Matthew): *hina apelthōsin eis tēn Galilaian* (v 10). *Eis tēn Galilaian* would seem to be a catchword used to tie the pericopes in chap. 28 together. Matthew's love of both catchwords and the theological symbol Galilee is well known.[10] (c) The *oros*-motif is also typical of Matthew. Omitting neutral uses, we can list as theologically significant: 4:8, mount of temptation; 5:1 and 8:1, mount of teaching (redactional); 14:23, mount of prayer; 15:29, mount of healing and feeding (redactional); and 17:1 + 9, mount of transfiguration. So, although a mountain has not been mentioned in the immediately preceding context, its appearance should cause no surprise and *in*

[8]While my position owes a great deal to Strecker's insights (cf. especially *Weg*, 208-211), in what follows I shall be disagreeing with or modifying a number of his views. Strecker's basic position is shared by G. Bornkamm, "Der Auferstandene und der Irdische," in G. Bornkamm-G. Barth-H. Held, *Überlieferung und Auslegung im Matthäusevangelium* (5th ed.; Neukirchen: Neukirchener Verlag, 1968) 289. Bornkamm, in turn, appeals to R. Bultmann, *Geschichte der synoptischen Tradition* (8th ed.; Göttingen: Vandenhoeck & Ruprecht, 1970) 312-313.

[9]Cf. R. Pesch, "Levi-Matthäus (Mc 2:14/Mt 9:9; 10:3), ein Beitrag zur Lösung eines alten Problems," *ZNW* 59 (1968) 40-56.

[10]Lange, *Erscheinen*, 358-391; Lange claims Matthew has a special interest in half-Gentile, underprivileged Galilee as the place of Jesus' "exile."

itself is no argument for previous tradition.[11] (d) I must stress the *in itself* of the last sentence. For, while the *eis tēn Galilaian* is based on 28:7 + 10 and the *eis to oros* is explicable as a Matthean theologoumenon, the *hou etaxato autois ho Iēsous* cannot be explained simply by an appeal to Matthean redaction. Nothing either in the context of chap. 28 or in Matthean redactional tendencies explains the *hou etaxato*.[12] The directives in 28:7 + 10 mentioned Galilee, but said nothing about a mountain. Our suspicions are further aroused by the fact that the simple *tassō* is a hapax legomenon in Matthew and the fact that, while *hou* is used two other times in Mt (2:9 and 18:20, both times in the sense of "where"), this is the only place in Matthew where *hou* is used in the sense of "whither." A characterization of the Galilean mountain which is not prepared for in the previous text, plus two unusual linguistic usages, make the hypothesis of pre-Matthean tradition likely for the *hou etaxato* clause.

(2) *V 17: kai idontes auton prosekynēsan, hoi de edistasan.* (a) The participle *idōn/idontes* + an accusative or dependent clause is used throughout the whole gospel, almost as an unnoticed appendage. The usage is preponderantly redactional, and may indeed be redactional here. But, again, there may be a certain tension with the preceding context. The whole message of the angel in 28:1-7 leads up to the promise: *ekei auton opsesthe.* And this cannot be put down simply to Markan tradition; Matthew stresses the promise by repeating it in v 10: *kakei me opsontai.* If the seeing is so stressed in the first part of chap. 28, why is it practically ignored in 28:16-20, and in v 17 in particular? (b) *Proskyneō* is a typically Matthean word (Matthew: 13x; Mark: 2x; Luke: 2x). (c) *Distazō* occurs in the NT only here and in Mt 14:31, where Jesus says to the sinking Peter: *oligopiste, eis ti edistasas* (a Matthean insertion into the Markan story of the walking on the water). The use of *distazō* and the whole motif of the obedient/worshiping disciple who

---

[11]For "Galilee" and "the mountain," see further E. Lohmeyer, *Galiläa und Jerusalem* (Göttingen: Vandenhoeck & Ruprecht, 1936) 16, and Hubbard, *Matthean Redaction,* 73.

[12]Strecker *(Weg,* 98 and 208*)* misses this point, as do Hubbard and many others.

nevertheless wavers, mark *hoi de edistasan* as redactional.[13] Thus, as a provisional judgment on the narrative framework of our pericope, we can say that most of it seems redactional, with the exception of the end of v 16, and perhaps the inconsistency involved in the lack of stress on seeing Jesus.

(3) *V 18: kai proselthōn ho Iēsous elalēsen autois legōn, edothē moi pasa exousia en ouranǭ kai epi gēs.* (a) *Proserchomai* occurs 87x in the NT; in Matthew it occurs 52x, while it occurs in Mark 5x and in Luke 10x. In Matthew, the only other time the word is used of an action of Jesus is in the transfiguration story (Mt 17:7), where it is clearly redactional vis-à-vis Mark. Such seems to be the case here as well. (b) The phrase *elalēsen autois legōn* has many parallels in Matthean redactional material (e.g. 13:3; 14:27; 23:1). (c) Our automatic inclination would be to declare *exousia* a Matthean redactional term without further ado; indeed, as we shall see, Lange is very strong on this point. But the data are not so clear-cut. For one thing, from a merely statistical viewpoint, *exousia* is not peculiarly Matthean (Matthew: 10x; Mark: 10x; Luke: 16x). Moreover, the thought cannot be called peculiarly Matthean. Matthew never uses *exousia* elsewhere of Jesus' lordship over the whole cosmos, though the use of *exousia* for cosmic lordship has parallels in the extra-Matthean traditions (LXX Dan 7:14; Jn 5:27). (d) The conjunction of *ouranǭ* and *gēs* with both nouns in the singular does not seem to be redactional. The conjunction or opposition of heaven and earth (in the singular) occurs in pre- and extra-Matthean traditions, but never in what can be clearly shown to be Matthean redaction. This certainly holds true of Mt 5:18 (Lk 16:17); Mt 5:34-35 (Jas 5:12); Mt 6:10 (a pre-Matthean liturgical form of the Our Father); Mt 11:25 (Lk 10:21); Mt 24:35 (Mk 13:31). While Mt 18:18 remains unclear, I tend to think it belongs to a pre-Matthean church order. Even the occurrences of *en tois ouranois* with *epi tēs gēs* in Mt 16:19 and 18:19 probably stem

---

[13]I might note as an aside that the whole question of *how* the wavering of some of the disciples is overcome is beside the point. The wavering (like understanding and adoring) is part of being a disciple in the present *corpus-mixtum* situation, which runs through the soul of every disciple. The very existence of the Matthean disciple is constituted by the tension of *pisteuō/syniēmi* versus *distazō/oligopistos.*

from pre-Matthean traditions concerning church order.

(4) *V 19: poreuthentes oun mathēteusate panta ta ethnē, baptizontes autous eis to onoma tou patros kai tou huiou kai tou hagiou pneumatos.* (a) V 19a *(poreuthentes ... ethnē)* may be conceded as redactional; both vocabulary and style are typically Matthean. (b) On the other hand, the triadic baptismal formula in v 19b is probably not redactional, since it never appears elsewhere in Matthew and since Matthew would not likely introduce a new baptismal formula into his church.[14]

(5) *V 20: didaskontes autous tērein panta hosa eneteilamēn hymin kai idou egō meth' hymōn eimi pasas tas hēmeras heōs tēs synteleias tou aiōnos.* The verse contains many typical Matthean words: *tēreō* (Matthew: 6x; Mark: 1x; Luke: 0); *panta hosa* (Matthew: 6x; Mark: 3x; Luke: 2x) *idou* (Matthew: 62x; Mark: 7x; Luke: 57x—but Matthew has the form *kai idou* 17x, and all but two of these cases are redactional); *synteleia* (5x in Matthew, 1x in Heb 9:26, which has *synteleia tōn aiōnōn*, while only Matthew has *synteleia tou aiōnos*). Despite all these signs of redaction, Strecker thinks that the promise of Jesus' presence *(egō meth' hymōn eimi)* is shown to be a pre-Matthean element by its appearance in another form in 18:20, while it is absent from Matthew's redaction.[15] The problem with Strecker's argument here is that he is appealing to a verse that has no parallel. It might possibly be redactional, though most critics refer it to a pre-redactional unit on church order. But we will put off further discussion of this point until we treat Lange's position on this verse.

To sum up our preliminary results: the narrative framework in vv 16-17 seems mostly redactional; but hints of previous tradition may be seen at the end of v 16 and perhaps in the tension about the theme of seeing Jesus. In the catena of logia (vv 18-20), vv 18a, 19a, and 20a are redactional, while 18b, 19b, and perhaps the basic statement in 20b are pre-Matthean tradition. The tradition(s) could have come to Matthew as

---

[14]Hubbard (*Matthean Redaction*, 151-175) has said all that needs to be said in defense of the textual authenticity of the triadic formula in Mt 28:19b.

[15]Strecker, *Weg*, 209.

individual logia, which Matthew united for the first time.[16] But Strecker thinks that the baptismal formula in v 19b did not float isolated in the tradition; it demanded some context.[17] The same might be said also of 18b. It is a citation of LXX Dan 7:14 and echoes Mt 11:27, both of which stand in a wider context. Finally, Strecker argues from analogy that probably v 20b was not floating isolated (a point to which we shall return when we treat Lange's position). Strecker suggests that the three logia, or at least the motifs behind them, already formed a tripartite word of revelation dealing with: (a) the power of the exalted one, v 18b; (b) his command to baptize, v 19b; (c) the promise of his presence, v 20b. Strecker thinks this word of revelation had its *Sitz im Leben* in the liturgical tradition of Matthew's church, as v 19b indicates. Note how the three parts all suppose or express the church's belief in the presence or power of her exalted Lord, working in and through the community. So what Matthew has done is to take this tripartite liturgical tradition and heavily redact it to make it the vehicle of (a) the one great post-resurrection appearance of Jesus to the eleven in Galilee: and (b) the great missionary commission (*mathēteusate panta ta ethnē ... didaskontes autous tērein panta hosa eneteilamēn hymin*). What was at hand to Matthew was a liturgical tradition: what Matthew added to it was the idea of universal mission to all nations, who are to be taught the commands which Jesus gave during his earthly life.[18]

B. THE POSITION OF LANGE

In order to test the hypothesis sketched above, I shall now compare it with the opposite opinion of Lange, namely, that

---

[16]Cf. Michel, "Abschluss," 20, and G. Barth, "Das Gesetzesverständnis des Evangelisten Matthäus," in G. Bornkamm-G. Barth-H. Held, *Überlieferung und Auslegung,* 124-125 n. 3.

[17]Strecker, *Weg,* 210.

[18]Cf. Strecker's additional comments in the *Nachtrag* to *Weg,* 255. He rejects F. Hahn's view that the pre-Matthean tradition witnesses to the Hellenistic Jewish-Christian understanding of mission; rather, the pre-Matthean tradition dealt with the manifestation of the *exousia* of the exalted one in the administration of baptism.

Mt 28:16-20 is entirely a Matthean creation. We need not review the phrases which both Lange and I consider redactional. What we must investigate are those places where Lange's claim of Matthean redaction disagrees with the position I have outlined. There are five points of major disagreement.

(1) *eis to oros hou extaxato autois ho Iēsous.* As we stressed above, while the mountain in Galilee could in itself be a Matthean theologoumenon, there is no way in which the exact identification "whither Jesus had ordered them [to go]" can be explained on a redactional basis. Lange seems not to realize the extent of the problem. Symptomatic of his treatment is the fact that, while the two words *Galilaia* and *oros* are studied for some ninety pages,[19] the whole clause *hou etaxato* etc. receives only a cursory glance.[20] Lange tries to explain this clause by appealing to the Matthean schema of command/fulfillment of command which has been studied so well by R. Pesch.[21] But it seems to have escaped Lange's attention that a major emphasis in this schema is the exact correspondence between command and fulfillment (e.g. Mt 1:24; 21:6; 26:19; 28:15). In fact, it is the command that is usually more circumstantial, while the fulfillment of the command is narrated quite succinctly. The problem with the last clause in 28:16 is that *oros hou etaxato* etc. corresponds to nothing in the commands (28:7 + 10). By a strange paradox, Lange's ineffectual handling of the problem causes the reader to favor the very thesis Lange is trying to refute: namely, that behind Mt 28:16-20 there may lie a tradition similar to Acts 1:6-12.[22] Putting these two pericopes together may at first seem strange, since the Matthean and Lukan presentations of the risen Lord are so different.[23] And

[19]Lange, *Erscheinen*, 358-446.

[20]Ibid., 436-440 and 448-450.

[21]R. Pesch, "Eine alttestamentliche Ausführungsformel im Matthäus-Evangelium," *BZ* 10 (1966) 220-245 and *BZ* 11 (1967) 79-95.

[22]Lange (*Erscheinen*, 437 n. 91) names as proponents of this thesis M. Goguel, H. Bartsch, and J. Schmid. In support of his own view, Lange appeals to G. Lohfink, *Die Himmelfahrt Jesu* (Munich: Kösel, 1971) 153-158, 186-202, 208-211, and 239-241.

[23]For the standard presentation of the material, cf. H. Grass, *Ostergeschehen und Osterberichte* (4th ed.; Göttingen: Vandenhoeck & Ruprecht, 1970) 28-32 and 43-50.

yet, if we abstract from the redactional tendencies of each author, we discern a tradition, dealing with an appearance of the risen Lord on a mount (Mt 28:16/ Acts 1:12), with a tripartite schema. The tradition spoke of (a) the *exaltation* of Jesus (Mt 28:18b/ Acts 1:9-11); (b) the command to start a *mission* (Mt 28:19a or 20a/ Acts 1:8b); (c) the promise of assistance (Mt 28:20b/ Acts 1:8). Of course, one cannot press such correspondence too far. In any case, each evangelist has developed the traditional schema and motifs according to his own theological ideas and vocabulary (Matthew: mount in Galilee, Luke: Mount of Olives near Jerusalem: Matthew: exaltation *is* the resurrection, Luke: exaltation is a separate ascension forty days later; Matthew: the support is the perduring presence of Jesus who does not depart *from* but comes *to* the church, Luke: the support is the coming of the Holy Spirit, sent by Jesus after he departs). Also, one might wonder if, in accordance with Strecker's schema (also tripartite), Mt 28:19b (some type of baptismal formula) might not be substituted as the traditional element indicating mission or aggregation to the church. However that may be, I do think Lange's attempt to assign the whole of 28:16-20 to the redactor's creativity is weakened *certainly* by the last clause in v 16 and *perhaps* by a possible schema that lies behind Mt 28:16-20 and Acts 1:6-12.[24]

(2) *Edothē moi pasa exousia en ouranǭ kai epi gēs.* In two other works, I have defended the position that Matthew does intend to allude to LXX Dan 7:14 in 28:18b.[25] In this sense, v 18b is obviously not a pure Matthean creation. but, above and beyond this, I think Lange (largely following A. Vögtle[26]) has made three serious mistakes in his attempt to see this half-verse as purely redactional. (a) He tries to level all the *exousia-*

---

[24]While Hubbard examines the parallels of Mt 28:16-20 in Lk 24:36-53, Jn 20:19-23, and Mk 16:14-20, he does not (strange to say) consider Acts 1.

[25]*Law and History in Matthew's Gospel* (Rome: Biblical Institute, 1976). In reduced form, chapter two of this monograph appeared as "Salvation-History in Matthew: in Search of a Starting Point," the first essay in Part II of this volume.

[26]A. Vögtle, "Das christologische und ekklesiologische Anliegen von Mt. 28, 18-20," in *Studia Evangelica II* (ed. F. L. Cross; Berlin: Akademie, 1964) 266-294; cf. also F. Hahn, *Mission in the New Testament* (Naperville: Allenson, 1965) 66 n. 3.

passages in Matthew down to the common denominator of authority and power to teach. This involves the further error of ignoring or twisting those passages which refer Jesus' *exousia* to something else (8:9, healing [*exousia* here only indirectly of Jesus]; 9:6, 8, forgiving sins; 10:1, exorcism and healing; 21:23, 24, 27, perhaps teaching, but also cleansing of the temple, miracles in the temple, and approving the children's praise). *Only* Mt 7:29 uses *exousia* solely for teaching, and this verse is taken from Mk 1:22. (b) Consequently, Lange fails to see the new idea contained in *pasa exousia* in Mt 28:18. During the public ministry, various activities (teaching, healing, exorcism, forgiving sins, etc.) were put under the rubric of *exousia,* but this *exousia* was never given unlimited, cosmic dimensions. Now, for the first time, *all* power in heaven and on earth has been given; this is something definitely new, as is also the commission to the disciples to teach (contrast Mt 10:1, 7-8). While Lange sees that the joining of *pasa* to *exousia* is the redactor's work, he tries to defend the position that nothing new is contained in this *exousia*.[27] (c) The root of all these difficulties lies in the third and fundamental mistake: Lange makes too strict a parallel between Mt 28:18 and 11:27 *(panta moi paredothē).* Whatever the exact context of Mt 11:25-27 in Q (and of that we cannot be sure), in Matthew these verses give Jesus' reaction to the mystery of acceptance and rejection of his revelation after his initial ministry and that of his disciples. As the language makes clear (*ekrypsas ... apo sophōn kai synetōn kai apekalypsas auta nēpiois; epignōskei* used mutually of Father and Son; *apokalypsai* used of the activity of the Son), *panta moi paredothē* refers to the transmission and revelation of secrets and divine wisdom, given by the Father to the Son, and transmitted by the Son to mere children. This is not exactly the same motif as is found in

---

[27]Lange has great difficulty in explaining what the *pasa* means. In *Erscheinen,* 177, he states: "Er [Jesus] ist hier lediglich das 'geworden,' was er von Anfang an war [i.e., eschatological judge]." His embarrassment is clear on p. 177 n. 6: "Es erhebt sich die Frage, worin die *exousia* des Erhöhten denn überhaupt von der des Irdischen unterscheide. Die Antwort ist schwer zu geben, da der Evangelist und die Tradition vor ihm die *exousia* des Erhöhten ja gerade im Leben des Irdischen entdeckten und im Medium des Lebens des Irdischen zur Darstellung zu bringen trachteten. Dies aber dürfte nicht einmal ohne einen Grund in der Sache selbst so praktiziert worden sein."

28:18b, where the risen Jesus announces to the Eleven that the prophecy of Dan 7:14 has been fulfilled: he now possesses all authority in the cosmos and can command a universal mission. The perfect comment on this cosmocrator-image is Matthew's explanation of the parable of the wheat and the tares (13:36-43): the Son of Man rules over his Kingdom (v 41), which is the cosmos (v 38). This picture is not verified of the Matthean Jesus during his public ministry, restricted as it was to the land and people of Israel.[28] It is true only of the exalted Son of Man after the resurrection. To him all power in the whole cosmos (*ho kosmos*, 13:38; *en ouranō kai epi gēs*, 28:18) was given.[29]

(3) *en ouranō kai epi gēs*. Lange tries to hold that, while the phrase existed before Matthew (cf. the Our Father), it was inserted by Matthew in 28:18.[30] But, as we noted above (in A3d), this conjunction, with both nouns in the singular , never occurs in Matthean redaction, although it is witnessed in all the traditions (Mark, Q, and M). The weight of probability definitely lies on the side of tradition.

(4) *V 19b* (triadic baptismal formula). Lange claims that this is received tradition.[31] But he refuses to see it as embedded in some larger piece of tradition which might lie behind 28:16-20 (e.g., a tripartite word of revelation). Granted the various elements of tradition we have detected up until now, Lange's position seems unlikely.

(5) *V 20b* is perhaps the most difficult logion on which to make any decision. Lange presents solid arguments for its being totally the work of the redactor.[32] Redactional characteristics include (a) *kai idou;* (2) the use of *egō* when not strictly necessary; (c) *hēmera* for duration of time and points of time; (d) *synteleia tou aiōnos*. But, when we take a closer

---

[28]Cf. my "Salvation-History," the first essay in Part 2 of this volume.

[29]Writers who, with various nuances, hold some concept of exaltation enthronement, or a new conferment of power over the cosmos in 28:18b, are listed by Lange, *Erscheinen*, 175-178. Lange himself rejects such a concept for 28:18b.

[30]Ibid., 96-147, especially 147.

[31]Ibid., 313.

[32]Ibid., 328-329.

look, we see that most of Lange's arguments do not prove all that much. (a) *Kai idou* appears 17x in Matthew, but also 17x in Luke, 6x in Acts (sometimes as *kai nyn idou*), and 11x in Revelation. Within the NT, then, it is hardly unique to Matthean redactional activity, especially since at least two Matthean examples come from Q (Mt 12:41, 42). (b) As for *egō*, the use in 28:20 is, I think, not lax, but rather in accordance with classical usage for the sake of emphasis or solemnity. At any rate, Matthew is not unique in his frequent use of the singular of the first person pronoun in the nominative case (Matthew: 28x; Mark: 16x; Luke: 22x; John: 132x [!]; Acts: 44x). (c) While Matthew uses the word *hēmera* 45x, the phrase *pasas tas hēmeras* occurs in Matthew only at 28:20. Indeed, in this precise form (accusative of duration, no further modifiers), the phrase is a hapax legomenon in the NT. Furthermore, the frequent use of *hēmera* is not unique to Matthew; Mark has it 27x; Luke: 83x; Acts: 94x; and John: 31x (only constructions with some form of *pas* are rare). The upshot of all this is that only the very last words of 28:20 (*heōs tēs synteleias tou aiōnos*) are clearly redactional.

What of the core statement, *egō meth' hymōn eimi?* This statement takes up the interpretation of Emmanuel in 1:23, *meth'hēmōn ho theos* (forming a sort of inclusion), and is also reminiscent of Jesus' promise of his presence to the church in 18:20: *ekei eimi en mesǭ autōn.*[33] Clearly the arrangement of the theme at the beginning and end of the gospel is redactional. But are the basic statements themselves creations of Matthew? It is difficult to say, because, if they are not redactional, they come to Matthew from his special traditions globally labeled M). And it is often extremely difficult to distinguish M from redaction. Let us take the verses one by one. (a) Firstly, concerning 18:20: in chap. 18, Matthew uses various traditions to draw up regulations for community life. The rules and sayings that immediately precede vv 19-20 (i.e., vv 15-18) reflect how the community conducts itself in disciplinary questions,

---

[33]Ibid., 328-349, which also treat other passages that touch on the theme of the presence or absence of Jesus. For a treatment of *meth' hymōn*, see also H. Frankemölle, *Jahwebund und Kirche Christi* (Münster: Aschendorff, 1974).

and are probably not the creation of Matthew. He is not creating church order for the first time. By analogy, the same can probably be said of vv 19-20; they reflect the community's understanding of itself at prayer. This self-understanding is taken over by Matthew from his community; it is probably not created by Matthew and imposed on the community. Moreover, the similarity of 18:20 to Jewish conceptions of Torah-study and the Shekinah may also argue for a pre-Matthean, Jewish-Christian origin, as Bultmann thinks.[34] (b) Secondly, concerning 1:23: the basic tradition of the virginal conception existed before Matthew, as we can see from the independent traditions in Luke. The existence of a *Reflexionszitat* such as 1:23 prior to Matthew is more problematic. But at least we may note that E. Schweizer holds in his commentary on Matthew that the explanation of the name Emmanuel, which would be self-explanatory only to readers knowing Hebrew, must have existed before Matthew, and that probably the citation of LXX Isa 7:14 was already connected with the story of the birth of Jesus before Matthew's redaction, as can be seen from Lk 1:31.[35] The fact that *methermēneuomenon* (Mt 1:23) is a hapax legomenon in Matthew may be seen as supporting this view.[36] If, then, we may trust the views of Bultmann, Schweizer, and Strecker, both 1:23 and 18:20 belong to pre-Matthean tradition. There is thus a fair possibility that the basic statement in 28:20b is likewise traditional.

Consequently, we do not think that Lange has proved his thesis that 28:16-20 is totally the product of Matthean redaction, a new edition of 11:27. We submit that there is much to be said for the view that behind the heavily redacted pericope 28:16-20 there lies some pre-Matthean tradition. While we cannot say what the exact wording of this tradition was, it seems to have involved the following elements; (a) an

---

[34]Bultmann, *Geschichte*, 158, 161; he even suggests that 18:20 may go back to the primitive Palestinian church (p. 176).

[35]E. Schweizer, *Das Evangelium nach Matthäus* (Göttingen: Vandenhoeck & Ruprecht, 1973) 12.

[36]So with Strecker (*Weg,* 56 n. 3) and against Frankemölle (*Jahwebund,* 17 n. 41).

appearance of the risen Christ in Galilee, on a mount to which he had ordered his disciples to go;[37] (b) a statement concerning exaltation or enthronement;[38] (c) a command to baptize, or alternately, some sort of command to begin a mission; (d) perhaps even a promise of continuing divine support in this mission—although this element remains the most doubtful of the four.[39]

II. The Question of Gattung

Our second disputed question is: to what form-critical category does 28:16-20 belong? I would maintain that an attempt to solve this question without attending to the question of tradition and redaction has led to an endless multiplication of suggestions, none of which has proved totally satisfactory. I admit this is a rather sweeping statement. To sustain it, I must quickly review the major suggestions made in this century and try to indicate briefly why each is inadequate.[40]

[37]Note that here I would assign to the tradition some details that Hubbard would assign to Matthew's redaction (*Matthean Redaction*, 122-123, 131). On the other hand, I do not feel certain as to whether any reaction of the disciples was mentioned in the tradition.

[38]Hubbard sees this as Matthean editing (*Matthean Redaction*, 128-129).

[39]I will be treating Hubbard's thesis on the *Gattung* of (and tradition behind) Mt 28:16-20 in Part II of this article. But I might note here one difference between Hubbard and myself which is the origin of many other differences: namely, the difference in method. I have worked "backwards" from the present text of Matthew, using criteria of language, style, and motifs to decide what is Matthew's redaction and what is underlying tradition. Hubbard works "forward" by discerning an OT commission-pattern and then trying to apply it to Matthew and other NT authors. The problem of his method, as we shall see in Part II, is the inherent danger of pressing a highly idiosyncratic text of Matthew into a predetermined pattern.

[40]For surveys of solutions, see Lange, *Erscheinen,* 349-354 (only for 28:18b-20, like many other writers); Frankemölle, *Jahwebund,* 46-48; and (more extensively) Hubbard, *Matthean Redaction,* 2-23. From Hubbard's list I omit what seems hopelessly wrong (e.g., J. Munck's categorizing of 28:19-20 as a farewell speech) or irrelevant (F. Hahn's treatment of 28:18-20, which never really focuses on the question of *Gattung,* except for references to the enthronement pattern; Hahn's concern is rather with the concept of mission). I have tried to expand or add material where the treatment seems incomplete (e.g., Bultmann, Trilling). Since I have treated Strecker's theory concerning vv 18-20 as a "word of revelation" in Part I, I shall not repeat his view here, especially since the major interest is the *Gattung* of vv 16-20 as a unit.

Strange to say, many critics have not really posed the form-critical question in reference to 28:16-20 as a whole. A good amount of recent work concentrates to a large degree—or even exclusively—on the form of vv 18b-20.[41] Now, there is nothing wrong with discerning various sub-forms or component-forms within parts of a pericope. But the primary datum, the unit or pericope lying before us in the gospel as it now stands, is vv 16-20, not vv 18b-20. A consideration of various sub-forms which does not issue in a judgment concerning the form of the pericope as a whole is inadequate. Yet we are faced with the fact that many authors treat only vv 18b-20. What we shall do, then, is first examine the attempts to categorize vv 18b-20 and then see whether any of the suggested categories helps us with our main concern, the *Gattung* of vv 16-20. But, even a priori, we can see that the first group of suggestions will not supply an adequate answer to our question.

A. THE GATTUNG OF vv 18b-20

(1) I begin with M. Dibelius, since he designates vv 18-20 as a missionary command (combination of self-presentation and call to preaching) with mythic character (all power in heaven and on earth, presence to the end of the age).[42] This designation raises the fundamental question: is "missionary command," which strictly speaking refers only to vv 19-20a, an adequate description of the whole of vv 18-20, to say nothing of vv 16-20? For reasons which will become clear as we treat the other suggestions, we think not. It focuses on only one element, and does not adequately designate the whole.

(2) Depending on the work of OT scholars dealing with the ideology of kingship in the Ancient Near East, J. Jeremias[43]

---

[41] Hubbard, in particular, is a happy exception to the general tendency (cf. *Matthean Redaction*, 2).

[42] M. Dibelius, *Die Formgeschichte des Evangeliums* (6th ed.; Tübingen: Mohr, 1971) 285.

[43] J. Jeremias, *Jesus' Promise to the Nations* (London: SCM, 1967) 38-39; cf. also his *Die Briefe an Timotheus und Titus* (9th ed.; Göttingen: Vandenhoeck & Ruprecht, 1968) 22-25.

and O. Michel[44] have suggested that we have in vv 18-20 the pattern of a ritual of royal enthronement. Jeremias has traced such a pattern in 1 Tim 3:16, as well as in Phil 2:9-11 and Heb 1:5-14. Michel in particular has applied the pattern to the exegesis of our pericope. According to this approach, the most important point in the pericope is not the missionary charge in itself, but rather the idea of the enthronement or exaltation of the Son of Man. The form-critical category most appropriate would thus be "enthronement hymn." I find this solution attractive, since it would conveniently agree with the views I have propounded in other publications on Matthew:[45] Matthew has a good amount of realized eschatology in his theology; he presents the death-resurrection of Jesus as the "turning of the ages"; and he makes 28:16-20 something of a "proleptic parousia." But, despite the attractiveness of the enthronement-hymn pattern, there are some real problems. The ancient near eastern enthronement ritual had three acts: (a) exaltation to the divine realm; (b) presentation to the pantheon or proclamation of the name; (c) enthronement proper: the handing over of power, accompanied by acclamation. With monotheistic modifications, one might trace such a pattern in Phil 2:9-11 or 1 Tim 3:16. However, it does not really fit Mt 28:18-20, for three reasons. (a) While we may not want to categorize the entire section as a "missionary charge," still the missionary command in vv 19-20a is very important to the pericope. These verses speak not of an enthronement but rather of a commission: the emphasis is not on what is done to Jesus, but on what the disciples are to do on his authority. (b) The authority mentioned in v 18b is not thought of as conferred on Jesus at the moment the words of vv 18-20 are spoken; rather, the conferment of power is presupposed and narrated as a past event (aorist: *edothē*). Note, too, that Jesus is not spoken about in these verses; he speaks in the first person, which is contrary to the hymnic pattern of Philippians 2 and 1 Timothy 3. (c) Finally, 28:20b simply cannot be pressed into the schema;

44Michel, "Abschluss," 22-23.

45See n. 25 above.

it says nothing about handing over power or acclaiming.[46]

(3) E. Lohmeyer[47] suggested that the verses might follow the schema of the S^ema^c: (a) self-revelation of the speaker (v 18b)= "Hear, O Israel, the LORD, our God, is one LORD"; (b) commission (19-20)=command of love; (c) promise (20b). Lohmeyer admits he faces a problem with part (c), which finds no clear-cut correlative in the S^ema^c. All Lohmeyer can do is note that a divine promise is often found in other passages, following upon a divine command.

(4) W. Trilling[48] rightly stresses the difficulty of finding any one satisfactory category for our pericope. Emphasizing the missionary charge (vv 19-20a) as the midpoint (the words about authority and presence provide a framework), and the section's place at the end of the gospel, Trilling at first calls the pericope a "Testament" or (with Harnack) a "Manifest." The fact that each of the three logia in vv 18-20 may have had a creedal or liturgical formula as its origin may explain why it is so hard to choose one form-critical category for the whole. Vv 18-20 contain both a profession of faith in Christ and a community rule, but neither designation does justice to the whole, in which Christological and ecclesiological motifs are combined in typically Matthean fashion. Having said all this, Trilling then goes on to observe that vv 18-20, with its succession of word of revelation, command, and promise, seems akin to the OT pattern of divine speech (*Gottesrede*). Trilling admits that no one OT text has all three elements in such a compact form. At times, the OT has the first two elements (e.g., the beginning of the decalogue), at times the last two elements (e.g., Jer 1:7-8). Despite the lack of a perfect OT parallel, Trilling thinks that this OT pattern may have provided

---

[46]A point made by Lange, *Erscheinen*, 350; cf. also the objections of Hubbard, *Matthean Redaction*, 9.

[47]E. Lohmeyer, "'Mir ist gegeben alle Gewalt!'," in *In Memoriam Ernst Lohmeyer* (ed. W. Schmauch; Stuttgart: Evangelischer Verlag, 1951) 22-49, especially 33-34.

[48]W. Trilling, *Das wahre Israel* (3rd ed.; Munich: Kösel, 1964) 45-49. It should be noted that all the references in the present article are to the *third* edition of Trilling's monograph; his treatment of Mt 28:18-20 in the *second* edition of his work (Leipzig: St. Benno-Verlag, 1961) is somewhat different.

an exemplar for Matthew.[49]

(5) B. Malina[50] has the merit of distinguishing between the two questions of the form of vv 18-20 and the form of vv 16-20 (though he never explicates his view on the form of vv 16-20). For vv 18-20, Malina thinks the closest parallel is the royal decree of Cyrus that concludes the second book of Chronicles (2 Chr 36:23). The decree is a variant of the basic OT messenger form (with a report in the perfect and a command in the imperative). This form (isolated by C. Westermann) is similar to the official yet filial message of Joseph to Jacob in Gen 45:9-11: (a) Message formula: *tade legei ho huios sou Iōsēph;* (b) Narration (report): *epoiēsen me ho theos kyrion pasēs gēs Aigyptou;* (c) Command (summons): *katabēthi;* (d) Motivation: *kai katoikēseis en gē̦ Gesem.* This form is seen in 2 Chr 36:23.

(a) Message formula: *tade legei Kyros basileus Persōn*

(b) Narration: (i) Statement of authority: *pasas tas basileias tēs gēs edōken moi kyrios ho theos tou ouranou*

(ii) Reason for command: *kai autos eneteilato moi oikodomē sai oikon autō̦ en Ierousalēm en tē̦ Ioudaia̦*

(c) Command: (i) Those commanded: *tis ex hymōn ek pantos tou laou autou*

(ii) Motivation: *estai ho theos autou met' autou* (probably in the sense of: *may* his God be with him)

(iii) Command proper: *kai anabētō*

Malina sees Mt 28:18-20 as structured in the same way:

(a) Messenger formula: here refashioned as a narrative introduction to Jesus' decree.

---

[49]Ibid., 48-49. Lange (*Erscheinen,* 351) goes beyond Trilling in claiming that in Exod 3:6-12 and Jer 1:4-8 all three elements can be found; but even Lange has to admit that in these passages the form is not as compact and precise as in Matthew. Lange goes on, however, to state his preference for the solution of B. Malina (see n. 50).

[50]B. Malina, "The Literary Structure and Form of Matt XXVIII. 16-20," *NTS* 17 (1970) 87-103.

(b) Narrative: statement of authority, the basis of the obligation that follows (aorist).

(c) Command: a community regulation expressing the law-duty-custom of a specific group (imperative+participles).

(d) Motivation: same as 2 Chronicles, except for the present tense.

A brief comparison of these three texts points up many dissimilarities as well as similarities. In the decree of Cyrus, we have a very complex situation: God gives a command to the king, so the king gives a command to the people. This structure is not present in either Genesis or Matthew. The messenger formula, which is part of the spoken statement, simply does not appear in Mt 28:18-20; to say that it is refashioned as a narrative is tantamount to admitting that the form is not present. "Motivation" proves to be a capacious umbrella-concept. It covers what Jacob can do in the future if he accepts Joseph's invitation, the prayer of Cyrus in the future or imperative, and the promise of Jesus in the present. We also observe that, in 2 Chr 36:23, the motivation precedes the command proper. Malina himself seems to feel that the decree pattern is not entirely sufficient to explain Mt 28:18-20. He suggests that the decree pattern shades off into the prophetic proof pattern, as described by W. Zimmerli (message formula, motivation, announcement of salvation, proof formula). All of this suggests that Cyrus is not the answer.

(6) Independently of Malina, H. Frankemölle[51] perceived a connection between 2 Chr 36:23 and Mt 28:18-20, though he sees the parallel differently:

2 Chr 36:23	Mt 28:18-20
(a) *tade legei ... en tē̦*	
Ioudaia̦	v 18
(b) *tis ex hymōn ... met'*	
autou	v 20b

[51]Frankemölle, *Jahwebund*, 46-61.

(c) kai anabētō   v 19

More importantly, Frankemölle goes on to claim that the whole of vv 16-20 fits the covenant-formula isolated by K. Baltzer.[52] Thus, vv 16-17 are the preamble with the determination of time, place, and persons; v 18 is the prehistory with conferment of power; v 19a is the statement of basic relation or obligation; vv 19b-20a are the detailed commands; and v 20b is the blessing (promise of Jesus' presence). There are many problems with Frankemölle's parallels. Baltzer's fifth element (the invocation of the gods as witnesses) finds no correlative whatever; the preamble in Mt 28:16-17 takes the form of a narrative, not a declaration in the first person; and the supposed prehistory lacks a narration of deeds done in favor of the vassal. The parallel with 2 Chronicles is open to the objections made against Malina's theory; the parallel with the covenant-formula is simply incredible.

To sum up: the suggestions of *Gattung* for vv 18-20 suffer from two problems: (a) they are concerned only with a subsection; (b) each suggestion may be able to supply a partial parallel with vv 18-20, but no one is so exact that it excludes the other suggestions. Enthronement hymns, liturgical formulas, OT *Gottesrede*, and royal decrees all shed some light on the text; but no one contender can be declared *the* form, eliminating the claims of the others. We are left asking whether a consideration of the larger unit may bring some order into the chaos.

B. THE GATTUNG OF vv 16-20

If we may safely omit Frankemölle's suggestion of covenant, there are five major views. (1) H. J. Holtzmann[53] called the

---

[52]K. Baltzer, *Das Bundesformular* (2d ed.; Neukirchen: Neukirchener Verlag, 1964) 20. The six parts of the covenant-formula are: *Präambel, Vorgeschichte, Grundsatzerklärung über das zukünftige Verhältnis, Einzelbestimmungen, Anrufung der Götter als Zeugen,* and *Fluch und Segen.*

[53]H. J. Holtzmann, *Die Synoptiker* (3rd.; Tübingen: Mohr, 1901) 299.

whole passage a piece of Jewish-Christian community-rule, on a level with Mt 5:17-19; 16:17-19; and 18:16-20. But no one who appreciates the Christological import of Mt 28:16-20[54] can be satisfied with the designation of *Gemeindeordnung*, especially when it applies strictly only to vv 19-20a. The designation is useful insofar as it reminds us that the pericope contains not only a commission vis-à-vis non-Christians but also an ordering of the life of the already constituted community.

(2) R. Bultmann's treatment of vv 16-20 is rather disconcerting. In his *Geschichte der synoptischen Tradition*[55] we find no one firm *Gattung* specified, but rather a number of judgments that identify individual motifs. On. p. 310, he uses the very general category of *Ostergeschichten* (though at least this takes into account something from which most of the suggested categories totally prescind!). Yet he also thinks that the baptismal formula makes this Easter story a sort of cult legend (so also on p. 333). On pp. 312-313, he says that vv 16-20 is governed by the motif of *Missionsauftrag des Auferstandenen;* but this motif is combined with the motif of *Auferstehungsbeweis durch die Erscheinung des Auferstandenen* (v 17: *hoi de edistasan*). On p. 169, vv 18-20 are put under the category of *Ich-Wort* (Though this hardly does justice to v 19). Bultmann's treatment may be confusing, but the very confusion points up the problem of having so many motifs coming together in so small a compass.

(3) Treating the whole of vv 16-20, M. Dibelius calls it a Christological revelation that issues from the passion narrative; the Risen One reveals himself as the one to whom all power has been given.[56] This really does not get us beyond Bultmann's general designation of *Ostergeschichten*.

(4) C. H. Dodd is one of the few critics who takes vv 16-20 seriously as a resurrection narrative and then tries to determine

---

[54]Cf. J. Kingsbury, "The Composition and Christology of Mt 28:16-20," *JBL* 93 (1974) 573-584, and his book, *Matthew: Structure, Christology, Kingdom* (Philadelphia: Fortress, 1975). I think Kingsbury is correct in stressing a Son-of-God Christology in Matthew, but I think a Son-of-Man Christology is equally important, especially in 28:16-20.

[55]Bultmann, *Geschichte,* 310-313, 333, 169.

[56]Dibelius, *Formgeschichte,* 199.

what kind of resurrection narrative it is.[57] Dodd divides all appearances of the Risen One into two types: concise (=Bultmann's apophthegmata, Dibelius's paradigms, Taylor's pronouncement stories) and circumstantial (=tales, *Novellen*). Mt 28:16-20 comes closer to the concise type, whose structure is (a) situation: Christ's followers bereft of their Lord; (b) the appearance of the Lord; (c) greeting; (d) recognition; (e) word of command. But immediately we notice certain dissimilarities in vv 16-20. (a) Our story has no greeting. (b) That the disciples are bereft is not stressed. After all, they have received their Lord's order; they are obeying it with full knowledge of where they are going and why. (c) It is hard to distinguish between appearance and recognition. V 17 has to serve for both, and nothing is said about how the disciples recognize Jesus and how or whether the doubters overcome their doubt. (d) The word of the Lord is more than a commission; and even the commission, as Dodd admits, is extraordinarily long for a concise story. While Dodd's pattern has the advantage of pointing up some contacts between vv 16-20 and other resurrection narratives, the differences are too great.

(5) Finally, the most recent and most satisfying attempt to find a form-critical category for vv 16-20 is the dissertation by B. Hubbard.[58] Hubbard discerns in the Hebrew bible a recurring form in the narratives of the commissioning of patriarchs and prophets. In its fullest form, it has seven parts: circumstantial introduction, confrontation between the commissioner and the one to be commissioned (sometimes with divine self-asseveration), reaction to the presence of the deity, commission proper, protest to the task outlined in the commission, word of reassurance from the deity, and conclusion. When applied to Mt 28:16-20, the *Gattung* takes the following form: v 16: introduction; v 17a: confrontation; v 17b: reaction; v 18: confrontation; vv 19-20a: commission; v 20b: reassurance. A number of words and motifs found in the OT *Gattung* are also present in 28:16-20: the verbs "go" and "command," the

---

[57]C. H. Dodd, "The Appearances of the Risen Christ: an Essay in Form-Criticism of the Gospels," in *Studies in the Gospels: Essays in Memory of R. H. Lightfoot* (ed. D. Nineham; Oxford: Blackwell, 1967) 9-35.

[58]Cf. n. 3.

ressurance "I am with you," and the plentiful use of the adjective "all." Mt 28:16-20 and the parallel material in Jn 20:19-23 and Lk 24:36-53 point to a primitive apostolic commissioning underlying all three narratives: confrontation (Jesus appears); reaction (joy yet disbelief); commission (preach to—and, perhaps, baptize—all); reassurance (sending the Spirit). Matthew took the proto-commission and redacted it to give it a closer correspondence to the form and language of a Hebrew bible commission.

Hubbard's thesis is definitely the finest work done on the problem of the *Gattung* of vv 16-20 to date. And yet some serious questions remain.[59] We might divide these questions into (a) questions that bear upon the commissioning *Gattung* taken by itself, and (b) questions that bear upon the application of this *Gattung* to Mt 28:16-20.

(a) In the commisssioning-*Gattung*, are there enough specific elements—and are they constant enough—to justify the claim of a special *Gattung* that goes beyond theophany or angelophany? As H. McArthur rightly asks, would not most of the elements in this commissioning-*Gattung* appear in almost any narrative in which an authoritative X meets Y for a significant exchange? Especially when the introduction, reaction, protest, reassurance, and conclusion can be lacking in one or another example (the only absolute constants that are never lacking are the confrontation and the commission), how fixed a *Gattung* is this?

Moreover, the *Gattung* is extremely broad in applicability. For instance, one could apply it to Lk 1:5-23 (Gabriel's annunciation to Zechariah), Lk 1:26-38 (Gabriel's annunciation to Mary), and Lk 2:8-15 (the angels' annunciation to the shepherds). Granted, the element of commissioning may be somewhat attenuated. But new roles are predicted and concrete directives are given (and followed). And, in the first two cases, we also have "indirect commissionings" of the Baptist and

---

[59]For the critique that follows, I am very much indebted to the perceptive remarks of H. McArthur in his review of Hubbard's work in *CBQ* 38 (1976) 107-108. But since I have modified and added to his critique, I must take final responsibility for what is said here.

Jesus. If the element of commissioning is somewhat attenuated here, so is it also in some of the OT examples Hubbard uses. The commisssion seems to extend to almost any divine command or promise. For example, in Gen 28:13b-14, we have more of a promise or prophecy made to Jacob than a commission to do something. If this can qualify as a commission, so can the directives, promises, and prophecies in Lk 1-2. And the problem is, the list of candidates could be extended far beyond the first two chapters of Luke, especially if we hold to a minimal structure of (introduction) confrontation, commission, (conclusion). All of the synoptic versions of the finding of the empty tomb could qualify. So could the appearance of Jesus to Saul in Acts 9:1-9—and, even more obviously, the appearance of Jesus to Ananias in Acts 9:10-19. Some might want to add the appearance of the angel to Cornelius in Acts 10:1-8. And, if one really wanted to stretch a point, one could almost apply the minimum *Gattung* to the "theophanic" scene of Jesus in the garden in Jn 18:1-12.

Consequently, we are left asking ourselves: is there any special commissioning-*Gattung* over against the general *Gattung* of theophany or angelophany? On p. 26 of his work, Hubbard remarks: "'Commission' ... appears to be the broader term applicable to every pericope under investigation." Yes—and to a large number of pericopes not under investigation. That is the basic problem. The supposed *Gattung* is too broad; it lacks specificity.

(b) This basic problem flows over into the attempt to apply the *Gattung* to Mt 28:16-20. Since the *Gattung* is so broad, we must ask whether it really aids us in understanding a particular kind of Easter appearance. As so often happens with *Gattungen* applied to Mt 28:16-20, the post-resurrectional nature of the epiphany does not enter into the choice of *Gattung*.

Furthermore, even if we grant that behind vv 16-20 lies a *Gattung* such as Hubbard describes, some of the data will not support the statement that Matthew redacted the proto-commission to make it correspond more closely to the Hebrew bible *Gattung* of commission. According to Hubbard, the proto-commission had a confrontation, reaction, commission, and reassurance. I personally think one could also argue the possibility of an introduction and conclusion in the proto-commission.[60] If this be true, then Matthew adds no new element to the structure; his additions are mainly (or perhaps entirely, if one admits an introduction in the proto-commission) additions of motifs. Precisely in this context it is noteworthy that part of what Matthew *does* add disturbs the supposed *Gattung*. Particularly troublesome is v 18b, which Hubbard cannot really explain within the structure of his *Gattung*. He makes v 18b the second half of a confrontation that is split in two by the reaction (which naturally becomes the reaction to the first part of the confrontation only). Nowhere do we find this split-confrontation in Hubbard's OT parallels. Num 22:22-35 does not supply an exact parallel, since in that text there are two confrontations, each with its own reaction. And, when it comes to explaining the exact function of v 18b, Hubbard tries to interpret it as a self-asseveration. He paraphrases it as "I am the One to whom God has given" etc. but that is not what v 18b says. There is no "I am the One"; there is simply no verb in the present tense. The main verb (*edothē*—aorist!) is not even to be translated, strictly speaking, as "has been given," but rather as "was given." The past event of the resurrection is identified as Jesus' enthronement as cosmocrator. This is the element that gave rise to the enthronement-hymn hypothesis. But, just as some elements of vv 16-20 would not fit an enthronement-hymn pattern, so too v 18b (declaration of the past act of enthronement which is the basis of the present commands) will not fit a commissioning-*Gattung* perfectly, especially when it follows upon the reaction.

And so we reach the rather negative conclusion that no form-critical category yet proposed fits Mt 28:16-20. Why? Are we to await a bigger and better *Gattung*? A moment's reflection on what we have seen in Parts I and II of this article would suggest not. The reason why we spent so much time

---

[60]It is especially strange that, while Hubbard includes an introduction in his schematization of Mt 28:16-20, Mk 16:14-20, Lk 24:36-53, and Jn 20:19-23 (*Matthean Redaction*, 103), he does not include an introduction in his hypothetical proto-commissioning (p. 122). It seems to me that, if one holds to this proto-commissioning, all the data indicate that some sort of introduction belonged to it from the beginning. If that be the case, then out of the seven possible elements belonging to the *Gattung*, Matthew has added no new element to the proto-commissioning lying before him.

with tradition and redaction (Part I) was to show that vv 16-20 represent tradition that has been heavily redacted by Matthew to express his own ideas concerning Christology, ecclesiology, and eschatology.[61] The reason why no *Gattung* (dealing with the *typical*) is satisfactory is that the pericope is so *sui generis,* so much a product of Matthew's redactional activity—redactional activity, however, which worked upon some existing tradition. It is precisely this interplay, this dialectic, between tradition and heavy redaction, that has produced a pericope so idiosyncratic that it defies the labels of form criticism. This, then, is why the thesis of Hubbard, for all its excellent points, cannot supply a satisfying answer to the question of *Gattung.* It is the very question that is wrongly posed.

Afterword

General treatments of Mt 28:16-20 may be found in Jane Schaberg, *The Father, the Son and the Holy Spirit* (SBLDS 61; Chico, CA: Scholars, 1982); Pheme Perkins, *Resurrection* (Garden City, NY: Doubleday, 1984) 131-37; and Terence L. Donaldson, *Jesus on the Mountain* (JSNTSup 8; Sheffield: JSOT, 1985).

Individual articles on aspects of the pericope include J.-C. Bassett, "Dernières paroles du ressuscité et mission de l'Eglise aujourd'hui (A propos de Mt 28:18-20 et parallèles)," *RTP* 114 (1982) 349-67; G. Friedrich, "Die formale Struktur von Mt

---

[61] For the precise delineation of these theological concerns of Matthew, I refer the reader to "Salvation-History in Matthew," the first essay in Part 2 of this volume.

28:18-20," *ZTK* 80 (1983) 137-83; L. Abramowski, "Die Entstehung der dreigliedrigen Taufformel—ein Versuch. Mit einem Exkurs: Jesus der Naziräer," *ZTK* 81 (1984) 417-46; K. Grayston, "The Translation of Mt 28:17," *JSNT* 21 (1984) 105-9; and the different view of the same verse presented by P. W. van der Horst, "Once More: The Translation of *hoi de* in Mt 28:17," *JSNT* 27 (1986) 26-30; D. Hill, "The Conclusion of Matthew's Gospel: Some Literary-Critical Observations," *Irish Biblical Studies* 8 (1986) 54-63.

9

John the Baptist in Matthew's Gospel

I. Introduction

The purpose of this essay is to examine the special theological significance which Matthew's gospel assigns to John the Baptist.[1] To appreciate the specificity of Matthew's presentation, we should first review briefly how far all four gospels concur in their treatment of the Baptist and how Mark, Luke and John portray the Baptist for their own purposes.

---

[1] The bibliography on John the Baptist is enormous. For general orientation and basic bibliography, cf. M. Dibelius, *Die urchristliche Überlieferung von Johannes dem Täufer* (Göttingen: Vandenhoeck & Ruprecht, 1911); M. Goguel, *Au seuil de l'évangile.-Jean Baptiste* (Paris: Payot, 1928); E. Lohmeyer, *Das Urchristentum. 1. Buch. Johannes der Täufer* (Göttingen: Vandenhoeck & Ruprecht, 1932); J. A. T. Robinson, "The Baptism of John and the Qumran Community," and "Elijah, John, and Jesus," in *Twelve New Testament Studies* (London: SCM, 1962) 11-27 and 28-52; J. Steinmann, *St. Jean-Baptiste et la spiritualité du désert* (Paris: Seuil, 1957); C. Scobie, *John the Baptist* (London: SCM, 1964); R. Schütz, *Johannes der Täufer* (Zurich: Zwingli, 1967); O. Böcher, "Ass Johannes der Täufer kein Brot (Luke, vii. 33)?" *NTS* 18 (1971-72) 90-92; E. Bammel, "The Baptist in Early Christian Tradition," *NTS* 18 (1971-72) 95-128; J. Hughes, "John the Baptist: the Forerunner of God Himself," *NovT* 14 (1972) 191-218; J. Becker, *Johannes der Täufer und Jesus von Nazareth* (Neukirchen-Vluyn; Neukirchener Verlag, 1972); M. Enslin "John and Jesus," *ZNW* 66 (1975) 1-18. The best study so far on Matthean redaction is W. Trilling, "Die Täufertradition bei Matthäus," *BZ* 3 (1959) 271-289; the article is a part of Trilling's doctoral dissertation which could not be included in the published form, *Das wahre Israel* (1st ed; Leipzig; St. Benno, 1959; 3rd ed; Munich: Kösel, 1974). The best over-all redactional study is W. Wink, *John the Baptist in the Gospel Tradition* (Cambridge: Cambridge University, 1968). As Wink notes at the beginning of his chapter on Matthew (p. 27), he simply takes over, without too many changes, Trilling's presentation, including Trilling's mode of structuring the data.

As a bare minimum, we can say that all four gospels agree that John the Baptist is a significant figure, who must be taken into account when the story of Jesus is told. All four evangelists see John standing, in some sense, at the beginning of the gospel of Jesus Christ. This meager statement, however, just about sums up whatever consensus there is. Beyond this, each evangelist develops a highly individual interpretation of the Baptist; and, to be blunt, most often the interpretation aims at neutralizing the Baptist's independence to make him safe for Christianity. To illustrate this, let us turn to Mark, Luke, and John.

Mark makes the Baptist an Elijah incognito.[2] He is the eschatological forerunner of both Jesus and the Christian disciples, inasmuch as John first proclaims (*kēryssō*) and then is handed over to death (*paradidomai*). Jesus and his disciples live out the same pattern of first proclaiming and then being handed over.[3] Interestingly, however, in Mark this pattern is the only way in which John points to Jesus; he never expressly recognizes Jesus as the Messiah or points him out as such to others. He remains the Elijah incognito, a fitting forerunner of a secret Messiah.

Luke expands the possibilities of speaking about the Baptist by introducing him into his infancy narrative, where Luke is comparatively free to compose as he sees fit.[4] In his infancy narrative, Luke carefully profiles the Baptist and Jesus. The two annunciations and the two births form two diptychs which express the close relationship of the two figures—indeed, they become relatives! Yet Luke always puts a "plus sign" on the side of Jesus, be the plus sign a virginal conception, the belief of Mary, a nativity canticle by angels, or two oracles by

---

[2]Wink, *John the Baptist,* 17.

[3]On the pattern of proclaiming and being handed over, cf. N. Perrin, *The New Testament: An Introduction* (New York: Harcourt Brace Jovanvich, 1974) 144-145.

[4]A weakness of H. Conzelmann's *The Theology of St. Luke* (New York: Harper & Row, 1961) is that it does not give sufficient attention to the infancy narrative as an integral part of the gospel and thus distorts Luke's view of the Baptist; cf. pp. 18-27, especially p. 22 n. 2. On the Lucan infancy narrative and the place of the Baptist in it, cf. R. Brown, *The Birth of the Messiah* (Garden City: Doubleday, 1977) 235-499, especially pp. 241-243.

Simeon.[5] Contrary to what Conzelmann has claimed, John is quite definitely the Elijah-like forerunner who prepares the way for the Lord (1:17: "And he shall go before him [the Lord God] in the spirit and power of Elijah to turn the hearts of the fathers towards the children [cf. Mal 4:5-6; Sir 48:10] and the disobedient to the prudence of the just, to make ready for the Lord a people well prepared").[6] At the beginning of the public ministry, Luke forestalls any rivalry between John and Jesus by mentioning the arrest of the Baptist before he narrates the baptism of Jesus. Strictly speaking, Lk 3:21-22 does not tell us *who* baptized Jesus; we are simply told in one part of a participial phrase that Jesus was baptized (3:21).[7] Luke's placing of the Baptist's arrest before Jesus' baptism has been interpreted by some as an attempt to exclude John from the mid-point of salvation history (the time of Jesus) and to consign him to the period of the law and the prophets.[8] I would rather see Luke as placing the Baptist neither completely inside nor completely outside the mid-point of history. In the interest of continuity within the flow of salvation history, Luke has the Baptist bestride the two periods like a colossus, with one foot in each period.[9] He is the clamp, the link, the bracket between the time

[5]Cf. Dibelius, *Die urchristliche Überlieferung,* 67; R. Laurentin, *Structure et Théologie de Luc I-II* (Paris: Gabalda, 1957) 32-33; and the more nuanced view of Brown in *The Birth,* 250-253. Brown suggests that the original, neat pattern of diptychs was distributed by a second stage of Lucan composition. Curiously, it is in the parallelism of his infancy narrative that Luke comes closest to Matthew's way of portraying the relation between John and Jesus.

[6]On the mistaken view of Conzelmann, cf. n. 4 above.

[7]Wink, (*John the Baptist,* 83 n. 1) interprets *baptisthentos* as a middle participle ("baptized himself"), since no one else is there to baptize Jesus. But this is to ignore the words just preceding: *egeneto de en tǭ, baptisthēnai hapanta ton laon kai Iēsou baptisthentos.* Certainly the *baptisthēnai* is to be understood as a true passive, with John as the understood agent (cf. 3:7: *ochlois baptisthēnai hyp'autou*). In this wider context, it is extremely difficult to take *baptisthentos* as a middle rather than a true passive. Moreover, an aorist middle form existed, if Luke had desired that nuance.

[8]So Conzelmann, who rests his case especially on Lk 16:16; cf., e.g., *Theology,* 16, 20-26, 112-113. A similar view is held by C. Kraeling, *John the Baptist* (New York: Scribner's, 1951) 180. Whether Lk 16:16 really means what Conzelmann claims is disputed; cf. Brown, *Birth,* 243 n. 23; E. Franklin, *Christ the Lord* (Philadelphia: Westminster, 1975) 85-86; and P. Minear's comment quoted in Wink, *John the Baptist,* 51 n. 1.

[9]Perhaps what Kraeling says of Mt 11:12-13 is more aptly applied to the Lucan portrait of John: ". . .John the Baptist stands at the dividing line between the period

of the law and prophets and the time of Jesus. A similar function is played in Luke-Acts by the twelve apostles; they bestride and connect the time of Jesus and the time of the church.

As for the fourth gospel, John the Baptist ceases to be the Baptist; the title is never used. Similarly, John explicitly denies that he is Elijah (1:21); the negation of such a fiery, apocalyptic role reflects the dampening of apocalyptic fire in the fourth gospel in general. John is instead the first witness to Jesus (Jn 1:7-8, 15, 19, 32, 34; 3:26; 5:33-36).[10] Even when John's baptism is mentioned, it is no longer a tool either of remission of sins or of repentance. Instead, John's baptism has become a tool of revelation, of Christological manifestation (1:31: "And I did not know him, but in order that he might be revealed [*phanerōthē*] to Israel, for this I came baptizing with water"). Like other human witnesses and like the signs, the function of John is to point beyond himself to the One witnessed to, the One signified (3:30: "He must increase, I must decrease"). John decreases so much that the baptism of Jesus by John is neither narrated nor recalled after the fact.[11]

By way of exclusion, then, we come to the question of the place Matthew assigns the Baptist in his gospel. As I hope to show, Matthew's presentation of the Baptist is of the four gospels, perhaps the most puzzling and difficult to understand. I shall investigate the data and try to interpret them in the following two parts of this essay. In Part Two, I shall marshal the data according to the order in which they appear in Matthew's gospel. But, as we shall see, the marshaled data

of anticipation and the period in which the Kingdom is present but in conflict. . ." (*John the Baptist,* 156-157).

[10]This position is so widely acknowledged that there is no need to argue it in detail; cf. Dibelius, *Die urchristliche Überlieferung,* 102-109. For a different explanation of why the fourth gospel denies that the Baptist is Elijah, cf. J. L. Martyn, "'We Have Found Elijah'," in *The Gospel of John in Christian History* (New York: Paulist, 1979) 9-54.

[11]Jn 1:32-33 speaks of the descent of the Spirit in the form of a dove, but the fourth gospel never explicitly states that this took place at the baptism of Jesus; this point is missed by Dibelius, *Die urchristliche Überlieferung,* 105-106. Bammel ("The Baptist," 111) notes the absence of the baptism of Jesus in the fourth gospel and claims that F. C. Baur was the first to point out this absence.

only lead to a riddle. If I may for a moment anticipate the results of the survey: we shall see that Matthew combines a startling and thorough attempt to make the Baptist a figure parallel to Jesus with a few pointed statements about the Baptist's unworthiness and inferiority. In Part Three of this essay I shall try to face this two-sided riddle and attempt to explain why Matthew strove to make John parallel to Jesus while at the same time retaining or even heightening statements about John's inferiority.

II. The Data

The data on John the Baptist in Matthew have already been presented—in thematic order—by W. Trilling[12] and have been made available in English by W. Wink.[13] From the start, however, I must stress one major difference between Trilling's presentation of the data and my own. Trilling arranges the data according to certain set themes and thus plays down the order of the data in the gospel. The problem with this method is that an interpretation is being imposed upon the data from the outset. If, instead, we wish to start from "point zero,"

[12]Cf. n. 1 above.

[13]Wink, *John the Baptist*, 27-41. Both Trilling and Wink presuppose and employ the two-document hypothesis, and I shall do the same in the examination of texts which follows. I am well aware that the two-document hypothesis is under attack from various quarters (W. Farmer, M. Goulder, X. Léon-Dufour, to name but a few). Although I respect and admire these scholars, I do not consider their objections cogent or their alternative theories preferable. I have explained my preference for the two-document hypothesis in my *Law and History in Matthew's Gospel* (Rome: Biblical Institute Press, 1976) 2-6. In addition to the various theoretical arguments in favor of the two-document hypothesis, I would add one pragmatic observation from Matthean studies: it works over the long haul. The two-document hypothesis has been applied with success to almost every area of Matthean research: miracle stories (H.-J. Held), legal and moral questions (G. Barth, A. Sand, J. Meier), Christological material (J. D. Kingsbury), parables (Kingsbury), Jewish-Christian polemics (D. Hare), eschatology and ecclesiology (G. Bornkamm, H. Frankemölle), passion narrative (D. Senior), resurrection stories (H. Grass), and the Baptist material (Trilling, Wink)—not to mention many prestigious commentaries on the whole gospel. No other theory of synoptic relations has proved itself by being applied so minutely and successfully to almost every aspect of Matthew's gospel. In writing a commentary on Matthew for the *New Testament Message Series* (Wilmington: Glazier, 1980), I became convinced that only the two-document hypothesis offers a natural, coherent explanation of the data.

without any set theory or a priori interpretation of the data, I think it is methodologically preferable to review the data according to the order in which they appear in the gospel. This mode of presentation will help us appreciate more the strange interweaving of parallelism yet subordination with regard to the Baptist. This attempt at a "neutral" methodology is all the more important when we notice that not all Matthean scholars recognize the technique of parallelism in Matthew's presentation of John. So eminent an authority as G. D. Kilpatrick, for instance, denies Matthew's tendency to assimilate John to Jesus,[14] while E. Bammel denies both a tendency to distinguish between the two and a tendency to emphasize their common cause.[15]

We begin our survey with Mt 3, since Matthew, unlike Luke, does not retroject the Baptist into his infancy narrative. As we shall see, chaps. 3 and 11 contain the largest amount of material on the Baptist. To oversimplify a bit, we might entitle chap. 3, "The Baptist's View of Jesus and Himself," and we might entitle the first half of chap. 11, "Jesus' View of the Baptist and Himself."

A. THE BAPTIST'S VIEW OF JESUS AND HIMSELF (CHAP. 3)

Chap. 3 divides into two major parts: the activity of the Baptist (3:1-12) and the baptism of Jesus (3:13-17). The first part, the activity of the Baptist, divides in turn into three subsections.

1. The Activity of the Baptist (3:1-12)

(a) *The appearance of the Baptist (3:1-6).* Chap. 3 is the only

---

[14]G. D. Kilpatrick, *The Origins of the Gospel according to St. Matthew* (London: Oxford University, 1946) 107, 90. Kilpatrick holds that "the evangelist carefully distinguishes between Jesus and John" (p. 107); ". . . in Matthew the tendency is not to assimilate Jesus and John but to emphasize differences between them" (p. 90).
[15]Bammel, "The Baptist," 104.

chapter in the gospel where the Baptist is present for the whole of the chapter. Since, at the beginning of chap. 3, Matthew is skipping some thirty years and is introducing a new character, it is only natural that he clears his throat and begins solemnly: "Now in those days. . ." This solemn beginning expresses both Matthew's view of the time of Jesus as something sacred, finished, and unrepeatable (Matthew's so-called "historicizing" tendency)[16] and also the sense that a new, heightened period of eschatological revelation is dawning.[17] Significantly, John is introduced with the verb *paraginetai* (3:1), the same verb used for the appearance of Jesus in 3:13. Except for the coming of the Magi in 2:1, this verb is never used again in the gospel. The paralleling process thus begins, ever so modestly, in 3:1. In 3:1-2, Matthew changes the object of John's heralding, as compared with Mark. In Mark, the object of the heralding was a baptism of repentance "unto the forgiveness of sins" (*eis aphesin hamartiōn*, Mark 1:4). For Matthew, forgiveness of sins comes only through the sacrificial death of Christ, and so the phrase *eis aphesin hamartiōn* is transposed from John's baptism to the word over the cup at the Last Supper (26:28).[18] Instead of "a *baptism* of repentance" the Baptist in Matthew heralds a *call* to repentance; the object of his proclamation is not a rite but an inner attitude of conversion. The startling thing is that Matthew makes the initial proclamation of John in 3:2 an exact copy of Jesus' initial proclamation in 4:17; *metanoeite ēggiken gar hē basileia tōn ouranōn.* As so often

[16]For this tendency, cf. G. Strecker, *Der Weg der Gerechtigkeit* (3rd ed.; Göttingen: Vandenhoeck & Ruprecht, 1971) 41-49, 86-122, 184-188.

[17]Cf. J. D. Kingsbury, *Matthew: Structure, Christology, Kingdom* (Philadelphia: Fortress, 1975) 28-30. Kingsbury states on p. 30 that the phrase "in those days" in 3:1 "signals the inauguration of the ministry of the Baptist" and "designates that eschatological period of time that breaks upon Israel with the public ministry of John the Baptist. . . ." It is not clear how this jibes with Kingsbury's theory that the prologue of the gospel extends from 1:1 to 4:16. I disagree with Kingsbury's view that the *de* of 3:1 connects chap. 3 with the infancy narrative to form a prologue which ignores the passing of some thirty years; cf. J. Meier, *The Vision of Matthew* (New York: Paulist, 1979) 56 n. 21.

[18]Contrary to D. Senior (*The Passion Narrative according to Matthew* [Louvain: Louvain University, 1975] 80-83), I think the presence of the phrase in the cup-word was already traditional in Matthew's church; but it is Matthew who strikes the phrase from Mk 1:4, thus showing that he fully agrees with the point of view of his special tradition.

Matthew tightens up the Markan text. Matthew drops the phrase "the time is fulfilled" (Mark 1:15), perhaps because *peplērōtai ho kairos* does not jibe with his use of *plēroō* (never used in Matthew with words for time). Matthew also drops the command "believe in the gospel," perhaps because he never uses *euaggelion* absolutely and never makes *euaggelion* the object of *pisteuō*. More significantly, both in 3:2 and 4:17 Matthew inverts the Markan order of indicative and imperative. For Matthew, the imperative cry *metanoeite* comes first; the indicative of the coming of the kingdom is then mentioned as the reason for and the ground of repentance. Matthew thus keeps the nexus between indicative and imperative in Christian proclamation, but he definitely puts the accent on the imperative. Matthew's typical concern for eschatological morality is obvious here. Indeed, his concern is so powerful that he coopts the Baptist as a preacher of Christian repentance by placing the words of Jesus in John's mouth.[19]

This striking affirmation of parallelism is followed immediately by a counter-balancing citation of Isa 40:3; John is himself not the Messiah, but simply the preparer of the Lord's way, as prophesied by Isaiah.[20] This eschatological tone is continued by the Markan description of John in terms of a prophet, perhaps even of Elijah[21] (Mt 3:4a; cf. 2 Kgs 1:8) and by the renewed nomadic existence of the desert (3:4b), remi-

---

[19]Hughes ("John the Baptist," 200) tries to defend the historicity of Mt 3:2 in the mouth of John; unfortunately, the whole article lacks a consistent use of redaction criticism.

[20]Another interesting example of parallelism-yet-subordination is Matthew's attaching of two citations of Isaiah (40:3 and 9:1-2 [8:23-9:1 in the Hebrew]) to the two initial proclamations, Mt 3:2-3 and 4:15-17 respectively. One should note not only the chiastic order (John's proclamation followed by the Isaiah citation versus the Isaiah citation preceding Jesus' proclamation) but also the subordination of John which is brought out by the choice of texts. The citation of Isaiah in Mt 3:3 presents John as a voice in the desert exhorting people to prepare for the Lord who is to come (cf. 3:11), while the citation of Isaiah in Mt 4:15-16 celebrates the Messiah who has come (note the aorists in Matthew's version of the citation). On this, cf. Wink, *John the Baptist*, 37-38.

[21]That the clothing of camel's hair signifies a prophet is generally accepted; but Becker, among others, rejects any direct reference to Elijah (*Johannes der Täufer*, 26, 111). For the reasons for the dispute, cf. Robinson, "Elijah, John, and Jesus," 29 n. 2. Matthew, however, may have intended an allusion to Elijah if he already had 11:14 in mind.

niscent of the first exodus and portending the final exodus. Matthew concludes the pericope of the Baptist's appearance by mentioning his baptism and the baptized people's confession of sin. Matthew has no objection in principle to mentioning these two elements of John's ministry, provided John's baptism is not seen as *conferring* remission of sins.

(b) *The Baptist's sermon of repentance* (3:7-10). While Q probably had John direct his sermon of repentance to the crowds (cf. Lk 3:7), Matthew changes the audience to the unlikely fellowship of the Pharisees and Sadducees.[22] The joining of Pharisees and Sadducees is, of course, unhistorical; but Matthew sees Judaism as a "united front" which opposes Jesus and his disciples just as Israel of old opposed and martyred the prophets sent to it. Accordingly, Matthew readily joins together various Jewish groups and individuals (including Herod the Great and Herod Antipas) as one solid phalanx arrayed against Jesus. Thus, Matthew's paralleling tendency again surfaces in this scene: the united front Jesus will face (cf. 16:1-12) is the united front already facing the Baptist. The parallel even expresses itself in the exact repetition of words: the epithet "brood of vipers" is repeated by Jesus in 12:34, against the Pharisees (cf. 12:24; contrast Mk 3:22: "the scribes"), and in 23:33, in the woes against the scribes and Pharisees. Since "brood of vipers" was apparently already in the Q sermon of the Baptist (Mt 3:7 = Lk 3:7), and since the other two places in Matthew which have "brood of vipers" have no synoptic parallel, it is likely that, in this case, Matthew has borrowed a phrase from the Baptist and placed it on the lips of Jesus. This "creative copying" is especially striking in Mt 23:33, where Jesus' rebuke, "brood of vipers, how shall you flee from the judgment of Gehenna?" seems to be an

---

[22]On Matthew's reference to "the Pharisees and Sadducees" as redactional, cf. Wink, *John the Baptist,* 34 n. 1. In the NT, only Matthew joins together the Pharisees and Sadducees. In a number of cases we can see that the change is due to Matthew's redaction (e.g., 16:6, 12). Hence it is probable that the Pharisees and Sadducees of 3:7 also come from Matthew's hand. The joining of Pharisees and Sadducees into one group—united in doctrine (16:12)—is unhistorical, whether one regards the pre-A.D. 70 or post-A.D. 70 situation. Matthew's blithe yoking of the two traditionally hostile groups may be a sign that he is not personally acquainted with Jewish parties and even that he himself is perhaps a Gentile; cf. Meier, *The Vision of Matthew,* 17-25.

adaptation of John's "brood of vipers, who has shown you how to flee from the coming wrath" in 3:7. Likewise, John's statement in Mt 3:10, "every tree not bearing good fruit is chopped down and thrown into the fire," is repeated word-for-word by Jesus in the sermon on the mount (7:19). Matthew is at pains to stress that the danger to which the Pharisees and other Jewish groups succumbed is the danger which also threatens would-be disciples. Thus, in the very beginning of chap. 3, we see that Matthew is consciously and methodically transferring parenetic sayings of Jesus to the Baptist and vice-versa, while at the same time balancing this parallelism with texts emphasizing the Baptist's subordination. In what follows we must investigate whether this is just an isolated quirk in the gospel or a thorough-going theological approach to the Baptist.

(c) *The Baptist's promise of the coming one* (3:11-12). Matthew mixes Mark and Q in this final section of his portrait of the Baptist. It is a section which hammers home the message of John's subordination to Jesus. The Baptist is inferior on three counts. (1) His baptism is just a water-ritual meant to lead people to repentance; the coming one will plunge men into the fiery, punitive yet purifying experience of God's spirit, poured out in the end time. (2) The one who succeeds John temporally, in the order of salvation history, is nevertheless superior to John in spiritual power.[23] He is the stronger of the two,[24] perhaps in reference to the apocalyptic struggle with the

---

[23]On the paradox implied here, cf. O. Cullmann, *The Christology of the New Testament* (London: SCM, 1959) 26, and his fuller treatment in "Ho opisō mou erchomenos," in *The Early Church* (Philadelphia: Westminster, 1956) 177-182. The *opisō mou erchomenos* is first of all a temporal statement; so BAG, *sub voce* 2b. That there might also be a hint that Jesus was once a disciple of the Baptist is possible; "to be a disciple" is the sense of *opisō mou elthein* in Mt 16:24. But such an idea at 3:11, in a context which emphasizes the Baptist's inferiority, is unlikely; we must beware of transferring what we know from John 1 to the synoptics. Consequently, I must disagree with Wink's categorical judgment: "It is all the more remarkable then that Matthew portrays Jesus as the *disciple of John* [the italics are Wink's]. There is no other way to interpret his retention of *opisō mou* in 3:11" (*John the Baptist*, 38). In a similar vein, cf. Cullmann, *Christology*, 24, 32. For the opposite view, cf. Kraeling, *John the Baptist*, 55.

[24]Note the difference in wording among the synoptics. While Mk 1:7 and Lk 3:16 both read *erchetai (de) ho ischyroteros mou (opisō mou)*, Matthew changes the emphasis by writing *ho de opisō mou erchomenos ischyroteros mou estin*. The emphasis in Mark and Luke is on the announcement of the coming while Matthew

strong man Satan (cf. Mt 12:29). (3) The coming one is the master; John is but his slave, indeed he is unworthy to perform one of the usual services of a slave, carrying his master's sandals. John then concludes his sermon with a warning about the separation of good and bad and the fiery punishment which the last judgment will bring—a theme often touched upon in the discourses of Jesus (e.g., 7:19; 13:40-42, 50; 25:31-46). Thus, even in a pericope stressing the Baptist's subordination to Jesus, a note of parallelism is struck.

2. *The Baptism of Jesus (3:13-17).*

As we have already seen, Matthew's use of *paraginetai* to introduce Jesus in 3:13 subtly assimilates him to the Baptist. Matthew inserts into the short Marcan story of the baptism a theological dialogue between John and Jesus, and by now it is no surprise that the dialogue weaves together subordination and parallelism. John begins by stressing his inferiority, his need to be baptized with the spirit which Jesus, the coming one, bestows (cf. v 11). The Baptist is objecting to the reversal of proper roles, a reversal which associates Jesus with a sinful humanity needing cleansing. But, in his first words recorded in Matthew's gospel (3:15), Jesus sweeps aside John's objection: "Let it be, for thus it behooves *us* to fulfill all justice: *(aphes arti, houtōs gar prepon estin hēmin plērōsai pasan dikaio-synēn).* Instead of seconding John's admission of inferiority, Jesus graciously associates the Baptist with himself. "It behooves *us*"—John and Jesus together[25]—to carry out the Father's saving plan of history, marked out beforehand in prophecy,[26] in other words, "to fulfill all justice." Especially when one considers the weighty Christological significance of

emphasizes the superior strength of the one who comes; cf. Dibelius, *Die urchristliche Überlieferung,* 55. Matthew's use of *ho erchomenos* in 3:11 prepares nicely for 11:3.

[25]It is possible to see in the "us" an appeal Matthew makes to Christians, the baptized disciples of Jesus, to join Jesus in "fulfilling all justice"; so Strecker, *Weg,* 180. That is at best a secondary reference; on the level of the narrative, the "us" obviously refers to John and Jesus; so G. Barth; "Matthew's Understanding of the Law," in G. Bornkamm-G. Barth-H.-J. Held, *Tradition and Interpretation in Matthew* (Philadelphia: Westminster, 1963) 138 n. 4.

[26]Cf. the various OT echoes in the declaration of the voice in 3:17: Isa 42:1; 44:2; Ps 2:7; and possibly Gen 22:2; Jer 31:19-20 [LXX 38:20].

plēroō in Matthew,[27] which means more than "to do" or "to obey," this assimilation of John to Jesus is astounding. John no longer simply points to the fulfiller, as did the Law and the prophets. Now along with the fulfiller, John is also fulfilling God's prophesied plan for salvation.[28] We have here a theme which will be developed in 11:13: "For all the prophets and the Law prophesied until John." Quite fittingly, then, the theophany after the baptism of Jesus is not restricted to Jesus alone, as in Mark, but is extended at least to the Baptist.[29]

B. JESUS' VIEW OF THE BAPTIST AND HIMSELF (11:2-19).

After chap. 3, the most important chapter for Baptist-material is the first half of chap. 11. The material is entirely from Q,[30] and divides neatly into vv 2-6, the Baptist's question about Jesus, and vv 7-19, Jesus' question about the Baptist.

1. *Vv 2-6.* Chap. 11 begins the "third book" of the public ministry, the book which focuses upon the opposition and disbelief Jesus meets at the hands of Israel. In fact, in 11:2-6, there seems to be a note of uncertainty, if not disbelief, in the question John addresses to Jesus. At least there is no reason—piety apart—to think that John asks his question only as a

---

[27]Cf. J. Meier, *Law and History*, 73-81. The most important use of *plēroō* is in the *Reflexionszitate* (passive voice of verb). *Plēroō* in the active voice is used positively only here and in 5:17 (Jesus alone). Negatively, the verb is used in the active voice in 23:32, of the scribes and the Pharisees. See also the same work, pp. 76-80, for the justification for taking *dikaiosynēn* to mean "God's saving plan" or "God's saving action" (as in Mt 5:6; 6:33). I do not think that "to fulfill all justice" refers simply to Jesus' desire to give a good example to his disciples, a position espoused by Kraeling, *John the Baptist,* 134.

[28]Wink, *John the Baptist,* 36-37, makes the intriguing suggestion that "in the baptism of Jesus *John's baptism is fulfilled,* i.e., Christianized, and becomes by this act the rite of the church ... Jesus comes not to destroy but to fulfill John's rite in such a way that its consummation is at the same time its transformation." Though this idea is consonant with 5:17 and 28:16-20, the object of *plērōsai* is *dikaiosynēn,* not *baptisma.*

[29]Cf. Kingsbury, *Matthew,* 14. I tend to think the theophany is meant not only for John but for all bystanders; cf. Dibelius, *Die urchristliche Überlieferung,* 61. Revelation goes public in Matthew. One must admit that the question remains moot and cannot be decided simply on the basis of 3:13-17.

[30]Indeed, in the synoptic gospels, Mt 11 (= Lk 7:18-35; 10:12-15, 21-22) is one of the best arguments for the existence of Q.

pedagogical exercise for his disciples, and not for his own sake as well.[31] John poses his question because he has heard in prison of *ta erga tou Christou,* the works of *the* Messiah. Considering Matthew's attempt to associate the twelve disciples with Jesus' ministry in the missionary discourse of chap. 10 we should probably understand *ta erga tou Christou* to mean the "messianic works" of proclaiming and healing, performed both by Jesus (chaps. 5-7 and 8-9) and by his disciples (chap. 10). The reason why this "messianic" activity has raised a question in John's mind is that the merciful, healing activity of Christ and his disciples, the joyful proclamation of forgiveness and wholeness in the end-time, does not fit John's prediction of the fearsome, fire-breathing judge who was to come after John (recall *ho de opisō mou erchomenos* in 3:11). John naturally is moved to ask: is Jesus, after all, *ho erchomenos* of whom John spoke? Is Jesus the object and fulfillment of all prophecy, the Messiah?[32] Or should John and his disciples look for some-one else? Jesus replies not with any theoretical argument but by pointing to all he and his disciples have done, as narrated in chaps. 5-10. Matthew had carefully arranged those chapters so that they would correspond to and verify Jesus' list of activities in 11:4-5. The list of miracles, culminating in the still greater miracle of proclaiming good news, not fiery judgment, to the poor, echoes Isa 29:18-19; 35:5-6; 25:8; and 61:1-2. Obviously, then, these activities, which so precisely fulfill the messianic prophecies, demonstrate that the time of salvation is at hand and that Jesus is the prophesied Messiah. But this end-time is not as John had pictured it. Hence, John's bewilderment and question. In a concluding beatitude,[33] Jesus gently appeals to

[31]On the question of John and the answer of Jesus, cf. J. Dupont, "L'ambassade de Jean-Baptiste," *NRT* 83 (1961) 805-821 and 943-959.

[32]Strictly speaking, "he who is to come" does not appear as a messianic title in the OT (though cf. Ps 118:26; Mal 3:1; and Gen 49:10). But the messianic implications are clear enough on the redactional level from the context of both chap. 3 and chap. 11; cf. n. 24.

[33]Dupont, "L'ambassade," 952, emphasizes the unusual *kai* that introduces the beatitude. He gives it the sense of "blessed also" and remarks: "... la conjonction lie étroitement ce verset au verset précédent.... L'homme dont Jésus dit qui'il est heureux se voit associé aux bénéficiaries du salut messianique...."

John not to stumble and fall from faith, not to be led into the sin of disbelief like most of Israel, not to take offense (*mē skandalisthē en emoi*) because Jesus is a different type of Messiah from the one the Baptist and indeed all Israel had expected. Blessed is he who does not "look for another" because, if he does, he is looking for the fulfillment of his own fantasies rather than of God's prophecies. In a sense, then 11:2-6 presents the low point in Matthew's treatment of the Baptist. Nowhere else in the gospel does John seem so distant from, and so inferior to, Jesus.[34]

2. *Vv 7-19,* however, restore the balance by giving the Baptist singular praise. After Jesus has replied to John's disciples concerning who he (Jesus) is, he in turn asks the crowds who John is. More specifically, if Jesus is the coming one, who is John in relation to Jesus? Jesus proceeds by rhetorical questions, which one by one exclude various possibilities and leave the inquirer with only one conclusion (vv 7-9). Large throngs were not drawn out to Jordan's banks to see a vacillating crowd-pleaser with his finger in the wind, a time-server fittingly symbolized by a reed on the banks of the Jordan, a reed swaying according to the promptings of the prevailing political wind. John is in prison precisely because he had the courage to denounce Herod's marriage (14:3-4). Nor did the crowds seek out some influential royal advisor, a courtier of Herod clothed in fine linen. The Baptist is in Herod's prison, not Herod's palace; and his clothing was camel's hair and a leather belt (3:4). John was neither a weak nor an "influential" man, as this world counts influence. John was a prophet—a most important category for Matthew—and therefore the Spirit of oral prophecy, thought to have grown silent in Israel, was speaking again, in the end-time. But precisely because John stood in the end-time, he was more than a prophet. He was a prophet who was living in the age of which the OT prophets had spoken; indeed, John was part of this fulfillment which he himself had

---

[34]Matthew may possibly be hinting at a further point of inferiority: John worked no miracles, while the messianic works of Jesus *and his disciples* are abundant. Yet one must beware of an *argumentum ex silentio;* only Jn 10:41 explicitly refers to John's lack of miracles.

foretold.[35] To him also Jesus could direct the beatitude he speaks to his disciples in 13:16-17: "But happy are your eyes for they see, and your ears for they hear. For Amen I say to you that many prophets and just men longed to see what you see and they did not see it, and hear what you hear and they did not hear it." John does not belong to that list of "many prophets." More than a prophet, he is the eschatological messenger of whom the prophet Malachi spoke, the messenger sent by God to prepare the way for the Messiah (Mal 3:1, conflated with Exod 23:20).[36] In v 11, immediately following the citation, the importance yet limitations of John receive a terse and puzzling summary. On the one hand, Jesus solemnly assures the crowd in v 11a that there has not arisen among those born of women one greater than John the Baptist.[37] Yet, says v 11b, the least in the kingdom of heaven is greater than he.[38] The meaning of this affirmation poses a serious problem.

[35]Cf. A. Schlatter, *Das evangelium nach Matthäus* (Stuttgart: Calwer, 1947) 176: "[The people should see in John] nicht bloss einen, der weissagte, sondern einen, der selbst geweissagt war, der ihnen nicht nur für die Zukunft Hoffnung gab, sondern ihre Erfüllung begann."

[36]Mk 1:2 conflates the Malachi and Exodus texts and then attaches them in v 3 to Isa 40:3, the whole citation being attributed to Isaiah. Matthew and Luke both remove the Malachi-Exodus text from their third chapters, leaving a text which they can correctly attribute to Isaiah. Perhaps both were led to do this, independently of each other, by the presence of the Malachi-Exodus conflation in Q (Mt 11:10 = Lk 7:27).

[37]Dibelius *(Die urchristliche Überlieferung, 9)* holds that Matthew's perfect form *(egēgertai),* vis-à-vis Luke's present form *(estin),* is an attempt to exclude Jesus from the comparison.

[38]Theoretically, "in the kingdom of heaven" could be read with "greater," but the word order favors the customary translation, which is adopted by almost all modern English versions (*RSV, NEB, NAB* [with the addition of "born into" after "least"], *JB, TEV,* Phillips, Goodspeed). If one were to take *mikroteros* and *meizōn* as true comparatives, one might understand the sentence as contrasting the Baptist (the older person? the master?) and Jesus (the younger? the former disciple of the Baptist?), with the phrase "in the kingdom of heaven" possibly modifying *meizōn;* cf. M. Zerwick, *Graecitas Biblica* (5th ed.; Rome: Biblical Institute, 1966) #149. Matthew, unlike Luke, says nothing about John's being older than Jesus; unlike the fourth gospel, Matthew gives no hint of Jesus' emerging from the Baptist's circle of disciples. Therefore, whatever 11b may have meant in the tradition, Matthew probably understands *mikroteros* and *meizōn* in the superlative sense (cf. Zerwick, ibid., #147) and reads "in the kingdom of heaven" with *mikroteros.* O. Cullmann has been a notable proponent of the position that Mt 11:11b should be taken to mean that Jesus is younger than John, yet greater; cf. "Ho opisō mou erchomenos," in *The Early*

On the one hand, Matthew places the Baptist firmly in the central time of salvation history as a figure parallel to Jesus, and in that limited sense in the kingdom. On the other hand, no commentator known to me would contend that Matthew in v 11b means to exclude the Baptist from the final stage of the kingdom at "the end of the age," at the parousia. But then, if "in the kingdom of Heaven" refers neither to the public ministry of Jesus nor to the final stage of the kingdom—to what does it refer? Significantly, neither Trilling nor Wink can give an adequate explanation of v 11b.[39] After we have finished our review of the data, an explanation of this verse in terms of Matthew's view of salvation history will be offered in Part Three of this essay. For the time being, however, v 11 reminds us of the puzzling duality of Matthew's treatment of the Baptist: unheard-of-praise in v 11a, cryptic critique in v 11b.

In a manner we have come to expect, the limitation placed on John in v 11b is in turn balanced by the important place attributed to him in vv 12-14.[40] Matthew rewrites a simple, if puzzling statement in Luke 16:16 to create vv 12-13—two verses not originally belonging to this context, and two verses heavily laden with Matthean theology. Luke 16:16 reads: "The Law and the prophets [lasted] until John; from then on, the kingdom of God is proclaimed as good news, and everyone

---

Church, 177-182; and his *Christology,* 32, with a list of the Fathers who favor this interpretation. For another view on the origin and development of 11:11 in the oral tradition, cf. Dibelius, *Die urchristliche Überlieferung,* 8-15, 121 n. 1. Dibelius holds that v 11a comes from Jesus, while v 11b is a creation of the church. On the contrary, Becker *(Johannes der Täufer,* 75) holds that the whole of v 11 comes from Jesus.

[39]Trilling ("Täufertradition," 277) rightly says that John is drawn into that period in which the kingdom of God has already broken in. All the more striking then is his inability to deal effectively with 11:11, although he gives a great amount of space to 11:12-13. Wink *(John the Baptist,* 40 n. 1) lamely says that "11:11b does not *exclude* John from the Kingdom in Matthew's eyes; it merely subordinates him *within* it." The problem with this statement, which in a certain way is perfectly true, is that it works with an undifferentiated idea of the kingdom; cf. Part Three of this essay.

[40]The Q material represented by vv 12-13 was probably not originally connected with vv 2-11; cf. the different context of Lk 16:16. Vv 14-15 seem to be a creation of Matthew, who draws upon similar material contained elsewhere in his gospel (e.g., 17:12; 13:9, 43). These rearrangements and additions make Matthew's desire to compose a comprehensive and balanced statement on the Baptist in chap. 11 all the clearer.

forces his way into the kingdom."[41] Matthew combines the end of Luke 16:16a with the whole of 16:16b and states: "From the days of John the Baptist until now the kingdom of God suffers violence, and the violent bear it away." As Trilling and Wink have pointed out,[42] Matthew's consistent use of such temporal phrases as "from the days" (*apo de tōn hēmerōn*) indicates that John stands in the mid-point of time, the time of Jesus, the present period of violent struggle over the kingdom. The phrase "from the days of John the Baptist *until now*" (*heōs arti*, the moment in which Jesus is speaking)[43] forms one time period, in which the precursor and the Messiah stand together over against the forces opposing the kingdom's coming—a point we have already seen in chap. 3. Within the context of opposition to Jesus which chaps. 11-13 set, Mt 11:12 may well carry the negative sense of: "the kingdom suffers violence, and its violent opponents snatch it away from those who would receive it."[44] Not only *have* both John and Jesus experienced this violence, the two of them *will* experience this violence unto death, as chaps. 14 and 17 will make clear.

[41]As exegetes well know, Lk 16:16 bristles with problems, problems we cannot consider at length here. The two main problems are whether John is included in or excluded from the time of the Law and the prophets (Conzelmann favors the former choice, Franklin the latter; cf. n. 8 above) and whether the verb *biazetai* carries a friendly or hostile sense ("forces his way into the kingdom" or "uses violence against the kingdom"). The friendly or positive sense seems more likely and is favored by most modern English versions. On all this, cf. W. Grundmann, *Das Evangelium nach Lukas* (7th ed.; Berlin: EvangelischeVerlagsanstalt, 1974) 323; J. Ernst, *Das Evangelium nach Lukas* (Regensburg: Pustet, 1976) 470; G. Caird, *Saint Luke* (Baltimore: Penguin, 1963) 189.

[42]Trilling, "Täufertradition," 277-278, shows that the usual sense of a temporal *apo* in Matthew is an inclusive, not an exclusive one; cf. Wink, *John the Baptist,* 29-30. Becker, *Johannes der Täufer,* 76, holds that the original sense of 11:12 in the mouth of Jesus was exclusive, although he admits Matthew may have understood it in an inclusive way.

[43]Dibelius, *Die urchristliche Uberlieferung,* 24, misses the point when he takes the *hēos arti* to mean that a new period is beginning "now."

[44]Admittedly, this interpretation comes from the general context rather than from any decisive data in the verse itself. It is entirely possible that the verse means that the kingdom of God is entering the world with explosive power, and those who earnestly desire to enter it pay any price to become disciples. BAG, *sub voce,* notes that all the examples of *biastēs* in extra-biblical literature use the word in the negative sense: a violent, impetuous man. The modern English versions are divided on the interpretation but the negative interpretation seems to predominate.

And so, the supreme privilege of John is, as we have already seen in vv 9-10, that he no longer stands in the period of prophecy as one of a line of prophets; the prophetic figure of the Baptist stands in the time of fulfillment alongside of Jesus. Instead of Luke's "the Law and the prophets [lasted] until John," Matthew boldly turns the OT canon on its head makes John part of the period of fulfillment toward which the whole of the OT, prophetic to its core, pointed: "For all the prophets and the Law *prophesied* until John."[45] John's pivotal, eschatological position is then declared openly in v 14; " And if you wish to accept [it], he is Elijah who is to come."[46] The conditional clause, "if you wish to accept it" does not express hesitancy or indifference on Jesus' part. Rather, it voices an urgent appeal and warning to the listener,[47] a warning also heard in the terse command of v 15: "he who has ears, let him hear!" The emphatic demand for acceptance of this mysterious teaching coincides with the clearest identification of the Baptist with Elijah within the NT.[48] He is paradoxically the prohesied pro-

---

[45]Matthew's reversal of the traditional designation for the OT canon, the law and the prophets, is astounding and unparalleled. Instead of seeing the Torah as the canon within the canon, which the prophets guarded, interpreted, and passed on, Matthew turns the canon around and makes the prophets the canon within the canon. For Matthew, the whole of the OT is prophetic—a point to be remembered when dealing with "law and prophets" in 5:17; cf. Meier, *Law and History*, 85-87. Trilling, "Täufertradition," 279, fails to grasp the full import of the transposition, and Wink misses it entirely: "Matthew's version...is a grotesque jumble; 'the prophets and the law' appear in reverse order..." (Wink, *John the Baptist*, 29), Bammel ("The Baptist," 101-102) likewise misses the point of Mt 11:13 and claims it is "unlikely that Matthew wanted to incorporate John into the new era."

[46]Since *dexasthai* has no expressed object, it is open to a number of interpretations. The most likely solution is to supply a simple "it": "If you are willing to accept this truth that I am telling you [namely, that John is Elijah]." Also possible in the context of v 13 is: "If you are willing to accept the testimony of the prophets and the law." An intriguing, though less likely possibility would be: "If you are willing to receive John as Elijah, then he does play the role of Elijah for you"; Dibelius (*Die urchristliche Überlieferung*, 31-32) favors this last possibility.

[47]Other interpretations of the condition: this truth cannot be proven, it is a matter of faith; one must be sincere and well-disposed to receive this mystery; cf. Trilling ("Täufertradition," 281). Cullmann (*Christology*, 36) suggests that the condition "probably means only that it does not make any difference whether the name of the returning prophet is Elijah or one of the other ancient prophets." Such an interpretation does not fit the problematic of Matthew.

[48]Wink mistakenly claims that the clearest expression of this identification occurs at the descent from the mount of the transfiguration; cf. his *John the Baptist*, 30.

phet, the Elijah who is to come who has already come.[49] Thus the question of John's relation to Jesus, raised in v 7, receives its full answer.

After this brief detour to include a reworked version of Luke 16:16, Matthew returns to the main Q context (Mt 11:2-11, 16-19 = Lk 7:18-35). He does this to conclude his statement on the Baptist with a final touch of parallelism.[50] In keeping with the general theme of the opposition of Israel, the parallelism takes the form of a parallel rejection suffered by both John and Jesus, though for opposite reasons. The unfaithful contemporaries of Jesus, "this generation," have not heeded Jesus' urgent appeal to hear and receive his message (vv 14-15). Instead, they are like spoiled, finicky, self-willed children in a market-place who are never satisfied.[51] Neither the ascetic John nor the expansive Jesus suited their taste. The asceticism of John challenged them, but the challenge was neutralized by equating his forbidding manner with diabolical possession. Jesus' free and easy table fellowship with religious outcasts was an invitation to rejoice in God's grace; but, in a sudden spirit of puritanism, the offer was rejected by equating free grace with cheap license. The parallel formulations in vv 18 and 19, especially the key parallel statements, "John *came* . . .

Trilling, on the contrary, is correct when he states in his "Täufertradition," 281: "Dieser Vers [11:14] stellt die entwickeltere Form dar, insofern als hier Jesus selbst in eindeutiger Klarheit und nicht mehr im Rätselwort die Gleichung ausspricht, ferner insofern, als die Gleichheit noch prägnanter ausgedrückt wird durch *estin*."

[49] While this equation of John with Elijah is striking, I am not sure that it and other passages we are investigating justify Trilling's assertion that the idea of John as Elijah transcends and leaves behind the idea of John as forerunner ("Täufertradition," 288). For all of Matthew's insistence on parallelism and Elijah-identification, the evangelist does not choose to omit 3:3 or 11:10.

[50] As can be seen from Q, Matthew has not invented the theme of parallelism without a basis in the tradition. As so often happens in Matthew, the evangelist takes his "cue" from some element in the sources (Mark or Q); he then expands upon and systematizes what he finds especially useful in the tradition.

[51] The parable of vv 16-17 has been interpreted in three different ways. (1) The rebuked generation equals the children who pipe and wail; they want to set the tune and dictate how everyone else is to play. John and Jesus have refused to play by their rules, which do not fit the new period of salvation. (2) The rebuked generation equals both groups of children, who in their determination to have their own way waste time and do nothing. (3) The rebuked generation equals the moody children who refuse to be moved either by the piping (Jesus' joyful style) or by the wailing (John's ascetic style). On all this, cf. D. Zeller, "Die Bildlogik des Gleichnisses Mt 11:16f./ Lk 7:31f.," *ZNW* 68 (1977) 252-257.

the Son of Man *came*,"[52] give striking testimony to the parallel positions, yet contrasting styles, of John and Jesus in the mid-point of history. Despite the fact that both have been rejected by "this generation,"[53] God's wisdom (i.e., his well-ordered plan of salvation) will be vindicated (*edikaiōthē*)[54] by the results of its activity in the ministry of both men (i.e., by "its [Wisdom's] works.[55] The very last words of the whole Matthean composition thus push John and Jesus together again as two manifestations of the works of divine Wisdom.[56]

C. THE MARTYRDOM OF THE BAPTIST (14:3-12)

In 14:3-12, Matthew gives us an abbreviated form of Mark's story of the martyrdom of the Baptist. More telling than the abbreviations are two positive changes Matthew makes in the Marcan text. First, in Mark the one who desires John's death is Herodias (Mark 6:19), while Herod blocks her desire because he fears John, knowing him to be a just and holy man (6:20). In Matthew, it is Herod himself who from the beginning desires John's death; but he fears, not John, but the crowd, which considers John a *prophet*. Already we can hear the leitmotif of the violent fate of the prophets, who are put to death by the

---

[52]In Matthew, besides Jesus (under his various titles and roles), only two human beings are said to *come* in the weighty, eschatological sense of that word: the Baptist (11:18; 21:32) and Elijah (11:14; 17:10-12; 27:49 probably does not apply here).

[53]As Zerwick points out (*Graecitas Biblica,* #455), the *kai* in v 19 may have the "concessive" or "adversative" sense of "nevertheless"; so C. Moule, *An Idiom-Book of New Testament Greek* (Cambridge: Cambridge University, 1960) 178.

[54]The aorist *edikaiōthē* is curious. It may be an overliteral translation of a semitic perfect tense. Or it may be a "prophetic" aorist, affirming the certainty of what will be by putting the verb in a past tense. Moule (*An Idiom-Book,* 13) also suggests either a gnomic aorist ("wisdom is always justified") or a statement of a single past fact ("wisdom received her justification"). These last two explanations do not seem likely in the Matthean context.

[55]For *erga* as the original Matthean reading, cf. B. Metzger, *A Textual Commentary on the Greek New Testament* (Stuttgart: United Bible Societies, 1971) 30; H. Schürmann, *Das Lukasevangelium* (Freiburg: Herder, 1969) 1.428.

[56]Trilling ("Täufertradition," 284) takes the plural "works" to refer to John and Jesus. This is possible in the light of the immediate context (11:16-19). Schürmann (*Das Lukasevangelium,* 1. 428), among others, takes "works" in connection with the works mentioned in 11:2. In the latter case, it would be the disciples who are associated with Jesus in his works. One might ask whether the two interpretations are of necessity mutually exclusive.

evil leaders of Israel (cf. 23:29-37). One is reminded in particular of why the Jerusalem leaders fear Jesus during his last
days in Jerusalem; the crowds consider him a prophet (21:11,
46) as they considered John a prophet (21:26). The second
major change Matthew introduces into the Baptist's death
comes at the end of the story. In Mark, the disciples of the
Baptist come and take his corpse and place it in a tomb.[57] In
Matthew, the disciples of the Baptist take the body, bury it,
and then "announce" (*apēggeilan*) to Jesus what has happened
(Mt 14:12).[58] When Jesus hears this announcement, he withdraws into a desert place (v 13).[59] With this small change,
Matthew makes a number of points. (1) With their old master
dead, the disciples of the Baptist naturally turn to Jesus. (2)
Their news of the Baptist's martyrdom causes Jesus momen-
tarily to withdraw from the public scene; for, with the Baptist
dead, Jesus is the next prophet marked for martyrdom. (3)
Consequently, Matthew again achieves a paralleling of John
and Jesus. Both are destined to be martyred prophets of the
end-time, suffering rejection at the hands of a faithless Israel.
Yet, as always, the parallelism also involves subordination.
The Baptist goes before Jesus in death as in life, prophesying
and preparing the way for the "one who comes after" John,
even in passion and death. When the Baptist's disciples "announce" John's death to Jesus, they are announcing Jesus'
death as well.

[57]Since almost the same concatenation of words (*ptōma...kai ethēken auton en
mnēmeio*) occurs again in Mark only at 15:45-46 (the burial of Jesus), Mark may have
intended that the death of the Baptist prophesy the death of Jesus. If that is the case,
then we have another example of Matthew's expanding upon a "cue" he finds in
Mark.

[58]There is a clever reworking here of Mk 6:30, where the apostles, the disciples of
Jesus, return from their mission. *They* announce (*apēggeilan*) to Jesus all they have
done in their ministry.

[59]Here *anachōreō* indeed means "to withdraw or retreat in the face of danger."
Trilling ("Täufertradition," 273) is misled by the verbal parallel *(akousas de...
anechōrēsen)* between Mt 14:13 and 4:12. In 4:12, when Jesus hears of the arrest of
the Baptist, he goes into Galilee *(akousas de...anechōrēsen eis Galilaian)*, defiantly
taking up the Baptist's fallen standard in Herod's own territory. As G. Soares Prabhu
correctly remarks (*The Formula Quotations in the Infancy Narrative of Matthew*
[Rome: Biblical Institute, 1976]) 125: "The coming of Jesus into Galilee is, if anything
not a flight but a challenge." Thus, *anechōrēsen* in 4:12 should not be translated as
"withdrew" or "retreated" (*contra RSV,* Goodspeed, *NEB,* and *NAB*).

D. MT 17:10-13

The last notable statement about the Baptist in Matthew occurs in 17:10-13, after the transfiguration. Matthew reorders and clarifies the rather obscure dialogue of Mk 9:11-13. In the Matthean form, Jesus solves the problem of how he can be the Messiah if Elijah is supposed to precede the Messiah's coming. Jesus does this first *(men)* by confirming the belief that Elijah is to come (Mk 9:12a = Mt 17:11) and then *(de)* by announcing that Elijah has already come (Mk 9:13a = Mt 17:12a). In a manner more ordered in Matthew than in Mark (Mt 17:12b = Mk 9:13b, 12b), Jesus then explains that Elijah's rejection and suffering ("they did not know him but did to him what they willed") corresponds to the imminent passion of the Son of Man at the hands of the same united front (*mellei paschein hyp' autōn*).[60] Putting Elijah and the Son of Man closer together and stressing that the Son of Man will suffer at the hands of the same people again betray Matthew's paralleling tendency. Matthew drops Mark's puzzling reference to the Scriptures' prophecy of Elijah's sufferings, and typically adds the statement that the disciples then understood that Jesus was speaking of John the Baptist. The phrase *tote synēkan* reminds the reader of the same statement in 16:12, where Matthew also adds to the enigmatic Markan text the affirmation that the disciples finally understood Jesus' metaphor (leaven = teaching/ Elijah = Baptist). Actually, the disciples' understanding in 17:13 is simply an echo of what Jesus has explicitly stated in 11:14: John *is* Elijah.

---

[60]The two statements about the Son of Man and Elijah are separated in Mark by the affirmation that Elijah has come (Mk 9:13a). Matthew places Mk 9:13a first and so creates a closer correspondence between the two suffering figures (*houtōs kai* in Mt 17:12d). In drawing these two figures closer together, Matthew also makes the comparison clearer by rewriting Mark's question ("how is it written about the Son of Man") as a firm statement ("so also the Son of Man will certainly suffer"). I do not share the view of Bammel ("The Baptist," 102) that Mark intends all that is said to refer to only one person, namely Jesus, who is Elijah and Son of Man at the same time. For the more usual view, cf. R. Pesch, *Das Markusevangelium* (Freiburg: Herder, 1977) 2. 78-82.

E. OTHER MATTHEAN TEXTS

The few remaining passages which mention the Baptist can be dealt with quickly, for they occur in the same context, the dispute between Jesus and the Jewish leaders in Jerusalem just before Jesus' passion (21:25-32). The sad parallel of rejection spoken of in 17:12 is now acted out. Jesus' question about the origin of John's baptism not only shows up the Jewish leaders as vacillating and incompetent, without true authority, but also hints at the parallel fate of the two eschatological prophets; both were rejected, hounded, and finally martyred by the leaders, who hesitated to murder only because they feared the crowds (cf. v 26 and v 46). In 21:32, which is an additional and not completely fitting conclusion to the parable of the two sons (21:28-31), Jesus remarks that "John came to you [the Jewish leaders] in the way of justice." The leaders did not believe and remained hardened in their disbelief even when they saw the salvific influence of John's ministry upon the tax collectors and prostitutes. What exactly "in the way of justice" means is not clear. It could mean that John taught God's will, or that he himself did God's will, or even that he fulfilled his proper role vis-à-vis Jesus in salvation history (one is reminded of "to fulfill all justice" in 3:15). At any rate, the fact that John and Jesus are both prophets sent to the unresponsive leaders of Israel is affirmed for the last time.[61]

III. An Interpretation of the Data

Having marshaled the individual data, we must now try to interpret the whole. Quite clearly, Matthew has taken pains to make John and Jesus parallel figures, while at the same time preserving John's subordinate role within the mid-point of time. The pressing question is *why?* What theological reason or reasons have led Matthew to this surprisingly consistent redactional endeavor of paralleling yet subordinating? A

---

[61]For a complete study of this theme of the rejected prophet in Matthew, cf. A. Sand, *Das Gesetz und die Propheten* (Regensburg: Pustet, 1974), especially pp. 125-177.

number of suggestions have been made by various authors.[62] The tendency to parallel the two figures could be seen simply as a natural thrust of Christian faith as it developed and reflected further on key figures in the gospel story. Yet this tendency to parallel appears with great clarity only in Matthew, who engages in careful redactional techniques to bring to the fore his unique theological viewpoint. It might be possible that Matthew is claiming John for the Christian church against the claims of non-Christian Baptist sectarians. But Matthew's gospel does not betray any hint of a polemic against the followers of the Baptist, such as we find in the fourth gospel.[63] Nor is the parallelism simply an expression of a literary tendency to assimilate one character to another. The way in which Matthew consistently undertakes his program of paralleling at key theological moments shows that his purpose is deeply theological, and not just stylistic. To appeal to Matthew's high Christology does not of itself solve the problem, for one would think that a high Christology would reduce John's role instead of enhancing it. That John and his disciples in some way provide the seedbed for the church is a common NT theme, and so does not explain the unique vision of Matthew. The fourth gospel contains both a high Christology and some idea of the Baptist's group as a seedbed for Christ's disciples, but these factors do not produce any tendency toward parallelism in the fourth gospel.

---

[62] A convenient list of opinions can be found in Trilling, "Täufertradition," 288-289; cf. Wink, *John the Baptist,* 40-41.

[63] The disciples of the Baptist appear in three pericopes; in none of the three is there a strong tone of hostility. In 9:14-17, their inadequacy vis-à-vis the Christian dispensation is shown, but Mt 9:14 changes Mk 2:18 to avoid placing the disciples of John together with the Pharisees in the introductory narrative. The two groups occur together in the question, but not in the narrative. In 11:2-6, they are presented in a neutral light as being sent by John to Jesus with the question about Jesus' Messiahship; presumably they bear Jesus' impressive answer back to the Baptist (cf. 11:7a). The high praise of John in 11:7-19 hardly makes sense if it is delivered immediately after a hostile confrontation. In the most redactional of the three passages, 14:12, the disciples of the Baptist naturally come to Jesus after John's death to tell their ally of their master's martyrdom. This is the last mention of John's disciples in Matthew. Does Matthew thus intimate that they become disciples of Jesus? At any rate, there is no notable polemic against them.

Trilling comes closer to the truth by emphasizing Matthew's prophetic indictment of Israel and his claim that the church, not Judaism, is the true people of God.[64] The deuteronomistic conception of the rejection and violent fate of the prophets helps Matthew answer the scandalous problem of why Israel rejected both the final messenger, John, and Messiah himself. Thus, the history of damnation which extends through the prophets extends down to John and Jesus. Intertwined with this theme may be the apologetic need to answer Jewish objections about the necessity of Elijah's coming by identifying Elijah clearly with the Baptist.[65] I think Trilling's explanation moves in the right direction to the extent that it focuses on a vision of salvation history as the reason for Matthew's treatment of John. Unfortunately, Trilling does not develop any further his insight into the nexus between salvation history in Matthew and the picture of the Baptist in Matthew. By itself, the deuteronomistic theme of the violent fate of the prophets does not adequately explain Matthew's passion for parallelism-yet-subordination.

Elsewhere I have tried to develop an adequate overview of Matthew's conception of salvation history.[66] Basically, Matthew's outline involves three stages; the OT, the time of Jesus, and the time of the church. In each stage, the kingdom is realized more fully in history. The OT is the time when the law and the prophets pointed toward the Messiah. In this period, the kingdom was in some sense already present to Israel (21:43). The time of Jesus is the period in which the Messiah undertakes a limited mission only to the lost sheep of the house of Israel (15:24) and sends his twelve apostles on an equally limited mission (10:5-6). The time of the church begins

---

[64]I would not agree, however, with Trilling's designation of the church as the true or new "Israel" (so "Täufertradition," 289). Matthew uses "Israel" only of the OT people of God, the concrete nation which has rejected its Messiah and so has ceased to be the chosen people; cf. D. Hare, *The Theme of Jewish Persecution of Christians in the Gospel according to St Matthew* (Cambridge; Cambridge University, 1967) 153.

[65]While this is one consideration, I do not think we can view this as "Matthew's point of departure in adapting and modifying his sources," as Wink claims (*John the Baptist,* 40).

[66]Meier, "Salvation-History in Matthew: in Search of a Starting Point" (the first essay in Part 2 of this volume); cf. *The Vision of Matthew,* 26-39.

with the earthshaking, apocalyptic event of the death-resurrection (27:51-54; 28:2-3, 16-20) which breaks down the barriers of law and race and extends the mission to all nations.

I would suggest that this schema coincides with and is able to explain all the puzzling statements about the Baptist in Matthew. (1) First of all, the place of the OT in this schema coincides with Matthew's reworking of the Q logion found in its more original form in Lk 16:16. The Matthean reformulation (11:13) reads: "For all the prophets and the law prophesied until John."[67] The prophets and the law form a prophetic economy pointing forward to a time of fulfillment. In Matthew's view, the time of fulfillment is obviously distinct from the period of the law and the prophets, and John stands on the far side of this distinction, over against the prophets and the law and together with Jesus. (2) Why that should be so can be seen from Matthew's view of the second period, the time of Jesus, the mid-point of time. Matthew prefaces his presentation of the public ministry with an infancy narrative which acts as a prologue, indeed as a theological overture and proleptic passion narrative, introducing a number of key theological themes in the gospel. In this prologue Jesus the Messiah is born, and specifically, born as the Davidic King and Son of God (1:1, 20-23; 2:2, 6, 11, 15). The eschatological "temperature," the presence of the kingdom, has obviously been heightened by this prologue. The birth of the King necessarily involves a fuller coming of the kingdom, from the birth of Jesus onwards. For that reason, when the Baptist appears on the stage in chap. 3, he can hardly still belong to the old period of the Law and the prophets. A new period, the mid-point of time, has already begun with the birth of Christ; and the Baptist necessarily stands within it by the inner logic of Matthew's schema. The Baptist's proclamation, rebukes, threats, fate, and martyrdom all reflect his place squarely within the central period of salvation history. This is the most important, indeed, the only adequate explanation for his being

---

[67]Interestingly, Kraeling (*John the Baptist,* 156) sees in Mt 11:12-13 a schema of salvation history falling into three periods—though they do not correspond exactly to the periods I am proposing.

paralleled with Jesus. Matthew need have no fear of this paralleling, since his high Christology prevents any real threat to Jesus' status. Matthew, of course, keeps the various traditional statements which express John's subordination, and even adds a few. But he feels no need to emphasize this subordination in the way he consistently emphasizes the parallelism. (3) The third period, the time of the church, also helps explain one curious aspect of Matthew's view of John. In Matthew's vision, the time of the church is a period distinct in nature from the time of Jesus, as the apocalyptic events of the death-resurrection, the exaltation of Jesus to the status of cosmocrator (28:18; cf. 13:37-38), and the universal mission make clear.[68] Through baptism, not circumcision, all nations can now enter into the new people of God, sharing the "family life" of Father, Son, and Spirit, and observing as the norm of morality not the Mosaic law *qua* Mosaic but rather all whatsoever Jesus commanded (28:19-20).[69] An appreciation of the different quality of this age of the church makes intelligible that puzzling saying of Jesus in 11:11b: "But the least in the kingdom of heaven is greater than he." As we have seen, these words are difficult to square with the statement of v 11a ("there has not arisen among those born of women one greater than John the Baptist") and with what I consider the obvious intention of Matthew not to exclude the Baptist from the final stage of the kingdom at the end of the age. But once we realize that the time of the church is distinct from the time of the earthly Jesus and enjoys a heightened eschatological quality over that of the time of Jesus, the saying in 11:11b becomes clear. On the one hand, the Baptist, who has the unique privilege of being paralleled with Jesus in the mid-point of time, is greater than any other person in that period of the sacred past. But even the least disciple in the church, enjoying all the riches of the period after the death-resurrection, living as he is in a time when the kingdom has broken into this age in a new, definitive way,

---

[68] Here I differ from Kingsbury, who sees only two epochs: the OT and the time of Jesus (cf. his *Matthew*, 31).

[69] This is not to deny the connecting links between the time of Jesus and the time of the church, chief among which is the person of Jesus himself; cf. Meier, *The Vision of Matthew*, 209-210.

even this least in the kingdom (during the time of the church) is greater than the Baptist, who died before this new stage of the kingdom burst upon the scene. Consequently, 11:11b does not so much denigrate the Baptist as felicitate the disciples who have entered into a new and better period of salvation history.[70] Matthew's pattern of parallelism-yet-subordination thus proves to be a function of his ecclesiology as well as of his Christology. That is hardly surprising, since the nexus between Christology and ecclesiology is the distinguishing hallmark, the specificity, of Matthew's gospel.

Matthew has thus succeeded in reworking the image of the Baptist to fit it neatly into his vision of salvation history, Christology, and ecclesiology. One has to marvel at the care with which every pericope dealing with the Baptist is "retooled" to bring the statements into line with Matthew's overarching vision. Consequently, I cannot agree with Wink's conclusion that Matthew's treatment of the Baptist is "more comprehensive than Mark's" but "less profound"[71]—unless one equates "profound" with "obscure" and "cryptic." In its ability to synthesize disparate, even conflicting traditions into a coherent whole, Matthew's gospel is one of the most profound documents in the NT, and his treatment of the Baptist is a showcase example of his genius.

☙

Afterword

Most of the recent literature has concentrated on the historical figure of the Baptist, individual Baptist pericopes in

---

[70]Cf. Dibelius, *Die urchristliche Überlieferung*, 13.
[71]Wink, *John the Baptist*, 41.

the Four Gospels, or the pericope narrating the baptism of Jesus by John. Relatively few works focus on Matthew's unique presentation of the Baptist throughout his Gospel. For a sampling of recent opinions, see A. Fuchs, "Intention und Adressaten der Busspredigt des Täufers bei Mt 3.7-10," *Jesus in der Verkündigung der Kirche* (ed. A. Fuchs; Studien zum Neuen Testament und seiner Umwelt, series A, vol. 1; Linz: A. Fuchs, 1976) 62-75; S. Bénétreau, "Baptêmes et ablutions dans le Judaïsme. L'originalité de Jean-Baptiste," *Foi et Vie* 80 (1981) 96-108; O. Böcher, "Johannes der Täufer in der neu-testamentlichen Überlieferung," *Kirche in Zeit und Endzeit* (Neukirchen-Vluyn: Neukirchener V., 1983) 70-89; S.L. Davies, "John the Baptist and Essene Kashruth," *NTS* 29 (1983) 569-71; J. Lindeskog, "Johannes der Täufer," *ASTI* 12 (1983) 55-83; J. Ernst, Offnet die Türen dem Erlöser. Johannes der Täufer—seine Rolle in der Heilsgeschichte," *TGl* 74 (1984) 137-65; H. Fleddermann, "John and the Coming One (Matt. 3:11-12//Luke 3:16-17)," *Society of Biblical Literature 1984 Seminar Papers* (ed. K.H. Richards; Chico, CA: Scholars, 1984) 337-84; P. Nepper-Christensen, "Die Taufe im Matthäus-evangelium," *NTS* 31 (1985) 189-207; C.R. Kazmierski, "The Stones of Abraham: John the Baptist and the End of Torah (Matt 3, 7-10 par. Luke 3, 7-9)," *Bib* 68 (1987) 22-40.

10

The Canaanite Woman in Matthew 15:21-28 and the Problem of World Religions

To the theologian or pastor exploring the theme of Christianity and world religions, Matthew's account of the encounter between Jesus and the Canaanite woman hardly seems promising. After all, the story starts with Jesus the Jew brushing off a pagan woman because his mission is restricted to a Jewish Israel. What this could possibly say to Christianity's relation to world religions today is at best unclear. "Relevant" applications of the text strain the most ingenious of hermeneutical imaginations. Yet biblical hermeneutics does not consist of finding—or inventing—one-for-one correspondences; those rarely, if ever, exist. Hermeneutics is possible because, by the light of faith, believers can perceive surprising structural similarities in different encounters between human need and divine grace—even across the gaping chasm of cultural shifts. Granted, in 15:21-28 Matthew obviously did not intend to treat the modern problem of Christianity's relation to world religions. Yet the theologian who approaches this story with the contemporary problem in mind and who watches the encounter between Christ and the pagan with open eyes comes away with a new vision.

But first things first: All hermeneutical projects, however grand, begin with listening to the text on its own terms and with its own structures. Indeed, the structure Matthew has devised for 15:21-28 is most intriguing. As is well known, Matthew's miracle stories tend to boil down the narrative to a single encounter between the petitioning word of the person in need and the healing word of Jesus. In Mt 15:21-28, however, the verbal encounter occurs four times, for particular structural and theological reasons. Scholars often point to the "law of threes" in biblical narrative. In the parable of the Good Samaritan, for example, there are precisely three persons who come upon the victim; the audience instinctively knows that the climax will occur the third time round. Only with this law of threes in mind can we appreciate the structure of Matthew's story. The audience senses that the woman will get three chances: "Three strikes and you're out!" But God is not held to the rules of narrative anymore than he is held to the rules of theology. Divine grace supplies a fourth time at bat. The four verbal encounters thus give our story an extraordinary structure and an extraordinary theological insight.

(1) The story begins with the initiative of Jesus, as he withdraws to the pagan regions of Tyre and Sidon. Yet, strangely, the tension in the rest of the story springs from Jesus' refusal to take any initiative when it comes to the natural result of his action: encounter with a pagan. It is rather the Canaanite woman who seizes the initiative by "coming out" (symbolically?) from "those [pagan] regions" to plead with Jesus. In a sense, the woman already has three strikes against her before she even starts: She is a woman; she is the mother of a demoniac; and worst of all she is a pagan Canaanite, a member of the ancient enemy of Israel, the indigenous people of Canaan who fought Israel over its inheritance in the Promised Land. Still, for all her handicaps, the woman is not shy about shouting her need. The first verbal encounter begins with her cry of "Lord" and "Son of David." In Matthew, "Lord" is addressed to Jesus only by true believers, and "Son of David" is used by the marginalized of society, the no-accounts who recognize the Messiah of Israel, whom the leaders of Israel reject. The woman knows full well that her insight of faith gives her no claim on the Jewish Messiah; all she can do is beg for mercy for her tormented daughter. From the reader's point of view, the woman has a lot going for her, but the three strikes against her seem to carry more weight with a disturbingly hard-hearted

Christ. Jesus refuses the verbal encounter; he speaks not a word in reply. His first rebuff is silence.

(2) The second verbal encounter arises out of the initiative of the officious disciples. They are annoyed with the woman's persistent cry of faith; so, just to get rid of her, they presume to tell Jesus to grant her request (this seems to be the sense of "send her away"). This time, Jesus deigns to speak, but it is a word of rebuff. God has sent him on a mission restricted to his own people Israel, who have all gone astray like lost sheep— no more so than in their refusal to recognize the Son of David. Faced with the urgency of his mission, Jesus cannot transgress the limits set by the Father's plan of salvation. His second rebuff is theology.

(3) As the third verbal encounter begins, the audience senses that the climax is now being reached. Persisting in the face of discouragement, the woman of faith "comes" to Jesus and "worships" him (*proskyneō*, a favorite Matthean verb for the proper act of reverence toward Jesus). She repeats her petition with heart-rending simplicity: "Lord, help me." Like the Psalmist, she is at the end of her rope. Surely now, importuned by a third request, Jesus will relent and show compassion. The audience is as disappointed as the woman when Jesus smashes the law of threes and adds the insult of a racial slur to the injury of turning a deaf ear. He repeats the excuse of his limited mission, but now in the form of a harsh parable. He tells the pagan that the bread of his healing and teaching ministry is meant only for God's children, the Israelites; he may not waste it by tossing it thoughtlessly to the "dogs" (a Jewish epithet for pagans). The story seems to end in disaster: The woman of faith is bereft of her request and an aloof Jesus is bereft of compassion. His third rebuff is sheer insult. The reader is left bewildered.

(4) That is where it should end—by the law of threes. But a genuine encounter of human faith with divine mercy can put an end to all ends and limits, however sacred they may be to either theology or narrative criticism. That is what "eschatology" is all about. This extraordinary woman of persistent faith shows herself to be a woman of wit and humor as well. She deftly takes up the gauntlet of the parable cast down by Jesus and turns it to her advantage. "Yes, *Lord*," she says, replying

to insult with politeness as well as with faith and humility (cf. Mt 5:38-42). "I accept your view—at least for the sake of argument—that I am a pagan dog when compared to the privileged children of Israel, my masters. And I acknowledge that I have no right to snatch bread out of the children's hands. But, after all, even the dogs lying under the table are allowed to nibble the unwanted scraps that haphazardly fall from their masters' tables." The woman boldly engages Jesus in a game of wits, matching *mashal* with *mashal;* and her faith, spiced with determination and humor, trumps the Lord. Yet Jesus hardly seems dismayed by the outcome. The reader comes to realize that this whole verbal duel has displayed the maieutic method by which Jesus has led this woman up four steps to the heights of faith, a faith that can transcend the barriers of race, religion, and even the set periods of salvation history. At the end of Matthew's Gospel, after the death-resurrection, Jesus will indeed tear down the barriers he affirms in 10:5-6 and 15:24 by sending his disciples to all nations, but the desperate need of this woman cannot wait. Her impatient faith leaps the barriers of time and religious groups to touch directly the healing power of Christ. Salvation history was made for man, not man for salvation history. Hence Jesus' final cry is one of approval and praise, not of weariness and defeat: "O woman, great is your faith!" It is such irregular, unlawful, but all-powerful faith that can bring healing to a possessed humanity, even if it ignores the "proper channels" for coming to Christ.

By now, our unpromising pericope has begun to show promise—even for such an "un-gospel like" theme as Christianity and world religions. To start with, the notably different roles of Jesus and his disciples suggest a key distinction in our hermeneutical reflections on this story. When one speaks of the exclusivity of the claims of the Christian religion, one must carefully distinguish between Christ and his church. The true exclusivity lies in the person and the role of Jesus—he is the one mediator between God and humanity (I Tim 2:5); no one comes to the Father except through him (Jn 14:6). He alone can grant healing to the well-disposed pagan standing before him. It is important to remember that this exclusive claim about Christ was not hammered out by the early Christians in ignorance of the other great religious movements around them. The first-century Mediterranean world presented a smorgasbord of religions and cults, from the high ethical monotheism of Judaism to the lowest pagan magic and self-mutilation. Over against all of its competitors, the church consciously and deliberately proclaimed the unique role of Jesus Christ—a theological obsession that struck most pagans as odd. To be sure, the church in the twentieth century has gained much wider knowledge and sympathetic appreciation of non-Christian religions. This in itself is a grace, not least because such widened horizons can deepen the church's understanding of God's workings in the world, both in and apart from the church. Still, none of this changes the church's basic faith-affirmation that just as there is one God (the monotheism of the *Shema'*), so there is one mediator (the Christology of the creed). To replace that confession with a "broad-minded" syncretistic smorgasboard is not to reinterpret Christianity but to replace it with a new gnosticism. It is Jesus, and Jesus alone, who brings the fullness of God's healing to humanity. Christianity rises or falls on the centrality of God and the finality of Christ: *Shema'* and creed.

The exclusive claim of Christ does not, however, entail an equally exclusive claim by his church—though the church is constantly tempted to arrogate to itself the unique and indispensable role of Jesus. The disciples officiously try to act as middlemen between the pagan and her Lord, only to be dismissed by Jesus. (Notice how the disciples disappear from the rest of the story; they are neither wanted nor needed by either party in the duel of wits.) Jesus is quite capable of dealing with the pagan woman directly. After all, it is he, not the disciples, who is the object of the pagan's trust and prayer.

Granted, we cannot draw facile present-day lessons from a unique past situation in which Jesus was physically present and the church was not yet established. But the church must constantly remind itself that it is dependent on Christ, and not vice versa. If Jesus is really *Kyrios*, then he is Lord of all the world and of all men and women. The church is the special locus of his lordship in the sense that the church alone explicitly and knowingly acknowledges, worships, and obeys him as Lord. Yet Jesus exercises his lordship over all men and women, whether they are aware of it or not, whether they like it or not, and whether the official (not to say officious) church is on the scene or not. The Lord is free to lavish his grace and mercy on whom he wills (cf. Rom 9:15-16). If he sees fit, he can sanctify pagan hearts and draw them close to himself, using whatever "natural sacrament" or elements of pagan religion he chooses. This is what it means to be Lord: to be sovereign in bestowing grace, both in and outside the church. The church is Christ's special instrument in the world, but not his only one.

This is not to say that the church must not pursue her mission of evangelization with zeal. The Matthew who shows us Jesus dispensing with his disciples as he interacts with a pagan is also the Matthew who presents the risen Lord commanding those same disciples to undertake a universal mission (Mt 28:16-20). To be sure, in ways hidden from our eyes, Jesus may continue acting to save sincere pagans apart from the church's preaching of the gospel. We hope it is so; we pray it is so; but, of course, we have no way of knowing it is so with complete certitude. What we do know from the New Testament is that the risen Lord wills the myriad divisions of mankind to be overcome in one visible family of God, with one baptism, one code of discipleship, and one Lord acknowledged openly by all his people in his church. He who is de facto Lord of all refuses to be hailed as such without the preaching of weak, inadequate disciples like ourselves. The Word still insists on becoming flesh, however inefficient that procedure may be.

Some claim that it is imperialistic of the church to persist in its universal mission, as though it were some international conglomerate intent on a hostile takeover of other religious corporations. Such a haughty, imperialistic attitude can be—and has been—a serious error in the church's missionary activity. At times, silence, theology, and insult have become Christian weapons in the encounter with non-Christians. Yet true mission, true servanthood to the nations, is anything but imperialistic. Imagine, for a moment, what would happen if the church fully succeeded in carrying out the great commission of Mt 28:16-20, if the church so perfectly reflected the measureless mercy of the Son of David that it drew all nations to itself. Imagine Canaanites and Israelites, or Arabs and Jews, or all Asia and Africa united in the one family of God. Would—

could—the church look anything like it does today, with bureaucratic and theological leadership still very much entrenched in the first world? Would not Christian liturgy and lifestyle undergo a sea change, as billions of Asian and African Christians had their proper say and impact in the one church of Christ? If the great commission is ever fulfilled, it will mean not the imperialistic triumph of the present form of the church but rather its death, followed by the resurrection of a genuine world-church, catholic in a sense we can hardly dream of. The one thing that would remain the same would be the church's Lord: the Son of David who is the same yesterday, today, and forever (Heb 13:8). He is already at work in Tyre and Sidon; we obtuse disciples have yet to catch up.

꙳

Afterword

Although this exegetical essay is done for a more popular audience than most of my Matthew studies, I must confess a certain fondness for it, simply because it is the only Matthean essay I have ever done that totally prescinds from Synoptic parallels and questions of tradition and redaction. Instead, it pursues a path similar to the literary and narrative criticism used by Jack Dean Kingsbury in his recent works. A summary of his literary-critical views on Matthew can be found in the second, revised and enlarged edition of his *Matthew as Story* (Philadelphia: Fortress, 1988) For a general introduction to contemporary literary approaches to the New Testament, see Norman R. Petersen, *Literary Criticism for New Testament Critics* (Philadelphia: Fortress, 1978); George A. Kennedy, *New Testament Interpretation through Rhetorical Criticism* (Chapel Hill, NC/London: University of North Carolina, 1985); Terence J. Keegan, *Interpreting the Bible. A Popular*

Introduction to Biblical Hermeneutics (New York/Mahwah, NJ: Paulist, 1985). For a literary-theological approach applied to the Passion Narrative in Matthew, see Donald Senior, *The Passion of Jesus in the Gospel of Matthew* (Wilmington, DE: Glazier, 1985).

Two articles that consider the Matthean pericope in tandem with the Marcan parallel are G. Schwarz, "*Syrophoinikissa—Chananaia* (Markus 7.26/Matthäus 15.22)," *NTS* 30 (1984) 626-28; and F.-J. Steinmetz, "Jesus bei den Heiden. Aktuelle Überlegungen zur Heilung der Syrophönizierin," *Geist und Leben* 55 (1982) 177-84. The first article dwells on a hypothetical Aramaic background to the difference between Mark's "Syrophoenician" and Matthew's "Canaanite"; the latter takes up the pericope in the context of the problem of relations between Christians and non-Christians.

11

Antioch

Syrian Antioch (modern Antakya in Turkey) was a city founded by Seleucus Nicator in 300 B.C. and conquered by Rome in 64 B.C. Located on the Orontes River in the north-western corner of the Roman province of Syria, it was the province's capital, the third largest city of the empire, a center of Greek culture, and a commercial hub. Jews inhabited Antioch from its foundation and enjoyed the right to observe their own customs. The various synagogues of the city sent representatives to a council of elders presided over by a "ruler." Large number of Antiochene Gentiles were attracted to Jewish worship. Nicolaus of Antioch, one of the seven Hellenist leaders in Jerusalem (Acts 6:5), was among those Gentiles who became Jewish proselytes. The first Jewish war (A.D. 66-73) occasioned anti-Jewish riots in Antioch, but on the whole Judaism enjoyed a peaceful life at Antioch and thus provided early Christians a stable matrix. Public order, a prosperous urban culture, a Judaism used to contacts with Gentiles, an intellectual and religious milieu open to many currents, interest in mystery cults, fine roads and lines of communication—all these factors favored Antioch as an energetic center for Christian missionary outreach.

Christianity at Antioch

Christianity was brought to Antioch ca. A.D. 40 by Hellenists who fled from Jerusalem after the martyrdom of Stephen (Acts 11:19-20). Thus began the first Christian generation at Antioch (A.D. 40-70). At Antioch Hellenists from Cyprus and Cyrene made the momentous decision to begin, as a matter of policy, to convert Gentiles without circumcision. This striking difference from Jewish proselytism set these believers apart, and so it was at Antioch that they received a new name, "Christians" (Acts 11:26). The Jerusalem church sought to control this new development by sending Barnabas, a fellow Cypriote, to guide the Antiochene community. To aid him in teaching this "large company" of believers, Barnabas brought Saul (Paul) from Tarsus to Antioch, where "for a whole year they met with the church" (Acts 11:22-26). Along with Symeon Niger, Lucius of Cyrene, and Manaen (a childhood companion of Herod Antipas), they formed a leadership group of "prophets and teachers" (Acts 13:1). This group sent Barnabas and Saul on their first missionary journey (Acts 13:2-14:28).

Around A.D. 49, objections to Antioch's circumcision-free mission were raised by some Jerusalemite Christians. Paul, Barnabas, and Titus went to Jerusalem for a meeting with Peter, James, John, and other leaders. This "Council of Jerusalem" decided that Gentiles did not have to be circumcised (Acts 15:1-19; Gal 2:1-10). Some time after this meeting, Peter visited Antioch. At first he practiced table fellowship with Gentile Christians but then withdrew under pressure from members of the James party, recently arrived from Jerusalem. Paul, fearing that Gentile converts would think that circumcision was necessary to be fully Christian, publicly rebuked Peter for hypocrisy (Gal 2:11-21). Since Paul soon left Antioch without Barnabas (who sided with Peter), and since Paul never mentions Antioch again in his letters, returning there only briefly, it may be that Paul lost the argument. Luke smoothes over this painful incident by omitting all reference to Paul's clash with Peter. He assigns Paul's break with Barnabas to a squabble over Barnabas' cousin, John Mark (Acts 15:36-40). After Paul's departure, the tension within the Antiochene church may have been relieved by the compromise enshrined in the "Apostolic Letter" of Acts 15:23-29. The circumcision-free mission was confirmed, but the Gentiles had to observe certain "kosher laws" mentioned in Lev 17-18, laws considered incumbent on Gentiles living in the Holy Land. Such observance would make possible common life with Jewish Christians. Amid the tensions between the Hellenist left and the Jamesian right, Peter probably represented a centrist position around which various groups could rally; but the James party had the upper hand.

Second Christian Generation at Antioch

There is practically no source of information for the second Christian generation at Antioch (A.D. 70-100), with the possible exception of Matthew's Gospel. If, as many think, Matthew does come from Antioch, we may gather that the Antiochene church continued to feel strains between the Jamesian right and the Hellenist left. However, the Jewish war, the martyrdom of James, the destruction of Jerusalem, and the eventual break with the local synagogue(s) had weakened the conservative Jewish element in the Antiochene church. Meanwhile, the success of the Gentile mission both pointed the way to the church's future and created new problems for the Christian reformation of pagans. It was Matthew's task to reinterpret and synthesize the competing traditions at Antioch to provide a smooth transition from a Jewish past to a Gentile future. Matthew's Gospel takes the form of a "foundation story," to give a pastoral answer to the crisis of identity the Antiochene church faced in the second generation as it strove to define itself over against both Judaism and paganism. Jewish roots, fulfillment of prophecy, and large blocks of Jewish moral teaching serve to anchor an increasingly Gentile church in the sacred past. But the norm of morality, the center of faith, is now Jesus Christ, who validates a universal, circumcision-free mission at the end of the Gospel (Mt 28:16-20). This balancing act allows Matthew to preserve both "new and old" (Mt 13:52). Hence he extols Peter, Antioch's centrist figure as the "chief rabbi" of the church (Mt 16:18-19). Yet, while admitting the need for Christian leaders, Matthew is wary of the trappings of power and titles (Mt 23:1-12).

Third Christian Generation at Antioch

In the third Christian generation (after A.D. 100), the new pressures of imperial persecution and gnosticising tendencies overrode Matthew's dislike of titles. The need for clearer church structures to defend church discipline and teaching called forth the triple hierarchy of one bishop, a council of elders, and deacons. The first testimony we have of this development is from Ignatius of Antioch (d. ca. A.D. 117). Ignatius inherited Antioch's problem of opposing tendencies in the form of a weak Judaizing movement on the right and a more dangerous Docetism on the left. Like Matthew, Ignatius sought unity through balance. He synthesized strains of Matthean, Pauline, and Johannine traditions to strengthen the emerging "catholic church"—a phrase first used by Ignatius. Matthew's Gospel and the triple hierarchy were Antioch's twin gifts to this catholic church.

※

Afterword

The detailed arguments for my positions in this sketch can be found in R. E. Brown and J. P. Meier, *Antioch and Rome* (New York/Ramsey, NJ: Paulist, 1983) 12-86. The basic source for the history and archaeology of Antioch is G. Downey, *A History of Antioch in Syria from Seleucus to the Arab Conquest* (Princeton, NJ: Princeton University, 1961). For an overview of Antioch down to the time of John Chrysostom, see W. Meeks and R. Wilken, *Jews and Christians in Antioch in the First Four Centuries of the Common Era* (SBLSBS 13; Missoula, MT: Scholars, 1978).

In the light of all the discussion that the *Antioch and Rome* book generated, perhaps the most interesting result is that no one, to my knowledge, has either refuted my arguments for placing Matthew's Gospel at Antioch or supplied a better candidate. It appears that the scholarly consensus today is that

Matthew's Gospel was written in Antioch ca. A.D. 80-90; anyone holding otherwise should feel obliged to present weighty arguments if he or she wishes to overturn the consensus.

12

Presbyteros in the Pastoral Epistles

The purpose of this essay is to investigate the use of the word *presbyteros* in PE.[1] Taking into account the diverse conditions in the churches of Ephesus and Crete, we shall try to reach a conclusion concerning the identification or non-identification of *presbyteros* (elder, presbyter) and *episkopos* (overseer, bishop) in PE. Since our goal is a very limited one, we omit a detailed consideration of the history of the word *presbyteros*, partly because general knowledge of the subject may be presumed from the studies already available,[1a] and partly because an investigation into the history of the word would not contribute very much to our particular purpose. Our method is to try first of all to understand the Pastorals from within the Pastorals.

This method of working out from within PE should be emphasized in the face of so many works on church ministry in the NT which do just the opposite. Usually the gospels, Acts (notably chap. 20), the undisputed Pauline epistles, Colossians and Ephesians, the catholic epistles, Hebrews, etc., will be

---

[1]For PE read "The Pastoral Epistles." PE is also used at times as the abbreviation for the title of any commentary on the Pastorals, irrespective of what the precise wording of the title is, or what language it is in. Complete titles can always be found in the first reference to the work.

[1a]Among the many surveys available, we may mention M. Guerra y Gomez, *Episcopos y Presbyteros* (Burgos: Seminario Metropolitano, 1962); G. Bornkamm, "Presbys, presbyteros," in *TDNT* (Grand Rapids: Eerdmans, 1969) VI, 651-683; A. Lemaire, *Les Ministères aux Origines de l'Église* (Paris: Cerf, 1971) 21-27.

given the lion's share of attention; general conclusions will be implicitly drawn during the investigation; and then these conclusions will be imported into PE. Needless to say, this can do violence to the valuable testimony contained in PE. Moreover, the interesting differences between 1 Timothy and Titus tend to be ignored in the rush to schematize and fit the data into the prefabricated synthesis. Even the recent excellent book of A. Lemaire does not seem to avoid this last pitfall. Accordingly, we shall try first to present a line-by-line, section-by-section study of those passages in PE which contain the word *presbyteros* or related material. Then we shall try to draw some general conclusions, which may or may not fit into some neat schema.[2]

We will now take the *presbyteros*-passages in PE and examine them one by one. The data are as follows: 1 Tim 5:1, 17, 19; Tit 1:5. The abstract noun *presbyterion* occurs in 1 Tim 4:14. The feminine form *presbytera* occurs only in 1 Tim 5:2; and, since the commentators agree that it refers to older women, we shall not give it any special consideration.

I. 1 Timothy 5:1-2

Our first passage, then, is 1 Tim 5:1-2: "Do not treat an older man (*presbyterą*) roughly, but appeal to him as to a father; treat younger men as brothers, older women as mothers, younger women as sisters, with perfect propriety." It seems

---

[2]Since we do not try to fit PE *a priori* into any predetermined concept of the historical development of church ministries, we need not settle here and now the question of time and circumstances of composition. We think, though, that our conclusions will have some light to cast on the question. Note well, then, that we do not invoke any particular position on authorship and date before we begin to exegete the individual passages. At most we presume that what is said about the churches of Ephesus and Crete do reflect the conditions of those churches at the time of the composition of PE. Even if the author of PE is a disciple or admirer of Paul, writing sometime after the Apostle's death, it is only reasonable to suppose that his admonitions reflect the state of the churches at his time. The "fragments-hypothesis" of P.N. Harrison need not be considered, since none of the *presbyteros*-passages we will consider fall under what he considers fragments. For the time being then, we may remain neutral on the question of authorship. When we use the name "Paul" as equivalent to the phrase "the author," it is simply a useful convention, not a critical decision.

obvious that the meaning of *presbyteros* here is "an older man." Not only the opposition to "younger men" (*neōterous*), but also the whole structure of vv 1-2 argue for this: *hōs patera ... hōs adelphous ... hōs mēteras ... hōs adelphas*. The careful balance here would make any reference to an office-bearer very forced, since the other groups are classified according to age and sex. Moreover, the admonitions of vv 1-2 have forerunners, as to both structure and content, in hellenistic ethical teaching common at the time. Commentators refer especially to Plato's *Republic* (5, 463c), where it is said of the Guardian that he will regard everyone he meets as either brother or sister, father or mother, son or daughter, grandchild or grandparent. C. Spicq quotes an inscription from Priene in which a man is praised for honoring older people as parents, people his own age as brothers, and younger people as children.[3] Such praise was common on funerary inscriptions in the centuries just before and after Christ. We might also note that 1 Tim 5 does treat of the proper way to discipline ordained elders, namely in vv 19-20. It is unlikely that the same subject would be brought up twice in the same chapter in such a disjointed way. On the basis of all this evidence, we must object to the New English Bible translation of *presbyterǭ* in 5:1 as "an elder," especially since no alternate reading is given in the margin. The rendering, "an older man," which is found in the RSV, is definitely to be preferred.[4] In short, the importance

---

[3]C. Spicq, *Les Épîtres Pastorales* (Paris: Gabalda, 1969) I, 522. J. Elliott, "Ministry and Church Order in the NT," *CBQ* 32 (1970) 367-391, wishes to see *neōteroi* as a technical term for the newly baptized. Whatever we may think of such passages as 1 Pt 5:1-5, such a technical meaning in 1 Tim 5:1 is highly unlikely because of the hellenistic parallels. Also, what then are we to make of the *presbyteras* and *neōteras* in v 2? In an article entitled "La place ou rôle des jeunes dans certaines communautés néotestamentaires," *RB* 76 (1969) 508-527, Spicq suggests that the *neōteroi* in Tit 2:6 might refer to young Christian men seen as a special group, formed into a type of "club" common in the hellenistic world. But even in Tit 2:2 (Spicq does not consider 1 Tim 5:1-2 in detail in the article), he considers the *presbytas* to be older men, not presbyters.

[4]It is interesting to note that Spicq, PE, *ad loc.,* does not consider "elder" as even an alternate translation; neither does J. Jeremias, *Die Briefe an Timotheus und Titus* (Göttingen: Vandenhoeck & Ruprecht, 1968) 31. J.N.D. Kelly, *The Pastoral Epistles* (London: Black, 1963) and A.T. Hanson, *The Pastoral Letters* (Cambridge: C.U.P., 1966), both criticize the *NEB* translation. Others who take *presbyteros* here in the

of 1 Tim 5:1 is that it reminds us that, despite the technical use of *presbyteros* in PE, the profane meaning can appear with no need of apology or special explanation. We can say even at this point that, whatever may be the precise meaning of *presbyteros* in the rest of PE, the word has not become exclusively a *terminus technicus* for ecclesiastical office.

II. 1 Timothy 5:17, 19

The next two occurrences of *presbyteros* are in 1 Tim 5:17, 19. But immediately a methodological problem arises. To be able to expound what is said about *presbyteros* in this passage, one has to know where the treatment of *presbyteros* ends. The farthest possible limits of the *presbyteros*-pericope are obvious. V 16 concludes the treatment of widows, and 6:1 begins the instruction on slaves. At most, then, the *presbyteros*-pericope extends from v 17 to v 25 inclusive. But there is certainly the possibility that the treatment of *presbyteros* ends as early as v 19 or with v 21 inclusive. It is our contention that the *presbyteros*-pericope does extend through to v. 25, and that the pericope, far from being hopelessly unstructured, has a chiastic pattern.[5] This view naturally has an important effect on the interpretation of the statements made about the *presbyteroi* in the passage, especially in vv 20 and 22. Our *modus procedendi* will be to examine each verse in order,[6] showing

non-technical sense include Guerra y Gomez, *Episcopos* 272; E. Schweizer, *Church Order in the N.T.* (London: SCM, 1963) 85; W. Michaelis, *Das Ältestenamt der christlichen Gemeinde im Lichte der heiligen Schrift* (Bern: Haller, 1953) 51; and J. Leal, *Paulinismo y jerarquía de las cartas pastorales* (Granada: Comancho, 1946) 47.

[5]The question of the precise structure of vv 17-25 is often overlooked, even by commentators who tend to see all the verses as referring to *presbyteroi*. W. Lock, *The Pastoral Epistles* (Edinburgh: Clark, 1966) 61, comes close to presenting a chiastic structure, but his view that v 22 refers to reconciliation weakens the pattern. In his excellent essay, "Die Handauflegung im NT bereits ein Bussritus? Zur Auslegung von 1 Tim 5:22, " in *Neutestamentliche Aufsätze. Festschrift für Prof. Josef Schmid* (edd. J. Blinzler-O. Kuss-F. Mussner; Regensburg: Pustet, 1963) 1-6, N. Adler notes a "fallende Tendenz" in vv 17-24. This is true enough, but it does not allow him to integrate v 25 into his schema.

[6]As has been noted by a number of authors, it is always best to take these verses in the order in which they would be normally read. To decide what v 20 means by invoking what v 22 (supposedly) means is questionable methodology.

how each verse is best understood as referring to presbyters. We will then present our view of the chiastic structure as a confirmatory argument. In this way, even one who does not accept the argument from the chiastic structure may still be able to accept our fundamental position on the unity of vv 17-25, simply on the basis of our verse-by-verse analysis.

We begin, then, with v 17. "Those presbyters who preside notably well should be counted worthy of a stipend twice as large; this holds true especially of those who exercize their ministry by preaching and teaching." Almost all the commentators agree that *presbyteroi* here means presbyters, church officials.[7] The verb *proïstēmi* no doubt has the technical, ministerial sense of 1 Thes 5:12 and Rom 12:8, although 1 Tim 3:4, 5, 12 and Tit 3:8, 14 show that the non-technical use is certainly known to the author of PE. How many different groups of presbyters are mentioned in v 17 is disputed. One could conceivably see four ever-smaller groups: presbyters, presbyters who preside, presbyters who preside well, presbyters who preside well especially by preaching and teaching. But, if we take *presbyteroi* as a technical term, it is questionable whether— this early in the Church's history—there were any otiose presbyters who simply did not preside, i.e., exercise some form of leadership.[8] Rather, "presiding" is the very definition of what a presbyter is. So it is better to see three groups mentioned here: presbyters who (simply) preside, presbyters who preside with great diligence or notable success, and those in this second group who exercise their leadership especially by preaching and teaching. *Kalōs* (translated above as "notably well") is

---

[7]The singular view that *presbyteros* in PE always means simply "an old man" and is never a technical term for ministry, has been continually defended by J. Jeremias in his commentary; cf. also his articles "PRESBYTERION ausserchristlich bezeugt," *ZNW* 48 (1957) 127-132, and "Zur Datierund der Pastoralbriefe," in *Abba (Göttingen:* Vandenhoeck & Ruprecht, 1966) 314-316. We will treat this position (which does not seem to have met with wide acceptance) separately, after reviewing the individual texts.

[8]P. Benoit, in his article, "Les origines de l'épiscopat dans le N.T.," *Exégèse et Théologie* (Paris: Cerf, 1961) 232-246, holds that the text does mean that there were some presbyters who did not preside, just as there were some who did not preach. But it seems that "preside" refers here to the whole office of presbyter, and not just to one function among others, as does preaching.

probably not to be opposed to those who preside badly;[9] it might be doubted whether these latter would be given *any* honorarium. Instead, "well" probably denotes those who give over a good part or even all of their time to the ministry, with the natural result of greater success. Especially if the ministry became one's total occupation, there would be an obvious need for extra support, since one's secular employment would have to be given up. This brings us to the problem of *diplēs timēs*, translated above as "a stipend twice as large" (i.e., twice as large as that received by the ordinary presbyters). The word *timē* can mean either "honor" or "honorarium." The second meaning seems the more likely here, although the notion of payment certainly does not exclude but rather presupposes respect. But it is difficult to find a satisfactory explanation of *diplēs* if *timē* is taken to mean simply "honor." Translations such as "much more honor," "more than that which the widows receive," "more than the less industrious elders," "honor beyond the esteem that an elder merits because of his age," all seem a bit forced; there is no adequate reason for the specification "double." On the other hand, the use of *timē* to mean price, money, or salary is witnessed in the NT, the papyri, and the inscriptions of the period.[10] Double pay was given to elite soldiers, and there is a text that speaks of the emperor giving *dipla opsōnia* to the prophet for his services.[11] A parallel usage is supplied by Greek and Egyptian clergymen, who were remunerated in money or goods. Finally, the meaning "stipend" fits better with the Scriptural quotation (or quotations?) in v 18. The contexts of Lk 10:7 and 1 Cor 9:9 definitely recommend the meaning "honorarium" in 1 Tim 5:17.[12]

[9]J. Reville, *Les Origines de l' Épiscopat* (Paris: Leroux, 1894) 289, does hold that there is a reference here to presbyters who are negligent.

[10]For examples, cf. Spicq, *PE* I, 542.

[11]W. Bauer, *A Greek-English Lexicon of the New Testament and Other Early Christian Literature* (translated by W. Arndt and F. Gingrich; Chicago: Chicago University Press, 1968), *sub voce*.

[12]Michaelis, *Das Ältestenamt,* 112-119, argues at great length against a monetary interpretation of *timē* here, but his case is greatly weakened by a number of doubtful hypotheses, notably the rejection of v 18 as a later addition. H. Lietzmann, "Zur altchristlichen Verfassungsgeschichte," *Kleine Schriften* (Berlin: Akademie Verlag, 1958) I, 155, mentions as a proof-text for *timē*-stipend the passage in *Didache* 13:2—a

The last problem of v 17 concerns those special presbyters engaged in preaching and teaching. The clause "who exercise their ministry" translates *hoi kopiōntes. Kopiaō* is often (though not always) used in Pauline letters as a term for ministerial activity (1 Thes 5:12; 1 Cor 15:10; Gal 4:11; Rom 16:12; Phil 2:16; Col 1:29; 1 Tim 4:10). This is the sense here. The importance of discerning a special group among the presbyters devoted to preaching and teaching can only be fully estimated when one turns to the list of qualities needed in *ho episkopos* (1 Tim 3:1-7). In v. 2 it is said that the overseer must be *didaktikos,* a skillful teacher. It seems likely, therefore, that at Ephesus there was a board of presbyters, a kind of "executive board" or "board of directors" that had general responsibility for and authority over the community. Different members of the board were engaged, more or less actively, in different ministries. In a situation where the faith was endangered by doctrinal errors, it was only natural that great stress would be placed on the ministry of teaching and preaching, and slowly those who were dedicated to the doctrinal ministry came to the fore as a special group within the larger circle of presbyters. These teachers are the presbyters referred to under the title *episkopos* in 1 Tim 3:1-7.[13] And so, at Ephesus, we have the ingredients for a college within a college. Three caveats, however, should be noted. First, this is definitely not the same situation as the monarchical episcopate reflected in the Ignatian epistles. And secondly, what is true for the church at Ephesus need not be true for the church on Crete. Only an investigation of the epistle to Titus will settle whether or not we can simply equate *episkopos* and *presbyteros* in PE.[14] And finally, we should be careful when we say that *presbyteros* and *episkopos* are "identical" or "synony-

---

text which Michaelis, *Das Ältestenamt,* 117-118, rejects because he holds it refers to a later usage. The monetary sense is also supported in M. Dibelius-H. Conzelmann, *Die Pastoralbriefe* (Tübingen: Mohr, 1966) 61.

[13]Thus, with many commentators, we take *ton episkopon* to be a generic singular, taken, perhaps, from a set list of qualities.

[14]The necessity of this distinction is overlooked by many commentators and writers on the subject of early church structure; see, for example, H. Küng, *The Church* (N.Y.: Sheed & Ward, 1967) 410.

mous."(1) *Episkopos* probably could be applied only to certain *presbyteroi* at Ephesus. (2) The term *episkopos* occurs only twice in the whole of PE (1 Tim 3:2 and Tit 1:7; the abstract *episkopē* only at 1 Tim 3:1), possibly because *presbyteros* is the normal term favored by the author, while *episkopos* is embedded in the traditional list of qualities. (3) While the two terms could be applied to the same people, their nuances remained different (function of overseer *vs.* dignity of age); also, their origin may have been different (pagan hellenistic office *vs.* the Jewish executive board of the synagogue). But we should note that speculation about the possible connection between the *m^{c}baqqer* of Qumran and the Christian *episkopos* prevents any apodictic assertions about the origin of the latter term as a designation for church office.

We can restrict our treatment of v 18 to a few short observations. Obviously, the whole verse is meant to support and prove (*gar*) the teaching of v 17 concerning the *diplēs timēs*. There is no great problem about 18a: "For the Scripture says: 'Thou shalt not muzzle the ox as it treads.'" The citation is taken from Dt 25:4 LXX, and appears in a similar context in 1 Cor 9:9.[15] Much more difficult is the second citation: "The laborer deserves his wage." Many various views are proposed to explain this quotation. Some would take the citation as a free rendering of Dt 24:14-15. Others think that the word *graphē* holds only for the first citation, and that the second citation is added rather loosely, without coming strictly under the rubric of *graphē*.[16] In this understanding, Paul could be

---

[15]Cf. H. Strack-P. Billerbeck, *Kommentar zum Neuen Testament aus Talmud und Midrasch* (Munich: Beck, 1926) III, 384-385, where it is noted that this passage was extended by the rabbinic exegesis to apply not only to other animals but also to a man hired to help with the harvest. Paul's sharp distinction between the law's literal sense and its inner meaning is closer to the allegorization of hellenistic Judaism (the *Letter of Aristeas,* Philo) than to the allegorization of the Palestinian rabbis, who emphatically upheld the literal sense even when they allegorized.

[16]J. Fitzmyer, "OT Quotations in Qumran and in the NT," in *Essays on the Semitic Background of the NT* (London: Chapman, 1971) 14, shows parallel cases in the Qumran literature, and notes that 1 Tim 5:18 might be a case in point. On p. 15 he states: "Such a feature, found both in the NT and in the Qumran literature, would hardly warrant the conclusion that other works were regarded as 'canonical' other than those which subsequently came to be regarded as such in the various canonical lists; it is much more likely that the introductory formulae were at times used loosely also of other literature which served some didactic or ethical purpose."

quoting either a familiar proverb or a *logion* of Jesus that circulated widely in the oral tradition before coming to rest in Lk 10:7. Or alternately, Paul could be quoting from Q or some other collection of *logia* of Jesus, a collection he considered as having the authority of *graphē*.[17] Then again, the author—who in this case would certainly not be Paul—might be explicitly quoting Luke's gospel, already venerated as Scripture. Again, the author might be quoting from an unknown apocryphal work which contained this proverb, a work our author ranks as Scripture. Fortunately, since we simply are interested in the meaning of *presbyteros* in vv 17-25, this subordinate question of v 18b can be passed over unsolved.[18] V 18b interests us insofar as it supports (as Scripture? unwritten *logion*? proverb?) the contention that the apostolic laborer deserves compensation. Actually, given this purpose, v 18b is really a much apter proof of v 17 than v 18a: *ergatēs* corresponds to *hoi kopiōntes* and *misthou* to *timēs*.

V 19 treats the problem of denunciation of a presbyter: "Do not entertain an accusation against a presbyter, unless it is confirmed by two or three witnesses." Denunciations were becoming a problem for secular governments during this period, and we have civil documents with similar admonitions not to accept denunciations without proof. The appeal to proof by testimony in penal cases was an innovation for people familiar with Greek and Roman law, but was a firmly embedded institution in rabbinic legal procedure. It comes from Dt 19:15 (cf. Dt 17:6 and Num 35:30), and is referred to in Mt 18:16; Jn 8:17; 2 Cor 13:1; Heb 10:28. There may just be an ironic note in the direction that Christian presbyters should have at least the protection that every Jew enjoyed under the Mosaic Law. There is no real way of determining whether the accusation is thought of as touching the presbyter's official conduct or his private life. Perhaps the most important thing about this verse is that it supplies us with one example in PE of the use of *presbyteros* in the singular when referring to a

---

[17]Cf. J. MacArthur, "On the Significance of *hē graphē* in 1 Tim 5:18," *ExpT* 53 (1941-2) 37.

[18]For arguments for and against the different solutions, cf. the commentaries *ad loc.*

minister. This invalidates one of Spicq's arguments for the distinction he sees made between *episkopos* and *presbyteros* in PE as a whole: ". . . dans les Pastorales, *episkopos* est toujours au singulier et avec l'article défini; *presbyteroi* toujours au pluriel. . . . "[19] It is difficult to understand how this statement could be made by such a careful scholar, who proceeds to translate 1 Tim 5:19 as "Contre un presbytre" etc.[20]

The problem about the limits of the *presbyteros*-pericope arises for the first time in v 20. "Reprimand those who sin, in the presence of all, in order that the others may be filled with salutary fear." Does the key phrase *tous hamartanontas* refer to the aforementioned *presbyteroi* (v 17)/*presbyterou* (v 19) or to sinners in general (thus beginning a new pericope)? It is not impossible that the phrase could mean "sinners" or even (stressing the present form of the participle) "those who persist in sinning."[21] P. Galtier was a perennial defender of the view that v 20 referred to sinners in general,[22] especially since he saw that his attempt to interpret v 22 in reference to the reconciliation of sinners depends very much upon this interpretation of *hamartanontas* in v 20. But there are weighty, and, we think, decisive objections to taking v 20 as referring to all sinners.[23] First of all, if the verse refers to sinners in general, why does the author use the participle instead of the adjective-noun *hamartōlos*? This may not appear to be a telling objection—until we ponder NT statistics. *Hamartōlos* is used much more in the NT than the participle. There are 47 uses of *hamartōlos* in the NT (in both the gospels and the epistles), as

---

[19]Spicq, *PE* I, 452.

[20]*Ibid.*, 545. Note that, if one agreed with the *NEB* translation of 1 Tim 5:1, one would have a second example of the ministerial term *presbyteros* in the singular.

[21]In this case, both *pantōn* and *hoi loipoi* would seem to refer to the same people, *scil.,* the whole congregation.

[22]P. Galtier "La réconciliation des pécheurs dans la première épître à Timothée," *RSR* 39 (1951) 317-320.

[23]For what follows, cf. Adler, *Die Handauflegung* 2-3; but his argument from the use of the participle and the noun needs further nuance, which we try to supply. Cf. also J. Osyra, "Die Wiederaufnahme der Sünder beim hl. Paulus," *BZ* 12 (1914) 176-180. It seems to us that J. Murphy-O'Connor dismisses the argument from the participle too quickly in his article "Péché et Communauté dans le Nouveau Testament," *RB* 74 (1967) 175 n. 37.

opposed to only 11 uses of the participle (found only in the epistles). Almost all of the participial uses are attributive (e.g., "who commits a sin unto death," "through the one man who sinned") or adverbial (e.g., "if we sin," "when you sin"). The passage that comes closest to the generic substantive sense Galtier sees in 1 Tim 5:20 is 1 Jn 3:6: *pas ho hamartanōn*. But even here, the generic sense is made clear by the *pas*. On the other hand, *hamartōlos* is regularly used as a substantive,[24] and often in a generic plural. Now the author of 1 Timothy uses *hamartōlos* in 1:9 and 1:15—both times as a plural substantive with the generic sense of sinners! On the other hand, the participle is used only once in PE, precisely in 1 Tim 5:20. Thus, by an argument from converging philological data, we can state that in 5:20 the weight of probability favors the translation, "those ones of the aforementioned group who sin," rather than the generic substantive "sinners." Within a given context, this use of a non-substantive participle without the explicit mention of a substantive naturally leads to the presumption that the participle stands in function of a prior substantive from the context, in our case *presbyteroi/presbyterou*. Examples of such usage occur in 1 Timothy especially in chapter five: 5:5-6; 5:11-12; 6:12—in fact, even 5:17a+b! A second objection against taking *tous 'hamartanontas* as referring to sinners in general is that this reference would not fit into the general context. The section 5:1-6:2 treats of Timothy's relations with various groups in the community, who are classified according to age, sex, ecclesiastical function, or social status. First we have a general admonition about treating Christians with regard to their age and sex (5:1-2); then the instruction on widows and the order of widowhood (5:3-16); then the rules for the support and governance of the presbyters (5:17-19 at least); and finally instructions on the behavior of Christian slaves (6:1-2). It fits the context perfectly to extend the treatment of presbyters through 5:25. But a section on sinners would disturb the list of groups. The general tendency today seems to be to date the PE either from the last years of

---

[24]Cf. Bauer, *sub voce;* in a few cases it is difficult to decide whether *hamartōlos* has kept its adjectival force or is being used as a noun.

Paul's life (if authentic) or to place them towards the end of the first century (if not authentic). At neither date do we have any proof for a fixed "order" of penitents that could be catalogued along with the other groups in 5:1-6:2.[25] A third objection against seeing v 20 as applying to sinners is that the participle-forms in vv 17-20 argue for continuity rather than for a caesura.[26] Thus, three groups of presbyters are mentioned, all accompanied with participial descriptions: *hoi kalōs proestōtes* (v 17a), *hoi kopiōntes* (v 17b), *tous 'hamartanontas* (v 20a). But there is still an objection to our view that must be met, namely the plural participle *hamartanontas* cannot refer back to the singular *presbyterou*. But such disconcerting alternations between singular and plural are not unknown in 1 Tim 2:9-15 betrays exactly the same pattern—plural, singular, plural. Note also the change from singular to plural in 5:1 as well as the oscillation between singular and plural in the widow-pericope (5:3-16). With such looseness of construction it is not impossible that the number of *presbyterou* and *hamartanontas* is simply influenced by the OT citations which come just before them: *ergatēs* before *presbyterou* and *martyrōn* immediately before *tous hamartanontas*. At any rate, the frequent alternation between singular and plural with no ostensible reason prevents us from making much of the sequence *presbyterou ... hamartanontas*.[27]

We come, now, to v 21: "I charge you in the sight of God and Christ Jesus and the chosen angels to observe these instructions without showing preference, doing nothing out of a spirit of favoritism." This verse is only a pawn in the exegetical game. Its meaning depends entirely on our judgment of what

[25] This point will be treated further when we come to v 22.

[26] So N. Brox, *Die Pastoralbriefe* (Regensburg: Pustet, 1969) 202, as opposed to Bornkamm, "Presbys" *TDNT* VI 666 n. 93. H. Holtzmann, *Die Pastoralbriefe* (Leipzig: Engelmann, 1880) 351-352, even sees an opposition between *hoi kalōs proestōtes* and *tous hamartanontas*. But it is questionable whether *kalōs* in v 17 has the sense of "well" as opposed to "badly"; further, one would expect a *de* at the beginning of v 20 if such an opposition were intended.

[27] We do not bother with minor points of v 20 that do not affect our investigation of *presbyteros*. As for the question of who exactly the *pantōn* and *loipoi* are, we tend to think that the *pantōn* refers to the whole congregation, while the *loipoi* refers to the other presbyters.

tous hamartanontas means in v 20. Since we hold that v 20 refers to presbyters, the obvious sense of v 21 is that, in hearing accusations against presbyters (v 19) and reprimanding those found guilty (v 20), Timothy is to avoid showing preference (*prokrima*—a latinism) and excessive sympathy (*prosklisis*) for the presbyter(s) in question. A minor confirmation of our view concerning the connection between v 20 and v 21 is that the Deuteronomic law of two or three witnesses finds an analogue in the judicial Triad before whom Timothy is now adjured: God, Christ, and the chosen angels. They witness to the author's charge to Timothy, and perhaps there is even the suggestion that Timothy, who now represents this heavenly tribunal, will one day appear before it himself to answer for his judicial decisions. Some commentators suggest that we have here a veiled reference to some recent case, perhaps painful and scandalous, that had not been handled with complete impartiality.[28] But this is quite hypothetical.

V 22 is a true *crux interpretum:* "Lay hands hastily on no man, and do not thus share in another man's sins. Keep yourself unstained." We will treat the rite of laying-on of hands at greater length when we come to 1 Tim 4:14. J. Coppens notes that, through the centuries, exegetes have connected the ceremony in 1 Tim 5:22 with almost every purpose ever associated with the rite: healing, penance, confirmation, and ordination.[29] But only two interpretations are really feasible: the phrase refers to either reconciliation of penitents or ordination. Those who support the former alternative appeal to (1) the practice of the imposition of hands to reconcile penitents, certainly in vogue in the African church as early as the third century, if not before; (2) the fact that the verb *koinōneō* usually refers to something already present (e.g., the sins of the penitent) and not to something future (e.g., the possible future sins of the presbyter being ordained); (3) 2 John 11, which uses the verb *koinōneō* in a context that urges Christians to avoid a person holding false doctrine (since he who even greets such a person

---

[28]So Kelly *PE* 127; Spicq, *PE* I, 546.

[29]J. Coppens, *L'imposition des mains et les rites connexes* (Paris: Gabalda, 1925) 125; on pp. 125-130, Coppens gives a good treatment of the question in relation to the exegesis of the Fathers—a point we omit here for the sake of brevity.

shares—*koinōnei*—in his evil deeds); (4) the fact that many other NT examples (without *koinōneō*) can be cited, which enjoin Christians to avoid contact with sinners or false teachers; (5) the whole context, which speaks of discipline and judicial procedure.[30] But we think that stronger arguments lie on the side of ordination. (1) No proof for the existence of the rite as applied to penitents goes back beyond the third century. Tertullian interpreted our text as referring to penitents, and Cyprian clearly witnesses to the actual performance of the rite in his church. (2) The sins mentioned in v 22b need not be referred solely to the possible future sins of the presbyters; the *tacheōs* in v 22 as well as the investigation mentioned in vv 24-25 suggest rather the sins that a man may have committed before ordination. (3) The two other references to the imposition of hands in PE (1 Tim 4:14 and 2 Tim 1:6) both clearly speak of ordination. (4) No NT writing ever uses "imposition of hands" or some like phrase to describe reconciliation of penitents. (5) When the commentators who interpret v 22 of reconciliation appeal to the context, they obviously presuppose that vv 20-21 do not refer to presbyters, but to sinners in general. We think we have shown that the opposite is more likely. Thus we have a cumulative argument. If we are correct that vv 20-21, together with vv 17-19, refer to presbyters, it seems highly unlikely that v 22, without any particle of transition, would suddenly broach the new subject of reconciliation of penitents in general. (6) Taken as referring to presbyters, v 22 expresses one of the dominant preoccupations of the author of PE: not to admit to church offices any but the most worthy candidates. By way of an aside, we might note that the *via media* of seeing v 22 as referring to the reconciliation of penitent presbyters (cf. Lock, *PE, ad locum*) does not offer a more satisfying solution. Some of the arguments we have used to reject the theory of penitents in general (1, 3, 4) are just as valid against this *via media*. If our theory is accepted, we have a coherent development of thought up to v 23. Having dealt

---

[30]Details of the arguments and specific proof-texts can be found in the commentaries, and especially in Galtier's articles. We omit some arguments that seem to be highly speculative (e.g., Hanson, *PE* 63, on what actions would or would not lie solely in the bishop's area of initiative).

with the problem of the correct way to discipline sinful presbyters, the author now urges that prevention is better than a cure. Avoiding hasty ordination will forestall not only the subsequent burden of reprimanding sins still to come but also any paticipation in the candidate's prior life of sin. The author then rounds off this last point with a general admonition to watchfulness: "Keep yourself unstained."

It is probably this last remark that occasions the strange digression of v 23: "Stop drinking only water; instead, take a little wine because of your stomach-condition and your frequent illnesses." Whether or not Paul is the original author of PE, this disconcerting interruption of the thought is most pauline. Of course, we should not overemphasize the break in thought. The general remark about pure conduct in v 22 might have raised in the author's mind the question of ascetical practices, embraced perhaps by the recipient of the letter. The author may be saying that there is a difference between moral uprightness and excessive (gnostic?) observances. But such intriguing questions as the genuine, *historische* state of Timothy's stomach and a possible allusion to gnostic teaching can be passed over, since they do not enter into our investigation of *presbyteros*. Even if we see a connection between the end of v 22 and v 23, v 23 still qualifies as a digression from the main thrust of the context.

After v 23, v 24 returns to the thought of v 22:[31] "The sins of some are so obvious that they run to judgment before them, while the sins of certain others follow after them." Note that the *hai hamartiai* of v 24 resumes the theme of sin present in v 20 (*tous hamartanontas*) and v 22 (*hamartiais*). If we have been correct in referring vv 20-22 to presbyters, then the resumption of the theme of sin probably denotes a resumption of the topic of presbyters as well. The sense of v 24 seems to go better with v 22 (avoid hasty ordination) rather than with v 20 (correction of sinful presbyters). Timothy is to avoid ordination of the wrong candidates by carrying out a careful investigation. It is to be careful precisely because, while some sins are so public that they cry out like denouncers running to the tribunal,

---

[31]So Holtzmann, *PE* 357, and many commentators after him.

other failings show up belatedly, only after prolonged inquiry.[32]

But there is a brighter side. V 25 states that the same rules hold for discernment of good candidates: "In the same way good works too are easy to see; and, even if this is not at times the case, the good works in question cannot remain hidden for long." The second half of the verse stresses a more agreeable reason for extending one's investigation: it is all too easy to pass over men whose reserve hides their splendid qualifications.

We have come to the end of our exegesis of vv 17-25. We have seen that the entire context of the passage is easily referred to presbyters.[33] It now remains to show that the structure of the passage confirms this view. We have already noted some verbal links in the pericope. We can now advance this line of argument even further. The different participles used to designate presbyters in vv 17a, 17b, and v 20 link up in v 20 with the theme of sin (vv 20, 22, and 24), since the same word (*tous hamartanontas*) is both the last in the series of descriptive participles and the first in the series of *hamartia*-words. To these linking elements we may add the possibility of an inclusion (*kalōs* in v 17, *kala* in v 25). More importantly, as we read through the passage, we note that this tract on presbyters starts on a positive note (the excellent presbyters who deserve support, vv 17-18), shifts to a negative theme (accusation against presbyters, correction of sinful presbyters, avoidance of ordination of unworthy candidates, vv 19-22), resumes the negative theme after a digression (some sins of candidates are obvious, others require investigation, v 24), and returns at the end to a positive note (good qualities follow the same rule, v 25). This pattern of positive-negative-negative-positive forms a

---

[32]Cf. the demand for a period of prior testing in the case of deacons, 1 Tim 3:10. Along with P. Dornier, *Les Épîtres Pastorales* (Paris: Gabalda, 1969), *ad loc.*, we think *krisin* refers to Timothy's judgment to confer or withhold ordination, though a reference to the divine tribunal is also possible.

[33]C. K. Barrett, *The Pastoral Epistles* (Oxford: Clarendon Press, 1963) 82, wishes to extend the presbyter-pericope to 6:2. In his understanding, 6:1-2 refer not to slaves in general, but to elders who are slaves. But there is really nothing in 6:1-2 to suggest this positively, and the parallel *Haustafeln* for slaves (Col 3:22ff.; Eph 6:5ff.; 1Pt 2:18ff.; Tit 2:9f.) give no special consideration to slaves who are church officials.

chiastic structure A-B-B̂-Á that can be diagrammed as follows:[34]

CHIASTIC STRUCTURE OF 1 TIMOTHY 5:17-25:
RULES CONCERNING PRESBYTERS

A. POSITIVE   v 17—principle: *hoi kalōs proestōtes presbyteroi*
(good elders)   *hoi kopiōntes*
                    v 18—proof: citations from *Scripture* (at least 18a)

B. NEGATIVE   v 19—accusation; quote from *Scripture: 3 witnesses*
(sin and   v 20—*tous hamartanontas:*   *before all*
prevention)   v 21—adjuration to impartiality: *before 3 witnesses*
                    v 22—avoid hasty ordination: *hamartiais*

                 keep yourself pure

                            digression: v 23—water &
                            wine: watershed of the
                            2 negative blocks.

B̂. NEGATIVE   v 24—investigate candidates for possible *hamartiai*
(sin and   some obvious, some not
prevention)

Á. POSTIVE   v 25—investigate candidates for *erga kala;*
(good candidates)   some obvious, some not

The chiasm we suggest is not one that would result from very sophisticated literary techniques. 1 Timothy is not Hebrews. Rather the pattern is a very natural one, arising spontaneously from the drift of thought. The thought begins

---

[34]Note that we take into account the digression of v 23, which splits the negative theme into two blocks. If one wished to omit v 23 entirely from consideration and count only three blocks of material, one would have another typically pauline pattern: A-B-Á.

with a positive observation, drifts into some negative themes, wanders in v 23, returns to the negative theme, and finally comes home to rest on a positive note. Precisely because the chiastic pattern is simple and unreflected, one cannot press individual elements for greater symmetry: Ḃ, for example, is much shorter than B. But the general pattern, together with all the small linking elements, refutes the view that vv 17-25 do not form a unit. Consequently, our contention that vv 20 and 22 refer to presbyters receives added confirmation.

III. Titus 1:5-7

We move now to Tit 1:5-7. "For this reason I left you behind in Crete, to put in order what was deficient and to appoint presbyters in each city, just as I ordered you—if anyone is above reproach, a man with one wife, and with Christian children who are not subject to charges of loose living or insubordination. For, as the manager of God's household, the bishop (*ton episkopon*) must be above reproach, [here follows a long list of qualities]." These three verses contain a number of vital points for our investigation, but before we examine them a word should be said about the general condition of the church on Crete as opposed to that of Ephesus. One gets the impression when reading Titus that a much more primitive state of ecclesiastical affairs is being described. This is certainly understandable if the situation presented in the letter is historical. If Paul wrote 1 Timothy, he did so at a time when Ephesus was already a well-established church, having been founded some twenty years previously. The pauline churches on Crete would have been of more recent origin. Even if the letters date from after Paul's time, the author has done a very cunning job of maintaining the fiction of describing differences between the state of the church in Ephesus and that of the churches of Crete in the 60's. Timothy is to look to the discipline of the presbyters, while Titus (apparently alone, without collaborators or a college) is to appoint them in each city (obviously for the first time). There is an order of widows in Ephesus; no mention is made of this in Titus. The same holds true for the order of deacons. The command in 1 Tim 3:6

not to make a neophyte an *episkopos* probably finds no echo in Titus because the Cretan churches were too recent for such a criterion to be feasible. And there is nothing in Titus to correspond to the emphatic admonition to rich Christians in 1 Tim 6:17-19; the Ephesian church seems to be growing rather comfortable. We must keep these differences in mind as we try to exegete Tit 1:5-7; they will prevent us from automatically reading what we know about the Ephesian church into the Cretan communities. In v 5, the impression is given that Paul and Titus have just finished a whirlwind tour of Crete. Paul has departed from the island, leaving Titus behind to consolidate the apostolic work and provide structure for the nascent churches. In particular Titus is to see that each city (*kata polin*—distributive) has a group of presbyters (*presbyterous*—plural, for each city!). V 6 begins in a manner we are now quite used to, i.e., with a change from plural to singular: "if anyone" (*ei tis*—a typically pauline phrase). What follows is a short list of qualities necessary for a presbyter. Being "above reproach" (*anegklētos*) is mentioned first, and then qualities related to the candidate's wife and children.[35] These "domestic" qualities are important, says the author, because (v 7—*gar*), as the manager of God's household (*theou oikonomon*), the bishop must be above reproach (*anegklētos* again), no self-willed, etc. Despite the rough syntax (v 6 is either tacked on loosely to v 5 or simply left hanging without any apodosis), one thing seems perfectly clear from the structure of vv 5-7: the presbyters seem to be equated with the bishop. The *presbyteroi* (plural) are certainly to be identified with the *tis* (singular) in v 6, who is to be *anegklētos*, as well as endowed with other, "domestic" virtues. The reason (*gar*) given for requiring these qualities is that the manager of God's household, the bishop (*ton episkopon*—singular), *must* be *anegklētos*. The ironclad identification might be diagrammed as follows:

---

[35]Happily, we may omit a consideration of the endless arguments over the meaning of "a man of one wife" (v 6), since the question has nothing to do with our investigation.

$$(gar)$$
$$presbyterous\text{-}tis\text{-}anegkl\bar{e}tos \longrightarrow ton\ episkopon\text{-}anegkl\bar{e}tos$$

(v 5)	(v 6)	(v 6)	(reason)	(v 7)	(v 7)

As we have already seen, the switch from plural to singular takes place in v 6, with *tis*, so that there is nothing at all surprising about the singular *ton episkopon* in v 7. It may be, of course, that the singular in v 7 is also due to the fact that the author is here quoting a set list of requirements, a list in which *ton episkopon* is firmly embedded. Such a list of qualities or virtues necessary for a particular office was well known in the hellenistic world. But such a possibility in no way neutralizes the fact that the author does equate this *episkopos* of the traditional list with the *presbyteroi* about whom he has been talking.

The simplest and most obvious conclusion, then, is that while the older church at Ephesus had already evolved to the point where a small group of teaching *presbyteroi* (the *episkopoi*) were coming to the fore had assuming a position of leadership within the presbyterium, in the primitive churches of Crete there had not been enough time for "functional specialization" to evolve a special group within the larger group of presbyters.[36] In Titus as well as in 1 Timothy, the bishop is connected with teaching (Tit 1:9; cf. 1 Tim 3:2). But, instead of the differentiation that we find in 1 Tim 5:17 (when compared with 1 Tim 3:1-2), we find in Tit 1:5-7 a simple identification of this teaching bishop with the presbyter. And, as we have

---

[36]Because of our position on the difference in structures between Ephesus and Crete, we do not bother with a detailed comparison of the qualities of Tit 1:7-9 with those of 1 Tim 3:2-7. Correct methodology demands that one start not with a comparison of 1 Timothy 3 and Titus 1, but rather with a comparison of 1 Timothy 3 and 1 Timothy 5 on the one hand, and a comparison of Tit 1:5 and Tit 1:7 on the other. A comparison of the two epistles should follow upon the comparison of the data within each epistle. —Needless to say, the attempts to detect later interpolations in the *episkopos* passages lack objective support in the documents. For such an attempt, cf. A. von Harnack, *Entstehung und Entwicklung der Kirchenverfassung und des Kirchenrechts in den zwei ersten Jahrhunderten* (Leipzig: Hinrich, 1910) 50-51. A different attempt to get around the difficulty of Tit 1:5-7 is to understand before v 7 some phrase like, "for precisely from among the presbyters the bishop must be chosen." But this is to read the situation in 1 Timothy (or even of the later monarchical episcopate) into Titus. Once again, it lacks all foundation in the text and derives from the original sin of refusing to let the epistle of Titus be the epistle of Titus.

already noted, the singular *ton episkopon* in 1 Tim 3:2 and Tit 1:7 can be easily explained as a generic singular embedded in a traditional list.[37]

IV. 1 Timothy 4:14

We have completed our examination of the *presbyteros*-texts in PE. There remains one text in which the abstract derivative *presbyterion* appears,[38] namely 1 Tim 4:14: "Do not neglect the grace of God which is in you, which was given to you through prophecy together with the laying-on of the hands of the presbytery (*presbyteriou*)." Here we must omit many questions which, though interesting and important in themselves, do not bear directly on our treatment of the word *presbyterion:* e.g., the concept of charism, its connection with the rite of ordination, its permanent quality, the exact force of *dia* ("through," or possibly "on the occasion of") as opposed to *meta* ("together with," "accompanied by"), the history of the "laying-on of hands,"[39] etc. We will concentrate solely on the meaning of *presbyterion,* traditionally translated as "presbytery," i.e., a college or board of elders. The interpretation is then quite simple. Paul, indeed, ordained Timothy personally by imposition of hands (2 Tim 1:6); but in this he acted as presiding officer and was accompanied by the whole body of

[37]Note that such grand arguments as *"episkopos* always appears in the singular in PE" are slightly deflated when one realizes that the word occurs only twice, in precisely the same context.

[38]The alternate *presbyterou* (witnessed in the original of Sinaiticus) is obviously a later attempt at creating an easier reading; in the light of later exegesis, such a relatively early sign of difficulty with the sense of *presbyteriou* seems prophetic.

[39]Taking up a suggestion from D. Daube, "The Laying on of Hands," in *The NT and Rabbinic Judaism* (London: Athlone Press, 1956) 222-246, some commentators stress the difference between a *placing* of the hands (Hebrew *sîm* or *shît*) to bless or heal and a laying-on (properly, "leaning" or "pressing") of the hands (Hebrew *sāmak*) to install in an office or to designate for sacrifice. But, by common admission, this distinction was lost in the LXX, which translated both *sîm* and *sāmak* (rarely *shît*) with the same Greek verb, *epitithēmi.* Consequently, we think it is difficult to say just how operative the original Hebrew distinction would have been for the author of PE, writing in Greek, especially since we have not decided (within the methodological limits of this paper) whether the author of PE was himself Jewish (e.g. Paul) or not.

presbyters, who also imposed hands.[40] This rite seems to have been drawn from OT precedents, especially the appointment of Joshua as Moses' successor or Num 27:18-23, and Dt 34:9, where it is said that Moses "pressed" his hands on Joshua. The ceremony obviously sets aside Joshua as the substitute or successor of Moses (though to say that Moses pours his personality into Joshua is perhaps going a bit far). An interesting parallel for 1 Tim 4:14 is Lev 4:15: *epithēsousin hoi presbyteroi ... tas cheiras* (but used here of a sacrifice!). The imposition of hands as a rite of assignment to office or mission is also witnessed in the NT in Acts 6:6 (the Seven) and Acts 13:3 (Barnabas and Saul). The "communal" mode of ordination, probably witnessed in 1 Tim 4:14, is certainly known in the Church at a later date, and has survived in still another form to our own day.

But in recent years this almost universal interpretation has been challenged by a number of commentators for various reasons.[41] (1) *Presbyterion* as meaning a body of elders would be used here for Christian elders for the only time in the NT (since Lk 22:66 and Acts 22:5 refer to the Jewish body in Jerusalem). The only other non-Christian uses seem to be *Susannah* 50 θ in a variant reading (where the sense is the dignity or privilege of being an elder) and possibly in Josephus, *Contra Apionem* II, 206 (where it is a collective abstract term for "old men"). With no real precedent for the meaning of "Christian board of elders," the question naturally arises why *presbyteriou* should stand here instead of *presbyterou* (as Sinaiticus and a number of other MSS read) or *presbyterōn*.

---

[40]Whether this ceremony took place at Timothy's installation as "apostolic delegate" at Ephesus, or at some early period (e.g., when Paul first chose him as an associate) need not concern us here.

[41]E.g., Kelly, Jeremias; we depend on these two for much that follows. As with the question of *sāmak* and *sîm*, the great impulse was given by Daube's article. While it is most instructive, certain terms are used in it in an unfortunate way. For example, to say (p. 245) that 1 Tim 4:14 describes "the creation of a bishop by a *sāmak* on the part of one who is bishop already" is to ignore the use of the term *episkopos* in PE. Certain other points in Daube's article are also debatable (e.g., his explanation of why *s^emîkat z^eqēnîm* was translated as *epithesis tōn cheirōn tou* PRESBYTERIOU); but we prefer to address ourselves to the presentations of Kelly and Jeremias, who are formally commenting on PE.

(2) It is sheer harmonizing to try to reconcile 1 Tim 4:14 with 2 Tim 1:6 by saying that Paul was acting as the head of the ordaining college; the first text does not mention Paul and the second text does not mention the college. (3) A much better explanation is had if we understand the whole phrase as being a translation of the rabbinic technical term $s^e m\hat{\imath}k\bar{a}\ z^e q\bar{e}n\hat{\imath}m$. The phrase literally means "a pressing-on (i.e., imposition of hands) of elders," but the genitive is a *genitivus finalis:* an ordination to make one an elder, ordination to the presbyterate. Such an explanation has a number of advantages: (a) it explains the use of the abstract *presbyteriou* instead of the concrete *presbyterōn;* (b) it eliminates any discrepancy between 1 Tim 4:14 and 2 Tim 1:6; (c) it gives an understandable picture of Paul acting alone in commissioning his personal representative; (d) it suggests an early date for PE, since "it is not easy to imagine a second-century writer, or even one living in the last decades of the first, using such a rabbinical idiom."[42] But we think that these arguments against the traditional interpretation are not as strong as they might at first seem. (1) Granted that *presbyterion* in the sense of a "college of Christian elders" is not witnessed elsewhere in the NT, the recourse to the $s^e m\hat{\imath}k\bar{a}t\ z^e q\bar{e}n\hat{\imath}m$ does not solve anything. On the one hand, if we have here a translation of a *terminus technicus,* it is surprising that we do not have a literal translation of $z^e q\bar{e}n\hat{\imath}m$ as *presbyterōn;* the curious nature of the singular abstract noun remains. On the other hand, the use of *presbyterion* as a *terminus technicus* to denote a body of Jewish elders certainly provided sufficient foundation for the transferal of the term to a body of Christian elders, once the basic term *presbyteros* had been transferred. (2) Saying that 1 Tim 4:14 and 2 Tim 1:6 do not contradict each other is not mere harmonizing. If Paul was acting as the head of a college when he ordained Timothy, he certainly was not obliged to mention his special part every time he mentions the ordination. And the special nature of 2 Timothy (the personal testament *vs.* the more objective "rule for the community" in 1 Timothy) can easily

---

[42]Kelly, *PE* 108.

explain the emphasis on "my hands." (3) Spicq states that the *s^emîkāt z^eqēnîm* did not appear in Judaism as a rite to install teachers and judges before the end of the first century, and was not current until the second and third centuries. So Kelly's use of the "rabbinic" view to argue for an early date for PE backfires. The rabbinic imposition of hands did not involve prayer or the communication of the spirit. It was not really a sacrament or a religious rite; it simply symbolized continuity in a chain of tradition.[43] We might add that, while some might argue for an earlier date for the tradition enshrined in the rabbinic texts that are cited in this debate, the very fact of disagreement among scholars points up the methodological difficulties involved in using rabbinic texts for the interpretation of the NT. (4) The parallel phrases in 2 Tim 1:6 (*cheirōn MOU*) and Acts 8:18 (*dia tēs epitheseōs ton cheirōn TŌN APOSTOLŌN*) suggest that the genitive *presbyteriou* should be taken as subjective or possessive, not as final. (5) By the time of Ignatius, *presbyterion* had the firm meaning of a college of elders; this point is especially important for those who hold a later date for the composition of PE. (6) According to the "rabbinic" interpretation, Timothy received an ordination to the presbyterate, "elder-ordination." Yet, strangely, Timothy is never called a presbyter in PE. He is associated with such titles as *euaggelistēs* (2 Tim 4:5) *anthrōpos theou* (1 Tim 6:11), *diakonos Christou Iēsou* (1 Tim 4:6); he is to be concerned about his *diakonia* (2 Tim 4:5) and his *didaskalia* (1 Tim 4:13, 16). But no word is ever said about his being a *presbyteros*. Actually, we can see quite easily the reason why Timothy would not rank in the author's mind as a *presbyteros*. For the author of PE, *presbyteros* refers to a more or less stable member of a stable group of rulers within a local community.

---

[43]Spicq, *PE* II, 724-725. For his judgment Spicq relies partly on H. Mantel, *Studies in the History of the Sanhedrin* (Cambridge: Harvard U.P., 1961) 206ff. Mantel notes the various opinions as to when and why the rite of *s^emîkāh* was discontinued. One need only compare Spicq's judgment on the date of the practice with that of Daube, 231-232 (the practice of *sāmak* continued at least up to the first half of the second century and was abolished at the latest about the middle of the third century), to realize how difficult it is even for scholars to reach some agreement when they are using rabbinic sources for NT studies.

It is a sedentary, not a peripatetic, office.[44] As the *ad hoc* "apostolic delegate" of Paul (who will ask him in 2 Tim 4:9,21 to leave Ephesus), Timothy could hardly be called *presbyteros* by the author. But if the author does not consider Timothy a *presbyteros,* how could he say that Timothy received an ordination to the presbyterate? If, however, we understand 1 Tim 4:14 to mean that the presbyters assisted Paul in his imposition of hands, the text need not mean that Timothy was ordained precisely to be a presbyter. Thus, weighing the arguments on both sides, we think that the traditional interpretation of *presbyterion* as "college of elders" is still to be preferred.[45]

V. A Note on Joachim Jeremias

Before we conclude, we should note the special view of J. Jeremias, who tries to interpret all the *presbyteros*-texts we have cited in PE as referring simply to "older men."[46] His reasons for doing so are as follows: (1) 1 Tim 5:17 speaks of double payment for *presbyteroi* who preside well. But if we translate *presbyteroi* as presbyters, we would have a differentiation of two levels of payment for presbyters according to accomplishments—an arrangement that does not seem very likely to Jeremias. If, on the other hand, we take *presbyteroi* to mean "old men" (as in 1 Tim 5:1—its first appearance in PE!), the meaning is clear: old men who do a good job of presiding should receive a double stipend, as compared to the

[44] Is is important to remember that we speak here *only* of PE and *their* use of *presbyteros.*

[45] J. K. Parratt, "The Laying on of Hands in the NT," *ExpT* 80 (1969) 210-214, has some interesting criticisms to make of Daube's view; he prefers to see the background for the rite of 1 Tim 4:14 in the setting-apart of the Levites in Num 8:10.—Others who interpret *presbyterion* as a body of elders include H. Schlier, "La hiérarchie de l'Église d'après les épîtres pastorales," in *Le Temps de l'Église* (Paris: Casterman, 1961) 154 n. 31: H. Lietzmann, "Zur altchristlichen Verfassungsgeschichte," in *Kleine Schriften* (Berlin: Akademie Verlag, 1958) 155; Behm, *Die Handauflegung* 48, n. 3.

[46] See the works by Jeremias cited in n. 7; for a succinct critique, cf. Kelly, *PE* 122. Jeremias' interpretation of Tit 1:5 can be found as early as H. Bruders, *Die Verfassung der Kirche* (Mainz: Kirchheim, 1904) 383.

stipend given to support other old men and widows. (2) The problem of Tit 1:5-7 thus disappears. *Presbyteroi* and *episkopos* are not two terms for office that are equated here. Rather, Titus is to appoint older men in each city to the office of *episkopos*. (3) Jeremias' view also explains the absence of *presbyteros* from the list of office-bearers in 1 Tim 3. (4) Jeremias is especially attached to his position because it makes PE agree perfectly with the undisputed pauline letters, which lack any use of *presbyteros* as a designation of office in the Church. The PE are thus shown to be prior to 1 Peter and Acts, which already show the office of "elder" existing in the churches of Asia Minor. *A fortiori* the hierarchy of PE is shown to be other than the developed hierarchy of the Ignatian letters. But we can reply to Jeremias' arguments as follows: (1) Against his interpretation of 1 Tim 5:17, we must stress that neither the immediate context nor PE in general speaks of a dole distributed to old men. (2) Jeremias takes *katastēsēs ... presbyterous* (Tit 1:5) to mean "appoint elderly persons (as overseers)," but this is contrary to the Greek. The verb *kathistēmi* can mean "appoint," "put in charge," "ordain," but the specification of what a person is appointed to is expressed by *epi* + genitive (or dative or accusative), or by an accusative of person + an infinitive of purpose, by *eis* + an infinitive, or by a simple predicate accusative.[47] So if *presbyterous* in Tit 1:5 simply refers to old men, some futher construction would have to express what they are appointed as, to, or for. A most instructive parallel for our construction is found in 1 Clement 54:2: *meta ton kathestamenōn presbyteron,* where the context clearly shows that Clement is speaking of the ordained presbyters who are to be obeyed.[48] (3) The absence of *presbyteros* from the list of officers in 1 Timothy 3 and its appearance in 1 Timothy 5 causes a problem only if we identify completely the *episkopos* and the *presbyteros*. But we have seen that this was not the case at Ephesus. Moreover, we should not attach too

---

[47]Cf. Bauer, *Lexicon, sub voce.*

[48]Lietzmann, *Verfassungsgeschichte* 170-171, in quoting this passage, explicitly notes this difference between this technical use and the profane use which occurs earlier in the letter (1:3—repeated in 21:6—and 3:3).

much importance to the fact that the treatment of the *episkopos* comes in chap. 3, while the *presbyteroi* are discussed in chap. 5. The PE often alternate in a somewhat haphazard manner between rules for church order (e.g., 1 Timothy 3 and 5) and warnings against false teachers (1 Timothy 4). (4) Jeremias seems intent on eliminating *presbyteros* as a term for ministry because he conceives the presbyterate in the ministerial sense as a third type of office alongside of the episcopate and the diaconate. But since we hold that the overseers are totally identified with the presbyters in Titus and that they form a specialized group within the presbyterate in 1 Timothy, such an objection falls to the ground. As for the silence about presbyters in the undisputed paulines, we should remember that, except for the passing reference in Phil 1:1, there is no mention of overseers and deacons, either. (5) Jeremias' view would suggest the unlikely conclusion that the church's *episkopoi* were drawn exclusively from the ranks of the aged. (6) Jeremias seems to adopt a self-contradictory position by championing Daube's view of 1 Tim 4:14. Most of the other supporters of Daube's theory hold *presbyteriou,* as a final genitive, refers to the office of presbyter, and with good reason. What "ordination to be an old man" would mean is rather unclear, but this is the only translation possible if one wants to hold that the genitive is final (because it translates the rabbinic *terminus technicus*) and yet at the same time that *presbyteros* refers merely to an "old man." The non-Christian example in Susannah 50 θ *l.v.* that Jeremias appeals to may also go against him, since the sense is probably "the privilege or dignity of an elder," i.e., of some sort of official, and not merely of an old man (cf. the use of *presbyteroi* in v 41 and especially in v 50 itself).

VI. Conclusions

Let us sum up what we have learned from our investigation. (1) An inquiry into the meaning of *presbyteros* in PE must distinguish carefully between 1 Timothy and Titus, between the church at Ephesus and the churches on Crete. (2) In the primitive situation on Crete, Titus has to establish presbyters for the first time, and these seems to be simply equated with overseers. (3) On the other hand, in the developed church at Ephesus, Timothy finds a college of presbyters already existing. "Functional specialization" has already set in, and some especially capable presbyters have been assigned to the particular duties of teaching and preaching (as well as other tasks suggested by the list of qualities in 1 Tim 3:1-7). Only such a specialized presbyter would receive the title of *episkopos* at Ephesus. (4) The relatively primitive condition of the churches on Crete suggests an early date for the composition of Titus. Even 1 Timothy is not especially advanced. The specialized *episkopoi* of 1 Timothy are still a long way off from the monarchical bishop of Ignatius or even of Polycarp.[49] (5) Without trying to decide the question of pauline authorship of PE from the vantage-point of our limited problematic, we can state that the argument against pauline authorship that is drawn from the "advanced state" of the hierarchy is invalid. And one cannot protest that the monarchical episcopate is represented by Timothy and Titus, since they are not stable leaders of local churches and they do not bear the title *episkopos*. It would be strange indeed to want Timothy and Titus to represent the later monarchical *episkopos,* and yet to apply that title only to a number of officials below Timothy and Titus, while never applying the title to the "apostolic delegates." (6) Finally, it is almost exegeting the obvious to point out that the great variety of church structures that is often noted in the NT in general is verified even within the modest compass of PE. As we ponder the problem of church structures today with a view to possible reforms, we should remember that those very NT writings, which are so often

---

[49]Even if we grant that Polycarp is not as assertive as Ignatius in his role as leader of his church, still no one will deny that he is in some sense a unique figure in his own church, even if one thinks of nothing more than a "chairman of the board." Such prominence of one stable member of the local hierarchy is simply unknown in PE (since neither Timothy nor Titus—much less Paul!—belongs to the local hierarchy). Needless to say, all this makes von Campenhausen's position that Polycarp (or someone close to him in time and outlook) wrote PE untenable. For von Campenhausen's arguments, see his *Polykarp von Smyrna und die Pastoralbriefe* (Heidelberg: Winter-Universitätsverlag, 1951).

considered quite bourgeois and conservative, witness to a refreshing flexibility and even a surprising variety in the ministry.

❧

Afterword

German scholars have been especially prominent in recent studies on the Pastoral Epistles. A good basic commentary is Norbert Brox's *Die Pastoralbriefe* (RNT 7/2; Regensburg: Pustet, 1969). Brox's was one of the first serious Catholic commentaries to espouse fully the position that the Pastoral Epistles were written by a disciple of Paul toward the end of the first century, and not by Paul himself. This view, perhaps still daring when Brox published in 1969, is now a common one among Catholic exegetes.

How comfortable Catholics have become with pseudepigraphy in NT letters can be seen in the essays in *Paulus in den neutestamentlichen Spätschriften* (QD 89; ed. K. Kertelge; Freiburg/Basel/Vienna: Herder, 1981); the essays by Gerhard Lohfink ("The Way Pauls' Theology Was Taken Over in the Pastoral Epistles") and Peter Trummer ("Paul's Letters and the Pastorals. On the Positioning of the Paul-Tradition in the Pastoral Letters") are especially noteworthy. Far from being embarrassed by pseudepigraphy in the Pastorals, the authors almost revel in this indication of an ongoing apostolic tradition that speaks in Paul's name and applies Paul's theology to new problems in a new day. (Lohfink has continued his research into the Pastoral Epistles' appropriation of oral as well as written Pauline traditions in his article, "Die Vermittlung des Paulinismus zu den Pastoralbriefen," *BZ* 32 [1988] 169-88. An extensive study of the Pastoral Epistles as an expression of

Pauline tradition can be found in Michael Wolter's *Die Pastoralbriefe als Paulustradition* [FRLANT 146; Göttingen: Vandenhoeck & Ruprecht, 1988]).

I stress this point because the concluding remarks in my essay could be misconstrued to mean that I hold that Paul wrote the Pastorals. Rather, I am simply making the point that the Pastorals do not reflect the advanced hierarchy of Ignatius of Antioch; therefore, rejecting Pauline authorship because of such a supposedly advanced hierarchy would rest on an invalid argument. As a matter of fact, I think the arguments brought forth by Brox and other do tip the balance of judgment in favor of composition by some disciple of Paul toward the end of the first century.

This is not to say that some learned exegetes do not still hold to authorship by Paul; a spirited defense of the conservative position is given by Gordon D. Fee, *1 and 2 Timothy, Titus* (San Francisco: Harper & Row, 1984). The unusual view that Luke wrote the Pastorals is defended by Stephen G. Wilson, *Luke and the Pastoral Epistles* (London: SPCK, 1979); this view, espoused also in varying degrees by C.F.D. Moule and A. Strobel, has not found a great following. In a very different vein, David C. Verner applies sociological analysis to the Pastorals in his *The Household of God. The Social World of the Pastoral Epistles* (SBLDS 71; Chico, CA: Scholars, 1983). Finally, on the precise question of ordination and ministry in the Pastorals, see Hermann von Lips, *Glaube—Gemeinde—Amt. Zum Verständnis der Ordination in den Pastoralbriefen* (FRLANT 122; Göttingen: Vandenhoeck & Ruprecht, 1979).

Part Three

13

Catholic Funerals
in the Light of Scripture

My object in this essay is not to trace the historical development of Roman Catholic funeral practice. That would demand a professional liturgist. My purpose is rather to confront present-day practice with the insights of Scripture concerning death and to ask whether, in the light of these insights, some modifications might be in order.

But I should first say a few words about my method and presuppositions. First, we are considering biblical "insights" regarding death: There is no uniform view of death and afterlife in Scripture. We find many stages of development in its reflection on death. True, for us the development culminates in the crucified and risen Christ. But the development, being genuinely historical—and not a system elaborated philosophically—is not always neat and rectilinear. Historical development often involves false starts, detours and blind alleys. But even views that appear incomplete and unsatisfactory may still have something to say to us about the revelation we have received in Christ. Basically, then, our method will consist in reviewing biblical revelation in roughly chronological order, considering the various stages in relation to our present liturgical practice at funerals.

In treating OT material, I accept the stages of development as outlined by most scriptural scholars today. But a minority viewpoint, championed especially by Mitchell Dahood of the Biblical Institute in Rome, would stress reading the OT from the vantage point of Ugaritic studies and therefore sees in it a much more developed interest in death. But Dahood's methodology and conclusions have been challenged by a number of prominent American scholars, and I shall stay with what seems to be the consensus today.[1]

There may, finally, be some surprise that I should begin with the OT. But against Marcion and more recent critics the church has defended and retained the OT—from which, moreover, a number of readings are suggested for funeral masses. The OT offers penetrating and beautiful expressions of both anguish and belief in the face of death. I will try to show now that the OT *does* speak to us Christians today about the meaning of death and even of the way in which it should be celebrated.

I

The "traditional patriarchal" view in Israel is an appropriate starting point. It is especially well exemplified in the lives of the patriarchs of the second millennium B.C., though it continued even after the Babylonian exile and found a home among the Sadducees of the intertestamental period. In this view, the good life that reflected God's blessing and approval consisted in length of years, prosperity, victory over one's enemies and a large number of children and grandchildren, even to the fourth generation. If one had all this, one could face death with peace and resignation. Consider, for instance, the portrayal of the death of Abraham in Gen 25:7-8: "The whole span of Abraham's life was 175 years. Then he breathed his last, dying at a ripe old age, grown old after a full life; and he was gathered to his fathers."

---

[1]Dahood published any number of scholarly articles in the *Catholic Biblical Quarterly, Gregorianum,* etc. But for the general reader his most accessible work is a three-volume commentary on the Psalms published in the Anchor Bible series. For a short introduction to his views, see *The Psalms I* (Garden City: Doubleday 1966) XV-XLIII, esp. XXXVI.

We should not ascribe these limited horizons to a crass materialism. Ancient Israel had only a vague idea of afterlife. In some way one was gathered to one's fathers in the abode of the dead, Sheol, where all the departed, good and bad alike, led a shadowy existence without any contact with living men or the living God. In this conception Sheol was little more than a poetic expression for the common grave, the universal tomb of earth that awaits us all. So, since the early Israelites had nothing to look forward to in the next life, it was only natural for them to emphasize the good life here and now.

Is this deeply human experience of the patriarchs to be discarded as totally outmoded? Do we, too, not have patriarchs among us—elderly people who die after they have enjoyed the "patriarchal experience" of a happy, prosperous life, surrounded till the end by family and friends? In our funeral thanksgiving, or eucharist, should we not express our gratitude to God for the patriarchal blessings given to such a person shared by all of us? At times an OT reading referring to one of the patriarchs could well be chosen.

But there is a larger point here, one that goes beyond the question of the happy death of the elderly. While the funeral eucharist should certainly include expressions of contrition and petition, the other two great acts of worship, praise and thanksgiving, should not be neglected. We express the paradox of the cross perfectly when we mark a death by giving thanks in the midst of suffering. This point brings us to the second stage.

II

A sentimental or escapist approach to death and funerals receives a rude awakening from this second stage, which attacks the traditional patriarchal position. The patriarchal view was systematized into a theology of the nation's history by the writers of the Deuteronomist school in Deuteronomy and the historical books from Joshua to Kings, as well as by some of the streams of Wisdom tradition. This Deuteronomist theology rested on the fact that Israel as a whole and every individual Israelite was involved in a covenant, a peace treaty, with Yahweh which entailed blessings or curses as its sanctions. The Deuteronomist view was a simplistic and popular one: if you keep the covenant, you will be rewarded in this life; if not, you will be punished in this life. This view also prevailed because it offered the only plausible explanation of life's inequities for people who believed in a just God but had no clear concept of reward or punishment in the next life. The answer expressed an ideal of justice that could serve as a goal for any society. This *is* the way things should be in a community; this *is* the direction in which a society should strive to develop.

The rub of course, was that things did not always work out that way. The good sometimes "got it in the neck" while the wicked prospered. And so we begin to find antiestablishment protests within the community of Israel. Here again the OT is its own best critic—an admirable quality in any living religious tradition. The critique was voiced especially in the Wisdom tradition, which was the stream of thought closest to empirical observation and thus most apt to question life as it really is. In Qoheleth, or Ecclesiastes (the Preacher), for instance, we find a note of skepticism, a "who knows?" attitude. Take as an example Qoh 2:16-17: "Neither of the wise man nor of the fool will there be an abiding remembrance, for in the days to come both will have been forgotten. How is it that the wise man dies as well as the fool? Therefore I loathed life . . . for all is vanity and a chase after wind." Or consider Qoh 3:16, 18-21: "And still under the sun in the judgment place I saw wickedness and in the seat of justice, iniquity. . . . I said to myself: As for the children of men, it is God's way of testing them and of showing that they are in themselves like beasts. For the lot of man and of beast is one lot: the one dies as well as the other. Both have the same life-breath, and man has no advantage over the beast; but all is vanity. Both go to the same place; both were made from the dust, and to the dust they both return. Who knows if the life-breath of the children of men goes upward and the life-breath of beasts goes earthward?"

So in Qoheleth we find a weary resignation in the face of the inequity of things, coupled with a rejection of the reigning theology. In Job we hear a more piercing, bitter cry, almost the shriek of a wounded animal. After the first two (prose) chapters Job is anything but patient. He wants to drag God to trial and wring from him the reason why the innocent (Job, naturally!) suffer while the unjust prosper. Ultimately, of course, the answer in the poetic part of the book is that God refuses to give an answer, precisely because he is God. If God could be browbeaten and cross-examined, he would be more intelligible—but he would then be an intelligible creature, not the transcendent and inscrutable Creator.

When considering liturgical application here, we have to admit again that this is not the full answer to death. And yet the mutterings of Qoheleth and the cries of Job can serve as a corrective to present-day Catholic funeral practice. There is a danger that the so-called "Mass of the Resurrection" (a designation apparently quite popular with funeral directors) can become a votive mass in honor of Saint Pollyanna. It is insipid and insensitive to speak only of joy and triumph when the mourners in the pews are trying to grapple with the real mysteries of pain, suffering and sometimes tragedy. Especially in the case of a suicide or the death of a young person, the liturgy should not gloss over the palpable tragedy, the apparent meaninglessness of the event.

This fact was brought home to me in a very personal way recently when two close friends from my seminary days were killed in separate accidents within the space of one month. True, I felt thankful to God for the times we had had together, for the mutual strengthening in faith we had given each other. And yet there was also a keen sense of loss, frustration and purposelessness. One did not exactly feel like saying before the gospel reading: "Alleluia, alleluia, alleluia. N. has died and gone to heaven. Alleluia, alleluia, alleluia"—as was actually done recently in one New York parish! In the prayers, hymns, chants, readings and homily of the mass, there must be a place for facing some searing questions, for expressing *legitimate* grief. Saint Paul warns the Thessalonians not to mourn the dead like those who have no hope (1 Thes 4:13); but there is a truly Christian mourning which is not incompatible with Christian hope. And this Christian sense of mourning should find expression in the liturgy.

A friend of mine who was on the liturgical commission of another diocese once told me the story of the first "experimental" funeral mass he directed. He had used the paschal candle, the white baptismal covering for the coffin, incense, holy water and enough sung alleluias for all the Easter Sundays combined. After the mass a Jewish psychiatrist, who had been among the mourners, stopped in the sacristy to congratulate my friend on the liturgy. He was genuinely enthusiastic about the sustaining symbols of life and hope that gave support to the bereaved. But he also issued a warning. The psychiatrist predicted that, unless the liturgy was modified to provide for the dignified expression of legitimate sorrow, he, the psychiatrist, would soon be treating a large segment of the Catholic population.[2] One should never try to suppress legitimate grief or make one's congregation feel guilty about not feeling overly joyful at a funeral.

I must emphasize here that I am not advocating a return to the lugubrious black mass with its semipagan *Dies irae* and *Libera me*. The Christian's conception of death and the end-time (eschatology) today should not be that of Michelangelo's Sistine Chapel murals. But we must try to strike the human, Christian balance so well expressed by a wise old Italian cardinal, who composed this line for his own memorial card before his death: Weep because it is human; hope because it is Christian.

III

Our third step is to sketch some of the answers the later parts of the OT offered to the clamorous objections of Qoheleth and Job.

1. First, and perhaps even fairly early, we have the general hope expressed that *somehow* God will preserve me from total

---

[2]The psychiatrist would be surprised to find himself seconded by the new *Ordo Exsequiarum, Praenotanda,* #17, which reads (translation and italicizing mine): "Moreover, when commending the deceased to God in the funeral liturgy, let all—but especially priests—remember that it is also their duty to arouse hope in the participants and to foster faith in the paschal mystery and in the resurrection of the dead. But let them do this in such a way that, by bringing to the fore the loving concern of Holy Mother Church and the consolation of faith, they may on the one hand give comfort to believers *but on the other hand not offend the mourners.*"

death, somehow God will take me to himself. This is the hope expressed in such Psalms as 16:11:"You will show me the path to life, fullness of joys in your presence, the delights at your right hand forever"; or 73:23, 24, 26: "Yet with you I shall always be; you have hold of my right hand. With your counsel you guide me, and in the end you will receive me in glory. . . . Though my flesh and my heart waste away, God is the rock of my heart and my portion forever." Notice that the exact nature of the salvation from death which is hoped for is not clarified. These expressions of hope arise from the worshiper's intimate experience of God in covenant and cult. There arises the deep conviction that God will be faithful to the covenant and to a faithful member of the covenant people, even beyond the limits of death, the limits of all human faithfulness. *Somehow,* beyond death, I shall be *with* God.

2. For the Hebrew OT, however, man was not and could never be just a disembodied soul or immaterial spirit. If man was to survive after death, it would have to be as man, as a whole living being, a living body—which was what a human being was for the ancient Hebrew. Consequently the idea of the resurrection of the body begins to be articulated towards the end of the OT period. As we know, this basic hope was taken over into the NT as well.

But we should stop at the first mention of this hope in the OT and notice a problem that the resurrection hope entails. How are we to conceive of the resurrection of the body? Some may find the massively realistic idea of resurrection in 2 Maccabees almost repellent. In 7:11 one of the martyred seven sons holds out his hands and says: "It was from Heaven that I received these, and for the sake of his laws I disdain them; from him I hope to receive them again." In 2 Macc 14:46 we hear of the martyr Razis that when he was about to expire "he tore out his entrails and flung them with both hands into the crowd, calling upon the Lord of life and of spirit to give these back to him again." There is here an emphasis on "these very bones and flesh" that could lead to an idea of resurrection somewhat similar to a scene in a horror film ("the night of the living dead") or at least closer to the resuscitation of a corpse than to the raising of a glorified body.

This is not to deny NT teaching on the reality of the

resurrected body. But the NT presents a more refined conception than does 2 Maccabees. Especially in 1 Corinthians 15 there is a careful balancing of the continuity and discontinuity involved in the resurrection of the body. Compare the ideas of 2 Maccabees with the metaphor of the seed in 1 Cor 15:35-38, 42-44: "Perhaps someone will say, 'How are the dead to be raised up? What kind of body will they have?' A nonsensical question! The seed you sow does not germinate unless it dies. When you sow, you do not sow the full-blown plant, but a kernel of wheat or some other grain. God gives body to it as he pleases—to each seed its own fruition. . . . So it is with the resurrection of the dead. What is sown in the earth is subject to decay, what rises is incorruptible. What is sown is ignoble, what rises is glorious. Weakness is sown, strength rises up. A natural body is put down and a spiritual body comes up."

The application I would encourage here concerns preaching and catechesis during and apart from the funeral mass. We should dissociate ourselves from the "pop" ideas of resurrection that demand the revivification of exactly the same "mass" of matter, atom for atom and molecule for molecule. Such an idea is ludicrous when applied to a living being that is constantly changing the cells of its body during its life. From ancient times the church has been aware of such objections to the idea of resurrection—the ancient pagans (e.g., the Neo-Platonists) were quick to point them out. Instead of elaborating a detailed teaching on the mechanics of resurrection, the church in its normative teaching has appealed to faith in God the Creator, who will bring about a "new creation" at the resurrection.

We could sum up Christian faith in the resurrection of the dead in one sentence: *God the Creator* will raise *us* to new life. "God the Creator"—for only his omnipotent power could bring about such a marvel as the new creation. "Us"—not some disembodied spirits, but the full persons he knew, loved and saved. "New life"—the fullness of life, not just the resumption of our former earthly lives with their built-in death warrant. Seen in this light, the resurrection of the dead is the ultimate affirmation of the goodness of material creation. God so loves the material order that he will transform it and glorify it to bring out every potential and perfection it might ever have.

But the exact way in which God will raise and glorify the human person is beyond our power to imagine. We believe in him who will raise us. It is useless to speculate on the "technique" he will use.

IV

Our most important critique of the funeral liturgy, however, must come from the basic NT viewpoint. How should we categorize the NT view of death, resurrection and eschatology in general? Some scholars have seen NT eschatology as developing along the problematic: imminent parousia, giving way to disappointment over the delay of the parousia, being overcome in turn by a theology of salvation history. Hans Conzelmann in his *Theology of Saint Luke*[3] is one of the chief exponents of this school of thought. Others, like Oscar Cullmann,[4] argue that the basic structure of NT eschatology lies in the tension between the "already" and the "not yet." This tension seems to underlie the preaching of Jesus himself.

There will, no doubt, always be disputes as to whether this or that saying in the gospels was really spoken by the historical Jesus. But despite the disputes over individual sayings, some sayings and actions of Jesus which are practically indisputable (such as proclamation of forgiveness of sins, table fellowship with sinners, exorcisms) do indicate a presence of salvation in his own ministry, while at the same time he seems to proclaim a future event that will bring in completely the kingdom of God—the kingdom that is already present by anticipation in his ministry. This "already/not yet" tension becomes broadened and modified by individual writers in the NT in the light of the resurrection, the experience of the early church, and the ongoing history of the world.

Even within the modest compass of the undisputed Pauline epistles, we can note a shift in emphasis. In 1 Thessalonians (c. A.D. 50) Paul stresses a lively hope in the early coming of the

[3]H. Conzelmann, *The Theology of Saint Luke* (New York: Harper & Row 1961).
[4]O. Cullmann, *Salvation in History* (New York: Harper & Row 1967).

Lord, while Romans (c. 58) has little to say on the subject, despite its detailed discussion of such central questions of Christian existence as the present justification by faith and the future resurrection of the body. The later Captivity Epistles shift even farther to the "already" aspect of salvation while firmly maintaining the "not yet" character of Christian hope. John's Gospel goes the furthest in embracing the "already" of realized eschatology. But at least in the present form of the gospel the "not yet" is not totally surrendered.

How can this NT data be applied to the problem of a Christian funeral? The basic question to raise of any Christian funeral liturgy is: Does this liturgy reflect the NT tension between already and not-yet? Is the present funeral liturgy in danger of expressing an overrealized eschatology? We have all been at funerals where the choir proclaimed, "The Strife is O'er, the Battle Won." But is that so—either on the level of personal religious experience or on the level of systematized Christian theology?

On the level of Christian faith experience, we must realize that most of the family and friends attending the funeral will not have an unmitigated sense of victory and triumph. Feelings at funerals—even Christian feelings—can be quite ambiguous. And on the level of formal theology, a proclamation of total triumph *now* does not do justice to the basic tension of already/not yet. True, as far as this empirical world is concerned, the deceased has *already* consummated the Christian Passover he began with baptism and the eucharist. *Already* he has, hopefully, been brought into closer union with Christ, now that he has departed from this empirical existence. But the exact state of the deceased right now is not known to us fully. We may speculate all we want on the relation or non-relation of the deceased to time and ongoing history, or on whether he is present at the last day as soon as he dies. But the truth is: we simply do not know.

The NT witness does tell us, moreover, that the state of the deceased cannot be considered as completely perfect, lacking in nothing. The deceased is a member of the church. And the church still looks forward to Christ's parousia, to the resurrection of the dead, to what Paul describes as the handing over of the kingdom to the Father, when God will be all in all. The very presence of the corpse at the funeral is a stark reminder that death, while defeated in principle, does enjoy a temporary victory. The church still looks forward to the day of the Lord when death itself will be destroyed. But it is *not yet*. Until that day comes, the church remains fragmented, since some of its members remain in this life while some have departed. The victory of Christ has not yet been made manifest to all. And so the church, while rejoicing in Christ's triumph, still prays that at some future date she and all her departed may share fully in that triumph.

I hope I do not appear to be opposing all reforms and experiments in funeral rites. Rather, I welcome them. Use of the paschal candle, baptismal covering, a wide choice of readings expressing Christian hope and victory, reception of communion by the bereaved, greater lay participation in the rites—all these are a vast improvement over the old funeral mass. But we must beware of gnosticism, that is, of dissolving the ongoing process of salvation into a timeless myth of complete salvation present and available on demand at any and every moment. The church is on a dynamic trajectory through history, moving towards her divinely appointed goal. To ignore our present situation on that time line, to pretend that everything is now perfect, complete, at the goal, is neither good theology nor good liturgy. Christian liturgy is a proclamation and a making-present of God's saving action —here and now, yes, but here and now in our real situation, not in our timeless imagination. A healthy liturgy, a meaningful liturgy, is a *realistic* liturgy. If liturgy today is in danger of losing touch with reality, one reason might be that it shows too many signs of being a theoretical construct assembled in some classroom or study or liturgical workshop. That is why I have used Scripture, especially the OT, as a corrective. There is nothing more alien to pretense and make-believe than the bracing realism of biblical faith.

A final, practical note. We have seen how a sane Christian funeral liturgy must balance bereavement and hope within the realistic tension of faith. One practical way in which the different strains of sorrow and joy can be joined in the liturgy is to seek different emphases in different services and different parts of one service. For example, at a wake the basic theme of keeping watch in the night might lend itself to a subdued, restrained tone, one of hope in the midst of the night of sadness. A brighter tone could surface at the funeral mass the next day. But even at mass there is an opportunity for starting out on a more restrained note—say, in the opening hymn—then developing the theme of Christian joy in the reading and the homily and finally reaching a high point at communion, with appropriate hymns of union and victory.

At the graveside the celebrant might begin with a final affirmation of hope in the resurrection, even as we consign the body to the earth. He should offer words of comfort to the bystanders at the grave—for this is often their most difficult moment. Also—and here the priest must judge the individual situation prudently—there may be place for a few words of admonition, underlining the sobering fact that we all will most certainly follow the deceased.

Here, at the last moment of the service, we see most clearly the guiding rule for all the rites of passage: the celebrant must mold the message of faith according to the precise need of the moment. What is most fitting at this stage in the ritual? What most truthfully corresponds to the circumstances of this particular death? Finally—and most fundamentally—what will nourish best the faith of the bereaved Christians before me?

❧

Afterword

From my limited experience, I would hazard the guess that some of the embarrassing excesses seen in Catholic funerals soon after the Vatican II reforms have since been corrected. One abuse, however, still remains: the tendency to turn the funeral homily into a funeral eulogy or oration. If the homily is to be a homily in any meaningful sense of the word, it should first of all be an intelligible and relevant explanation of the Scripture texts just proclaimed.

This does not mean that references to the life, virtues, and achievements of the deceased are totally forbidden; if tastefully done, they can form part of the relevant application of the texts. But what must stand at the center of any Catholic funeral homily is the message of faith, the proclamation of the death and resurrection of Jesus as the center of our faith, the basis of our hope that the deceased will rise again on the last day, and the source of our love for one another in a time of bereavement. All too often a boring curriculum vitae, sentimental reminiscences, and tasteless humor take center stage in what could just as easily be a memorial service at an Ethical Culture Society meeting.

Unfortunately, the prime offenders are sometimes preachers at the funerals of high ecclesiastics; the curriculum vitae approach seems de rigueur, as though the main point were to impress God. Sad to say, the lower clergy seems to take their cue from such performances; perhaps a grass-roots revolt is needed in order to affect (ultimately) the obsequies of the high and mighty.

14

Celebration of the Word In Communal Services of Penance

Since the publication and implementation of the New *Ordo Paenitentiae* a number of articles have remarked on the weaknesses of the rite: for example, the impracticality of "celebrating" the rite in confessionals, the mixing of various traditions of penitential discipline and the restrictions placed on general absolution. Little has been said about one precise problem, namely the celebration of the word in communal services of penance. One almost gets the feeling that there is no problem, or at least that no problem is perceived. Yet my own experience in conducting or witnessing such services suggests that an inadequate celebration of the word is perhaps the major reason why some penance services fall flat. Granted, this may not surprise anyone used to the Catholic celebration of the word at mass. Still, I would maintain that the penance service poses the general problem of word celebration with a particular sharpness. In this article-*cum*-laboratory specimen, I should like to specify the problem and offer some remedies.

At present, I see two main abuses in the celebration of the word (that is, readings and homily) in penance services. First, the celebration is almost always patterned on the liturgy of the word in the mass: opening hymn, greeting, prayer, first reading, psalm, second reading, homily. Now, there is nothing wrong with this pattern as one possible model. Unfortunately, it seems to have becomes the unvarying law of the Medes and the Persians. One of the sad effects of original sin is that unvarying ritual becomes mechanical ritual, which, for some, is equivalent to Catholic ritual. Precisely to avoid such rote ritual, the celebrant and ministers of a penance service should consciously strive to vary the pattern of the celebration of the word. I would offer but one example. In a service in which I recently participated, the people assembled in silence in a mostly darkened chapel. After a brief opening prayer, Mt 5:21-48 was read, a homily on the passage was delivered, a period of silence for self-examination followed, and then the service was concluded by a prayer leading into individual confessions (for those who desired them). This format has a number of advantages. A subdued, quiet meditative atmosphere is at times a welcome relief from the celebration-equals-maximum-decibel-count approach; it is especially suited to penance services during Lent or a retreat. One long Scripture reading, instead of the two or three snippets (usually read at a rapid pace) is not only in conformity with the directions of the new rite but also strikes a blow against the snippet readings that plague us both at mass and in the office. Moreover, if the homily takes the tack suggested below, there is no need for a boring communal examination of conscience, read aloud after the homily. And, if the service is concluded before individual confessions begin, confessors and penitents are free to have a genuine relaxed encounter, without the pressure of "getting back" for the concluding rites. Having a celebrant announce that the community will reassemble in a half hour has always struck me as a ludicrous take-off on some movie about D-Day, complete with synchronization of watches.

The second, more specific problem, is the homily itself. The precise problem with the homily at a penance service is that the preacher is easily tempted to give his all-purpose penance homily No. 73, with no concern for the particular reading that has just been proclaimed. The more avant-garde types will present some psychological considerations that would be fine as a class lecture in Psych 232, while the more traditionally minded will give an emotionally spiced rerun of some novena or mission ferverino. In neither case is there a word event. In neither case does the same "electric shock" of God's word run through a continuous wire of reading, homily and private reflection. In neither case is there a forceful presentation of the Christian message of sin and grace, of Christ's claims as Lord and our obligations as disciples. For a penance service to succeed as word event, the preacher must carefully choose a pertinent text, then apply sound exegesis to investigate what the text says instead of what he wants it to say, and finally develop out of the text a clear, direct message to his audience, a message that speaks *from* the gospel of Christ and *to* the problems of Christians.

I cannot claim that the homily which follows fulfills all these requirements perfectly. I can simply state that it is based on sound exegesis and has been well received by a number of audiences, before whom I have preached. Because I have used it with two different congregations, seminarians at the North American College in Rome and cadets from West Point, the homily has taken on divergent forms, with varying concrete examples and applications. The form I give below is the text as delivered before seminarians.[1] It is my hope that the text that follows will not be mechanically repeated or even adapted to lay audiences by lopping off the first two paragraphs and reworking a few clerical sentences. What I hope this homily might do is to spark the reader's own reflections and suggest texts and applications that might be used in his or her own congregation. When it comes to homilies, imitation is the highest form of flattery only when the imitation is creative.

A Penance Homily on Matthew 5:21-48

The kingdom of heaven is like—like what? Well, in a seminary, the kingdom of heaven is sometimes like the day Saint Michael brought an Italian TV set up to heaven to show God what man, his clever creature, was up to. God was delighted and asked Michael to tune in a channel. Unfortunately, Michael chose Channel One just when it was showing a documentary on the drudgery of peasant life in Reggio Calabria. Men's faces were disfigured with dirt and sweat, their bodies twisted and broken by years of brutal labor. "What is this creature" cried God. "Why, Lord," replied Michael, "this is man." "What" said God, "this can't be man. Why, I created man in my own image and likeness." "But Lord," objected Michael, "you also said that he was to earn his bread by the sweat of his brow." "I was only fooling," said God, "at

---

[1]As the reader will notice, this involved a slight change in the treatment of Mt 5:21-48 (the six "antitheses"): the third antithesis, on divorce, is omitted.

least, I didn't mean like this. Change to another channel; this is disgusting." So Michael quickly changed to Channel Two, and there in all its blazing splendor was the nave of Saint Peter's Basilica during a solemn celebration. Surpliced monsignori floated up and down the aisle, while scarlet-robed cardinals received the applause of the faithful. "Now," said God, "this is a bit better. Er—who are these people?" "Ah, Lord," said Michael, "these are the men who knew you were only fooling."

The point of the parable, of course, is that the clerical mindset is always with us. Neither Vatican II nor the fact that some of us may not yet legally be clerics dispenses us from the disease. The essence of the clerical mindset is that the cleric belongs to an elite. He is separated from, nay, saved from, the great unwashed herd on the main drag. Obviously, clericalism has not died in the socioeconomic sphere, as is plain to see. But, worse still, it has cropped up afresh in a new area: the area of sin and sacramental confession. Voltaire thought religion was good for the masses; it kept them in line. Some priests and seminarians view confession in the same light. There is great eagerness to be the minister of the sacrament, *not* the recipient. And yet what could be more ridiculous? A person who is not thoroughly versed in the experience of being reconciled sacramentally can never be a fit minister of that same reconciliation. It would be like most seminary professors exhorting you to be good pedagogues. If you think that's ludicrous, it is nothing compared to how ludicrous *your* sacramental ministry will be if you know only its comfortable side, if you dispense yourself from the obligation you preach to others.

It is precisely to counter this clerical mindset that we have listened to the Sermon on the Mount this evening. It is unfortunate that people speak glibly of the "spirit of the Sermon on the Mount," as though it were some glucose substance made up of salty tears mixed with maple syrup. The Sermon on the Mount is much closer to a slap in the face. It is meant to wake us up to the real challenge, the real difficulty, of being a disciple. At the beginning of the Sermon, Matthew places the vacillating crowd at a distance; only the disciples (the elite, if you will) come close to Jesus on the mount. For what Jesus is about to teach is not some benign humanitarianism. No, he is about to proclaim the fierce demands of discipleship (this is elitism with a bite!). He is about to call for that change of heart which must incarnate itself in changed lives. He is about to proclaim that he is Lord—Lord not just of this or that area of this disciple's life, but Lord of the total existence of the disciple. He is Lord over every thought, word and deed the disciple controls; and there is no sector of the disciple's life so private, so hidden, that it is withdrawn from the gaze and scrutiny and judgment of his Lord. To map out a private sector for ourselves where Jesus is not Lord, where he has no interests, is to cease to be a disciple; it is to declare that Jesus is *not* Lord at all. For Jesus, like Yahweh in the Old Testament, is a jealous Lord, a Lord of the whole person. And he will not share his reign with anything or anybody. A private sector removed from his lordship threatens to become another absolute, a rival god. That is why all sin is ultimately idolatry.

It is in this spirit, then, that we must listen to the Sermon on the Mount. It is one long, insistent proclamation that Jesus is Lord, really Lord, in every sector of our lives. How different is this kind of morality from that of the Old Testament, whose laws were careful to delimit precise areas of obligation: you are obliged so far and no farther. Being a radical in the best sense of the word, Jesus will have nothing to do with such lines of demarcation. For lines of demarcation easily become limits set by us on his lordship.

For example, the Old Testament said: You shall not murder. But Jesus says: If you are my disciples, realize that murder is no more heinous a crime than is your anger. A bullet aimed at an enemy is no worse than your anger aimed at a brother. Whole marriages have been ruined by harsh words becoming hateful words. And whole seminaries have been torn apart by boy-men who have never mastered their emotions. John Updike observes in his novel, *Couples*, that our anger is just the mask of our fear. We burst out in rage against someone because we are insecure persons, half-disciples who have never truly learned to trust Jesus as *our* Lord. When things go wrong, when the pressure builds up, when someone offends us, we begin to doubt that Jesus is really controlling our situation, so we try to grasp control of ourselves—and paradoxically we end up losing control of ourselves. This evening before we bring our gift or repentance to the altar, we must first be reconciled: with the brother we do not love, but even more with the Lord we do not trust.

Again, the Old Testament said: You shall not commit adultery. But Jesus says: If you are my disciples, realize that adultery, that gross act of sensuality and infidelity, is no worse than the sensuality and infidelity of an undisciplined eye or heart or hand. Here Jesus is using the terminology of the Jewish rabbis of his time, who also spoke of adultery of the eye (every lustful glance), adultery of the heart (every lustful thought), and adultery of the hand (every act of self-abuse). With his radical claim of lordship over the whole person, Jesus tells us that there is no private thought or action which is exempt from his demand on our total service, body and soul. Jesus sought disciples not among angels, but among men— whole men, not disembodied spirits. It is strange how, in this area, the pendulum of priestly spirituality swings between extremes. Not too long ago we were caught in a morbid, overscrupulous fixation on sexual sin. Today there often reigns the tacit agreement that I won't mention it if you won't mention it. And so the lordship of Jesus is mocked. If he is not Lord of the whole person, he is not Lord at all.

Again, the Old Testament said: You shall not swear falsely. But Jesus says: If you are my disciples, you have no need of any oath or vow or any use of the divine name to support the truth of what you say. Now, in stating this, Jesus is getting at something more basic that just bad language or lying—though some might need improvement in those areas as well. What Jesus is saying is that anyone who takes the name of God upon his lips to strengthen a statement or confirm its truthfulness is denying that God is God. Such a person does not take God seriously as the utterly other reality. God has become for this nondisciple just another object in his self-centered universe. God, like everyone else and everything else, may be called upon and used at his convenience. Jesus says that God is not for use, is not to be manipulated by a puny man who has never learned the meaning of God, let alone met him. And precisely because we are professionals in the religion business, precisely because we daily handle and dispense the word of

God as though it were so much ice cream for sale, precisely because we are seminarians and priests, theologians and Scripture students, we stand in greater danger of handling the holy to our own condemnation. Jesus tells us this evening that, as we examine our spiritual status quo, as we rummage through our stock attitudes of joy and contrition, we should first ask ourselves where did the reverence go? Where is the awe which we should experience when we make contact with the living God—as opposed to our liturgical counterfeits?

Again, the Old Testament said: Eye for eye and tooth for tooth. These words were not meant to be a sociological description of seminary life, but I have seen it happen. Why is it that a seminarian, even when he is secure in his own identity, can at times become so spiteful and vindictive? Perhaps because a seminarian is, in a sense, a person robbed of a definite, permanent role. Neither layman nor priest, he is caught between two roles. His possible future role is controlled by inscrutable higher powers who may or may not be sane. Because he is denied a role in ordinary human terms, he stands at a fork in the road of his life. *Either* he seizes a unique opportunity to become a trusting disciple of his Lord, *either* he accepts the role Jesus offers to the poor in spirit who have nothing of their own, *or* he begins his self-definition, his empire building, which will continue into the twilight years of monsignorate. *My* rights, *my* time, *my* way—and just let any of my beloved brothers in Christ try to cross me. The more we give up things (money, job, marriage, family) the more we are tempted to defend our petty turf of fixed ideas and goals and ways of doing things, the more we are tempted to strike out in revenge against anyone who smashes the toys we still treasure. Jesus tells us only the man who loses himself finds himself. But most of us are not ready to let go.

And finally, the Old Testament said: You must love your neighbor, but you have permission to hate your enemy. For his disciples, Jesus revokes this comfortable, sensible permission. No, says Jesus; if you are my disciples, you are sons of my Father. And sons must show their family resemblance by practicing the same universal compassion the Father shows. *Universal* compassion—not just to the poor in the slums, who are quite lovable because they are at a safe distance, but also to the insufferable insensitive religious hypocrite who may be at an unsafe proximity to you in this chapel. It is precisely towards people who are exasperatingly close to us, people who may unwittingly persecute us with psychic violence (or who may be the object of psychic violence on our part)—it is precisely towards these that Jesus commands love. Of course, being a sensible down-to-earth Jew, Jesus does not mean gushing emotions when he talks of love. No, he means practical action, concrete words and deeds which incarnate, enflesh, and prove our concern. In Jesus' eyes, a disciple is not defined by what a person feels in his central nervous system at a particular moment. A disciple is defined by what a person freely decides and does. That is where Jesus wants to be Lord, and not in the fleeting feelings aroused by a penance service. If strong emotions be the norm of religious experience, then our ideal should be the religious maniac, since no one has stronger religious emotions than he.

At the end of our gospel reading, Jesus sums up all his demands on his disciples, on us, in what seems to be an impossible command: You are therefore to be perfect, as your heavenly Father is perfect. But this command becomes a bit more intelligible and practicable when we remember that, in biblical language, the word "perfect" doesn't mean the static, ethereal aloofness of the cloistered mystic. "Perfect" in the Bible means wholehearted, totally sincere, completely loyal and dedicated to God in the midst of our humdrum routine of work and prayer—in short; having a one-track mind when it comes to the things of God. And the things of God, the perfection of our Father, boils down to unlimited love, compassion without customs barriers, love for what appears unlovable to men. This perfection is not something you can put off till later. If you do not embrace it now, this evening, no magical imposition of hands at ordination will bestow it. It is vital that you realize that you will be as priests and confessors what you are becoming *now* as seminarians and penitents. You are therefore to be perfect—now!

An impossible ideal? Perhaps—except for the fact that we see this love, this perfection, in action this day. This day, Jesus the Lord comes to practice the perfection he preaches. This day, Jesus loves what appears unlovable to men. This day,

Jesus forgives us. It is only by being on the receiving-end of that forgiving love in confession that we make the proclamation "Jesus is Lord" something more than a glib emotional cry. It is only in confession that Jesus *becomes* Lord—for me.

꙳

Afterword

I fear that the debate over general absolution has so dominated discussion of public penance services that the question of quality of the homily has tended to be overshadowed. This is only a symptom of a much larger problem: a shift in the way Americans in general and American Catholics in particular think and speak about religion. The real problem is that pop psychology has taken the place of metaphysics as the main way in which American Catholics conceptualize and verbalize things spiritual, especially sin and forgiveness. At times the vertical or transcendent dimension, the fact that sin is an offense against God and that mortal sin is a rupture in our relationship with God, gets lost in the midst of psychological observations about our feelings and those of other people.

This is not to deny the importance of the horizontal dimension of forgiveness among human beings, or the incarnational Christian vision that sees divine forgiveness mediated through a graced human community. But I think we are in danger of having the vertical not only mediated by but swallowed up in the horizontal. Ultimately, what is at stake here is the reality of the personal, transcendent God. Because he is personal moral will, sin is a reality apart from our perceptions of it or majority votes about it. Christian morality can never be the same as popular mores. And because God is transcendent, sin is not just another name for crime, wrongdoing, or antisocial behavior in the human community. Unless the homily at a penance service incorporates this vertical, "God-ward" thrust, it is little more than a "Dear Abby" column.

15

Liberty and Justice for All

"With liberty and justice for all." Those final words of the *Pledge of Allegiance* have been chiseled into the bedrock of our memories since grammar school. Their fine rhetorical ring won them an honored place in the U.S. Catholic Bishops' observance of our nation's bicentennial back in 1976. More recently, and sadly, these words—indeed, the whole *Pledge*— have become a ploy in partisan political posturing. I find this especially regrettable because, to my mind, these final words of the *Pledge* can serve as a splendid place to begin theological reflection on what political democracy means to a Christian and how these words in particular can contribute to a true "spirituality of democracy."

As a step in that direction, I would like, in this short essay, to examine these two key words, "liberty" and "justice," and compare—or rather confront—their ordinary political meaning with the special meaning these same words have in Scripture, especially in St. Paul. Is there an agreement, a partial overlap, or a hopeless contradiction between the secular-political and religious-scriptural senses of these two terms?

At first, I think we may feel overwhelmed by the differences between the political and biblical meanings, the yawning gap between Paul's thought-world and the political arena today, even to the point of seeing no contact whatever. But, on reflection, I think we will find that the very difference—one might say the very strangeness—of the biblical concepts will shed new light on old problems. Perhaps, from the colliding atoms of different conceptions of liberty and justice, new

energy will be released to spark our Christian action in this last
decade of the twentieth century.

I. "Justice"

We begin with the basic Pauline idea of "justice" (or
"righteousness," as some translators render the Greek word
dikaiosynē). Both secular society and the Bible start from the
simple experience of a right or just relationship among people
living in a community, and from the need for "putting things
right" in society when correct relationships are thrown out of
balance and chaos threatens to set in. But here the paths of the
Bible and secular society diverge. For secular society, justice is
naturally a balance of rights and duties set up, maintained,
and vindicated by the government for the sake of all. Justice,
as understood by Congress or the Supreme Court, is a matter
of everyone getting exactly what he deserves, good or bad,
reward or punishment.

The government is obliged to see that just shares of benefits
and burdens are distributed to each citizen and that each
citizen has his or her rights preserved while in turn fulfilling his
or her duties. It's all a question of careful balances and
measuring rods. Distributive and retributive justice necessarily
involves a certain tit-for-tat. That is why, for instance, an
enraged society can demand that a particularly heinous crime
be dealt with according to "strict justice." This is the normal
and natural goal of any human government. To depart very
far from the demands of strict justice for a great length of time
would be to invite chaos in society.

Yet this political idea of justice diverges widely from that
"justice" or "righteousness" of which St. Paul speaks, that
justice which lies at the heart of his gospel. For Paul, the
justice of God—and Paul always starts from God's justice, not
man's—is no quality or state or balance in God or man. The
justice of God is God's saving activity, breaking through the
impasse of man's sin, calling creation out of the moral chaos
into which it has fallen, re-establishing the covenant with a
redeemed people—in a word, putting things right, not through
man's merit (which is a pious illusion) but through the death

and resurrection of Jesus.

Indeed, this forgiving, healing, gratuitous act of God's mercy and love is so different from political "justice" that it is extremely difficult for teachers and preachers to hammer Paul's meaning into the minds of their audience. A number of points in this Pauline concept of justice must be stressed again and again because they are so contrary to our usual understanding of justice. I would emphasize three points in particular.

(1) It is extremely difficult to disabuse most people of the notion that God's justice is primarily concerned with punishment, or at least with rewarding merit. Paul, however, uses the word "wrath" (or "anger") when he wants to speak of punishment inflicted by God. Justice is saving activity. And here Paul has his roots firmly in the Old Testament. It is true, I grant, that at times in the Old Testament the justice of God is used in a punitive sense. But even there it is in a context of the punishment of the nations or individuals who impede God's saving plan for his people. Much more illuminating for Paul's thought, however, are those Old Testament passages where "justice" obviously means God's saving action (as can be seen from the words that stand in parallel position to "justice"). For example, in Ps 143:1-2, the sinful yet trustful Israelite prays:

> O Lord, hear my prayer;
>> hearken to my pleading your *faithfulness*
>> in your *justice* answer me.
> And enter not into *judgment* with your servant,
>> for before you no living man is *just*.

Notice, the sinner knows he could not endure a hearing in God's court of law, where the judgment would have to go against him because he has no claim of merit, no claim of being just. So the sinner appeals instead to God's faithfulness, to his justice, which will forgive and save the sinner, apart from any question of merit. The justice of God is the exact opposite of what we would call "just punishment" or "strict justice." That this justice is equivalent to God's saving activity or salvation is clear from texts like Ps 36:6-7; Ps 22:31-32; Ps

71:15; and most notably, in the joyful song of the redeemed Israel in Is 61:10:

> I rejoice heartily in the Lord,
> in my God is the joy of my soul.
> For he has clothed me with a robe of *salvation,*
> and wrapped me in a mantle of *justice.*

We can understand, then, why Paul can equate the "good news" with something that does not strike our ears as good: the justice of God, now definitively revealed in Christ. As Paul says in Rom 3:21, 25:

> But now the justice of God has been manifested apart from the law ... that justice of God which works through faith in Jesus Christ for all who believe ... God did this to manifest his own justice, *for the sake of remitting sins committed in the past.*

Our first point is clear: God's justice is forgiving and saving, not punitive and vindictive.

(2) The mention of God's faithfulness in such passages as Psalm 143 reminds us that God's justice should not be understood in a narrow individualistic sense, a "me-and-God" approach, in which the despairing individual conducts his private search for a gracious God. God's justice, like his faithfulness, binds him to a people, a people joined to him in a covenant, that is, in a mutual relationship of love and fidelity. Now, the nations in the ancient Near East, among whom Israel lived, were quite accustomed to using treaties or covenants to regulate international affairs. And all the talk of love and fidelity we find in these political covenants cannot mask the fact that strict and punitive justice often was the fuel on which international relations ran. Some things never change.

But the God of Israel *did* change the rhetoric of covenant into reality. In his covenant(s) with Israel, justice and faithfulness did go far beyond the limits of human justice and merit. Even when the whole people sinned and lost every claim on their God, the God of Abraham and Isaac and Jacob could not forsake his very own, even though the standards of strict justice allowed him to do so. This became especially clear during the Babylonian Exile, when the covenant seemed definitively broken, when all hope of God's saving his people in the future seemed extinguished. In this dark chaos of national sin and shame, the prophet Isaiah delivers this promise, in the name of the just God speaking to his disconsolate people:

> Be attentive to me, my people;
>   my folk, give ear to me. . . .
> I will make my *justice* come speedily;
>   my *salvation* shall go forth (Is 51:4, 5).

> Listen to me, you fainthearted,
>   you who seem far from the victory of *justice:*
> I am bringing on my *justice,* it is not far off,
>   my *salvation* shall not tarry:
> I will put *salvation* within Zion,
>   and give to Israel my glory (Is 46:12-13).

Again we notice the parallel between salvation and justice, but now not in a context of individual prayer but in reference to the salvation of the whole people Israel, within the context of restoring the covenant after their sin. It is this people-centered justice that Paul sees definitively revealed in the death and resurrection of Jesus, which sets up the new covenant for the new people of God, that new Israel which is the Church.

(3) But the God of Israel was also the Lord of heaven and earth. His saving justice could not be restricted to one people; it had to extend to the entire cosmos, to the heavens and earth he had created. Sin, i.e., rebellion against the Creator and denial of one's status as creature, may begin in an individual's heart, but it soon sweeps through the whole of society like a forest fire, dragging down the entire created order to a demonic level. Sin is a chaotic, disruptive force, and once allowed to spread, it can threaten to pitch the whole of God's good creation back into primeval chaos. To save the situation, the Creator must once again exert his claim over his rebellious creation. And so we need not be surprised that the Old Testament looks forward to a time when God's justice will be

revealed before all the nations:

> The Lord has made his *salvation* known;
>   in the sight of the nations he has revealed his *justice*.
> He has remembered his kindness and his faithfulness
>   toward the house of Israel.
> All the ends of the earth have seen
>   the salvation by our God (Ps 98:2-3).

It is this universal, cosmic event destined for the end of time that Paul sees now a reality in Jesus Christ. That is why he keeps stressing that this justice of God is meant for *all* men; it is available for *all* who believe, Jew and Greek, male and female alike. By way of anticipation, the end of the world has taken place in the death and resurrection of Jesus. That is what we mean when we say that the death and resurrection of Jesus are eschatological events. They are the definitive action of God in the end-time, the final manifestation of his saving justice. *Now* is the time for God's saving justice to gather together all mankind into the one people of God. The Creator *now* finally seizes his rebellious creation and brings it back to order, to right relationship with himself.

The end of time is thus also the new creation (a common apocalyptic idea), the time when the Creator will *declare* sinful men just, and by that very act *make* them just. For when the Creator speaks, his word becomes an event; what he says happens. In his merciful justice displayed on the Cross, God the Creator declares all sinners who believe in Jesus to be just, and by that creative word of God he makes them just.

To sum up then: God's justice is God's saving activity, (a) which rescues the sinner through no human merit, (b) which reconstitutes a sinful yet redeemed people in a new covenant, (c) which recreates the universe according to that perfect image of God's will, Jesus Christ.

At this point, the Pauline notion of justice seems so far from the ordinary concept of legal justice that there seems no hope of contact or dialogue between these two ideas of justice. And I certainly would grant that one could hardly run day-to-day political affairs according to the super-human, super-rational justice of God, which confounds man's careful calculations and standards by justifying the unworthy sinner.

Yet we Christians cannot allow our experience of this divine justice in our life to have no impact on social justice in the political arena. That would be to make the realities of faith unreal, to make our faith-experience equivalent to flight from the world to a totally other-worldly life confined to sanctuary and cloister. Paul stresses that the good news is that God's future, the future of cosmic salvation and forgiving justice, has become a reality now, in our human time and space, in Jesus Christ. Or, as John puts it, the Word became flesh, i.e., God's eternal, justifying Word has enmeshed himself in our nitty-gritty, galling, limited world.

And it is only there, in that most imperfect of worlds (which includes society and politics), that the Word can speak his cosmic word of justice. God's other-worldly, eschatological justice is either experienced in our concrete daily life (including our political life), or it is not experienced at all. So, while we must avoid any glib and uncritical transferral of God's justice to the political sphere, we cannot exclude the impact of God's saving future on the sinful "now" of politics without making our faith unreal or at least irrelevant. The absolute future, the absolute justice of God, has become present, incarnate, in Jesus. And all those who are a part of Jesus and of his Body, the Church, must strive to make that divine justice present in a society and government which could suffocate in the airless propriety of strict legal justice.

One concrete example of such saving justice was the movement in the 1970s to grant amnesty to draft evaders and deserters in the post-Vietnam era. Here was a case where strict legal justice only led to a stalemate rather than a solution. By the standards of strict legal justice, people who had illegally avoided or deserted from military service had no right to amnesty or pardon. They were bereft of any claim in the court of strict justice.

The practical result, though, was that Americans were left divided, unreconciled, at an impasse, with no possibility of throwing down a bridge across the chasm. It was at that point that the larger picture had to be considered: the sinful, chaotic situation that the Vietnam War introduced into our society—a disordered situation that for a while threatened to tear the "American universe" apart. The "social covenant" binding the American people together was at times near the breaking point. In the end, a partial amnesty did apply some measure of saving, healing justice to the open wounds, but those wounds have never fully closed.

And so, even today there is a need for that divine rather than human justice, extended to those physically or psychologically wounded by Vietnam, be they on the right or on the left, be they veterans or draft evaders. To heal the extraordinary trauma of sin and chaos inflicted by the Vietnam War, we must go beyond strict human justice and seek the answer to our national disorder in that saving justice of God that forgives sin and restores the people without concern for past misdeeds on either side, without vindictive punishment for former sins, no matter who is judged to be at fault. Only the saving justice of God can break through such a national impasse by offering free pardon to all, apart from merit or demerit. In a situation of deadlock, where blow and counterblow will never break the vicious cycle of retribution demanded and refused, the only answer is the saving justice of God, not the punitive justice of man.

II. "Liberty"

With this understanding of God's justice, we are now in a position to move to Paul's second key-concept, that of liberty or freedom. (I use the two words interchangeably for the one Greek word used by Paul, *eleutheria*).

It is difficult, in a few words, to define what freedom means in a secular or political context; many competing philosophies would demand the adoption of their definition.

But in general, we can think of freedom in terms of the absence of compulsion and arbitrary restraints from without, especially those imposed by a foreign or unrepresentative power. To be free means to be self-determining, with control of one's destiny in one's own hands. Our founding fathers considered this freedom to be the right of every man and wisely placed its origin, not in the will of any human ruler, but in the endowment coming from the Creator. In the philosophical and political sense, then, freedom is the natural, God-given ability or right of every man to choose for himself, to be self-determining.

Once again we are immediately struck by the very different approach of St. Paul. Paul's idea of the Christian's freedom flows from his idea of God's justice and not from a philosophical analysis of human nature. It is the saving activity of God in Christ that has set man free; any freedom before or apart from Christ is an illusion.

Now, Paul is obviously not speaking here directly of political freedom; he is looking rather at the spiritual state of mankind. He sees that one and all are enslaved to sin, death, and the law—the three great enemies of man. It is this slavery that Paul is concerned about, and it is this slavery that colors his description of what freedom means.

It is in the seventh chapter of the Epistle to the Romans that Paul gives his most vivid and detailed description of enslaved man, caught in the grip of sin. Such a man is not totally corrupt. He wants to do good, but every time he tries to do so, he winds up doing evil instead. The sinner finds a split right down the middle of his own self, his own psyche, his own action. He is alienated not only from God and neighbor but even from himself. Such a man cries out in despair: "I cannot even understand my own actions. I do not do what I want to do but what I hate" (Rom 7:15). Mankind is a drug addict hooked on sin, and no amount of good intentions can break the habit, the compulsion of sin, which, like a tyrant, drives one on to self-destruction. Thus, this tyranny of sin inevitably means enslavement to death, that eschatological death which involves both body and soul for all eternity. "For the wages of sin is death" (Rom 6:23); the addiction is fatal.

The saddest part of this addiction to sin, this split in oneself that necessarily leads to death, is that it is only aided and abetted by what should have helped man, namely, the commandments of God's law. Here Paul shows himself to be a very perceptive psychologist. He sees that, given the *de facto* situation of a weak sinner, addicted to evil, the imperious do's and don'ts of the moral law will only incite the sinner to greater evil. Nothing is more likely to make a criminal person commit a crime than a strict "don't you dare" or an apodictic "thou shalt not...." And so even the just and holy law of God became an instrument of enslavement, only increasing and confirming man's slavery to sin. For the sinner, the law was not a very happy tool of consciousness-raising. It made man fully conscious of his sin and therefore of his despair.

And so Paul ends Romans 7 with a desperate cry for liberation: "Wretched man that I am! Who can free me from this death-doomed body?" But then immediately Paul answers his own question in a triumphant shout: "Thanks be to God, through Jesus Christ our Lord! ... for the law of the spirit, the spirit of the life in Christ Jesus, has freed you from the law of sin and death" (Rom 7:25; 8:2). What Paul means is that Christ, by his death and resurrection, has freed man from the inexorable compulsion to sin, has healed the split in his nature, has given him the inner power to do good. In place of the tyrannical compulsion to sin, coming from without like an alien force, splitting man into warring camps, the Christian now experiences the impulse of Christ's Spirit, integrating will and action, moving the believer naturally, spontaneously, from within, to do God's will. And so the Christian is freed from the power of eternal death, the result of sin, and freed also from the constraining and condemning law.

Of course, by freedom from law Paul does not mean that we are now free to give ourselves over to moral license. He means rather that the Spirit of Christ moves us to do the will of God so readily, so generously, on such a high plane, that we are living far above the level of minimalistic observance of laws. Engaged in self-sacrificing, loving service of his neighbor, the genuine Christian would no more think of breaking the basic commandments than a loving mother would think of killing her child. It's not that the obligation isn't there and observed; it's just that the people involved are spontaneously living on a much higher level of morality and so do not even advert to the basic obligations they are fulfilling. It is no longer law but the Spirit of Christ that forms their moral life. They are thus free from the sin, the death, and the law that shaped and doomed their old world. Their existence, their moral life, is indeed eschatological, precisely because God's saving justice has liberated them from the old world and has brought them into an entirely new existence.

Having understood Paul's concept of Christian freedom, we can now see important differences between man's political freedom and Christian freedom:

In the political realm, any man can, in theory, rise up against tyrants, break their power over him, and seize his rightful freedom. At times the help of other men, other liberators, may be necessary. But, in principle, every man has the potential to be his own liberator—given the right circumstances—because every man possesses freedom (at least potentially) as a natural part of his being. All he has to do is rise up and seize what is rightfully his.

By contrast, for Paul, the situation of sinful man is so desperate precisely because the sinner cannot, by any human power—his own or another's—free himself from his slavery to sin. Only the "utterly other" liberator coming from outside the human situation, yet embracing it, only the God who acts in Christ to break through the walls of mankind's self-made prison, only he can liberate man from his self-alienation. There is no room here for self-improvement or human potential movements, no possibility for lifting oneself up by one's own bootstraps. There is room only for the hand of the imprisoned beggar, stretched out to receive the pure gift of freedom.

The second great difference between political and spiritual freedom is that the goal of political liberation is autonomy, self-determination, the ability to be one's own boss. The free person is the one who has "gotten out from under" any domination by another. Paul's view is different—and perhaps more realistic, at least when it comes to the basic forces that mold our life. For Paul, there is no neutral ground where a man may be his own boss, determined by no one else. Man always stands under one of two determining forces, one of two lordships. He is either enslaved by the tyrant sin, or he serves the Lord Jesus by faith. But either way, he is determined by a higher field of force, be it sin or grace. There is no bland third alternative where he is free not to choose between sin and Jesus, death and life. To try not to choose is already to have made the wrong choice.

And so Paul sees no inconsistency in speaking of our liberation from sin, of our freedom as children of God, and in the next breath of our status as servants—yes, servants of that very "justice" that has set us free. Paul makes this especially clear in Rom 6:14, 16:

> You are now under grace, not under law.... You must realize that, when you offer yourselves to someone as obedient slaves, you are the slaves of the one you obey, whether yours is the slavery of sin, which leads to death, or of obedience, which leads to justice. Thanks be to God, though once you were slaves of sin, you sincerely obeyed the rule of teaching which was imparted to you; freed from your sin, you became slaves of justice.

But let us not be led astray by this paradoxical phrase "slaves of justice." Christian freedom is by no means just a rhetorical slogan Paul uses to make the drudgery of Christian life look good. Provided we are living the life of the Spirit, the life of love and service centered on others rather than on self, we are truly free from all the powers that constrict and choke a spontaneous, joyful, fully human life in Christ.

Prominent among these constricting powers for Paul was the Mosaic Law, with its demands of circumcision and kosher foods. Paul was so strong on the Christian's freedom from all such ritual laws that he even had a fight with St. Peter at Antioch, when the latter tried to withdraw from table fellowship with Gentile Christians because such associations were offensive to strict Jewish Christians. As Paul says bluntly in Gal 2:11: "When Peter came to Antioch I withstood him to his face, because he was clearly in the wrong."

In fact, a similar crisis over the Gentiles' observing Jewish ritual laws was the occasion of Paul's writing the Epistle to the Galatians, the *Magna Carta* of Christian liberty. After spending four complicated chapters showing how we are justified by our faith in Christ, apart from works of the law, Paul sums up his whole point with the triumphant battle cry: "It was for liberty that Christ freed us. So stand firm, and do not take on yourselves the yoke of slavery a second time!" (Gal 5:1).

To put it in concrete, homely terms that are nevertheless true to Paul's clash with Peter: Christ has given mankind the freedom to eat together—at the one table of human life and at the one banquet of eternal life. By liberating men from self-alienation, Christ has also liberated them from alienation, from one another. No ceremonial laws of religious ritual may ever rightly raise the ghetto walls again. Precisely because a Christian is radically subject to the Lord Jesus, he or she is free from all the petty rituals, rules, and taboos that men think up to enslave their fellow-men.

As with God's justice, so with Christian freedom, we are faced with the question: How can we make this freedom in Christ, this reality of the Spirit and the end-time, at least a partial reality in our workaday world? Granted that this freedom of the Spirit will be revealed fully only at the end of this age (Rom 8:21-23), how can we raise hope-filled standards of freedom in an un-free world, yes even in our own nation, which in many ways is enslaved to sin, death, and the law?

Judgments may honestly differ here. But I think that any Christian sincerely interested in liberating his fellow human beings from sin, death, and the law must be interested in the most significant liberation movement of our time—and I refer, not to Palestinian liberation movements or liberation movements in South America, but to the liberation of women. Unfortunately, women's liberation has all too often become associated with abortion, lesbianism, promiscuity, and every weird cause imaginable. But for a Christian concerned about the dignity of the human person redeemed (i.e., liberated) by Christ, nothing could be more important than liberation of the women's liberation movement from some of the women libbers. Nothing could be more important than the genuine liberation of women from all the stereotypes and unjust restrictions that diminish their status as full human persons, set free by Christ. As Paul says in Gal 3:28: "There does not exist among you Jew or Greek, slave or freeman, male or female. All are one in Christ."

I repeat: There is always room for disagreement on individual laws or reforms, such as the Equal Rights Amendment. But it is the duty of every free Christian to tear down the false walls of ceremony and custom and taboo that enslave a majority of the population of our country and our Church. For the Church to play the constant role of nervous nay-sayer to such a majority would be worse than disastrous politics. It would be a betrayal of the gospel. And the rebuke Paul aims at Peter would then hold true for us as well.

The Church, then, and every Christian in it is called upon to be a liberator, a channel of Christ's liberating justice, in a sinful and therefore un-free world. But before we start picketing government buildings with chants of "liberty and justice for all," perhaps we had best look at our own backyard. The Church can hardly hope to be a catalyst of liberty and justice for all in our secular society if she is viewed by that society as un-free and unjust herself. For instance, if we call for *justice* in the civil forum, let us first be sure that various systems of due process guarantee justice, God's saving justice, to all members within the Church.

And as far as *freedom* and equality go, I do not think that we can ever speak credibly to a secular world about freedom until women are given a full and equal place in every area of Church life. And that includes positions of responsibility and decision-making, as opposed to window-dressing. And, in my humble opinion, that also includes abolishing the *a priori* denial of the priesthood to women simply because they are women. Here is one notable area where the liberating justice of God, the freedom wherewith Christ has made us free, must break through the walls of human ceremony, tradition, and taboo.

St. Paul used the message of divine justice and Christian freedom to smash the barriers of Jewish food-laws and ceremonial rites. Paul's message, translated into our own age, calls us today to smash another Jewish barrier we have inherited (a barrier paradoxically inherited from Paul and other Jewish-Christian writers!)—the barrier barring women from the priesthood. Breaking with inherited custom and prejudice can be painful and disconcerting, especially when the custom and prejudice parade in religious garb (i.e., the supposedly clear intention of Christ). But as Paul told Peter in no uncertain terms, the gospel, and not inherited religious taboos must be our norm of action.

"Liberty and justice for all"—a splendid ending to the *Pledge of Allegiance*. But are we really prepared to act on those words, now that we have plumbed them to their Christian depths? That is where theory ends and praxis begins.

❧

Afterword

The recent pastoral letters of the U.S. bishops on war and peace and on the economy are fine examples of Catholics trying to speak the message of God's saving, redeeming justice in a contemporary American context. The generally positive response to these pastorals is heartening. More problematic is the question of a proper understanding of freedom in the United States today. Frontier roots plus the horrors of twentieth-century dictatorships have made Americans especially sensitive about government encroachment on individual rights. Like any other good, though, freedom can suffer from a lack of balance. In the United States today, one has to wonder whether exclusive emphasis on "my individual rights" has led to an illusory freedom that claims no limits and causes a very real strain on the tenuous social ties holding us together as a country.

One reason this type of freedom is so illusory is that, as Paul clearly saw, no human being can ever be an autonomous moral Switzerland, totally neutral and exempt from the influence exerted by the great powers round about. No matter how much we Americans vaunt our individual freedom, we are being largely manipulated in our choices by the power brokers and opinion makers in Washington, Madison Avenue, and Hollywood. In such a field of force, the committed Christian needs a countervailing force, a counter-society, a true church, to help him or her live the counter-culture life that is genuine Christian freedom. Only a church, as opposed to mystical individualism or sectarianism, can provide the corporate strength to counter the major forces in American society today. This has been the constant theme of certain sociologists of religion, notably Robert Bellah. Among his many books and articles, Catholics might be especially interested in his remarks to the Catholic might be especially interested in his remarks to the Catholic Society of America on the importance of a church providing a check on—and not just soothing therapy for—" bureaucratic individualism" ("Religion and Power in America Today," *The Catholic Theological Society of America. Proceedings of the Thirty-Seventh Annual Convention* [New York: CTSA, 1982] 15-25). The problems of the relation between a Catholic and an American ethos were very much at the heart of the exchanges between the American archbishops and Roman Curial officials in the week-long dialogue held at the Vatican during March 8-11, 1989; for the texts of the various addresses, see *Origins* 18 (1989) 677, 679-696, 697, 699-728.

16

On the Veiling of Hermeneutics
(1 Cor 11:2-16)

I. The Hermeneutics of a Roman Document

On January 27, 1977, the Congregation for the Doctrine of the Faith made public a *Declaration on the Question of the Admission of Women to the Ministerial Priesthood.*[1] Commonly known by its first two words in Latin, *Inter Insigniores*, the Declaration relied heavily on the data found in Scripture and the Fathers for its arguments. This mode of argumentation, of its very nature, invites response from and dialogue with scholars in the various fields of research employed in the document.[2] As a contribution to this dialogue, I should like to raise some questions concerning the hermeneutical procedure employed or rather presupposed by the document when it treats Scripture.[3] In

[1] The official date at the end of the document is October 15, 1976; the official Latin text, which was used in the preparation of this article, is found in *AAS* 69 (1977) 98-116.

[2] Critical comments have not been long in coming. For a treatment of questionable appeals by the document to Irenaeus and Tertullian, see M. Slusser, "Fathers and Priestesses: Footnotes to the Roman Declaration," *Worship* 51 (1977) 434-445.

[3] It must be stressed from the start that I restrict myself to hermeneutical questions which touch upon Scripture. For dogmatic and speculative questions, both space and competence are lacking. For a good survey in this wider area, see J. Komonchak, "Theological Questions on the Ordination of Women," *The Catholic Mind* 75 (1977) 13-28. For an introduction into the whole Scriptural problematic, see K. Stendahl, *The Bible and the Role of Women* (Philadelphia: Fortress Press, 1966); J. Reumann,

particular: as any reader reviews the Declaration's use of Scripture, one basic question about presuppositions and method must necessarily come to the fore. Does this document take historical-critical exegesis seriously? In other words, does this document take seriously the fact that the books of the NT were written at a particular time in a particular culture, and that the inspired writers, like all human writers, were working under the influence of inherited presuppositions? Granted, the inherited presuppositions of a writer are not necessarily wrong simply because they are inherited or unexamined. But, when ancient documents are read some nineteen hundred years later, in very different times and cultures, the inherited presuppositions demand not a passing reference[4] but a critical reexamination. Such a reexamination is not an attack on the Word of God, but rather an attempt to serve the genuine Word of God by making sure that we are preaching the divine Word and not antiquated human notions. It is precisely in order to serve this Word of God that the present article seeks to begin, ever so modestly, a gargantuan task: a critical hermeneutic of NT texts concerning women and church worship. The task is made all the more difficult by the fact that it now necessarily involves as well a critique of the Declaration's own hermeneutic of NT texts. We are thus involved in something of a "double hermeneutic": of the NT and of the Declaration.

One could approach this "double hermeneutic" in a number of ways. One could run through the texts cited by the Declaration and engage in the usual, seemingly endless

---

"What in Scripture Speaks to the Ordination of Women?," *CTM* 44 (1973) 5-30; and the more specialized study of M. Boucher, "Some Unexplored Parallels to 1 Cor 11:11-12 and Gal 3:28: the NT on the Role of Women," *CBQ* 31 (1969) 50-58.

[4]The Declaration does mention the problem of "prejudiced opinions about women" in the Fathers (*AAS*, 101). And in treating the medieval theologians, it admits that the theologians *often* draw on arguments which learned people today would find difficult to accept or even would *rightly* (*jure*) reject (*ibid.*). And yet, in the very next paragraph (two sentences later) the Declaration concludes its historical survey with the statement: "Therefore the tradition of the Church in this matter has been so firm throughout the centuries that...." One is reminded of Cyprian's dictum: "Traditio sine veritate vetustas erroris"—tradition without truth is error grown old.

arguments over what Paul means when, for example, he calls Phoebe a *diakonon* of the church of Cenchreae in Rom 16:1. One could also advert to questions not treated in the Declaration, e.g., the intriguing problem of whether the Junias, who is said in Rom 16:7 to be "prominent among the apostles," is actually a woman,[5] thus giving us (in Paul!) a woman apostle. The Declaration, which rests its case heavily on the argument that the *apostles* excluded women from the ministerial priesthood, does not even mention such a possibility with regard to this text. One can see why.

Such texts, however, do not lend themselves readily to detailed discussions of method and hermeneutics. I prefer, therefore, to take as a laboratory experiment in the hermeneutics of the NT and of the Declaration one especially dense text, which is adverted to only briefly in the Declaration. The text I have chosen for close scrutiny is Paul's directive concerning headcovering for women during public worship (1 Cor 11:2-16). Those who know the Declaration well may at first be surprised at my choice. After all, the Declaration takes up this passage only to dismiss it as expressing a disciplinary prescription which is not obligatory today. The Declaration is surprisingly "liberal" on this matter:

> Furthermore, they [the supporters of women's ordination] object that, among the prescriptions Paul lays down concerning women, there are some things which in our day are considered timebound and antiquated [*caduca*], and that some aspects of his teaching raise difficulties. But, on the contrary, it should be noted that almost all these precepts, which—as seems likely—were derived

---

[5]H. Lietzmann, *An die Römer* (Tübingen: Mohr, 1971) 125, favors taking the name as an abbreviation of Junianus; yet he admits that the abbreviation cannot be demonstrated to have existed from the literature of the time. He reasons that the form cannot be feminine, since the following statements exclude that—precisely what is to be proven, not presupposed! W. Sanday and A. Headlam, *The Epistle to the Romans* (Edinburgh: Clark, 1968) 423, note that John Chrysostom did not appear to consider the idea of a female apostle impossible here. M.-J. Lagrange, *Epître aux Romains* (Paris: Gabalda, 1950) 366, holds that it is more prudent to take the name as feminine.

from the customs of the time, concern practical disciplinary questions of only minor importance, for
example, the obligation imposed on women to veil their
heads (cf. 1 Cor 11, 2-16). These prescriptions are no
longer obligatory [*quae praescripta iam non urgent*].[6]

I would suggest that the Declaration was most prudent in
quickly dismissing 1 Cor 11:2-16 and passing on to other
texts. For the more one examines the context, presuppositions, and arguments of Paul in 1 Cor 11:2-16, the more one
opens a Pandora's box about historical conditioning, a box
the Declaration prefers to keep shut. At first glance, the text
of 1 Cor 11:2-16 seems funny. Yet, as one considers what is
involved not only in Paul's arguments but also in a light-
hearted dismissal of Paul's arguments, the hermeneutical
question becomes more serious. To demonstrate this, I must
now pass to a hermeneutical analysis of the hermeneutics
Paul himself practices in 1 Cor 11:2-16.

II. The Hermeneutics of 1 Cor 11:2-16

We should begin with the larger context. A large part of 1
Corinthians deals with various abuses and disorders in the
Corinthian church, disorders which Paul is called upon to
correct. In particular, chaps. 11-14 deal with abuses at
public worship, notably those concerning veils for women
(11:2-16), the neglect of the poor at the Lord's Supper
(11:17-34), and charismatic manifestations (chaps. 12-14),
especially speaking in tongues and prophecy (chap. 14). In
short, to use our terminology, both the liturgy of the Word
and the liturgy of the Eucharist need some reforms. At the
head of Paul's list of problems stands the question of the
veiling of women when they pray and prophesy in church.

---

[6]*AAS*, 106; translation and italics mine. Since the document takes the passage to
speak of veils ("velandi"), I shall accept that interpretation for the sake of argument.
As we shall see, the precise practice referred to by Paul is uncertain. It may be that
Paul is simply referring to a particular way of wearing one's hair. But such a detail
does not affect substantially the basic hermeneutical questions at stake here.

Let us see verse by verse how Paul treats this question, and what hermeneutical principles are operative in his treatment.

In *Verse 2*, Paul begins by saying: "I praise you because in all things you remember me and hold fast to the traditions, just as I handed them on to you." Considering the many rebukes Paul has to issue in 1 Corinthians, and considering especially the strong "I do not praise [you]" in 11:17 and 22, we are struck by this upbeat beginning.[7] It may be that Paul is citing a phrase from a Corinthian letter to him.[8] One can imagine the Corinthians protesting that "in all things we remember you and hold fast to the traditions, just as you handed them on to us." At any rate, Paul is obviously trying to begin a touchy question with a *captatio benevolentiae*. For someone coming from *Inter Insigniores*, what is most disturbing is Paul's use of the technical rabbinical terminology for tradition.[9] Paul has "handed on" (*paredōka*) to his church sacred traditions (*paradoseis*) which must be held fast (*katechete*). In this same section of the epistle, Paul will use *paradosis*-terminology for the narrative of the institution of the Eucharist (11:23). In 15:1-3, he uses the terminology for the basic credo of Christ's death and resurrection (vv 3-5). Indeed, in 15:2, he uses the same verb for the Corinthians' faithful adherence (*katechete*, cf. 1 Cor 11:2). In 1 Cor 11:2-16, therefore, Paul does not think, as *Inter Insigniores* does, that he is dealing with "practical disciplinary questions of only minor importance." He sees in the question of the veil a problem which touches the substance of the apostolic tradition, which included both

---

[7]The contrast is not so great, however, that it demands a division of 1 Corinthians into different letters, *contra* J. Weiss, *Der erste Korinther brief* (Göttingen: Vandenhoeck & Ruprecht, 1970) 268.

[8]So Lietzmann, *An die Korinther I/II* (Tübingen: Mohr, 1969) 53; similarly, F.F. Bruce, *1 and 2 Corinthians* (London: Oliphants, 1971) 102; cf, C.K. Barrett, *The First Epistle to the Corinthians* (NY: Harper &Row, 1968) 247.

[9]The idea of such tradition is not, however, exclusively Jewish or rabbinic; parallels can also be found in the philosophical schools and Gnosticism; cf. H. Conzelmann, *Der erste Brief an die Korinther* (Göttingen: Vandenhoeck & Ruprecht, 1969) 214 n. 18. On the different types of material which could come under "tradition," cf. also H. Wendland, *Die Briefe an die Korinther* (Göttingen: Vandenhoeck &Ruprecht, 1968) 90.

"faith" and "morals" (cf. 1 Cor 11:23; 15:1; 2 Thess 2:15; Rom 6:17; 2 Thess 3:6).[10] We can see already where Paul is going to rest his definitive argument: on church tradition. Verse 2, in a sense, announces v 16, which appeals to universal church tradition. One might almost suspect that everything in between is filler. That, however, would be a rash judgment. Paul no doubt thinks there is at least some validity in the arguments he will adduce from Scripture and reason. But the important thing to remember for the moment is that, if we, along with the Declaration, judge in the twentieth century that Paul's problem of veiling women is indeed a practical disciplinary question of only minor importance—and I think that *is* the case, then we are disagreeing with this inspired apostle of the NT, who appears to think this matter is of major importance, a part of apostolic tradition to be held.

Before we go any further with lofty hermeneutics, though, we should face one embarrassing point about concrete exegesis. We are not completely sure as to what had caused the problem Paul is addressing. Is Paul now attempting for the first time to introduce the custom of headgear for women in church? Or, to take another possibility, had Paul been an innovator in the Christian mission by introducing the practice when he founded the church at Corinth? Looking at Paul's appeal to church tradition in both v 2 and v 16, we must answer both questions in the negative. Paul and the Corinthians in general apparently followed a practice common to the early church, a practice no doubt inherited from the Jewish synagogue in and outside Palestine. Furthermore, similar customs were at least partially observed at some times and in some places in the pagan Greco-Roman world. What, then, had caused the mini-revolt over veils that Paul was facing? A number of possibilities arise, possibilities which are not mutually

---

[10]Not too much can be made of the fact that in 1 Cor 11:2 Paul does not say that the traditions were received by him "from the Lord," as he says in 11:23. This specifying phrase is also lacking in a number of other tradition-passages.

exclusive. (1) Pagan customs in the matter of veils in public and at worship varied, and especially in a loose, cosmopolitan port-city like Corinth more "liberal" views might well be expected. (2) The Corinthian church probably included in its bosom many strata of society: a few wealthy or middle class ladies, a good number of slaves or freed persons, and perhaps some former ladies of the night. After all, Paul's portrait of the former lives of some members of the congregation is anything but flattering (cf. 1 Cor 1:26; 6:9-11). Habits and views probably varied according to the stratum of society from which one came. (3) It is also possible that the practice of the Greek mystery cults, in which women sometimes participated without headgear, influenced some Christian converts. (4) Not to be excluded also are the possible "liberated" views of the Christian charismatics or enthusiasts, people perhaps with gnosticizing tendencies, who felt that the new creation in Christ and the gift of the Spirit had liberated them totally from this present world, from the order of creation, and therefore from the distinction of sex. (5) This last point brings us back to what was probably the ultimate cause of the revolt, namely Paul himself, and more precisely, Paul's preaching about Christian freedom. If Paul had told the Christians at Corinth, as he told the Christians in Galatia, that in Christ "there is neither male nor female, for all of you are one person in Christ Jesus" (Gal 3:28), then the unveiled women (especially the charismatics among them) might feel that they were simply taking Paul at his word and putting the Christian gospel of freedom into practice in Christian worship. And, after all, where else should that gospel of Christian freedom be more evident than at Christian worship? Perhaps the women even felt that, when he resisted the "unveiled look," Paul was contradicting himself and was retreating from his own good news. Paul, however, does not think so, as we see in what follows. He argues to the contrary from Scripture, natural law, and church tradition—with all three fonts very much colored by cosmological and anthropological speculation of the time, speculation current in such Jewish-Hellenistic thinkers as Philo of Alexandria. Paul gives us here a perfect example of the fact that any argument from Scripture or tradition or nature is filtered through the philosophical presuppositions of the person arguing.

In *Verse 3*, Paul jumps into the argument *in medias res*; he does not specify at first what problem he is addressing. "Now I want you to know that the Messiah is the head of every male (*andros*), and the head of a woman is the male, and the head of the Messiah is God." "Head," *kephalē*, is obviously being used here in a metaphorical sense. But what exactly is the metaphor? The metaphor does not seem to derive from the usage of biblical Hebrew, where *rôš* can be used metaphorically of the head of a group or society. That is not the sense here. Rather, we have here a later Hellenistic use of *kephalē* with metaphysical overtones. The idea is "source" or "origin," especially the origin of something's existence. A chain of sources and emanations is being set up. God is the source of the Messiah, since the Son comes from the Father and is sent into the world by Him, to do His will. Since the Son is God's instrument in creation (a Jewish-Hellenistic Wisdom-motif reflected in 1 Cor 8:6), the male is created immediately by Christ, and so proceeds directly from him.[11] Christ is the source and perhaps also the Platonic archetype of the male. On the other hand, the creation narrative in Genesis 2 states that woman was made from the rib of man, and so man is the immediate source of woman. The chain of being, the order of creation mapped out in Scripture, necessarily involves subordination, with set places and roles. Although Paul may not really wish to do so (cf. v 12), the chain he sets up almost inevitably implies that woman stands at a greater distance from God and Christ than man does.

In *Verse 4* and following, Paul confuses his argument—as

[11]Paul speaks in v 3 of *every* male in the context of creation, and not just of the Christian male in the context of redemption. Therefore he thinks of Christ in terms of *kephalē* rather than *kyrios*. For Paul, Christ is equally *kyrios* of Christian males and females (cf. v 12). Almost all of Paul's arguments in these verses are reducible to an argument from the order of creation. But in v 3, the order seems to be seen through the prism of Genesis 2; as colored by Jewish-Hellenistic speculation on Wisdom, Word, and image.

is his wont—by shifting the meaning of the key word "head." The word is now used for the physical head of the individual, while the other meaning, one's metaphysical source, still lies in the background.[12] For example, when Paul says in v 4 that "any male, if he prays or prophesies with his head covered, shames his head," the first occurrence of "head" obviously carries the concrete physical sense. The second occurrence, "shames his head," may refer both to his physical head as the symbol of his dignity, and also to his metaphysical source and exemplar, Christ. Actually, the case of a man's covering his head in church is for Paul a purely hypothetical case, brought up for the sake of the argument. He feels it allows him to argue by analogy in *Verse 5* that any woman, if she prays or prophesies without a cover on her head, shames her head—perhaps both her physical sign of dignity and her metaphysical source, man. All of Paul's contorted reasoning at this point may obscure the astounding fact—astounding at least for a religious group arising from the Jewish synagogue—that women were free in church to pray openly and to prophesy under charismatic inspiration.[13] To this extent, the old Jewish barrier imposing silence on women in the synagogue had been broken down. In public prayer and prophecy, male and female basically stand on a level of equality (note the parallel structure of vv 4 and 5). Paul may feel that it is precisely this new, heady equality which requires some external sign of difference, in order to preserve the healthy distinction of the sexes. This healthy distinction is seen even

[12]The shift and oscillation in meaning create difficulties, but Weiss' radical solution of striking out v 3 is unnecessary; cf. his *Der erste Korintherbrief*, 271. The attempt of W. Walker to prove that 11:2-16 is a non-Pauline interpolation (indeed, three interpolations) is unconvincing; see his "1 Corinthians 11:2-16 and Paul's Views Regarding Women," *JBL* 94 (1975) 94-110; contrast J. Murphy-O'Connor, "The Non-Pauline Character of 1 Corinthians 11:2-16?," *JBL* 95 (1976) 615-621.

[13]It is difficult to say how this can be reconciled with 1 Cor 14:34-35. The appeal of different letters or an interpolation smacks of a *deus ex machina*. If we examine the precise verbs used in each passage, we can perhaps find a distinction. 1 Corinthians 11 speaks of women praying or prophesying, while 1 Corinthians 14 seems to envisage a women engaging in teaching, discussion, and debate.

in the differences in length of hair.[14] As *Verse 6* observes, if a woman will not recognize her distinction as a woman, she might as well have her hair cut or shaved. If, as everyone would agree, such exposure would be shameful,[15] so too is the exposure of the head without the veil.

In *Verse 7*, Paul completes this line of argumentation by applying it to the male: "For the male, indeed, is not obliged (*opheilei*) to have his head covered." One wonders whether some vocal female Christians had insisted that, if they had to do it, so should the men, if indeed we are all "one person in Christ." Paul explains why complete uniformity does not hold here. The male is the image and the (reflected) glory of God, while woman is the (reflected) glory of the male. We are back to the lower status of woman in creation which was raised in v 3. Paul applies to the male the "image" terminology of Gen 1:26-27: "Let us make man in our image, after our likeness. . . . So God created man in his own image, in the image of God he created him; male and female he created them." But obviously Paul has given the image-motif a twist not found in Genesis 1. Genesis 1 speaks of the creation of *'ādām*, collective mankind, made up of male and female—a creation which is thought of as taking place at one time. There is no separate, secondary creation of woman in Genesis 1. But Paul reads the summary statement of Genesis 1 through the detailed narrative of Genesis 2. He understands the *'ādām* of Genesis 1 in terms of the concrete individual *'ādām* of Genesis 2, the first male. He, and he alone, is made directly by God, and is therefore the direct, precise image of God. He is the *eikōn* of God as well as the reflected glory of God (*doxa*).[16] Since woman is

---

[14]Note, by the way, the chiastic structure of Paul's presentation of his thought on equality-yet-difference: man (v 4)—woman (v 5)—woman (v 6)—man (v 7).

[15]The precise reason for the shame is not clear. Various commentators point to Isa 3:24, or to the punishment suggested in various ancient sources for an adulteress or the mother of an unworthy child. The shaven head is not a sign of a prostitute, who would be more likely to favor complicated coiffures. There may be a reference here to the practice of lesbians, especially so if Paul's concern about homosexuality is one of the unspoken reasons for his insisting on visible distinctions between the sexes.

[16]M. Hooker, "Authority on Her Head: an Examination of 1 Cor XI.10," *NTS* 10 (1963-64) 410-416, notes on p. 415 that Jewish exegetical traditions had also restricted

created later, from man, she is not the direct image of God. In fact, the image-terminology cannot be used of her at all. While rejecting the idea of woman as the image of God, Paul obviously would not say that woman was the image of man. That would blur the very distinction Paul wishes to uphold. So the only word applicable to woman is the one cultivated by Hellenistic-Jewish speculation, *doxa*. While woman cannot be the image of man, to say nothing of God, she can be the reflected glory—of man, not God. Paul explains the reason for this distinction and subordination by clearly referring to Gen 2:21-23 in *Verse 8*: "The male did not come from the woman, but the woman from the male." The one who comes from the other is the *doxa*, the reflected glory of the original. But as *Verse 9* points out, not only does woman come from man as her source, she was also created for man as her goal and purpose; quite literally, man is her *raison d'être*. Man needed a helpmate; none was found among the animals, so woman was created to help man.

Of course, even if we were to grant all this reasoning, we might object that Paul still has not shown how this inferior status of woman as the reflected glory of man means that women should wear veils and men should not. What is the connection between inferior status and veils—besides oriental custom? Paul begins to draw the connection in *Verse 10*. Unfortunately, v 10 is notoriously obscure. Literally, it reads: "For this reason [i.e., because woman is an inferior creature], the woman should have authority [*exousian*] on her head, because of the angels." There are two major problems here. What is the meaning of the "authority" on the head, and what is the meaning of the phrase, "because of the angels"? To take the second question first: it is clear from Qumran that at least some Jewish groups were greatly interested in angels, who were thought to be present at the worship of the community.[17] Paul

the reference in Gen 1:27-28 to the male. Hooker also remarks on the connection Jewish speculation had created between *eikōn* and *doxa*.

[17]Cf, J. Fitzmyer, "A Feature of Qumrân Angelology and the Angels of 1 Cor XI.10," *NTS* 4 (1957-58) 48-58. An excellent survey of older opinions and literature can be found in this article.

probably shares this idea. The question then is, what do the angels, present at the church's worship, have to do with women wearing veils? Some commentators appeal to the idea of the angels as the guardians of the order of creation, while others specify that the angels are the guardians of good order at worship and will punish any infraction, especially a physical defect (and Paul has equated having no veil with a woman's being bald). The problem with both views is that they place Christians very much under the cosmic and/or cultic control of angels, an idea that Paul, and especially the later Pauline literature, would not be quick to propagate (cf. already 1 Cor 6:3, and a good deal of the polemic in Colossians and Ephesians). For Paul and the Pauline school, Christians have been freed from the control of the angelic powers. More likely, in my opinion—though this is disputed by many—is a reference to Gen 6:2,[18] where the sons of God, angelic beings, lust for and take as wives the daughters of men. This relic of Near Eastern myth may strike us as weird in the extreme. But we should remember that the ancients, including ancient Christians, conceived of angels as sexual beings. The story of this fall of angelic beings into sexual union with human beings was widespread among Jewish writers in the first centuries B.C. and A.D.; cf. *1 Enoch* 6ff; 19:1; *Jub.* 4:22; 5:1ff; *2 Apoc Bar.* 56:10ff; Tob 6:14; 8:3; *T. Ruben* 5; Josephus', *Antiq.* I, 3. Recent discoveries at Qumran have only underlined the great interest certain Jews had in the matter. The Christian Fathers of the Church took up and exploited the story. It occurs in Justin Martyr (*Second Apology*, 5, 3); and Tertullian, at the end of the second century, actually uses the story of Genesis 6 to explain "because of the angels" in 1 Cor 11:10 (cf. his *De virginibus velandis*, 7). In this, Tertullian seems to be correct. The women, rapt in ecstasy while they pray and prophesy in the power of the Spirit, must not unwittingly tempt the angels present at the church's

---

[18]Paul, therefore, is still operating with the primeval history of Genesis—from chap. 1 through chap 2 to chap. 6. This opinion is rejected by A. Jaubert, "Le voile des femmes (1 Cor XI.2-16)." *NTS* 18 (1971-72) 419-30.

worship.[19] This gives us at least some direction in understanding the meaning of the authority on the head. Obviously the authority on the head refers concretely to the veil, although how Paul makes that connection is not completely clear. If I am correct in seeing a reference in the verse to the fall of the angels, somehow the veil is supposed to prevent untoward attention being paid to the women by the angels. How exactly this prevention takes place is not clear, because the exact meaning of "authority" is not clear. Does it mean that the veil symbolizes man's authority over woman and woman's acknowledgment of her proper place in creation, something which would obviate any possible sexual relation outside her proper sphere? Or, understood in a crasser sense, is the veil, the "authority" or "power," understood as some magic, apotropaic instrument by which the woman exercizes "power" to ward off the angels? In a more palatable vein, M. Hooker has suggested that the authority does not refer to man's authority over woman, but rather to the woman's own authority to pray and prophesy publicly, an authority denied her by the Jewish synagogue and granted her by Christ.[20] At any rate, v 10 seems to affirm

[19]There is no need to understand angels here in terms of demons in our pejorative sense. The angels in Genesis 6 were not necessarily demons before they fell. This would be supported by the use of *aggelous* in Jude 6 if, as I think, the reference there is to the fall of the angels in Genesis 6. Other possible references include 1 Pet 3:19-20 and 2 Pet 2:4; the former speaks of *pneumata,* the latter of *aggeloi.* What makes the references in Jude, 1 Peter, and 2 Peter likely is that the punishment of Solom and Gomorrah and/or the punishment of Noah's generation by the flood are mentioned in the same context. I would therefore disagree with Fitzmyer's position in "A Feature," 54 n. 6. Likewise, I think Hooker creates an unnecessary difficulty by presuming that, if Genesis 6 is referred to, then the angels present at Christian worship must already be evil; cf. her "Authority," 412.

[20]Hooker, "Authority," 410-416. Hooker prefers to see the angels as guardians of the created order, but I think her interpretation of *exousia* is also compatible with a reference to Genesis 6. The sign that the woman is acting with her proper Christian authority prevents any improper relationship from developing. It is, of course, a highly mythological conception—though hardly unique in the NT. The one problem I find in Hooker's explanation is that it suddenly introduces into the discussion a very positive idea of woman's authority, an idea which Paul has not been noticeably stressing in the preceding verses. The explanation of *exousia* by way of the Aramaic root *šlṭ* (both "veil" and "power") is highly unlikely; cf. Conzelmann, *Der erste Brief an die Korinther,* 222; Hooker, "Authority," 413; *contra* Fitzmyer, "A Feature," 52-53. The Aramaic reference would be lost on the Gentiles at Corinth (the majority

the necessity of the veil because it protects women from the angelic powers present at worship. And, if I am correct, the connection with what precedes lies in Paul's emphasis on observing the created order established in Genesis 1-2 and upset in Genesis 6. It is precisely the veil which helps them do that.

At this point, even Paul begins to fear that he may have gone too far, or at least been too one-sided, in stressing woman's subordination. In *Verses 11-12*, without taking back what he has said, Paul stresses the other side of the coin, the indispensable role of woman. If it was true in v 8 that, at the beginning, woman came out of man and not vice versa, it is also true in the natural course of birth today that a man comes into this world through a woman. Thus one does not exist without the other—first in the order of creation, and *a fortiori* "in the Lord" (v 11).[21] In an attempt to soften his position on women, which, as we saw, distanced them from God, Paul adds at the end of v 12: "But all things are from God"—but not, apparently, with equal directness.

Having tried to argue from the order of creation as known from Scripture in vv 3-12, Paul now argues from the order of creation as known by human reason and the "natural law" in vv 13-15. Paul begins in *Verse 13* with an appeal to the Corinthians' own good judgment.[22] Their critical faculty (*krinate*) will tell them what is fitting (*prepon*, a refined Greek word).[23] Paul supposes that human reason, especially

of the church). And we have no guarantee that the Hellenistic-Jewish Christians from the Diaspora (the minority) would be especially knowledgeable in Aramaic.

[21] Verse 11 seems to include in a compact way both the natural order (so v 12) and the order of grace ("in the Lord"). The addition "in the Lord" brings up a problem which many commentators do not solve adequately. They speak of Paul's admitting equality in the Lord while holding to distinctions in the order of creation. But the problem raised in 1 Cor 11:2-16 is not everyday conduct in the world but prayer and prophecy in the Christian assembly. What could be more "in the Lord"? Why is there not complete equality here? We must weigh the possibility that Paul was indeed being inconsistent here.—Weiss is again too rash in striking out *en kyriǭ* in v 11; cf. his *Der erste Korintherbrief*, 275.

[22] The *en hymin* in v 13 could mean either "in yourselves," "in your own minds," or "among yourselves."

[23] We see here one of the problems of any appeal to "natural law" as known by reason. It can so easily be equated with the convention of a given time.

reason enlightened by faith, can see that, while man, the image and glory of God, can meet his archetype face to face, "with unveiled face"(cf. 2 Cor 3:18), woman, who is only the reflected glory of man, not God, should not undertake such a direct confrontation of unequals. She needs a covering.

With a slight shift in the argument, Paul claims in *Verse 14* that nature itself hints at this need of woman for a covering. After all, if nature, even apart from questions of prayer, provides a woman with a natural covering, is not that a hint, a natural indication, that woman also needs a covering in the order of grace, when she prays? Paul's basic argument here is that woman must follow in prayer the lead nature gives her in daily life. It does not seem to occur to Paul that someone might just as easily argue that, since a woman's hair is given her by nature "as a covering" (v 15), there is no need for any further covering such as a veil. Paul seems to be using something of a grace-builds-on-and-imitates-nature approach. In v 14, Paul indicates that the same basic principle, though of course in a different way and in the opposite direction, holds true of man too: nature provides him with short hair and so hints at the fittingness of his praying uncovered.[24]

Paul seems to have a sinking feeling that none of these arguments from Scripture, reason, and nature is going to carry the day against his opponents, people who are contentious, obstinate, dogmatic, more interested in having a fight and winning it than in the truth (*philoneikos*). Well, if anyone wants to be contentious—, at this point, Paul does not even complete his sentence. He breaks off all reasoned argument and delivers his *fiat* on the basis of universal tradition, which reminds us of the *paradosis*-idea of v 2. *Quod semper, quod ubique ... securus judicat orbis*

---

[24]The reference to the shame of long hair on males may be another indication of Paul's fears that the Corinthians could fall into a confusion of sexual differences and therefore into homosexuality. Needless to say, the appeal to what "nature itself teaches" comes from Plato through the Stoics. Nature, of course, is integrated into Paul's OT creation-faith, and so ceases to be an independent, self-contained, and self-running entity. Nature can teach precisely because it is creation and thus the tool by which the Creator reveals (cf. Rom 1:18-32).

terrarum, etc. Neither "we" (probably Paul, his helpers, and the Gentile churches they have founded) nor "the churches of God" (probably the early Jewish-Christian churches, especially those in Judea, cf. 1 Thess 2:14; 2 Thess 1:4) have such a custom. As some commentators note, it is ironical that in the charismatic Paul, the great Apostle of freedom, we have the beginnings not only of natural law and natural theology in the Christian church, but also of apodictic canon law. One does wonder, in the light of v 16, why vv 3-15 even exist. The appeal to universal church practice as the definitive arbiter of a question does make theological reasoning look like so much window dressing. And that holds true both for Paul's day and for our own.

III. Some Conclusions on the Hermeneutics of Paul and Inter Insigniores

Our investigation of the laboratory specimen from 1 Corinthians has yielded some interesting insights, on a number of different points. (1) It is surprising how paradigmatic—or ominous, depending on your point of view—Paul's method of argumentation is. Faced with a new problem, Paul argues from Scripture, tradition, and theological reasoning: the paradigm to be found in any theological manual. Whatever one thinks of the method, one sees from 1 Cor 11:2-16 that it does not, of itself, guarantee optimum results. (2) Ironically, Paul's approach is paradigmatic not only of later theological method in general, but also of the mode of argumentation in *Inter Insigniores* in particular. One need only peruse the structure of the document to see that it is built upon the same types of arguments: Scripture, tradition, and theological reasoning. And among the main concerns of this approach are fidelity to apostolic tradition and the order willed by the Creator. All the more ironical, then, is the fact that the Declaration, using the same basic method as the inspired Apostle, comes to an opposite conclusion in the specific case of veiling women, and dismisses the view of the inspired Apostle in favor of its own—all the while proclaiming fidelity to apostolic tradition to be the touchstone of orthodoxy. (3) This brings us to the most striking point of similarity-yet-divergence in the approaches of Paul and the Declaration. For both, the only definitive argument is fidelity to apostolic tradition. But Paul the Apostle identifies veiling of women as apostolic tradition to be held. And who should know better what binding apostolic tradition is than an Apostle writing under the charism of inspiration? Yet the Declaration—and the church of the last ten years (let us not forget how recent the change is!)—blithely set aside as minor discipline what Paul declares to be apostolic tradition, a tradition which in fact has been kept by the Church for close to two millennia. By what right, then, can the Declaration base its negative judgment concerning women's ordination on the supposed fact that women were excluded from ordination in the apostolic church and that the later church has no power to change apostolic tradition? The Declaration's own treatment of the apostolic tradition in 1 Cor 11:2-16 is a glaring example that the church can and has changed apostolic traditions (let us not even mention women lectors and extraordinary ministers of the Eucharist). It seems that the Declaration is involved in a hopeless contradiction. *Either* the church must remain faithful to apostolic traditions, and so must remain faithful to the veiling of women, which Paul earnestly identifies as an apostolic tradition, supported by Scripture, theological reasoning on nature, and universal church practice. In that case, the Declaration has erred in its treatment and dismissal of 1 Cor 11:2-16. *Or*—the other possibility—the Declaration is correct in presuming that the later church, in different cultural circumstances, can come to see that what the early church *thought* was central apostolic tradition was only a culturally conditioned rule of discipline. In the latter case, the Declaration is quite right to dismiss veiling as a minor disciplinary rule not obligatory today, but consequently the Declaration has erred in trying to build its main argument on unswerving fidelity to what the apostles were already doing and teaching in the name of fixed tradition. Since I am an unrepentant Thomist of the old school, I do not think the Declaration can have it both ways, without

offending the principle of non-contradiction. *Either* it holds
to unchanging apostolic tradition and brings back the veil,
or it had better find some other foundation for building a
theoretical justification of present church practice as
regards women's ordination. In fact, here is the basic,
underlying parallel between 1 Cor 11:2-16 and the Declaration. In each case, a pastor has been taken by surprise by a
new practice on the horizon, and is desperately thrashing
about for a theory to justify his present practice and to
exclude the new practice. As someone once glumly
remarked, theology is church practice in desperate search
for a theoretical justification.

With this, we approach the conclusion of our hermeneutical observations on harried pastors of the first and
twentieth centuries. *Le plus ça change. . . .* But we should
note in closing that there are many other hermeneutical
problems in the Declaration which need to be addressed,
hopefully by other writers in other articles. Perhaps first
among these outstanding problems is the naive appeal to the
will of Christ, to what Christ did or entrusted to the
apostles, etc. It must be admitted, in the Declaration's favor,
that it does avoid some of the more crass approaches to the
problem. The document does skirt such lapidary statements
as: "Jesus ordained only men priests at the Last Supper."
And yet the whole Declaration does suffer from an
importation of the later reality, the Catholic priesthood,
into the early decades of the first century A.D. The simple
fact is that there is no irrefutable proof in the whole of the
NT that only a particular group of ordained people (male or
female) could preside at the Eucharist and speak the words
of institution. This is an especially fatal flaw in the argument
of the Declaration, since the Declaration tends to reduce the
specificity of the Catholic priesthood to the consecration of
the Eucharist. But it is precisely the power to consecrate the
Eucharist which is never specifically restricted in the NT to
any one ordained group. Quite to the contrary, 1 Corinthians
leaves us wondering *who* in Corinth is celebrating all these
Eucharists, when Paul and his confreres are absent and the
epistle itself gives no indication of the sort of resident
hierarchy which we find later in the epistles of Ignatius of

Antioch. Throughout 1 Corinthians, Paul has to appeal to the Corinthians as a group to restore order, because, unlike the situation in the Pastoral Epistles, we have no positive proof that there is any local ordained leader or leaders in Corinth who can be called upon to set things straight. And yet the Eucharist is celebrated. Paul becomes extremely sensitive when the question of the authority to preach the gospel or to found churches is raised. But nowhere does he claim for himself or his delegates the exclusive right to celebrate the Eucharist. In fact, we find the exact opposite tendency when it comes to Baptism. Paul does not consider baptizing to be his specific apostolic ministry, and he does not care *who* administers it. Although one must be cautious about arguments from silence and analogy, the same situation seems to hold true for the Eucharist. If there are grave disorders in the liturgical assembly, why does not Paul issue orders to the leaders of the liturgical assembly? *Are* there any permanent, ordained leaders of the liturgical assembly, specifically, the Eucharist?

Thus, the most fundamental problem of the Declaration is that it presumes for Jesus and the writers of the NT concern about the ordained Catholic priesthood as we understand it today, a reality which, as far as we can judge, appears for the first time in the First Epistle of Clement (ca. A.D. 96) and the Epistles of Ignatius (ca. A.D. 113), a reality which reaches full maturity with the writings of Cyprian in the third century and those of John Chrysostom in the fourth century. This fundamental flaw of anachronism infects and invalidates a good deal of the Declaration. To the question, what does the NT have to say about women becoming Catholic priests, the answer must be *nothing*, because the NT does not operate with our conception of the ordained Catholic priesthood.

There are many other appeals to Scripture in the Declaration which call for further scrutiny from scholars: e.g., the uncritical references to the group called the Twelve and the group called Apostles. One would never guess from the Declaration that these groups were not historically coterminous, since the document seems to work with something like the Lukan construct (equating the Twelve with the Apostles).[25] But I think the basic hermeneutical point is sufficiently clear. To the question I raised at the beginning of this article, the answer must be given: no, the Declaration does not take historical-critical exegesis seriously. It is not that the document totally ignores historical-critical exegesis. Learned footnotes and references to historical conditioning would belie such a charge. But, if one is to take the historical-critical method seriously, then one must be willing to follow through consistently, no matter where the method leads. One cannot be just a little bit critical. The Declaration attempts just that, and therein lies its faulty methodology. Let us not, however, end on a negative note. *Inter Insigniores* does show the beginnings of an awareness of the problems of historical conditioning. It is my hope that, in future contributions to the ongoing dialogue, scholars will responsibly encourage and foster this new sensitivity among church authorities. In that way, *Inter Insigniores* may yet mark a fresh start in the needed dialogue between church officials and church theologians.

❧

Afterword

Little did I realize, when I first penned this essay on 1 Cor 11:2-16, what a flood of material would appear on the question of feminism and women's ordination in general

---

[25]The document's treatment of the Twelve raises many questions. In particular, it is curious that the Declaration, in note 10, should readily accept as historical fact Mark's editorial comment on the purpose of the Twelve (Mk 3:14) while dismissing the one saying which has a strong claim of coming from the historical Jesus and of expressing his intention in forming the Twelve (Mt 19:28; Lk 22:30).

and on this pericope in particular over the last decade.

At the present moment, the U.S. bishops are working on a pastoral letter addressing women's concerns (and *not* a pastoral "on women"—as though they were the problem). Its title is "Partners in the Mystery of Redemption," and a first draft appeared in *Origins,* vol. 17, no. 45 (April 21, 1988). In the meantime, Pope John Paul II has issued an Apostolic Letter entitled *Mulieris Dignitatem* ("On the Dignity and Vocation of Women"), with an official date of August 15, 1988. It appeared in *Origins,* vol. 18, no. 17 (October 6, 1988) 262-83. To no one's surprise, Pope John Paul reiterated the ban on ordaining women articulated by *Inter Insigniores,* published under his predecessor, Paul VI.

Space does not allow an adequate treatment here of the use of Scripture in *Mulieris Dignitatem.* Suffice it to say that Pope shows great concern that his teaching be seen as based on Scripture intelligently read and properly understood. Perhaps the greatest problem for the exegete reading *Mulieris Dignitatem* is the same sort of blurring of the categories "the Twelve," "disciples," and "apostles" that can be seen in *Inter Insigniores.* As for the practical question of what Catholic women can realistically expect by way of doctrinal development in this area, I would direct the interested reader to the remarks of Cardinal John J. O'Connor in the book written by Nat Hentoff, *John Cardinal O'Connor. At the Storm Center of a Changing American Catholic Church* (New York: Scribner's Sons, 1987, 1988) 37-42.

As for 1 Cor 11:2-16, exegetes never tire of wrestling with its riddles. One of the most prolific Catholic writers on the subject has been Jerome Murphy-O'Connor. His many articles include "Sex and Logic in 1 Corinthians 11:2-16," *CBQ* 42 (1980) 482-500; "Interpolations in 1 Corinthians," *CBQ* 48 (1986) 81-94; and "1 Corinthians 11:2-16 Once Again," *CBQ* 50 (1988) 265-74. One of my difficulties with his approach is his attempt to read *pas anēr* in 11:3 as meaning "every human being" (quickly limited to "every believer") rather than "every male." This is doubly harsh, since (1) *gynaikos* ("woman") stands right alongside *anēr* in this verse and (2) *anēr* obviously means "male" elsewhere in this pericope (e.g., vv 7-9). I think Murphy-O'Connor is led astray by his desire not to see blatant subordination of women to men in this pericope; alas, it is there—as a lasting reminder that we must read the NT as well as the OT with its cultural conditioning in mind.

Author Index

Index of Scripture